Love Canal

Love Canal

*A Toxic History
from Colonial Times to the Present*

RICHARD S. NEWMAN

OXFORD
UNIVERSITY PRESS

OXFORD

UNIVERSITY PRESS

Oxford University Press is a department of the University of Oxford.
It furthers the University's objective of excellence in research, scholarship,
and education by publishing worldwide. Oxford is a registered trademark of
Oxford University Press in the UK and certain other countries.

Published in the United States of America by Oxford University Press
198 Madison Avenue, New York, NY 10016, United States of America

© Oxford University Press 2016

Library of Congress Cataloging-in-Publication Data
Newman, Richard S., author.
Love Canal : a toxic history from Colonial times to the present / Richard S. Newman.
pages   cm
Includes bibliographical references and index.
ISBN 978-0-19-537483-4 (hardcover : alk. paper)   1. Pollution—New York (State)—
Niagara Falls Metropolitan Area—History.   2. Hazardous waste site remediation—
New York (State)—Niagara Falls Metropolitan Area—History.   3. Love Canal Chemical
Waste Landfill (Niagara Falls, N.Y.)—History.   4. New York (State)—Niagara Falls
Metropolitan Area—Environmental conditions—History.   I. Title.
TD181.N72N51355   2016
363.738'40974798—dc23   2015032081

1 3 5 7 9 8 6 4 2
Printed by Sheridan Books, USA

For my students, past, present, and future

Finally, there's no end to any of it, or none we'll know that simply.

—Prefatory Note to *The Collected Poems of Robert Creeley*,
Vol. 1, 1945–1975

CONTENTS

PREFACE/ACKNOWLEDGMENTS

My interest in Love Canal began long ago when I first tried to find it. "Do you know where Love Canal is?" an old grad school friend asked one day in 1999 as we set our sights on Niagara Falls. "I think so," I replied a little bit too confidently. Having grown up in Buffalo and its suburbs, and having visited Niagara Falls so many times that it became a rather boring rite of passage when extended family or distant friends dragged me there, I was old enough to remember the original news reports about the Love Canal crisis. (My ten-year-old brain thought it was cool to see nearby Niagara Falls on the national news). When my colleague asked to see the neighborhood, I couldn't wait to go. We were soon on the road to Love Canal.

When we got to Niagara Falls, however, I had no idea where Love Canal was even located. There were no signs or maps saying, "this way to America's most famous man-made disaster." Naturally, I dragged my friend to a tourist booth. "How can I help you fine folks today?" the man asked, a brilliant smile plastered across his face. "Where is Love Canal?" I blurted. I was serious; he didn't think I could be. I told him I really wanted to see it and his face collapsed in disappointment. "Seriously?" he stammered. My friend spoke up: "I'm here from Oregon and just wanted to see something cool beyond the Falls." The man paused and furrowed his eyebrows as if to say, *okay, then, you asked for it*, before pulling out a pen. "I shouldn't really do this, but here are some directions." On a small white napkin, he traced, in blue ink, directions to Love Canal. He pushed the napkin over to me. "Please don't tell anyone I gave you this."

The directions—which I soon threw out in disgust—took us the wrong way, past Niagara Falls' pungent industrial and chemical flats. "This isn't Love Canal," I kept muttering as we drove past factories fenced off from public entry. "There's supposed to be old homes and neighborhood streets!" Evidently, the man thought we were both from the West Coast and wouldn't know any better. Stopping abruptly on one street and turning around, I tried to remember anything about the real Love Canal. A journalist friend's conversation suddenly came back to me. "You don't know where it is?" she once said, in a tone suggesting that I'd failed a basic Niagara Falls geography quiz for locals. "It's over by the Summit Park Mall," she continued, referring to one of the area's earliest suburban malls. It was a place I had passed numerous times. With that in mind, we soon found the former Love Canal neighborhood. Rolling past streets I knew from newspaper coverage—Colvin, 101st, 99th—we suddenly came upon the fantastical fenced-in landscape. At that time, a few houses slated for demolition still stood nearby, condemned and empty. *Incredible*, I thought. Though it was not marked in any way then, I had finally found Love Canal.

But how did Love Canal—the place, the movement, the symbol—find us? That is the subject of the pages that follow.

This book has been a part of my life for much longer than I care to recount and it was supposed to be finished on several earlier occasions. Each time, fate happily intervened. First, another book project took off—*Freedom's Prophet*, a biography of former slave and AME Church founder Richard Allen—which took me on a multi-year ride of talks, seminars and interviews for which I remain grateful (Allen now has his own commemorative stamp courtesy of the United States Postal Service). Then, I got busy on a series of undergraduate and K–12 teacher workshops. Generously funded by the National Endowment for the Humanities and the Mellon Foundation, they were a joy—but they took me further away from Love Canal at a time when I thought I might be close to wrapping up the book. Finally, I took a new job at Ben Franklin's Library Company of Philadelphia. It is a dream position for any scholar of American history. But taking that job meant finishing this book at the earliest opportunity.

Yet each delay allowed me to dig deeper into the Love Canal saga. New archives became available and old problems (at Love Canal and elsewhere) resurfaced, reminding me that Love Canal was not—would never be—buried and gone. As I sit in my house now typing these last words, I realize that the book could not have been done any earlier. Nevertheless, when Susan Ferber, my great editor at Oxford, said, "Deliver!" I smiled: not only was it time to finish the manuscript but this time I knew I would do it.

The sadness of parting with a manuscript is eased by the opportunity to thank everyone who made the project possible. Anna Schatz, lawyer and academic from SUNY–Buffalo days gone by, was the friend who asked to see Love Canal in 1999 and in no small way inspired me to begin thinking about the area's long history. Chris Densmore and Kathleen Delaney, the former now head of the Swarthmore Library Friends Collection and the latter a longtime project librarian at SUNY–Buffalo, helped me dig into the Love Canal Collections in Buffalo when I first started digging into Love Canal's past; I'm still mining the archival resources they introduced me to at Buffalo fifteen years later, a process that brings me into contact with new librarians at this gem of the SUNY system. Thanks to Bill Offhaus and John Edens, the most recent stewards of the collection. I'm grateful to both the University Archives at SUNY–Buffalo and to Penelope Ploughman, who studied Love Canal during its crisis years and now has bequeathed a magnificent archive of photographs to the university, for permission to publish historic images. I'd also like to thank archivists and staff at the Washington State Historical Society, Tufts University Special Collections, the Buffalo and Erie County Historical Society (now the Buffalo History Museum), the University of Rochester's Rush Rhees Library, the Chemical Heritage Foundation, The Library Company, and the University of Illinois–Springfield.

In the course of writing this book, I was lucky to meet and/or interview a range of interesting figures who were involved in various aspects of the Love Canal saga, each of whom was generous, helpful, and kind. Without their insights, this book would have been much different. Many years ago, Lois Gibbs gave me an extended interview that provided new insight on her approach to activism at and beyond Love Canal. Luella Kenny provided several illuminating interviews and was an early source of inspiration and support. She also visited my "Environmental Disasters" class several times and took us on Love Canal tours more than once. In the midst of a very busy day, David Shribman kindly gave a phone interview about covering Love Canal that helped me think more deeply about environmental activism and journalism. Joe Dunmire and Alice Stark provided insightful perspectives on the fraught nature of Love Canal health testing. Conversations with Love Canal protestors (from the Love Canal Homeowners Association, or LCHA, to the Ecumenical Task Force of the Niagara Frontier, or ETF) at a Pat Brown memorial in June 2000 provided further insight on grassroots environmentalism. Almost a decade later, John LaFalce provided a thoughtful and wide-ranging interview from his law firm that expanded my understanding of Love Canal politics well beyond Niagara Falls. To these and others—including both former Hooker employees and Black Creek Village residents, whom I have not identified here to protect their privacy—I offer a profound thank-you.

Several institutions shaped the contours of the book by offering places to teach, research, think, and write through the years. I would like to thank numerous colleagues at the Rochester Institute of Technology, where this book began and matured through research spurts, class discussions, and collegial conversations with others working in environmental history. Dean Jamie Winebrake has been a truly supportive colleague and friend, offering encouraging words—and funds to facilitate research. Associate Dean Ann Howard has also been generous and helpful, providing further access to travel funds. Christine Keiner and Tim Engstrom offered several guest lecture opportunities, which further challenged my thinking about Love Canal. A talk at the East Bloomfield Historical Society allowed me to think more about how the Love Canal story might be pitched to a broader audience. Likewise, Niagara University's Environmental Leadership Institute asked me to give the John J. LaFalce Environmental Leadership Lecture in 2005, an honor which allowed me to talk about Love Canal's deep history in a place well versed in the story. Thanks to Andrew Jenks for setting up that wonderful visit and to everyone at Niagara University for a transformative evening. Finally, RIT students were a constant source of fun and inspiration—thanks to Giles Holbrow, Amanda Morrison, Baylee Richards and many others who enriched my classroom life in Rochester.

At SUNY–Buffalo, my beloved alma mater, the Department of History allowed me to teach several graduate and undergraduate classes on Love Canal and American environmentalism. The students were always great

and the discussions powerful—the book is all the better for those experiences. Thanks to Tamara Thornton, James Bono, and Erik Seeman for allowing me to teach and work at the University of Buffalo. From Oneonta,
Dan Payne provided inspiration and environmental literacy beyond my
comprehension; he also shared the stage at a UB talk we gave on John
Muir and Lois Gibbs, which turned out to be a preview of our co-edited
book, *The Palgrave Environmental Reader*. Thanks to Bob Daly and my
father, Robert Newman, for making that talk happen. At SUNY–Geneseo,
Jordan Kleiman offered multiple chances to talk to his environmental history classes. He also organized field trips to Love Canal, which allowed
me to think about memorialization of that landscape in our own time. He
then put together a great panel at the American Society for Environmental
History (ASEH) on environmental activism. Jordan offered has consistent
counsel on the project for which I owe him much thanks. The Rochester
Area Unites States History (RUSH) research group in Rochester provided wonderful critiques of several draft chapters—big thanks to Alison
Parker for keeping RUSH going and to everyone who challenged me to
clarify my thinking on several key matters.

Friends and colleagues have been a continuing source of glorious dis-
traction and scholarly inspiration. Without knowing it, they have made
me think about everything from Love Canal memory to grassroots environmentalism in new ways. Thanks to David Blight, William Freehling,
John Van Horne, Stacey Robertson, Tom Thurston, John Stauffer,
Elizabeth Varon, Erik Seeman, and Tamara Thornton. Research help
came from several terrific students, who are now doing great things in the
fields of medicine, photography and history: Brian Powers, a Mainer
through and through, helped locate material on Edmund Muskie; David
Liebers, a brilliant scholar in his own right (though also a New York
Giants fan!) found great material relating to Love Canal politics; and
Giles Holbrow, an awesome photographer from RIT, took several indelible images of Love Canal for use in this book, which I have used with his
permission. At the Library Company, I would like to offer a special thanks
to Nicole Joniec and Concetta Barbera for skillful last-minute imaging
work. I also must thank the roster of amazing editors beyond Oxford who
pushed me to write a better book: Michael McGandy, Deb Gershenowtiz,
and Derek Krissoff, friends all but great book people too. Susan Ferber

signed the book, challenged me to write more cogently, and then got me to finish the manuscript. I remain grateful for her keen eye and encouragement through various delays. Thanks as well to Amy Whitmer at Oxford for her wonderful editorial work. Deidre Mullane, agent extraordinaire, stands behind the earliest incarnation of the book, for which I remain most grateful.

As always, the last word must go to family and friends, who made sure all was well when it was not (or didn't seem to be!). My brother Eric and sister Ruth made smile when I bogged down. And my nephews Julia and Nolan tickled me pink when I came rolling through Buffalo on various research trips. My mother and father, Robert and Milda Newman, always asked how my work was going and made sure that I had constant diversions on visits home. (They always knew that a gift certificate from Buffalo's Talking Leaves, one of the best bookstores in the nation, would allow me a little reading pleasure in the midst of much research worry). Thanks to you all for your love and support.

My wife Lisa Hermsen was a terrific partner throughout the research and writing of the book. A great scholar, teacher and administrator, she had more than enough on her own plate. But she went on Love Canal tours with me, came to my lectures, and talked with me about environmental history and activism in ways that I will always remember. Yet her biggest gift was near the end, when she was a rock in the midst of much career turmoil. She blew me away all over again. For that and so much more, Lisa, I love you madly.

I dedicate this book to my students, who through the years have taught me that teaching is a blessing—and that Love Canal can still inspire deep thought and big change.

KEY ABBREVIATIONS

BN: The *Buffalo News*
CHEJ: Center for Health, Environment & Justice
CCHW: Citizens' Clearinghouse for Hazardous Waste
EDA: Emergency Declaration Area
ETF: The Ecumenical Task Force of the Niagara Frontier
LCARA: Love Canal Area Revitalization Agency
LCHA: The Love Canal Homeowners Association
LCMF: Love Canal Medical Fund
NG: The *Niagara Gazette*
NYT: The *New York Times*
TRC: Technical Review Committee

Love Canal

Introduction

Of Burial Mounds and Toxic Tombs

Love Canal is not over. Love Canal will never be over.
—Lois Gibbs, on *Hardball with Chris Matthews*, 2000

Driving north on the 290 Expressway from Buffalo to Niagara Falls each day, thousands of cars race alongside the mighty Niagara River. North America's fastest-flowing body of water, the Niagara seems jet-propelled. If the Mississippi is the Father of Waters for its grand length, then the Niagara is its furious little cousin: a short but manic river that, in a span of roughly 30 miles, sprints from Lake Erie to Lake Ontario, with a famous plunge of nearly 200 feet at Niagara Falls. Few visitors ever come away from a tour of Niagara unmoved. "I was in a manner stunned and unable to comprehend the vastness of the scene," Charles Dickens said of his first glimpse of the Niagara River Basin and Falls in the 1840s. "Niagara was at once stamped upon my heart, an image of Beauty; to remain there, change-less and indelible, until its pulses cease to beat, for ever."[1] For Dickens, as for countless others, Niagara Falls exemplifies the American natural sublime.[2]

The highway chasing the Niagara River illuminates a different force cutting through Western New York: industrialization. For what was once a scenic landscape astride a beautiful waterway has long since become a poster child of mega-industrial growth. In Buffalo, where the "Niagara" section of the thruway begins, mammoth factory buildings, hulking steel mills, and a cityscape of grain elevators testify to the industrial pathway that made the region a production powerhouse. At Niagara Falls, the road rolls past majestic power canals and generating stations, illuminating the region's (and the nation's) path to hydroelectric energy. The advent of hydroelectric power, as the saying goes, turned night into day and helped fuel the American industrial dream. No wonder area nuns used to tell troublesome teens that they should pray for their souls. If the Soviet Union wanted to take out American industrial power in Cold War times, Buffalo-Niagara was a main target. They weren't joking.

While deindustrialization has taken much of the bite from the region's economy, the environmental impact of the great American build-out remains visible throughout Western New York. On the thruway to the Falls, tectonic trash heaps rise out of the ground like earthen waves. There's nothing unique about these mountainous formations, of course. From Des Moines to Dallas and Washington, D.C., to Seattle, Washington, dumps large and small dot the American landscape. In their ubiquity, these modern burial grounds offer constant reminders of the way that American environments have been remade to conform to consumer and industrial demands. Engineering marvels, these dumps are filled and then discarded—covered over with dirt and grass, piped with venting shafts, and then left fallow. They revert, in our imagination, back to pristine landscapes: grassy monuments to a disposable culture.[3]

Yet there is one type of dump that cannot be forgotten. Located next to a small subdivision near the end of the LaSalle Expressway at the southeastern edge of Niagara Falls, it has been landscaped into banality—a big green field with a scattering of trees and shrubs. From a distance, it looks like any patch of suburban land. Up close, the dump warns away visitors. Surrounded by an imposing chain-link fence, it is the dominant landmark of the area—but it remains unmarked. [Fig. 1] Sidewalks disappear beneath the metal cage while shrubs block monitoring wells positioned at strategic locations along the grassy knoll. Rows of empty streets around the fence bear signs of former settlement, as traces of old driveways and housing foundations appear beneath overgrown weeds. Much of the area—though not all of it—seems forlorn. Just what is this impressive but forbidden landscape?

It is Love Canal, perhaps the world's most famous toxic trash heap. Once part of a thriving neighborhood comprising roughly 1,000 families living on a ten-block grid of streets, it is now a partially settled subdivision anchored by a remediated hazardous waste mausoleum. While the heyday

Figure 1 Love Canal, 2015: This contemporary image of Love Canal shows the covered-over landscape, including a manicured lawn, through the prism of a massive chain- link fence. There is no signage at the covered-over dump indicating that the Love Canal saga played out here. (Courtesy of photographer Giles Holbrow)

of the Love Canal crisis is nearly four decades in the past, the chemical landscape that prompted it is still here in the form of over 20,000 tons of toxic sludge that could not—and will not ever—be removed from the ground below. It's just a dump, some local residents now say, and nothing more. But it is more than that. It is a celebrated and reviled toxic tomb. Though it is unmarked, people still visit the site regularly, from students learning about Love Canal to photographers trying to capture the area's odd beauty. As both place and symbol, Love Canal remains a shrine to the idea that the American landscape could seal away industrial waste forever—and to the counter-notion that buried toxic waste would haunt Americans for a very long time.

The reason we even know about this particular dump—and thousands of other hazardous waste sites scattered across the country—is that Love Canal residents organized a potent series of protest movements beginning in August of 1978. That crisis summer remains almost frozen in time by images of angry citizens screaming at New York State health officials and politicians about the hazardous brew of chemicals infiltrating their homes and lives. Initially seeking evacuation, area activists soon found themselves engaged in a much bigger battle over the meaning of both a toxic past and the future of American environmentalism. Indeed, after state and federal governments removed only about 25 percent of the families that summer, many remaining residents became activists, struggling for over two years before they too were evacuated. During that time (and long afterwards) residents-turned-activists broadened their struggle by focusing on a range of environmental concerns, from the need for a comprehensive national law that would remediate America's hazardous waste archipelago to the idea that all citizens had basic environmental rights: the right to clear air and water, the right to clean neighborhoods and school playgrounds, and the right to know what companies produced and discarded in their midst. Mobilizing just a few years after the inaugural Earth Day, Love Canal activism offered a bold and ramifying environmental vision that we still live with today.[4]

Back then, Love Canal protesters became media darlings and topics of conversation at the local, national and international levels. From the so-called "housewives turned activists" like Lois Gibbs, Luella Kenny, and Joann Hale, who led the grassroots movement to the hurly burly fathers angered that they could not protect their family from environmental ruin, Love Canal residents were the classic American underdogs taking on a callous world. "Hardly a person is now alive who does not remember the...ecological disaster at the chemical-waste deposits in Love Canal, New York," a reviewer noted of the 1982 made-for-TV movie, "Lois Gibbs and the Love Canal." As the true-to-life story starring an A-List actress showed, residents unleashed "a loud and aggressive movement to force the United States Government to relocate...[and] reimburse them for the loss of their property."[5] By being forceful and persistent, Love Canal activists eventually won their relocation battle and got out of a polluted environment.

Strangely, the oft-told story of Love Canal usually ends here: residents leave and Love Canal is no more. Worse, some books elide citizen activism from the Love Canal saga altogether. While it was surely an environmental milestone, governing officials, critics and even some scholars have referred to the Love Canal crisis in the passive voice: it was a chemical crisis that "happened" (or "was discovered") in the late 1970s before being speedily resolved by government officials. One of the leading and most important environmental texts notes that public health concerns about toxic pollution resulted from "the discovery of abandoned chemical dumps at Love Canal" and elsewhere, without delving deeper into just who unearthed the problem and made it significant beyond Niagara Falls: residents.[6] More ominously, Love Canal activists have gone missing from some environmental dictionaries. *Modern American Environmentalists*, a recent compendium of nearly 150 ecological reformers in the 20th century, has no entry on Lois Gibbs or Love Canal women—though it does include a long entry on Al Gore, which notes that he spearheaded the federal effort to examine abandoned toxic waste sites at places like Love Canal.[7]

Such elision and neglect flow from original debates at Love Canal, when some government and industry officials depicted residents as emotional and somewhat untrustworthy analysts of the toxic waste problem in Western New York. In the first official history of the chemical disaster (which laudably observed that Love Canal was a harbinger of things to come nationally), New York state health officials characterized activists as essentially background figures in the crisis. While noting that "public health concerns prompted" investigations of Love Canal, the September 1978 report did not credit residents for pushing officials to act in the first place. Indeed, the report highlighted the swift responses of state officials, who examined "every remedy available to...protect the public's health and safety" at Love Canal.[8]

Yet the opposite was true: residents were the primary instigators of consciousness-raising and change at Love Canal. Against sustained resistance, they sought to define their neighborhood as a toxic disaster zone born of faulty chemical policies, and land deals, of the past. While they pushed for evacuation, residents-turned-activists also prompted deeper debate about the fate of nature in Americans' daily living environment— the vernacular landscape that most Americans inhabited, played on, and used. Was that environment healthy? How had it been used and abused over time? Who decided its fate, now and in the future? Love Canal residents focused on these and other thorny questions, compelling Americans more generally to consider them too. "In our society," Senator Edmund Muskie of Maine observed soon after Love Canal residents testified in Congress in 1979, "we are discovering almost every day...new hazards

that have been released into the atmosphere over the period of our industrial revolution." Though they seem to "suddenly crop up in Love Canal,
up in New York State," these hazards have been lurking all along. Still, he
added, it took citizen activism to push such toxic troubles into the open.
In Love Canal's wake, Americans knew that toxic waste had created "enormous hazards to public health, to property values, to people."[9] The former
head of the EPA agreed, noting in 1979 that there were over 30,000 uncontained dumps (and perhaps many more) in the American landscape.
But Americans realized this most "disturbing fact" only after citizens mobilized in Niagara Falls. Thanks to them, the nation learned that Love
Canal "cannot be regarded as an isolated event."[10]

At a policy level, of course, Love Canal activism influenced the passage
of new environmental laws. In 1980, Congress created Superfund, the first
federal statute governing hazardous waste remediation; soon after, it established the Agency for Toxic Substances and Disease Registry (ATSDR) to
"protect the public from hazardous wastes."[11] States, and even industry,
also pledged to fight hazardous waste following Love Canal. At an organizational level, Love Canal residents inspired a wave of copycat grassroots environmental groups, whose collective exertions have made it more
difficult—though not impossible—to site hazardous waste facilities in
poor and low-income neighborhoods.[12] As even critics recognize, Love
Canal has "left a legacy that affects all Americans."[13]

The phrase alone is legend. "This could be another Love Canal," commentators often say about chemical spills or hazardous waste crises.
Indeed, "Love Canal" is now very nearly an adjective that lends weight to
any looming chemical, nuclear, or mining disaster. The polluted tar ponds
of Sydney, Nova Scotia, are called "Canada's Love Canal," while the
Agricultural Street Landfill in an African-American section of New
Orleans is colloquially referred to as the "Black Love Canal."[14] Natural disasters bring Love Canal to mind as well. In 2005, Hurricane Katrina,
which took the lives of over 1,800 Gulf Coast residents, prompted some
reporters to wonder about the witches' brew of toxic chemicals, spilled
oil, and other hazardous products unleashed by the swirling floodwaters
of New Orleans. "We've got a Love Canal down here," one commentator
noted rather ominously of a refinery leak.[15] More recently, the 2011
Fukushima nuclear disaster prompted a writer in the *Bulletin of the Atomic*

Scientists to link the tragedy in Japan (in which a tsunami crippled nuclear reactors, sending radioactive waste into the environment) to other "big mistakes" like Love Canal.[16] In its metaphoric ubiquity as a sign of toxic trouble, Love Canal has become Niagara Falls' doppelgänger—the evil twin of natural beauty everywhere.

In the era of hydrofracking and renewed concern about nuclear waste disposal, Love Canal's history remains relevant. "Could this be our generation's Love Canal?" a talk show host in Rochester wondered amid regional debates about hydrofracking, which uses a potent mixture of sand, chemicals, and water to unlock underground natural gas deposits, leaving large amounts of wastewater. When a Niagara Falls firm applied for a permit to collect mining waste from various hydrofracking companies, local citizens rang alarm bells by referring to the famed chemical crisis of 1978. "We had our Love Canal," one frustrated resident complained to city officials thinking about granting the permit.[17] (The firm's request was denied.) Meanwhile, national debates about what to do with more than 60,000 tons of nuclear waste generated over the past several decades often invoke Love Canal. As one writer put it, storing nuclear detritus at a single site (like Nevada's Yucca Mountain) could produce nothing short of "a nuclear waste version of Love Canal."[18] As these and countless other examples indicate, even in the 21st century there is still power in the Love Canal brand.

While the list of Love Canal legacies is long, one rather simple development perhaps best illustrates its continued relevance: the idea that Americans must confront their toxic past. For since Love Canal times, it is simply no longer possible to look away from polluted landscapes and say, as Americans once did, that toxic trash doesn't exist, or that it is someone else's problem, or that it will disappear into the earth. Love Canal protestors made us peer into a polluted past. The view was not pleasant but it made a lasting difference. According to the Environmental Protection Agency, one-fifth of the American population lives within a few miles of a Superfund site (defined by federal officials as one of the worst 1,000 or so toxic waste dumps in the nation and slated for remediation). That means, as Lois Gibbs proclaimed early and often, "Love Canal is [still] not over."[19]

But how did the Love Canal saga begin? And how did Love Canal—the place—ever become Ground Zero of toxic tragedy in the United States? While my history culminates in residents' rising activism and its lingering impact on environmentalism, health and politics, it necessarily begins long beforehand, when greater Niagara captured the attention of imperial regimes, industrialists, and a host of project-building dreamers who saw the Falls as beautiful but the landscape around it as a bounteous and nearly disposable commodity. The area that eventually became Love Canal played a key part in Niagara's evolving identity as a commercial and industrial powerhouse. In fact, from this single area—a modern neighborhood equivalent to a couple of dozen football fields—one can see centuries of environmental struggle and change in North America, from some of the earliest colonial development schemes and land-use debates to massive city-building projects after the Civil War and the rise of the American chemical industry in the early 1900s. René La Salle launched his global trade empire (in the form of *Le Griffon,* the first European-American trading vessel to ply the Upper Great Lakes) from a spot only a few hundred yards away from where citizen protestors like Lois Gibbs mobilized for removal from a toxic landscape. Likewise, celebrated engineer William Williams (a mentor to Robert E. Lee who helped build the Army Corps of Engineers) planned the Niagara Ship Canal at a spot that would later be claimed by William Love, whose power canal would feed the Model City megalopolis he envisioned rising in Western New York. And Elon Huntington Hooker, scion of two distinguished families, plotted a chemical empire only a short distance away from the area where his firm's waste would one day be buried: at Love Canal.

The fact that so much happened in what became the Love Canal area demands explanation. Yet Love Canal is often portrayed in relatively flat terms as a crisis flowing from a compact history of industrialization and chemical use in the mid- to late 20th century.[20] Even most scholarly studies begin after chemicals have been dumped into the Love Canal landscape, after thousands of people have already moved into the subdivision of the same name, and after Love Canal families have demanded evacuation from the area. But why were the chemicals dumped *there,* at Love Canal, in the first place? Why did this neighborhood—built over a dump—exist where it did and why did people move *there* years before revelations about old chemical hazards surfaced? Did anyone raise environmental objections to toxic waste disposal at or beyond Love Canal before the 1970s? Perhaps most importantly, just how did the citizens' movement form and influence broader environmental discussions in American culture—why was it so threatening and significant to so many people *beyond* Love Canal?

Answering any one of these questions would be an arduous task. But taken together, they form an environmental epic that, I hope, both explains and transcends Love Canal proper. Indeed, I would argue that the best way to understand the crisis, and the citizen's movement that prompted it, is to start at the very beginning of Love Canal's environmental history. As a place, as a problem, as a movement of people, Love Canal is a capacious entity indeed. Uncovering Love Canal's multi-layered meanings requires journeying far back in time to examine such topics as Native-colonial landscape disputes, Americans' attempts to build out the 19th century American environment via massive infrastructure projects, and the transformation of environmental journalism in the 1970s. In short, one can see a lot of environmental history from Love Canal. All of it is relevant to understanding the toxic tragedy there and its still potent legacy. In fact, one might say that Love Canal offers a terrific environmental case study in what engineers and social scientists refer to as "path dependency": the notion that established pathways determine future developments. At Love Canal, generations of industrial dreamers laid down a history of land use that led almost inexorably to the establishment of toxic burial grounds in the 20th century. The Love Canal citizens' movement was the first group to challenge this industrial path dependence—to break the cycle of disposable land use that had long dominated area politics and economics.

The very notion of path dependency is linked to another powerful brand of scholarly inquiry: Deep History. We now have extended environmental histories of the Hudson River and Long Island Sound, of Thoreau's Walden and John Muir's Hetch Hetchy, of cities stretching from Boston to Chicago to Seattle. And there are several Deep Histories of Niagara Falls. It is somewhat surprising, then, that no environmental history of Love Canal exists. So what do we notice when focusing on its deep past?[21]

For one thing, there was a very long history of environmental protest along the Niagara Frontier. No sooner had the great La Salle began building his 60-ton commercial ship in the 1670s than local Iroquois tried to destroy it, believing that it augured ill for the landscape they utilized. At the turn of the 20th century, nature reformers opposed the advent of hydroelectric power plants appearing along the Niagara River, including William Love's fantastical "Model City" scheme that relied on an artificial waterfall named "Love's Canal." Even during the era of Hooker Chemical's ascent in the early 1900s, local environmentalists were busy tabulating industrialization's balance sheet, noting that great developmental gains came with rising environmental costs.

Love Canal activists offered the most penetrating and sustained challenge to unbridled commercial and industrial development, especially the legacy of toxic waste that undergirded the miracle of the American Chemical Century. Increasingly conscious of the historical forces that shaped their struggle, Love Canal residents began asking tough questions about their environment and its place in a world nearly overrun by industrial waste. In newspaper articles, speeches, activist reports and other venues, they wondered how the industrial past had led to Love Canal. Anne Hillis, a young mother who became one of the most vocal Love Canal residents, argued that "our cry is not only for the people of Love Canal but for our country, for Love Canals are all over."[22] As she and other activists saw it, the nation must learn from Love Canal by reorienting societal ethics to account for toxic troubles in the past, present and future.

There is still more, for Love Canal's past illuminates the fundamental redefinition of landscape in American culture. Prior to the 20th century, European-American explorers and settlers alike saw "the landscape" as an almost abstract entity beyond human habitation. Often conflated with conceptions of "wilderness," a landscape might be a forest where evil spirits lurked or an open plain teeming with wildlife.[23] But it was usually devoid of people. For explorers and settlers coming to the Niagara region in the 1700s and 1800s, the Love Canal area fit this definition: it was, to their eyes, an uninhabited and open landscape—a developmental frontier. The very first portrait of the region, a famed woodcut from the 1690s affixed to a book about La Salle's North American travels, pictured greater Niagara Falls as vast, empty, and ready for major economic development. Forgetting about the area's Native peoples, explorers saw both Niagara and Love Canal as a wondrous natural landscape awaiting environmental conquest. Even now, standard dictionary definitions of "landscape" refer to it in rather classical frontier terms—the areas "out there" and away from population centers. According to one standard definition, "landscape" refers to "[a]n expanse of scenery that can be seen in a single view," such as a desert or mountain landscape.[24]

By the late 20th century, however, Love Canal became associated with a different definition of "landscape." Now it was also a place where people had fundamentally altered the environment via human landmarks, industrial development, and/or daily living arrangements. This "vernacular landscape," as scholars have referred to America's built environment, comprises urban infrastructure, average homes and neighborhoods, strip malls, highways and roads, and other human-constructed forms that, in one way or another, compete with nature as the dominant spatial force of a particular region.[25] As the EPA now puts it, in the post-industrial world, landscape must be defined not merely as open space but as the "traits, patterns, and structure of a specific geographic area, including its biological composition, its physical environment, and its anthropogenic or social patterns." Thus, just as there is a natural landscape of mountains at the Continental Divide, so too is there a hazardous waste landscape of dumps in the nation's industrial-urban core—a veritable ecosystem of toxic waste—that we must always keep in mind. Love Canal's Deep History constitutes an important step in that modern redefinition of the American landscape.[26]

Thinking about landscape in this fashion is no rhetorical exercise. For it also means redefining the very meaning of environmentalism in and beyond Love Canal. If vernacular landscapes comprise day-to-day human living spaces (including dumping grounds), then environmentalism must encompass them too; it cannot focus only on saving nature, or pristine landscapes, out there in the great non-human beyond. In fact, the corollary principle of landscape redefinition is that everyone has a right to landscape health—clean air, clean water, and clean land. We now call this notion environmental justice, and it is something that ruffles few feathers among either politicians or reformers. Yet at one time it most certainly did. To the extent that it is now commonplace to think about the landscape health of the nation's urban and industrial heartland, we might once again nod in Love Canal's direction. For the people in this infamous neighborhood were among the first to argue that their streets, sewers, homes, and yards comprised a threatened, and threatening, landscape. In the end, that may be the most important Love Canal legacy of all.

This book is broken into three sections, each detailing the way that the Love Canal landscape has been used, altered, and understood through distinct eras of our environmental past. The story continues up to the present, for a portion of the old Love Canal neighborhood has been revitalized. Borrowing words of wisdom from William Faulkner, it is clear that Love Canal's "past is never dead. It's not even past."[27]

Part I, "Love Canal in the Era of Great Dreams," examines early debates over commercialized land use in the Niagara region, generally, and the Love Canal area more specifically. Here the idea of path dependency reigns supreme through an extended timeframe, as a parade of developers, including both William Love himself (who gave his name to the canal zone above the falls that would one day be used as a chemical disposal pit), and Elon Huntington Hooker (whose chemical plant helped fuel the American chemical century) staked claims to the local landscape. My telling of this part of the story—especially the life of chemical magnate Elon Hooker—relies on new archival research. To date, no one has really examined the firm's astounding growth in the early part of the 20th century, mostly because the Love Canal saga made it difficult to do so. But new research reveals just how fast and furiously Hooker was expanding at precisely the moment that it (and other companies) began placing large amounts of toxic byproducts in landfills like Love Canal. As one of the most successful companies in Niagara Falls in the last hundred years, Hooker's story illuminates some of the main economic and ideological forces shaping land use patterns in Western New York. While this prehistory of Love Canal ranges over broad swaths of time, it is crucial to understanding how a toxic dump took shape in the region by the middle of the 20th century. I ask readers to stay with the story in these early chapters, for they frame and inform what comes next.

Part II, "Love Canal in the Era of Environmentalism," focuses on the rise of citizen environmentalism at Love Canal in the 1970s and early 1980s, including its ripple effects on things ranging from environmental activism to environmental journalism. Here time slows down to show just how painstakingly area activists worked to make Love Canal more than just a story about residential relocation. The chapters in this section are a bit longer and more detailed, reflecting (I hope) the wide-ranging impact of Love Canal activism in just a few years. It is still rather remarkable that a largely working-class community of just a few thousand people, especially activist women, could so quickly attune itself to the rhythms of environmental protest. But that is precisely what Love Canal residents did when they discovered the buried toxic dump at the center of their neighborhood. My tale of Love Canal protest is informed not only by newly opened archives left by activists but interviews with journalists, politicians and residents who lived through the crisis. After talking to these figures and working in the archives, I came to see Love Canal protestors as the most significant environmental activists of the post–Earth Day era. Digging into their actions and their consequences illuminates why I came to that conclusion.

Part III, "Learning From Love Canal," looks at Love Canal's legacies in the final decades of the 20th century. Here, a surprising but not wholly unpredictable tale takes shape, given the path dependency of developmental dreaming that led to Love Canal in the first place: the partial resettlement of the neighborhood in the 1990s. With activists gone, local and state officials were particularly eager to return area lands to productive use—a very important thing given the region's economic slide. Yet this action also compelled Love Canal protestors to rededicate themselves to environmental reform in the 1980s and 1990s. Indeed, the struggle to prevent Love Canal resettlement went hand in hand with keeping Love Canal's memory as a grassroots movement alive and relevant to new generations of people.

The book ends with an epilogue that examines the continuing debates over how to mark—or memorialize—Love Canal in the 21st century. In the end, as in the beginning, I view Love Canal as both a potent place and a powerful metaphor standing for something much larger than itself. Indeed, its multi-faceted history as an icon of both environmental disaster and environmental activism still looms large in any and all debates about Love Canal in the 21st century. If the past is any guide, Love Canal will remain relevant as long as people are concerned about their land and their health.

PART ONE

LOVE CANAL IN THE ERA
OF GREAT DREAMS

Past as Prologue

Developing Niagara Before Love Canal

We went two Leagues above the great Fall of Niagara, where we made a
Dock for Building the Ship we wanted for our Voyage. This was the most
convenient place we could pitch upon....
—Father Louis Hennepin in 1698 on the building of
La Salle's ship, the *Griffon*, near the future site of Love Canal[1]

In 1978, Love Canal resident Anne Hillis sarcastically explained the "recipe" for the chemical disaster taking shape in her neighborhood: take "approximately 16 acres" of land, add "22,000 tons of toxic wastes, mix with spring water, snow, etc..." Then, she wrote, add "human beings." The "yield" would be "miscarriage...birth defects...suicide and death." For people wondering just how the chemicals ended up in Love Canal in the first place, Hillis wrote that the whole saga began not in the recent past but in "the late 1800s, [when] a canal had been dug" by a starry-eyed industrialist who then abandoned the altered landscape. The groove of earth he left behind was "filled in with chemicals in the... 1940s," covered over and forgotten. Only later would "these chemicals" migrate from the dump into the local environment. For Hillis, as for other residents, Love Canal's troubled environmental present was a product of its toxic past.[2]

But how far back did that troubled past go? New York State health officials asserted that the "seeds" of Love Canal were sown in Niagara's "highly industrialized" history, which stretched from the late 19th century onward.[3] Similarly, the *Niagara Gazette* created a "Love Canal Chronology" that began in 1894, when entrepreneur William Love began excavating a power canal that never materialized but whose remains formed a perfect burial pit later on.[4] An activist group pushed Love Canal's chronology back further. Although "Love Canal became a household word in 1978," the group claimed, "the idea for the place that was to carry the name originated in 1836," when an engineer stamped out the route of an artificial river that would be even grander than the Erie Canal.[5]

No matter how far back they went, all of these commentators saw history as a key lens through which to view the modern Love Canal disaster. Yet few traced the area's toxic history back to colonial times. If they had, they would have seen that from the 17th century on, a succession of European and then American explorers, entrepreneurs, and developers plotted massive projects in the greater Niagara region generally—and the Love Canal landscape in particular—that defined the local environment as a usable, and even disposable, commodity. In no small way, Love Canal was a problem centuries in the making. Indeed, Love Canal's "mixed legacy," as a recent report put it, went back to the very beginning of North American development.[6] Blessed by its convenient position astride the Niagara River and Lakes Erie and Ontario, Niagara Falls became an important economic and transportation hub—a crossroads for competing empires, Native Americans, and eventually the expanding American nation. By the early 1900s, nearly three-fourths of North America's human population lived within a 500-mile radius of Buffalo-Niagara and thus the Love Canal landscape. When business leaders referred to Western New York as the "Niagara Frontier," they paid tribute to this cowboy-like industrial past. Buffalo-Niagara was the nation's first "West": an environment whose natural resources beckoned and inspired grand commercial and industrial dreams. It also witnessed epic industrial failure, which paved the way for subsequent disasters at Love Canal and elsewhere.[7]

In this way, well before it became synonymous with chemical catastrophe, Love Canal was associated with high environmental drama. Indeed, when developer William Love showed up in the 1890s, the landscape he traversed was already fraught with discord.

1. Love Canal in the Era of La Salle

Niagara's first great dreamer—and the Love Canal landscape's first environmental transformer—was the dashing French explorer René-Robert

Cavelier La Salle. He came crashing into the region almost by accident in the late 17th century. Like other explorers who plied the North American continent, La Salle searched for shortcuts to Asia and its highly valuable spice trade. Though he failed to discover the fabled Northwest Passage, La Salle found precious commodities in the landscape itself, especially timber and fur. His inaugural visit to the area probably occurred in 1669, when La Salle sailed into Irondequoit Bay, just off Lake Ontario near present-day Rochester. After making contact with members of the Seneca nation, La Salle sailed back to his imperial base at Montréal. In 1678, he arrived in Niagara, using Native American guides to reach the fabled Falls.[8]

La Salle soon saw the Niagara region's strategic importance to global trade networks. After reconnoitering the upper Niagara River—i.e., above the Falls—he envisioned the region as a key link in a transportation chain stretching from the Great Lakes to the Atlantic world. In La Salle's eyes, Niagara would become not simply a military or trading post but a great commercial entrepôt. Timber, fish, fur—La Salle hoped to make his fame by carrying these highly desired items from the New World to Europe, where overdevelopment had made them increasingly scarce.[9] As La Salle's traveling companion, a Jesuit priest named Louis Hennepin, would later put it, the French explorer sought to "fetch European commodities by a more convenient route than ... by the River St. Lawrence," the main French trade route off Lake Ontario. To reach the interior of the North American continent from the St. Lawrence, European traders usually took the Ottawa River. But this pushed them further north, an especially problematic undertaking in winter. By using the Niagara River, La Salle hoped to secure a better trade route and thus more power from European rulers.[10]

As it turned out, La Salle's commercial dream took more definite shape at Love Canal. After journeying around the Falls, he and his men decamped to Cayuga Island, a small piece of land bisected by the Niagara River. Four miles upstream from the cataract, it was also directly across from the future mainland locale of William Love's planned power canal: a fertile plain that led down to the marshy grasslands along the shoreline. A gentle stream—dubbed "the Little Niagara"—flowed around the island before rejoining the Big River. The Little Niagara also fed into Cayuga Creek, whose tributaries infiltrated the expansive countryside above the Falls. Commodious and well protected from the harsh currents of the big

Niagara, the island became La Salle's shipbuilding base. The site had the further virtue of offering protection from prying eyes, particularly the Seneca who watched La Salle's movements with great concern. As Father Hennepin put it, Cayuga Island was "the most convenient place we could pitch upon."[11]

La Salle's men set to work on the first European trading vessel to sail the upper Great Lakes. When completed in August 1679, La Salle's ship would weigh nearly 60 tons—the largest man-made boat produced on this side of the Atlantic. It looked like "a moving fortress," in Hennepin's words. Christening it "Le Griffon"—an imposing bird favored by La Salle's royal patron—the explorer believed that his vessel would soar above all doubters.[12] This included Native groups, which saw the *Griffon's* creation as a bad omen.[13] But La Salle did not heed Native concerns or worry about imperial doubters. He had lands to survey, routes to map, wealth to mine. After a prayer from Father Hennepin, La Salle sailed west in search of a lucrative future.

Along the way, he explained his vision to Hennepin, who later turned La Salle's words into a great epic of exploration and development with Niagara Falls serving as a pivot point. Entitled *A New Discovery of a Vast Country in America*, Hennepin's book foretold the immense wealth contained within the North American landscape. But it didn't start out that way. Indeed, as a missionary, Hennepin explained that he hoped to save Native souls. At Niagara, however, he realized that La Salle's men wanted to "buy all the furs and skins" they could "and... enrich themselves in one single voyage." Hennepin himself was impressed with Niagara's environmental wealth (game, timber, wild berries). When the *Griffon* set sail, Hennepin understood that religion placed a distant second to economic domination of the landscape.

This was certainly the message Hennepin conveyed to his readers. Issued at the close of the 1600s, *A New Discovery of a Vast Country in America* featured the first widely disseminated image of Niagara Falls. [Fig. 2] Hennepin's famous woodcut showed explorers looking at the majestic Falls in awe. Yet the panoramic view looked well beyond the Falls, where an open landscape above and beyond the Falls dissolves into the horizon. Significantly, the landscape is rendered empty, symbolizing the developmental opportunity awaiting European explorers. This amazing

Figure 2 La Salle's Niagara Falls: This is perhaps the earliest image of the
Niagara region and it suggests the bounteous landscape awaiting future
developers—at least from European-American perspectives. The area that
became Love Canal would have been located above the Falls on the left of the
image. (Source: Hennepin, A Vast New Discovery in America, 1698. Image
courtesy of the Library Company of Philadelphia)

view, Hennepin explained, was "our discovery": the economic potential
of the Great Lakes basin.[14] In fact, neither La Salle nor Hennepin had been
the first explorers to see the Falls (other European travelers had been
there decades earlier). And neither of them sketched this famous image.
In fact, the Niagara woodcut was executed years later by Dutch artists
who had never actually seen the Falls. Nevertheless, Hennepin's memories of greater Niagara shaped the making of the woodcut. In the image, as
in Hennepin's book (which was published in several languages), nature
beckoned European explorers and settlers to conquer the area beyond the
Falls. As someone who had traveled with La Salle to the fabled region,
Hennepin would become a minor celebrity. He was evidently happy with
the engravers who made Niagara seem empty and ready for commercial
exploitation. Like La Salle, he saw Niagara as the gateway to empire. And
as La Salle's confidant, he had seen its potential first.

As a religious man, Hennepin certainly knew the dark side of such grand visions. Euro-Americans saw evil lurking in forests and undeveloped landscapes. Religious figures also worried about the sin of moneymaking. To his dying day, Hennepin believed that La Salle's various missions should have focused more on piety and less on profit. His old companion's demise surely dimmed Hennepin's mood. In 1687, La Salle was exploring the lower Mississippi River in search of still-newer trade routes. After pushing his men too hard, they rebelled, killing La Salle with little fanfare. Luckily, Hennepin was not there. Yet Hennepin could not deny that the New World landscapes he visited with La Salle had inspired him too. Later, he even claimed to be a co-discoverer of the New World's environmental bounty, at Niagara and beyond.[15] He published his travel book not to warn others away from North American exploration but to curry favor with various imperial rulers who might dub Hennepin a power broker. And the great symbol of his dreams was that seemingly empty landscape above the Falls.

2. Building Niagara: Forts, Roads, People

La Salle (and Hennepin) set in motion the idea that the Niagara region—including tiny Cayuga Island—must serve as the base of a future economic empire. "This," famed 19th-century historian Francis Parkman declared of the trade route La Salle surveyed around Niagara Falls, remained "the most important pass of all the Western wilderness."[16] As a crossroads between the North American interior and Atlantic coast, it remained unsurpassed. Little wonder that French, British, American, and Iroquoian forces would all shed blood over this important landscape.

But before they developed the Niagara landscape, artists, travelers, and others paid homage to the magnificence of the Falls. Already by the mid-1600s, Niagara Falls was enshrined as a defining part of the North American sublime. It was, for many visitors, the very essence of unbridled nature. According to a French missionary in 1669, Niagara was "one of the finest cataracts, or waterfalls, in the world," its height, power and natural beauty unsurpassed by almost anything in the Old World.[17] Generations of writers felt that words failed them when confronted with such an awesome natural spectacle. "I already find my pen, or at least my ideas, inadequate to give any account of what is now before me," an English visitor scribbled in his journal in 1787.[18] By the Romantic era, Niagara provided travelers with a sense of rapture and transcendent insight into the heavenly works of Nature and Nature's God. "All must confess who view this wondrous scene, That if God were not, this had never been," a minor poet observed in 1849. "His voice here thunders in the mighty flood, And these rent rocks proclaim, their maker God; I love the dullness of the cataract's roar, And the wild grandeur of its craggy shore."[19]

So long as they did not harm the Falls proper, commercial schemers, developers, and traders could plan a multitude of massive projects in the Niagara region. Indeed, in La Salle's wake, French, European, and then American powers steadily built up the broader Niagara landscape with transportation infrastructure that facilitated territorial conquest and inter-regional trade. In this way, forts, roads, and storehouses served as a form of imperial eminent domain. By the 1720s, when the French built a military post/trading house at the confluence of the Lower Niagara River and Lake Ontario, the Niagara landscape had its first permanent commercial structure. Replacing the smaller trading and supply houses that had dotted the landscape before, Fort Niagara was an imposing building. Part military redoubt, part trading post and supply center, it signaled further European encroachment on Niagara's Native communities. By the 1750s, when it was expanded and reinforced by the French, Fort Niagara was one of the region's dominant landmarks—almost as notable as Niagara Falls itself.

Fort Niagara also symbolized European-Americans' desire to overcome the main environmental obstacle at Niagara Falls: the Lewiston Ledge. A geological wall of granite and trees, the Ledge (or Escarpment, as it is now known) separates the upper and lower Niagara land masses. Formed from millennia of erosion, the Escarpment runs east and west for over 900 miles. At Lewiston, it creates a ridge more than 200 feet high. "This rise, and others similar to it," an 1811 New York State report on navigation between the Hudson River and Great Lakes observed, "are called by the inhabitants, the ridge, the ledge, the slope and the hill. A more proper general appellation, perhaps, is, the steep, though occasionally by the elevation each way, it becomes truly a ridge, or from the horizontal strata of stone as, truly, a ledge." Noting that the Niagara escarpment was "almost perpendicular" near Niagara, the report described this natural phenomenon in forbidding terms.[20] Both Native Americans and European-American travelers called Lewiston "the carrying place"—a trail that took people up and down the Falls through a series of steep ledges. Noted Swedish botanist Peter Kalm learned the hard way about the carrying place when he first visited the Falls in 1750. "We did walk over the carrying Place, having in the beginning besides the steep and high side of the river to step up two high steep hills one after the other."[21]

For European traders, infrastructure and technology helped smooth the rough road around the Falls. The French experimented with a pulley system that allowed traders to get goods up and down the Lewiston Ledge more efficiently. And both the French and the British came to believe that forts and roads would speed area development and thus enhance their claim upon the landscape itself. In this sense, Fort Niagara rationalized the landscape, making the area more accessible to traders and settlers alike. With a critical mass of people in Niagaraland, the French and then the British (who defeated the French in the 1760s and became the region's main European power brokers) thought they might better utilize Western New York's abundant forests, plentiful fish and game resources, and beaver, bison, and deer pelts. Roads to and from Fort Niagara cut out more dependable pathways around the Falls than the old Carrying Place. By the time Americans took Fort Niagara from the British at the close of the Revolution, the area was poised for a major influx of migrants—and an even bigger change in the region's environment.

3. Native Resistance and Early Environmental Battles in Greater Niagara

But European-American settlement and development would not occur without Native resistance. For years, Native Americans had resisted La Salle–style dreams. The Iroquois, a vaunted political alliance that took shape in the mid-1500s, often opposed white interlopers, including the Dutch, French, British, and eventually Americans. Initially comprising five nations—the Mohawk, Oneida, Cayuga, Onondaga, and Seneca—the

League of the Iroquois (as it was known) held sway from modern-day Pennsylvania and Ohio through New York, Ontario, and Québec. From Niagara Falls to the Genesee River basin, the Seneca served as Iroquoia's "Keepers of the Western Door" (the Mohawk served as the "Keepers of the Eastern Door" near the Hudson River Valley.)[22] Seneca men, known as fierce warriors and formidable hunters, traversed the Western New York landscape with a sense of certitude that underscored their belief that this was "our land," as a famed Seneca orator put it in the early 19th century.[23] Cutting trails east and west, and utilizing north-south waterways (particularly the Genesee and Niagara rivers), they ranged over an area that comprised hundreds of square miles. Though the main Seneca villages were near Geneseo (about 70 miles away), the landscape around Niagara Falls, including the future Love Canal landscape, became a favored hunting and fishing spot. Seasonal camps along the Niagara River allowed Seneca fishermen to capture whitefish and trout in great quantities. Seneca hunters also rounded up deer, wild turkey, and even bear. The Falls itself provided occasional bounty in the form of dead fish and game tumbling over its mighty banks; Native hunters would simply gather the remains at the bottom, thankful for a gift from above.

Like other Native groups, the Iroquois changed their landscape— they were not the mythical "ecological" Indians of environmental lore.[24] They used slash-and-burn methods to clear fields for crops (which also nourished soils with ash deposits); they carved out towns and villages from wooded landscapes and moved settlements every ten to twenty years to new spaces (sometimes as a means of finding more fertile lands, sometimes to get away from waste and refuse that accumulated over time); they cut trails into the wilderness and used trees to build canoes of various sizes; and they engaged in hunting and fishing expeditions that provided protein to Native diets (often flushing out wildlife from bosky landscapes via controlled forest fires). They also traded with Europeans for various commodities and implements.[25]

Yet, like other Native cultures, the Iroquois defined themselves into the natural landscape: they were a part of nature's ecological balance, not apart from it. This led to major conflict with white explorers and settlers, who saw the land as a commodity to be dominated and developed (as many early modern Western clerics saw it, the biblical story of Genesis granted humans agency over the land). Indeed, one key precept of Native American life was self-sufficiency. Prior to European contact, Native populations rarely overused natural resources, even if that meant enduring periods of privation. Indians' relatively low population densities (perhaps born of diets less rich in protein than in Europe) and seasonal hunting/farming practices created a smaller environmental footprint than that of European-Americans. By moving to different locales, as the Seneca did, Native communities allowed animal and fish reserves to replenish themselves. By moving towns and villages every so often, Indians likewise allowed soils to revive. These actions reflected a Native environmental consciousness: use but do not abuse nature to sustain human populations. In one of the most wicked ironies of European colonization, Native sustainability helped produce the rich landscape that inspired La Salle and Hennepin. Forests with abundant wood, fishing stocks too plentiful to exhaust, and animal hides in massive quantities—such environmental wealth was scarce in Europe but almost inexhaustible in North America. It impressed explorers again and again. And much of that can be read as a tribute to Native communities' sensitivity to ecological balance.[26]

Iroquoian language, rituals, and communication patterns highlighted the signal importance of the natural environment in Seneca daily life and thought. "The great Law of peace," the covenant organizing the Iroquois Confederacy, used the iconic image of the tree—whose shady limbs offered shelter to those around it and whose sturdy roots symbolized strength—to enshrine the central concept of inter-group harmony. Similarly, Seneca creation tales illuminate the connections between people and nature. In the Seneca creation story, a figure named Sky Woman falling through a hole in the atmosphere is saved by a bevy of animals. The very foundation of the earth is built on the back of a turtle, who uses soil provided by a beaver to cushion Sky Woman's fall. Humans then take shape from this original Earth mother. For the Iroquois, nature remained much more than a mythic entity. Rather, it allowed humanity to survive and even thrive.[27] Nature pervaded Iroquoian ceremonial life too. "The thunder ceremony" occurred "when the first sounds of thunder are heard in the spring," offering thanks to the creator for sustaining the Iroquois in a new season. The ritual Thanksgiving speech, which preceded and followed all ceremonies, offered gratitude for the gifts of nature. "The traditional

Iroquois ask[ed] the supernatural for nothing," a modern archaeologist has explained, "but are grateful for what they get [from nature] as a matter of course." In offering thanks, "things of the earth are mentioned first... then the springs, streams, rivers and lakes," followed by "the plants, bushes and saplings," and then the "trees, animals, birds." The Thanksgiving address reminds listeners of their relation to the natural world.[28]

Though Native culture remained vibrant into the 1700s, it could not overcome the incessant development pressures wrought by European-American expansion. By the close of the American Revolution, when increasing numbers of white settlers encroached on Native lands, Iroquois populations dwindled. Access to ancestral lands (and therefore a self-sufficient way of life) decreased as well. At the Treaty of Canandaigua in 1794—seventy miles from the Falls—Seneca negotiators seemed to secure nearly four million acres from American diplomats. But that deal was soon renegotiated. At the Treaty of Big Tree, held outside Buffalo in 1797, the Senecas were guaranteed only 200,000 acres of reservation space in Western New York. By the early 1800s, one of the great land transfers in American history was essentially done.[29] Between 1820 and 1860, a new round of transportation projects—most notably the Erie Canal, which was completed in 1825—brought roughly 200,000 white settlers to the Buffalo/Niagara region.[30]

Still, Native people protested. Red Jacket, a well-known Seneca orator, tried to make a last stand against overdevelopment of Niagara's landscape. [Fig. 3] Born in 1758, he seemed destined for a confrontation with whites. If his birth name of *Otetiani* ("Always Ready") did not predict such a future, then his adult name of *Shaygoyewatha* ("disturber of dreams" or "he wakes them up early," among other translations) surely did. Even the name by which most Anglo-Americans came to know him until his death in 1830 symbolized the man's bold stand as Native defender. Red Jacket earned the moniker by serving as a messenger for the British, hoping to somehow fend off the land-hungry American colonists who now pushed back against the mighty English in the Revolutionary War. (England's Proclamation of 1763 sought to keep colonists east of the Appalachian Mountains and thus away from Native peoples; white colonists' first major rebellion aimed at striking down that edict so they could expand at will.) The red jacket given him by the British may have only been a token

Sa-go-ye-wat-ha

Figure 3 Defender of Native Lands: Red Jacket. This portrait of Red Jacket was cast before the "vanishing Indian" genre flourished in the late-1800s. Pictured in Native dress, Red Jacket appears as many people saw him: a respected Seneca orator and diplomat. By this time, however, he had died and Seneca lands in Western New York were under siege by new waves of American settlers. (Source: William L. Stone, *Life and Times of Red Jacket, or Sa-go-ye-wat-ha*, New York, 1841. Image courtesy of the Library Company)

for services rendered to the Empire, but its colorful connotations—red was the color not only of the Empire but of liberation from bondage—indicated that the Seneca man would dedicate his life to an alternative vision of American land use. Aged and infirm in 1819, he told representatives of the Ogden Land Company to lay no more claims on Seneca territory.[31]

By one estimate, Red Jacket gave well over 100 speeches, including several well-publicized anti-development lectures, to whites. His lecture to Rev. Jacob Cram, a Massachusetts missionary, remains his most famous appeal. First recounted in a monthly publication in March 1809, Red Jacket's speech derided Cram's claim that Native Americans "cannot be happy hereafter" without Christianity. But Red Jacket knew that beneath Cram's words was a deeper desire for Native lands. Red Jacket offered a blistering critique of the violence and greed associated with white settlement in Native country. "Brother," he told Rev. Cram, "listen to what we say":

> There was a time when our forefathers owned this great island. Their seats extended from the rising to the setting sun. The Great Spirit had made it for the use of Indians. HE had created the buffalo, the deer, and other animals for food. HE had made the bear and the beaver. Their skin served us for clothing. HE had scattered them over the country, and taught us how to take them. He had caused the earth to produce corn for bread. All this HE had done for his red children, because HE loved them.

And then, Red Jacket declared, "an evil day came upon us" when "your forefathers crossed the great water, and landed on this island." Even after Native Americans "took pity on them" and provided "corn and meat," Europeans and then Americans "gave us poison [alcohol] in return." Once "the white people had...found our country," he went on, trouble arose. As white settlers in Western New York increased, "they wanted more land; they wanted our country." Now, he said, facing Rev. Cram, "you want to force your religion upon us." Such overtures, Red Jacket insisted, must be rejected. Though Red Jacket did not wish to banish Christianity, a none-too-amused Rev. Cram quickly departed, refusing to shake hands with someone in league with "the devil."[32]

Though he was a complex figure in Native communities, Red Jacket remained at the forefront of Seneca struggles to control their land and way of life in Western New York. At a 1796 Council meeting at Fort Niagara, where Senecas had long camped, sold furs, and returned from hunting and fishing expeditions, Red Jacket vilified a U.S. commander who had requested that Iroquois people support more roads through Iroquoian territory. "Brother," he told the commander, Senecas wanted to protect "our land."[33] Indeed, while he would allow engineers access to Seneca land, Americans must halt further settlement. In particular, he wanted to stop "the great eater with a big belly," the Seneca label for Revolutionary financier Robert Morris (whose land holdings were spun off to the Holland Land Company and earmarked for development). But Red Jacket's appeal could not hold back a deluge of white settlers with their own developmental dreams. No sooner had the 19th century opened than the Holland Land Company offered cheap land to tens of thousands of people streaming into Western New York. By the Civil War, the company had produced an astonishing 600 different types of maps to speed demographic and economic development in the Buffalo-Niagara region.[34] When Red Jacket died, only a few thousand Seneca remained in Western New York and industrial development was more than just a dream. It was a reality visible in a whole host of infrastructure projects that not only commercialized the landscape but completely altered it.

4. The Niagara Ship Canal

Indeed, the drive to develop the Niagara landscape only intensified in the 1800s. Unsurprisingly, the Love Canal landscape took on its first recognizably modern shape in the form of a major engineering project that was planned but never built: the Niagara Ship Canal (NSC). One of the NSC's possible routes bypassed Cayuga Island, where La Salle launched the *Griffon*. Though never built, the NSC was more than a passing fancy. It arose from the canal-building craze of the early Republic. The Erie Canal, stretching 360 miles from Albany to Buffalo, was the first of America's great artificial waterways. Carved out of the New York landscape between 1817 and 1825 it was an engineering marvel that facilitated American migration and economic development.[35] Not only did the Erie Canal cut travel time, it paid for itself in a few years through tolls and constant river traffic. During the 1820s and 1830s, engineers, business leaders, and politicians throughout the Union sought to replicate the Erie Canal's success by building a maze of copycat rivers. And no copycat project seemed grander than the Niagara Ship Canal. By building a bigger and more advanced trade route around Niagara Falls, some New York businessmen asserted, the NSC would ensure the Empire State's economic dominance for years to come. As the famous abolitionist and investor Gerrit Smith proclaimed at mid-century, the Niagara Ship Canal was destined to happen.[36]

The project's visionary advocate was a West Point graduate named William G. Williams. Born in Philadelphia in 1801, Williams became one of the early republic's most celebrated surveyors and engineers. His disciples included a young Robert E. Lee, who ran boundary surveys of the Midwest at roughly the time as Williams and befriended the veteran engineer.[37] Before his death in the U.S.-Mexican War in 1846 (with Lee by his side), Williams gained renown with the Topographical Engineers.[38] Essentially a subset of the better-known Army Corps of Engineers, Williams' men focused on exploration and development. Stamping out roads, improving harbors, building lighthouses, clearing waterways, erecting forts—these were the essential technical tasks of the Topographical Engineers.[39] Williams is still known for an 1842 report on the dredging and widening of the St. Clair River Delta in Michigan, which eased the movement of larger ships between the nation's interior and its Eastern ports.[40]

His magnum opus was the Niagara Ship Canal. After settling in Buffalo in the 1830s, Williams undertook a massive "survey around the Falls of Niagara" to plan a route for this major new project. Far from a localized endeavor, his plan was a "National Ship Canal" that would allow for the speedy movement of both troops and goods through the Great Lakes. The advent of the Welland Canal in British Canada prompted Williams' sense of urgency, for he worried that the Canadian project would undermine American trade (and perhaps encourage British encroachment on America's northern borderland). Williams deemed the Niagara Ship Canal both indispensable and "patriotic." By 1836, he issued a thorough report to Congress, hoping that national leaders would agree to build his dream canal.[41]

Williams' surveyed several possible NSC routes around Niagara Falls, one of which went by Cayuga Island. By slicing into the Cayuga marshes and cutting a diagonal path towards the town of Lewiston seven miles away, this route was direct and relatively short. (Indeed, it was in many ways an enlarged version of the "carrying place" trails of colonial times.) Williams was so taken with the Cayuga area that he planned a second route there, this time using Cayuga Creek as a guide for a canal that ended farther north at the town of Wilson, twelve miles away on the shores of Lake Ontario.[42] He proposed several other routes as well. But whichever line was chosen, Williams knew that the NSC would require a huge build-out and major federal expenditures. Any new canal would run several million dollars, a princely sum at the time. And because the Niagara Ship Canal would have to overcome the Lewiston Ledge—a higher and more difficult terrain than that faced by Erie Canal builders—it would test American engineering expertise all over again.[43]

None of this mattered to Williams, who saw the Niagara Ship Canal as a true world wonder. On the Cayuga-to-Lewiston line, for instance, he planned gigantic locks that were 200 feet long, 50 feet wide, and 10 feet deep. These concrete blocks would have been more than half the length of a modern-day football field—so big that Williams also planned a series of intermediate basins to ease the hydraulic demands of raising and lowering ships along the steep slopes of the escarpment. After reading Williams' survey, many congressmen were impressed, though not enough to fund the $5 million scheme. [Fig. 4] Williams kept pushing the NSC, arguing that its construction would become an emblem of American technical ingenuity far into the future.[44] An 1840 image produced by an unknown artist pictured Williams' canal in these sublime terms. Dominating the natural landscape around it, the canal carries ships upward on a series of beautifully cut stone steps. Unlike Hennepin's famous image of Niagara Falls, no one faints before the Niagara Ship Canal. Rather, people traipse about the NSC's imposing edifice as if on holiday. For Williams, the NSC was nothing less than industrial art that smoothed out nature's rough edges.[45]

Williams' belief that technology improved nature was increasingly popular in the early 1800s. The so-called fashionable tour took Americans along the bridges, canals, and other internal improvements that made the

No. 23.

IN SENATE,

January 30, 1839.

REPORT

Of the Committee on Canals, on the Bill to authorize the United States to construct the Niagara
Ship Canal.

Mr. Skinner, from the committee on canals, to which was referred
the bill to authorize the United States to construct the Niagara Ship
Canal,

REPORTS:

That the committee have had the subject under consideration, and
have given to it that careful and deliberate attention which its importance demands.

By reference to a report made to Congress in 1837, by the Hon.
Gideon Hard, of this State, it appears that the project of a ship canal
to connect the navigable waters of Lakes Erie and Ontario, has for many years claimed the attention of the General Government as one of
conceded public utility, and one the construction of which was intimately
connected with the military and commercial prosperity of the country.

In the year 1808, in pursuance of a resolution of the Senate of the
United States, the Secretary of the Treasury, submitted to that body,
an able and elaborate report in relation to internal improvements, which
should command the attention and aid of the General Government; among
which was included the important project of the Niagara Ship canal.
He alludes to the limited project which had previously been started, by
the enterprise of private individuals, for cutting a canal from Porter's
store house, near old Fort Schlosser to Devil's Hole, (so called,) about

[Senate No. 23.]   A

Figure 4 The Niagara Ship Canal: As this state report indicates, many people
saw the Niagara Ship Canal as the next major American building project after
the Erie Canal. Associated with the technological sublime, the Niagara Ship
Canal was also viewed as a "military and commercial" imperative by state and
federal officials. Yet the dream of building the canal was dashed by fears that it
would simply cost too much, among other things. Yet the routes surveyed for
the Niagara Ship Canal inspired William Love's proposal for a power canal in
the region. (Source: "Report of the Committee on Canals, on the bill to
authorize the United States to construct the Niagara Ship Canal," Albany, 1839.
Image courtesy of the Library Company of Philadelphia)

Western New York landscape more accessible and thus more aesthetically pleasing.[46] Prompted by the Erie Canal's completion, the fashionable tour allowed Americans to value, not fear, their natural landscape precisely because it had been engineered into safety. At Niagara Falls, the "Biddle Staircase"—named after the Philadelphia financier who funded its construction—dropped nearly 80 feet down into the Niagara basin, allowing people to feel nature's raw power without risking their lives. Completed in 1829, the staircase became a great attraction and was the subject of many images through the years (it came down in 1927).[47] As one guidebook noted in 1838, the Biddle steps provided unmatched views of the Falls, as long as visitors did not lose their nerve. *"Descend that without fail,"* the guidebook encouraged readers traipsing around the Biddle Staircase entrance at Goat Island, and soon you would have a "tremendous flood pouring over you."[48] At other places, Niagara tourists received certificates of accomplishment for walking around, near and even behind "the great falling sheet of water," as one promoter put it.[49] Though pitched in stark terms, these odes to Niagara's awesome power actually touted human technical ingenuity, for the bridges, staircases, and towers now spreading throughout the region had turned the once-imposing landscape into a pleasing day at the park.

In fact, Niagara Falls was fast becoming a testing ground for the idea that nature could be re-engineered for almost any purpose, from recreational to economic to industrial. And yet, so grand was the Niagara Ship Canal that Williams never built it. In many ways, it was too big to begin. Nevertheless, each decade of the 19th century found new proposals for a Niagara Ship Canal.[50] In the 1890s, a man named William Love studied all of Williams' plans in great detail, hoping that he might bring to fruition what the great antebellum engineer had only dreamed about doing in Niagaraland.

5. Banished from the Garden of Eden, Niagara Style

The Niagara region that La Salle and Hennepin had long ago explored for its commercial prowess, and which Red Jacket had recently defended as a Native haven, remained a crossroads of American environmental debate long after Williams' plan failed to find financial backers. Indeed, in the industrial age proper, Niagara Falls became even more a symbol of American power and prosperity, as hydroelectric power plants became the region's "next big thing." That had ramifications as well for the Love Canal landscape, which often found its way into new industrial dreams. Yet the entire Niagara environment remained a conflicted symbol of American enterprise. In the late 1800s, people began to wonder: Were there environmental and even moral downsides to unregulated development at one of nature's most hallowed places? The great humorist Mark Twain thought so. He even relocated the human fall from grace to Niagara Falls, where, he thought, *fin de siècle* industrial dreamers had disfigured God's grandest natural creation. "Been examining the great waterfall," his American Adam observes in a wicked little story about "the first authentic mention" of the phrase "Niagara Falls." "It is the finest thing on the estate, I think." As the Falls fills with schemers who ignore God's warning to "keep off the grass," Adam and Eve contemplate the ultimate sin: a joke about making Niagara Falls flow backwards. "How wonderful it is to see that vast body of water tumble down there!" Adam thinks to himself one day, before regrettably adding that "it would be a deal more wonderful to see it tumble *up* there!"[51]

This old chestnut, blurted out by an idiotic Adam, offends God by essentially saying of nature, "so what?" With technology redefining the majestic Falls, humans could make water flow any way they want. And, Mark Twain implies, that very idea of environmental mastery offends God, who comments via the snake that Adam's joke illustrates the evil inherent in man-made "creation," a double entendre referring to both the advent of humans and human designs upon the natural world. And so, for the sin of overbearing knowledge and overdevelopment of a perfectly lovely landscape—Eve contemplates encouraging summer tourism at one point while Twain's story features a picture of the Biddle Staircase—the pair is kicked out of the Falls. Oh, well, Adam concludes, better to have Eve, children, and development outside the Garden than solitary nature inside it. The not-so-humorous lesson of Twain's delightfully told tale is that humans can never escape the contradiction at the heart of their modern existence: increasing power over the natural world comes at a hefty price. Many of Niagara's dreamers unwittingly learned a related lesson: even the fastest of currents tumble over the edge of great expectations.

2

Building Love's Canal

The fall from environmental grace that Mark Twain described was a product of sweeping industrialization at the close of the 19th century. Spurred by the advent of hydroelectric power, a whole new group of commercial schemers flooded the Falls in search of wealth, power, and prestige. "This is an electrical era," a Niagara booster bragged. "Back in the centuries that are past, we had the stone age, the ice age, etc., but the electrical age is purely the utilization of natural forces by the genius of man." "Naturally," he noted, "the first development of electric power was at the source of the greatest quantity of power anywhere to be found on earth, the Falls of Niagara."[1] That meant Niagara Falls would remain a watchword of industrial expansion far into the future.

Among the legion of businessmen, engineers, and investors flocking to the *fin de siècle* Falls was an unheralded entrepreneur named William Love. After surveying the area in the early 1890s, Love was smitten. The environment he encountered was beautiful and bountiful. He soon unleashed bold plans to build both the world's greatest hydroelectric power canal and "a model manufacturing city" that might someday encompass millions of people. By offering cheap power to businesses and an array of modern amenities to residents, Love's Model City would become "the most complete, perfect and beautiful" urban locale "in the world."[2] As Love told anyone who would listen, his plan was destined to succeed.

History knows Love for his dramatic failure. The economic crisis of 1893 undercut investments in Model City, while Love's tangled business plans killed construction of his power canal. By the early 1900s, Love was long gone. In Model City, located a few miles from the Falls, little remained of his epic vision, save for a few small buildings. Yet in the town of Lasalle, an environmental ruin associated with Model City remained a prominent part of the landscape for many years: "Love's Canal." Before Love's funding evaporated, his workers excavated a portion of a power canal and waterfall that would have been higher and more powerful than the natural Falls. That artificial river would have been an engineering marvel. Instead, the nearly mile-long groove of earth left by Love's men became a monument to industrial folly. Only "piles of dirt and a deep hole remain there," Niagara historian Edward Williams later observed.[3]

Without the abortive Love's Canal, of course, there would have been no ready-made pit for hazardous waste disposal later on and thus no chemical crisis at a future neighborhood dubbed "Love Canal." Yet Love's story encompasses much more than just the backdrop to a famous environmental crisis. For it also sheds light on turn-of-the-century environmental debates in the Niagara region. Indeed, even before Love's plan fell apart, he and other industrialists faced intense criticism from naturalists concerned about hydroelectric power's impact on the landscape. Though he responded to these critiques in interesting ways, Love remained unfazed. Like Carnegie, Frick, and Rockefeller—powerful industrialists who inspired him—Love saw the landscape itself as a great canvas upon which to draw monumental scenes. Environmental resources—land, water, and trees—served as Love's palette.[4] When the picture faded, Love simply moved on, leaving to subsequent generations the task of reckoning with environmental impacts he set in motion. But his was not a singular story. Love's loss of fortune, like his environmental impact, was part and parcel of the era in which he lived: the heyday of industrialization. From Boston to Chicago and Pittsburgh to Niagara Falls, industrialists carved up the American environment in ways that still remain visible—and problematic. It is not surprising, then, that even failures like William Love created environmental impacts that we can feel all the way into the 21st century.

1. Love's Grand Plan

Although an enigmatic figure, William T. Love hoped to give his name to history as an epic city builder and energy titan. Hailing from parts unknown (perhaps Knoxville or Chicago), Love arrived at Niagara Falls in the early 1890s. He described the Niagara landscape with a deep sense of awe. "Standing on the [Niagara] terrace," he wrote, "overlooking the Canyon [into which the Falls spilled] on a clear summer day, no lover of the beautiful in nature can fail to realize the impotence of language in attempting to portray the scene which lies in magnificent proportions before him."[5] Though he occasionally sounded like a starry-eyed naturalist, Love was equally entranced by the region's industrial possibility. In visions that flashed before his eyes, he saw Niagara's rushing waters and abundant land resources as the foundation of an urban-industrial empire. Love called it Model City, a megalopolis that would dominate the region from Lake Ontario to Lake Erie. It would be, he repeated to anyone who might listen, the "most perfect city in existence."[6]

Although he spoke in grandiose terms, Love saw himself not as a churlish booster but a hard-headed industrialist. "Ours is a rational business," he once observed, and "a conscientious endeavor to build a prosperous and booming city."[7] Love thought his plan fit perfectly with the times, an era when captains of industry built trans-continental railroads, massive steel plants, and hydroelectric power canals. But Love also saw himself as an industrial reformer. He offered free land to any businesses resettling in the Model City area; he also offered cheap housing to workers. By appealing to both laborers and business leaders, he hoped that Model City would thrive socially as well as economically. Love also believed that his city should be founded on principles of "great architectural beauty."[8] "We aim at perfection on the broadest possible lines," he proclaimed in his first promotional pamphlet.[9]

As his dream indicated, Love wanted to be known as an Urban Progressive. Love lived at a time when, as a noted scholar has put it, "the city stood at the vital center of Trans-Atlantic progressive imaginations."[10] If Puritan John Winthrop had initially envisioned building a perfect "City Upon a Hill" in the colonial wilderness, Progressive-era developers like Love hoped to rebuild that crumbling edifice through efficient urban planning and management. The Chicago World's Columbian Exposition of 1893 exerted a powerful pull on urban visionaries, who saw in Daniel Burnham's gleaming "White City" a model environment of clean streets, efficient sanitation services, and little graft or crime.[11] Love hoped Model City would be the next big thing in urban life—a well-planned and well-maintained megalopolis that still cared about average people.

Love also saw Model City as a technical wonder. He promised that all homes and businesses would have electrical, telephone, gas, water, and sewer services at a time when these things were far from universal in American life. "[P]neumatic conveyers" would provide nearly instantaneous mail service to Model City residents, while pure drinking water would flow through new piping systems. Love supported profit-sharing plans for workers, abundant parks for residents, and a brand of urban design that inspired rather than sapped city-dwellers' souls. Borrowing concepts from Henry George's 1879 *Poverty and Progress*, which saw class division as the key problem in urban America, Love called for an affordable Model City. Yet where George saw taxes as the way to equalizing class relations, Love believed that technological innovation—hydroelectricity—combined with access to undeveloped land would spur egalitarianism.[12]

Indeed, with businesses profiting from cheap power, and Model City leaders supporting low rents for workers, Love's town would avoid the squalor, discontent, and even rebellion associated with New York City, Chicago, Pittsburgh, and Philadelphia. In those cities, Love claimed, high rent born of urban congestion pushed workers into ramshackle homes. Uprisings often followed. "The Census of 1890 shows cities of 200,000 to 250,000 inhabitants covering 6000 to 23,000 acres," he wrote. But Model City would be different, Love claimed, because the New York State Legislature had granted him sway over 10,000 acres of unimproved land a few miles from Niagara Falls. That number was increased to 15,000 and eventually to roughly 30,000 acres, or the equivalent of roughly 50 square miles. And there was the prospect of even more land after that. For the company would have the sole power not only "to buy, sell and deal land" but "to carry on the work of building a town or City in Niagara County" by virtually any means available. In this famously unregulated era of American industrialization, Love had nearly unrivaled power to secure real estate, alter the landscape, and build a city ready-made for demo-graphic as well as economic expansion. Love charmed the skeptical Governor R. P. Flower, who had vowed to veto the massive land grant, into supporting Model City. "There will be a City of two million inhabit-ants there," Flower told a reporter after inking the Model City charter granting Love the largest tract of land in New York State history.[13] His surging confidence also gained Love advocates in the business world. J. M. Robinson, president of the First National Bank in nearby Wellsboro, Pa., trumpeted Love's plan. "I recently visited the Model City," he re-marked. "The site is a perfect one." The enterprise, he continued, "will prove a great success." C. M. Loring, head of the North American Tele-graph Company of Minneapolis, predicted that Model City would "as-tonish the world."[14] Love smiled at these testimonials. As he told all of his backers, Model City would not be just another town but the world's next great metropolis.

In making such predictions, Love joined other urban visionaries who saw Niagara Falls as a vanguard locale. With clean-burning hydroelectric power, Niagara's factories would be the antithesis of William Blake's infa-mous "dark satanic mills."[15] One turn-of-the-century industrial agent called Niagara "the coming manufacturing city of America." Though the city was younger than most metropolises, he observed, its proximity to renewable water resources provided "brighter prospects than any spot in the world."[16] He was not far off, for Niagara Falls attracted a bevy of new businesses in a short period of time. Lured by the success of several hydro-electric producers, including the Niagara Power Company and the Hydraulic Power Company, hundreds of industrial concerns moved to the region by the early 1900s: steel producers, milling plants, toolmakers, paper companies, chemical manufacturers, even distillers and brewers. As "The Electrical Handbook," a guidebook for businessmen, engineers and scientists surveying the industrial capacity of various American cities, put it, hydroelectric power had made Niagara Falls synonymous with "com-merce," "science," and the "mechanical arts."[17] And, the guidebook continued, the Falls had not nearly reached its maximum power capacity. Nikola Tesla, the famed inventor and father of alternating current (which allowed companies to get hydroelectric power from farther away), observed in 1897 that the powerhouses now lining the Niagara River epitomized nothing less than the human triumph over nature. "We have many monuments of past ages," he began, including "the temples of the Greeks and cathedrals of Christendom." These relics, he continued, "exemplified the power of man, the greatness of nations, the love of art and religious devotion." But "that mighty unit at Niagara has something of its own, more in accord with our present thoughts and tendencies." For Tesla, hydroelectric power meant "the subjugation of natural forces to man." As he saw it, Niagara Falls was literally a shining city on a hill: an electrified (and electrifying) embodiment of American will.[18]

William Love agreed that the Niagara region already offered the "greatest water power in the world."[19] But he predicted that his artificial waterfall would soar above every other hydroelectric power project in existence.[20] By diverting water inland over the Lewiston Ledge (the same high spot that had challenged colonial traders), Love bragged that he could "double" Niagara's power. "We are building a canal," he announced in his first promotional pamphlet, "to take water out of the upper and return it into the lower Niagara...which will be used to create one of the greatest manufacturing cities in America." One of Love's most ardent backers, New York State Assemblyman E. T. Ransom, told Love that, "[w]hat you have already accomplished...satisfies me of the great merit and vitality of the Model City." So keen was he on Love's vision that Ransom even recommended this "investment opportunity to my personal friends as an extraordinary one, and am backing it with my own money."[21]

With so much riding on what became known as "Love's Canal," it is surely significant that the only surviving picture of William Love shows him not at Model City but at the artificial waterway's groundbreaking ceremonies in Lasalle on May 23, 1894. [Fig. 5] The photo captures Love standing proudly at the head of a delegation of politicians, investors and well-wishers about to turn the first sod of land for his canal. After the ceremonial dig, Love's company began excavating the seven-mile river. The big dig comprised eight contiguous sections, with excavators starting at the Lasalle end of the power canal; another section was soon created near the end of Love's Canal. But the Lasalle portion would be the most important—that is where Love often took would-be investors to show them the progress of his industrial dream. In this way, Love's grandiose vision took shape almost exactly where Lasalle built the *Griffon*; it then followed

Figure 5 Turning Sod at Love's Canal: The ceremonial dig at Love Canal in 1894. William Love, the bearded figure to the left of the figure with the shovel, stands at the head of a delegation of local officials eager to extend the industrial revolution at the Falls via this majestic new power canal.
(Source: Love Canal Power, May 24, 1894. Courtesy, University Archives, State University of New York at Buffalo.)

a pathway designed by William Williams for the ill-fated Niagara Ship Canal. Love was sure town-building glory loomed in the distance.

Using a combination of excavators, derricks, men, and mules, Love's company plowed a groove of earth about a mile long, 80 feet wide and on average 15 feet deep. To continue cutting the canal path, Love had to secure land options from local farmers. He also had to maintain funding on the canal itself, not to mention Model City infrastructure: sewers, roads, telephone lines, and buildings. Love always faced funding troubles but his men kept working on the canal. "Signs are not lacking that the enterprise is going to land squarely on its feet," a reporter wrote of Love's canal six months after excavations began.[22] For a time, Love's project was no pipe dream but a rising reality.

In fact, local papers reported that "excavators have already made quite a hole and a big pile of dirt" in Lasalle. To capitalize on this publicity, Love offered public tours of the site. Special trains boarded daily in downtown Buffalo and deposited passengers at a Lasalle depot. Before embarking for Model City, visitors shuffled around the steam excavators plying the canal bed. Each of these machines could do the work of dozens of men, Love and his associates said, impressing would-be investors with their manufacturing prowess. Removing tens of thousands of cubic feet of earth, company workers remained busy day after day.[23]

With the canal cutting across the landscape and potential investors touring Model City, Love's confidence grew. He moved to a posh Buffalo home, where hydroelectric power moguls and industrialists lived. Even though his project was far from finished, Love also listed himself as a "manufacturer" in a city directory. He leased an office in downtown Buffalo and began circulating among bankers, businessmen and industrial moguls. Love was on his way to becoming perhaps the greatest industrialist the region had yet seen.

2. Environmental Debate in Love's Niagara

At Model City and Love's Canal, the world caught a glimpse of the future: hydroelectric power. "Any city which has a water-fall within an available distance has, so to speak, a goldmine," inventor G. W. G. Ferris (of Ferris Wheel fame) observed. "I am here to tell you that there is no power on the face of the earth that can stand against water-power," C. M. Loring, who in addition to his telegraph concern founded railroad and electric companies, added. No strangers to innovation, both Ferris and Loring hailed Love as a visionary. "When the water-power is let into the Model City," Loring predicted, "you will see a growth here that will astonish the world!"[24] Yet Love also stepped into an intense environmental debate over the impact of hydroelectric power at the Falls. Indeed, the speed and depth of industrial change along the Niagara River inspired the first major environmental struggles at the Falls: the "Free" and "Save" Niagara movements. Even the beguiling Love could not escape the impact of these twin late–19th century reform movements.

The Free Niagara movement took shape in the 1880s to protect the Falls from privatization and overdevelopment. As railroads brought greater numbers of tourists to the area after the Civil War, businesses and

private landholders scooped up land and then charged people for unob-
structed views of the famous cataract. For many visitors, the Falls' grandeur had been undercut, if not completely destroyed, by profiteers. Free
Niagara sought to liberate the region from such money-grubbing schemers. Yet reformers sought more than just better views of the Falls. They
also pushed for a public park that would forever protect the landscape
around the famous cataract. "The state of affairs existing here at present is
a disgrace to the American people," Thomas Welch, an assemblyman who
helped lead the effort to build the state park at Niagara, wrote to politicians around New York in the early 1880s. Welch called on New Yorkers
to "aid in the work of preserving and restoring the Falls of Niagara to the
people."[25] He had numerous allies. In the legislature, lawmakers passed a
bill allowing state officials to purchase land around the Falls in the name
of a public park. Outside the legislature, nature reformers advocated a
commercial-free zone at Niagara Falls. The Niagara Falls Association, a
coalition of activists, gathered petitions, published essays, and staged lectures in support of the park. Nevertheless, opposition to a public park remained strong in various parts of the state. Some opponents worried that
state funds would be wasted or funneled to political cronies who supported the park while others wanted the federal government to pay for
parkland at Niagara Falls. One Rochester banker wrote that he was under
tremendous "pressure" to oppose the entire plan because it would not
benefit the people of New York.[26]

Free Niagara forces therefore rejoiced in 1885 when the New York State
Assembly created the Niagara Reservation—the first state park in the
nation. After appropriating funds and securing land from landowners adjacent to the Falls, the legislature hired noted landscape designer Frederick
Law Olmsted to layout the park grounds. True to the environmental idyll
guiding 19th-century nature preservation efforts, Olmsted's plan allowed
people to get as close to the Falls as possible, while also providing access
to wooded areas that harkened back to Niagara's pre-industrial times.
Olmsted's park allowed visitors to contemplate the sublimity of Niagara
without paying for the privilege of it or endangering themselves.[27]

While Welch and famous park supporters like Theodore Roosevelt
gained fame for the passage of the Niagara Reservation bill, women also
played a key role in the Free Niagara movement. Throughout the state,

women circulated petitions, wrote of Niagara's power and beauty, and pressured political figures to support the park's creation. "I have noticed in attendance at this hearing," one of the leading advocates of the state park observed in 1885, "a large number of women. Such, I believe, has been the case in every instance when this bill shall be passed." State politicians added that "their wives earnestly appealed to them to vote" for the law that would forever protect Niagara's stunning views. It was "their love of everything beautiful," Welch himself observed in the gendered language of the time (a discourse that linked women's feminine sensibilities to nature's aesthetic beauty) that "arouses within [them] a desire for the preservation of the Falls." As evidence, Welch called attention to the "thousands of women looking upon Niagara for the first time, and always with an exclamation of delight." Yet women were not just onlookers; they served as true foot soldiers of Niagara's preservation.[28]

More broadly, the Free Niagara struggle illuminated the ascension of new environmental values in and beyond Western New York. Indeed, the park statute (and continuing debates over its meaning) showed the power of environmental jeremiads in the age of industrialization and urbanization: the notion that Americans had lost touch with nature and therefore an elemental part of themselves. To be sure, versions of this belief had existed throughout the 19th century. But they rarely pierced mainstream culture. Even the compelling antebellum figure of Henry David Thoreau, whose tale of a solitary life at Walden Pond railed against materialism and early industrialization, was not viewed as a heroic ecologist in his time; in fact, *Walden; or, A Life in the Woods* flopped, forcing a bitter Thoreau to undertake landscape surveying to make ends meet.[29] But nature reformers became heroes in the decades following the Civil War for their efforts to save the American outdoors. Soon after the Free Niagara movement solidified plans for a state park at the Falls, John Muir formed the Sierra Club outside San Francisco to save his beloved Hetch Hetchy Valley from industrial development. As he would write before his death, "devotees of raging commercialism seem to have a perfect contempt for Nature," praying to the "Almighty Dollar" rather than the cathedral of cascading rivers and inspiring mountains well beyond human development.[30] Like others Muir took heart from the Free Niagara Movement. It was a powerful example of environmental reform.[31]

The advent of hydroelectric power schemes in the 1890s inspired a new round of fears about industrial development at the Falls. The "Save Niagara" crusade took flight just as William Love was planning Model City. Worried that the region's myriad power projects would halt the raging Niagara River itself, and thus harm the Falls, Save Niagara activists argued that nature would be forever altered if they did not swiftly mobilize against men like Love. Though many Save Niagara activists wanted to preserve the Falls proper, a radical subset of the movement criticized industrial greed altogether. "The American capitalist is quite merciless to the natural beauty of the Falls," a British newspaper writer exclaimed, making clear that Niagara Falls must become a symbol not just of nature appreciation but of anti-industrialization. As he put it, Niagara Falls already appeared "disfigured," as the mighty wheel pits and generating plants created lasting environmental scars on one of nature's most pristine areas.[32] But one did not have to be a radical critic to express deep concern about the fate of the Falls. "If the people act, the Falls can be saved" once again, Niagara reformer J. Horace McFarland argued in the rather staid publication, *Ladies Home Journal*.[33]

The Free and Save Niagara Movements certainly affected William Love, who claimed that neither Model City nor his massive power canal would harm Niagara Falls. Not only did he argue that Niagara's abundant waters would fuel his power development scheme without much worry, but he also emphasized the key role that parks and green space played in his urban project. He envisioned a city not merely of factories but "of the greatest possible beauty and utility." In fact, Love guaranteed that roughly one-eighth of Model City land would be set aside for public parks. Love also emphasized his own reverence for nature. Still, there was no getting around the plain fact that he wanted to transform Niagara's landscape. If he was going to double all existing power supplies, as he claimed many times, then Love had to take large amounts of water from the rushing Niagara River. And many people wondered if this might be the body blow that finally cut the Falls down.

Thomas Welch expressed more than a little concern about Love's Canal. Welch, who became the longtime head of the Niagara Reservation after mobilizing support for its creation, thought that Love's waterway, if not scaled down, might harm Niagara Falls. As a Niagara booster, Welch was not totally opposed to Love's scheme; in fact, he supported it because Love's Canal would not directly develop the Falls. Yet Welch saw that hydroelectric power had made the land and water adjacent to the cataract much more valuable than ever before. Some politicians and business leaders—particularly in New York City—even pushed to reclaim the Niagara Reservation. Welch's ongoing battles against such schemes brought to mind his more famous preservationist allies, John Muir and John Burroughs, who constantly struggled to overcome American industrialists' will to develop nature. As he had argued in the 1880s, Welch again claimed that Niagara Falls belonged to the citizens of the state and the people of the world—it was nature's jewel and must not be overdeveloped. Welch mobilized new petition campaigns that brought critical support to the park. In 1896, he successfully opposed efforts to make the reservation—which was governed by an independent group appointed by the governor—part of a legislative commission that could be more easily influenced by business lobbyists. But he had to remain vigilant against every new scheme to develop the Falls, including that of Love.

Known as "Father Tom" for his preacherly support of the Niagara Reservation, Welch spoke at civic clubs, schools, and festive days. As he put it, the citizens of the state were the eternal stewards of its natural resources. In an Arbor Day speech at Niagara Falls in May 1896, Welch told hundreds of schoolchildren who gathered to plant trees in the state park, that they must forever protect the Falls. After regaling them with tales of his life as superintendent, Welch said that he sometimes called people just to let them "listen to the roar of the Falls on the phone."[34] Welch's activism worked, as a host of pro-park supporters rushed to his side. "Let Niagara Falls alone," the *Brooklyn Eagle* declared in support of Welch's plan to keep the Niagara Reservation independent, for it belongs not to corporations but "to the people of the republic, to the people of the world!" Without Welch's work, the Niagara Reservation may have been lost only a few years after it had been created. By the time of Welch's untimely death in 1903, Niagara's parkland had been saved. And three years later, the federal government passed the Burton Act, which prevented any further hydroelectric power project at the Falls itself.[35] In one historian's words, the Free Niagara and Save Niagara movements made it unacceptable to use nature "for limitless technological" development.[36]

But in the early 1890s, Niagara environmentalists could not stop Love from planning and excavating his power canal. The logic of industrialization remained compelling and strong—as long as would-be manufacturers like Love promised to keep Niagara Falls flowing.

3. Love's Boom Goes Bust

In 1894, Love's Canal was proceeding on schedule. "Everything is reported to be lovely with the Model City Project," newspaper reporter E. T. Williams wrote in September.[37] As Williams recognized, excavations at Love's Canal became the barometer of Model City's success. For it was here that the landscape bore the most unmistakable signs of the great environmental transformation in the works. Excited by reports of a grand canal taking shape outside Niagara Falls, one New York City paper mistakenly claimed that Love's Canal would be 400 feet wide!

In the wake of his canal building efforts, Love sold thousands of dollars in bonds, secured options on more Model City land, and began developing residential lots in Model City itself. Love also claimed that he had secured bids from "nearly one hundred [firms] from every part of the United States" to build the rest of the canal. Things looked especially bright in December 1894, when two out-of-towners gave Model City a glowing report after "inspecting the canal" and various Model City sites. Thomas Hersey, representing a London syndicate, and Charles Cramer of Louisville, "drove to Lasalle and inspected work already done on the Model City canal," Williams reported. "The open winter allows the work now being prosecuted there to proceed without interruption, which would not be the case if there was much snow." The two investors "could hardly say enough in praise . . . of the Model City scheme," Williams observed in an exclusive interview with them.[38] Hersey told Love that he should have "no problem" attracting the support of London financiers. That was enough for Love. By February 1895, he was in England to meet with British money men. "Love is not peddling smoke nor shoveling fog by a long shot," Williams wrote. With Love meeting overseas investors now, that prediction looked more solid than ever.[39]

Yet major problems loomed. For one thing, skittish investors worried about the lingering impact of the Panic of 1893, which put as many as

40,000 people out of work in New York alone and created financial chaos nationally. Many investors wanted sure-fire investments, not Love's promise of future returns. For another thing, Love failed to see that his own land-based dreams would conflict with his salesmanship, further tipping the scales against the power canal's completion. Love did not own a single acre of Western New York land. Rather, he had license to bargain for any land he sought to transform. Love thus had to attract investors while dealing with Niagara's farmers. And he did this at the very moment that other companies searched for real estate along the Niagara Frontier: railroad companies looking for routes to the Falls, new industries searching for access to hydroelectric power grids, shrewd investors hoping to flip land for a quick profit.

Niagara's land boom hit even the sleepiest of locales. A banner headline in one Buffalo paper proclaimed a Lasalle "real estate boom,", pointing readers' attention to land speculation in the small town where Love's Canal was being built. Soon a double-track trolley line would bisect the canal, the paper explained, further increasing area land values. "The option men are hustling themselves" in Lasalle, E. T. Williams commented. Others called them "option sharks," investors who bought land only to charge exorbitant sums for it later. "It is getting to be about like Southern California," Williams observed, "where in response to [the question], what was raised principally in the section, one was told, the price of land!"[40]

High land prices undercut the funding of Love's Canal. Land that previously went for $50 per acre now soared to $200, $500, even $1,000 an acre. The minimum amount was now $150 per acre, or three times the normal asking price when Love began. Love expressed particular concerns about skyrocketing land values on his trip to London in February 1895. British investors, he wrote to his "Lewiston friends," would underwrite much of the canal and Model City project, but only if William Love could secure big chunks of cheap land. Investors did not want "a checkerboard" of land deals, with some farmers holding out for even higher prices. Love simply did not have enough money to follow through on his grand plan.[41]

Love's land dealings with local farmers made matters worse. He initially crafted one-year options with local landowners. But before he could attract enough investors, these options expired, and Love had to renegotiate. Each year brought the same problem: Work had not proceeded fast enough for Love to attract new investors, which meant that he could not buy land or continue work on the canal; he then had to renegotiate with farmers for the following year, and these renegotiated options often meant a higher price per acre. Finally, in 1896, Love announced that he had signed five-year options with some farmers, thus removing the yearly onus of renegotiating contracts. But he still had to win farmers' (and capitalists') faith. In March 1896, William Love announced that he would begin paying farmers in the Lewiston-Porter area of Niagara County a 5 percent down payment for their land. Because he had now secured 30,000 acres, Love promised to pay out $750,000. This meant that, in 1896 dollars, Love intended to pay local farmers $15 million—$500 per acre. Land boom or not, no one had yet seen a purchase the size of William Love's. Yet few people had seen Love's money, either.[42]

Unbelievably, the project was still moving forward.[43] In Spring 1896, Love sent out a new prospectus to potential investors promising massive returns. In one stretch, he dispatched more than 175,000 pieces of mail. In March, he held a lavish banquet for over 50 businessmen at a swank Buffalo hotel, the Iroquois, at which Love "explain[ed] the Model City enterprise" all over again. "Love Conquers All," one headline read, calling the soirée "a very successful affair." Love told the audience that he had netted big finances for the scheme, that options had been secured on nearly 30,000 acres of Niagara County land, and that work on the canal would soon restart. "Mr. Love made a very favorable impression," one of his potential Buffalo backers noted.[44] A similar jamboree in May 1896, which attracted two dozen national investors, traveled out to the canal areas, where skeptics would see more than a hundred men working in teams to finish the artificial waterfall. Love even ran ads in a Buffalo paper that hyped the venture as if it were a *fait accompli*. "Model City . . . Booming," one proclaimed. "A great development is assured." "The Boom is on!" "Extraordinary Terms!" As summer approached, Love bragged that he had over $1 million of investments, with half of that amount pouring in over the last few months alone.[45]

This time, it really was all hype. Whether he intended to or not, Love essentially ran a Ponzi scheme to keep paying back investors and farmers whose land options had to be renewed. By August 1896, Love could no longer forestall the obvious: his plan was doomed. Creditors seized items from Love's Model City office: a printing press, some tables, and copies of his company newspapers. And work finally stopped on the power canal.[46] By the following year, all that remained of the Model City dream was the partially finished waterway. It turned out that Love could note conquer all.

4. Love's Ruins: "A Big Hole in the Ground"

For a time, others tried to revive Love's scheme. F. W. Moore, an original agent for William Love, took over the company newspaper in February 1897, which he now called *Model City Power*. The Niagara Power and Development Company, which held official title to the canal for decades, also underwent reorganization, with different teams of investors seeking to complete a power canal right up until the passage of the Burton Act. But nothing definite ever took shape.

Environmental ruin piled on top of financial failure. Even super-backer E. T. Williams had to declare that all William Love left Niagara was "a Big Hole in the Ground." According to a 1908 map of Lasalle, the old power canal was being used by the Niagara County Irrigation and Water Supply Company, perhaps to divert water to area farmers.[47] A few houses took shape in the abandoned canal zone over the next few decades. In summer, local kids used Love's Canal as a swimming pool; in winter, they skated on it. Few gave any thought to the great visionary who once saw the power canal as a gateway to Model City.

As for William Love himself, after yielding leadership of the company in 1897, he headed west. "It will be sometime before Model City will see him again," a former associate wrote. Love would now help a Canadian businessman run "ten valuable 40 acre tracts of mining land" for the "Manitou and Seine River gold mining company," including two rich lots known as "the jumbo vein." Capitalized at $2 million, but broken into dollar shares, Love's new interest was called a "most promising one, now causing great excitement in Canada." Some Model City backers, including state legislator E. T. Ransom, vowed to purchase stock in it. And many people wished Love well in his new venture. But a few chuckled when they discovered that Love's new home would be in a small town in western Ontario called "Rat Portage."[48]

Love tried to erase his notoriety years later in one last grasp at fame. In 1931, he wrote to President Herbert Hoover about ways to overcome the Great Depression. Now a New Jersey resident, Love hoped to convince Hoover that massive public works programs were the only way to save the economy and American democracy too. Ever the promoter, he claimed that such schemes (ranging from farm relief to urban employment programs) would propel America "to the greatest prosperity ever known!" Love then authored a series of articles under the heading, "Prosperity—A Plan to Achieve It." Yet fame eluded Love again. The articles appeared in the Burlington County *Mount Holly Herald* and were not circulated widely. Love died soon after. As the *Niagara Falls Gazette* put it, Love was still remembered for his abandoned waterway, which stood as "a monument to dead hopes" in the sleepy town of Lasalle.[49]

Karl Marx famously said that history is a twice-told tale—the first time as tragedy, the second time as farce. The saga of Love's Canal reversed that dictum. For William Love's city-building endeavors became a nearly comedic morality play on big dreams leading to even bigger failures. But the next time Love Canal entered the nation's public consciousness, it would be as one of the greatest environmental hazards in modern American history.

3

The Master of the Chemical Machine

The Rise of Hooker

The creative mind, working with and against the powers of Earth, Air, Fire and Water, has made Nature more fertile, industry more productive, and life more abundant.[1]

Through Human Energy controlling Natural Force, Man Becomes Master of the Machine.[2]

—Elon Hooker, 1934

Model's City's demise did little to slow industrial growth in Niagara Falls. During the early 1900s, the region's economy expanded at a tremendous rate. Niagara's next big thing came in the form of chemicals. When William Love departed the area, the Falls claimed no major chemical maker. By the 1920s, Niagara Falls was home to a dynamic and thriving chemical sector that produced huge amounts of industrial-grade chemicals via hydroelectric power. By World War II, dozens of companies called Niagara Falls home, making it a global leader in the production of chlorines, degreasers, explosives, pesticides, plastics, and myriad other chemical agents.

The chief architect of Niagara's chemical expansion was Elon Huntington Hooker, an engineer turned industrial titan who settled in the Falls soon after William Love left. [Fig. 6] Hailing from famous families, Hooker was destined for great things. On one side, Hooker could trace a lineage back to Puritan divines who had literally built cities on a hill; on the other, there were railroad titans who had traversed the American West. In both cases, Elon Hooker's family background inspired him to think big. The guiding spirit of a brash new chemical company that bore his surname,

Figure 6 Elon Hooker, circa 1930s. The patriarch of Hooker Electrochemical Company was also a captain of industry by the Great Depression. His death caught family and colleagues by surprise—and prevented him from seeing even greater growth at Hooker during the next decade. (Source: Elon Huntington Hooker, 1938)

Hooker harnessed Niagara's power to become the nation's leading producer of two key chemicals: chloride of lime (bleaching powder) and sodium hydroxide (caustic soda). Over the next fifty years, Hooker Chemical became a mainstay of American industry. Its products helped win wars, explore space, and fuel American consumerism.

These developments would not surprise Elon Huntington Hooker. Indeed, he thought of himself as an American Adam: a technological originator who reshaped nature and society in equal measure.[3] His vision of chemical superiority would come to fruition a few miles from Love's abandoned canal—at first glance, perhaps nothing more than a coincidence of history. But Hooker's success would soon collide with Love's failure at the big ditch in Lasalle, once again illuminating the Love Canal landscape's importance to the American environmental past—and future.

1. The Vision

Except for his grand industrial dream, Elon Huntington Hooker was in almost every way William Love's foil. Hooker's motto, which stemmed from his training under the demanding sanitary engineer Emil Kuichling, was the un-Lovelike phrase, "Bring Things To Pass." Hooker's associates called this "The Vision": a precise roadmap of moving from Big Ideas to Finished Projects.[4] But Hooker's visionary sensibility also came from his ancestors, who had passed down a combination of iconoclasm and certitude to Elon. Puritan founder Thomas Hooker was the first family member in Elon's paternal line to unleash grand plans that came to pass. After migrating from the Old World, he left the Massachusetts Bay Colony to establish the town of Hartford in 1636; a few years later he helped craft one of the first written constitutions in North America. Elon's maternal line included Colis Huntington, a key architect of the Transcontinental Railroad. Little wonder that Elon used both his father's and mother's surnames: as he rose in business and political circles, he wanted people to know that "Elon Huntington Hooker" represented both accomplishment and boldness.[5]

Still, by Elon's time, much of his family's glory was in the past. Elon's father, Horace B. Hooker, was by all accounts a good but not extraordinary man. A Rochester businessman, he served in the Union army during the Civil War. But Horace B. was not a towering figure.[6] Perhaps Elon's dreams of industrial empire flowed from a desire to re-establish family fame.

First he had to distinguish himself among a brood of brothers. Elon was one of eight children, including four brothers born within ten years of each other between 1865 and 1874. A tight-knit family, all of Elon's brothers would later work at Hooker Electrochemical Company. Albert

Hooker, the eldest sibling, became the company's senior research chemist until his untimely death in 1936. Harry became president following Elon's passing in 1938, serving for a decade before his own death in 1949. Horace W. was a company vice president while Paul, the youngest, worked for over two decades as an engineer at the Niagara Falls plant. Proud Western New Yorkers, all Hooker men attended the University of Rochester.[7]

Growing up in Rochester provided further inspiration to Elon. For this thriving entrepreneurial city along the banks of the Genesee River was also home to Kodak pioneer George Eastman, who many turn-of-the-century Americans saw as a model industrialist. Self-trained as an accountant, Eastman worked at the Rochester Savings Bank before turning to the new technology of photography after the Civil War. He worked tirelessly to launch innovative products that brought photography to the masses, including less onerous dry-plate and film technology. He founded Kodak in 1880, creating a paternalistic industrial order that impressed people around the world. Kodak's Brownie, the most popular handheld camera of its time, democratized photography by using film (and developing it for amateurs) rather than the messy wet-plates of many professionals. Just snap your own pictures of family and friends, Kodak ads famously boasted, "and we'll do the rest."[8]

Eastman's company became a Mecca for educated, technologically savvy businessmen and engineers, spawning famous spin-offs like Bausch and Lomb, not to mention parallel imaging industries like Xerox. One of the wealthiest men in America by the first decade of the 20th century, Eastman built a splendid home on Rochester's elegant East Avenue only a few miles from Elon's house, where politicians, dignitaries and philanthropists regularly gathered. Eastman's sprawling plant, known as Kodak Park, was located about a dozen miles north of Rochester, in the town of Greece, while corporate headquarters would eventually settle in downtown Rochester. Kodak was everywhere. As a young man, Elon had to look no farther than his hometown for an example of visionary industrial leadership. Indeed, Elon later contacted Eastman for advice about running a growing company.[9]

Elon needed just such a guide to manage the dizzying economic and technological changes swirling around him. In Elon's youth, the horse and buggy roamed Rochester city streets; when he died, Rochester had a subway system and America approached the atomic age. Hooker thought of his company as a key part of this transformation. "In 1869, when Elon Huntington Hooker…was born," a company history crafted during the Cold War claimed, "most of our organic chemicals came from Europe and electrochemistry…was little more than a laboratory exercise." But now "the chemical industry of the United States has no peer," pouring out products that have won world wars, scrubbed cities clean, and "made possible our modern industrial civilization."[10]

Like George Eastman, Elon's personal story was one of hard work and constant striving. He attracted attention as a high school student by taking night classes in illustration at the Mechanics Institute (now Rochester Institute of Technology), an institution founded on the Ben Franklin–like principles of self-improvement and economic uplift. Athletic, diligent, and driven, Elon earned an undergraduate degree from the University of Rochester in 1891, where he played on the university's inaugural football team, won a tennis championship, ran the Glee and Banjo Club, and successfully pledged a fraternity. After graduation, Elon worked at the Rochester Waterworks, headed by Emil Kuichling, whose innovations in sewer technology were well known by the 1890s, before attending Cornell. A prestigious fellowship allowed him to study engineering in Europe. After a year of study abroad, Elon returned to Cornell, earning a Ph.D. in Civil Engineering in 1894. For good measure, he also completed an M.A. at the University of Rochester. He was not yet 30 years old.[11]

Elon first worked as a hydraulic engineer. Relocating to Boston, he helped improve the city's water supply. He then assisted in a survey of the proposed Panama Canal. Elon soon caught the attention of New York Governor Theodore Roosevelt (TR for short), who made him Deputy Commissioner of Public Works in 1899. Elon was charged with improving the state's Barge Canal System, an enlarged version of the Eric Canal. Though he had no "political backing," TR called Elon "the best man" for the job.[12] But Elon was not satisfied working in government. He thought of himself as the next George Eastman, not a future William McKinley.

Towards that entrepreneurial end, Elon inaugurated the Development and Funding Company (DFC) in 1903. Based in New York City, the DFC was an industrial venture capital firm that supported "undercapitalized enterprises." He then turned to chemical production, hoping to invest DFC funds in a business that would lead America (and the world) into the age of electrochemistry. By making industrial-grade chemicals more abundantly, efficiently, and cheaply than before, Hooker hoped to dominate a market traditionally controlled by European concerns.[13]

He helped launch the American Chemical Century. Indeed, Hooker backed an economic sector ready to take off and take over. "There exists a common misconception that the Chemical Industry is largely a foreign importation which, transplanted upon American soil in recent times, has...rewarded those [few] who had the hardihood and capital to embark upon it," an analyst wrote in a 1928 summary of "representative industries in the United States."[14] But this was an "error" in judgment, for aggregate chemical production was anything but a hidebound part of American industry. In fact, electrochemistry was a homegrown success story—and an industrial sector now worth virtually as much as the iron and steel industry as a whole.[15]

Electrochemistry was at the heart of American chemical growth. Though electrolytic chemistry dated to the nation's founding era, no one had yet mastered its intricacies. According to one early historian of chemicals, "the first electrolytic chlorine in the United States was made at Rumford Falls, M[aine], in 1893."[16] Dow Chemical, based in Michigan, produced "small quantities" of chemicals via electrochemistry just a few years later. But Elon believed that he could do much better at the Falls, where the Castner Electrolytic Alkali Company had been the first in the area to produce chemicals through water power in 1898.[17] By passing massive amounts of electricity through a saline solution, an electrolytic chemist could create vast quantities of chlorine, hydrogen, and caustic soda, which, in turn, could be used to make either finished products (chloride of lime) or chemical compounds. The Solvay and Leblanc processes (which were more laborious) had long defined the production of chlorinated chemicals. But they did not produce the volumes of chemicals needed by Elon and others. If he could perfect the electrolytic cell (the little power plant driving electrochemistry), then Elon could rule the industry. Like Love, he knew that Niagara Falls offered the greatest hydropower opportunities in the world. Elon would soon use them to produce a chemical revolution at the Falls.[18]

2. Chemical Revolutions at Niagara

The promise of electrolytic chemistry also contained an inherent challenge. To produce massive amounts of chemicals, one needed an abundant (and cheap) hydroelectric power source that would send enough electrical current through a briny solution to produce chlorinated chemicals for market. A Rochester boy, Elon knew that Niagara waterpower systems had already tackled that concern. Yet another problem surfaced: finding a power cell durable enough to handle such huge electrical currents. To address this matter, Elon turned to a breakthrough technology: the Townsend cell. Developed in 1903, it grew from the work of Elmer Sperry, an engineer with over 400 patented technologies (including the gyroscope), and Clinton Townsend, a lawyer and chemist who became the new cell's namesake. "The Townsend cell was a small steel and concrete tank with a row of graphite anodes submerged in brine in the center," Robert Thomas observed in his 1955 history of Hooker Electrochemical. Electricity passed from the positive anode through "asbestos paper diaphragms" to negative cathodes. Chlorine then flowed from the anodes while hydrogen and caustic soda came from the cathodes. While the original Townsend cell would later appear antiquated—giving way to Hooker's more powerful and efficient "Type S cells"—it was revolutionary in the early 1900s.[19]

Pleased by its potential, Elon backed the Townsend cell with Development and Funding Company resources. The earliest prototype, tested at a Brooklyn plant, did not function smoothly; among other problems, the cell corroded. But perseverance paid off. Elon excitedly informed investors that the revised Townsend cell "has proven successful in all respects."[20] The next step was to find a dedicated production facility that offered access to the key ingredients of electrochemistry: salt, water and hydroelectric power. That brought Elon Huntington Hooker to Niagara Falls. Not only did the area boast unsurpassed water and power resources, but Western New York had abundant salt mines too. It was a perfect place for Elon's venture. In 1905, he launched the chemical company that would soon bear his name. He never once doubted the wisdom of his decision.

The plot of land he secured for what would become Hooker Electrochemical was hardly awe-inspiring, however. Located on the Upper Niagara River, the ramshackle farm originally housing the company had a creaky barn, a small three-room house, and pear orchards. Yet like William Love, William Williams, Rene La Salle and countless other Niagara dreamers, Elon drew inspiration from the broader landscape. "Niagara Falls," Hooker officials observed in 1938, "was no haphazard selection as the site of the initial [chemical] production." In fact, "[c]onsideration had been given to the availability of essential raw materials—salt, lime, and electric power."[21] As the first official company history proclaimed, the area Hooker selected "was ideal. It was within 60 miles... of the largest salt mine in the Western Hemisphere; it was only a few hundred yards from the largest freshwater supply in the world—the Niagara River and the Great Lakes system; and there was the power of Niagara Falls to generate electricity."[22]

In its first few years, the company almost shared the fate of William Love's Model City. Like Love, the engaging Elon Hooker could attract investors. He initially garnered $100,000 from financial backers. But the "small caustic soda and bleaching plant" Elon erected along the Niagara River drained funds more quickly than it could replenish financial reserves. "Production hardly started when money troubles began," the company historian later observed. During its first year of operation, bills doubled while sales lagged. Communicating from his New York City base, and often traveling by rail to the Niagara plant, Elon demanded more efficiency from his men. "I don't understand why the accounts are not being rapidly cleared up," he asked on one occasion. He also played cat and mouse with creditors, appealing for "just a few more days" to pay some debts. That gritty way of doing business stayed with the company years after Hooker shed its upstart status. Compared to Dow or DuPont, chemical concerns with deep roots in American society dating to the 19th century, Hooker always saw itself as a company with something to prove.[23]

In response to his early money-flow problems, Elon did something audacious: he doubled production, getting more products, particularly chloride of lime, on the market. By 1910, the Niagara plant had quadrupled its output of the magic powder, producing forty-two tons. Sales picked up and the company moved forward. Renamed the "Hooker Electrochemical Company," Elon's business grew steadily over the next decade. He formed a technical and advisory staff that included some of the nation's most innovative scientists: Townsend, Sperry, Dr. Leo Baekelend, whose plastic innovations pointed the way towards subsequent Hooker ventures, and his own brother Albert, a respected chemist who moved from Chicago in 1909.[24]

The dangers of massive chemical production nearly sent Elon's dream up in flames before they could be fully realized. "$300,000 Fire at Up-River Factory," a banner headline in the *Niagara Falls Gazette* screamed on May 27, 1910.[25] Hooker began rebuilding right away, promising to keep everyone on the payroll if possible. He then secured $200,000 in insurance money and reinvestment funds to build state-of-the-art production facilities. Back on its feet, the company attracted new investors and more talented personnel. R. Lindley Murray, a chemical engineer from California best known for defeating tennis legend Bill Tilden at the U.S. Open at Forest Hills, joined in 1912. J. H. Babcock, a Dartmouth graduate and inventor of a new explosive, arrived in 1916. And the Norwegian chemical engineer Bjarne Klaussen came to the Falls at roughly the same time. All three men would rise through the Hooker ranks, overseeing the production of new chemicals in Hooker Chemical's heroic age. Klaussen served as the foreman of the monochlorobenzyl plant, the largest in the world in 1917, which supplied the U.S. Army during World War I. Babcock helped Hooker perfect picric acid production, which allowed the United States to overcome an embargo by the German chemical industry that cut the flow of chemicals for TNT. Mixing profit and patriotism, Hooker produced "record tonnages of critically needed war materials."[26] After the war, the company's future was secure. As Elon would say, "Bring Things to Pass." With Hooker Electrochemical, he had done just that.

3. The Environmental Engineer: Elon Hooker as Reformer

Interestingly, Elon Hooker's vision encompassed more than chemical superiority. In fact, like William Love, he saw himself as an industrial progressive who harnessed technology to solve the nation's intensifying environmental problems. Throughout the nation, factories belched plumes of gray-black smoke into city skies, waterways overflowed with runoff from slaughterhouses and tanneries, and overcrowded urban tenement buildings spawned a wave of health epidemics.[27] Turn-of-the-century reformers began pressing local, state and even federal governments for laws dealing with all manner of pollution. The Rivers and Harbors Appropriation Act of 1899—the oldest national environmental statute—penalized polluters who disposed of waste in American waterways. In Buffalo, Pittsburgh, and other cities, reformers secured new smoke abatement codes that reduced the health hazards associated with blast furnaces and coke ovens fueling industrial production. In Niagara Falls, civic leaders touted efforts to keep their magnificent river clean.

Elon Hooker envisioned engineers as key a part of America's rising environmental consciousness. He was not alone. "Perhaps no other body of men come[s] quite so closely in contact with the problems involved in...the Conservation of our Natural Resources as Engineers," Henry Stott observed at Theodore Roosevelt's famous White House conservation conference in 1908. After hearing the laundry list of environmental problems compiled by various governors and reformers, Stott provided a "View of the Engineer," showing that technical men could alleviate almost every societal ill. For instance, soil erosion could be dealt with via scientific farming, while the development of waterpower would ease coal use, and thus thin particulate pollution, in the future. For Stott and others, science and technology were the friends of environmental well-being.[28]

Though a rising chemical manufacturer, Elon agreed. In fact, he dedicated a fair portion of his early career to supporting innovative technologies that would curb environmental degradation. In 1912, Elon joined Research Corporation, a firm that funded undervalued technologies contributing to the public good, including what we might today term "environmentally friendly" businesses. Applying for a certificate of incorporation from New York State in 1912, one company official argued that, while it had been organized by a "number of gentlemen who are interested in industrial development," Research Corporation also backed "discoveries and inventions" improving the civic order.[29]

That became clear when Research Corporation funded a new technology known as the "Electrostatic Precipitator" (EP). The brainchild of a Berkeley-trained physical chemist named Robert Cottrell, it promised to capture industrial smoke and hazardous vapors through a complex process of ionization. The EP was essentially a big industrial fan whose whirring blades grabbed particulate matter before it fouled the atmosphere.

While versions of the EP circulated in both European and American circles in the 1890s, Cottrell perfected a new model in 1906. By 1912, the EP was deployed in northern California to reduce emissions belched out by a local smelting plant.[30] As the American Chemical Society would put it, the Selby plant was no longer "a nuisance," illustrating the power of technology to heal the environment.[31]

For Elon Hooker, the EP validated environmental engineering. Like Cottrell, he believed in the power of practical science to solve pressing industrial problems such as air and water pollution.[32] Indeed, at Hooker proper, Elon selected chloride of lime over 250 other products because he believed that it would become an essential component of urban sanitation.[33] Produced by mixing chlorine gas in slaked lime, bleaching powder (as it became known) was essentially a recycled compound made from the byproducts of electrochemical production. Elon vowed to put the substance to good use. Within a few years, Hooker was the nation's leading producer of it.

Elon's optimism was bolstered by his brother Albert's applied research. In 1912, "AH," as he was affectionately called, published a well-regarded book on bleaching powder in urban America. Entitled *Chloride of Lime in Sanitation*, AH's text described the chemical properties and technical applications of the chlorinated compound, particularly its importance as a disinfectant in the nation's water systems.[34] From Boston to Cincinnati, he showed, urban officials now turned to bleaching powder as a way to reduce or even eliminate disease-causing bacteria and viruses. Earle B. Phelps, a leading authority on the matter and professor of sanitary sciences at MIT, hailed AH's book as both welcome and sound.[35]

According to AH, Americans need not fear chemically treated water supplies. To prove his point, he gathered a range of expert opinion. Perhaps the most persuasive testimonial came from W. P. Mason, a chemistry professor at Rensselaer Polytechnic Institute and former critic of bleaching power. Mason now argued that opposition to water disinfection was ill-founded.[36] Indeed, recent experiments in Chicago, Jersey City, and a host of other cities had changed his mind. As he explained, sanitary engineers and health officials could merely dose a water supply to the tune of ".03 of a grain [of bleaching powder] per gallon to purify it." "The amount of chemical required to do excellent work [is] in reality well-nigh infinitesimal," he concluded. The most stunning example, according to Mason, was in Chicago's "bubbly Creek," whose putrid water had been polluted by stockyard runoff, tannery waste, and refuse emanating from the city's infamous canned meat industry. This "grossly polluted" waterway was virtually lifeless, as bacteria gobbled up oxygen and created a nause-ating stench that became a geographical marker of the creek all around industrial Chicago. Mason claimed that there was "an average of 700,000 bacteria per cc" in the "filthy water"; yet a small dosing of chloride of lime had reduced bacterial build-up to almost nothing. Little wonder that both AH and Elon touted bleaching powder's environmental prowess.[37] They ardently believed that their chemicals had redeeming qualities far beyond industry.[38]

Indeed, even as Hooker Electrochemical grew, Elon continued to see himself as both a reformer and businessman. In 1912, he joined the Progressive Political Party. Known in popular lore as the Bull Moose Party—for Teddy Roosevelt's claim that he remained "fit as a Bull Moose"—Progressive Party members were often identified with TR's return run for the presidency. But the Progressive Party stood for much more than the old Rough Rider's vision of a robust national government that might stand up to industrial titans; rather, it emphasized a range of concerns, including workers' rights, fair competition among businessmen, and envi-ronmental conservation. TR was already a well-known advocate of con-servation. In his first stint as president at the dawn of the 20th century, he initiated over 200 wildlife and land preservation acts—more than any other president before him. TR's environmental vision broadened over the next several years too. "Here in the United States," he once lectured, "we turn our rivers and streams into sewers and dumping-grounds, we pollute the air, we destroy forests, and exterminate fishes, birds and mam-mals—not to speak of vulgarizing charming landscapes with hideous ad-vertisements.... But," he concluded hopefully, "at last it looks as if our people were awakening."[39] To be an ally of Roosevelt was to believe, at least in part, in his environmental ethic: that the nation's citizens must protect, not destroy, nature.

A friend of TR, Elon became the Bull Moose treasurer. According to his brother Harry, Elon thought that Roosevelt "represented the public, human welfare, wealth and property," whereas Democrats remained a conservative party, "representing wealth and property" alone. Only Bull Moose Progressives could "successfully bridge the [nation's industrial] transition without revolution."[40] Firmly anti-communist, Elon favored the Progressive vision of a strong central government that still allowed business to prosper. It was a third way between communism and laissez-faire capitalism. Though the party failed to win the White House in 1912, Hooker remained close to TR until the elder statesman's death in 1919.[41]

Elon imbibed TR's view of conservation because it was practical as well as visionary. By more efficiently organizing natural resources, and focusing on pragmatic environmental initiatives, Roosevelt (and his right-hand man, U.S. Forest Service head Gifford Pinchot) believed that Americans could revitalize their natural landscape. This would in turn restore the American soul. Hooker liked this sentiment. He knew that Niagara Falls was hallowed ground for naturalists and citizens; he also believed that it was an eminently usable resource for industrialists. Finding a middle ground for these two groups excited Elon.

Like TR, Elon also supported nature conservation initiatives that allowed sportsmen, hunters, and others to enjoy the great outdoors. He had memberships in several outdoorsmen's groups with a conservationist bent, including the Boone and Crockett Club, which had been founded by Roosevelt and George Bird Grinnell in 1887. Elon also supported new state and federal parks, always a high agenda item for Roosevelt and Progressives. It didn't hurt that Elon's wife also supported various environmental causes. The former Blanche Ferry, daughter of a Detroit seed company magnet whose lifelong passion became horticulture and public gardens, she became a key member of the New York Botanical Society. Though Blanche enjoyed the beauty of the Falls, she did not much like "dirty Buffalo," where the urban grid of factories, grain elevators, trains, and belching smokestacks seemed to epitomize the hazards of smoke, dirt, and ash. For Blanche Hooker, public and private gardens were an oasis from industrialization. Similarly, Elon believed that parks were vital to the nation's civic health. Even after his firm became an industrial powerhouse, he pushed for the creation of a major new park in Western New York: Allegany State Park.[42]

In short, Elon saw no major conflict between his industrial and environmental concerns. He thought of himself as both a Roosevelt Progressive and progressive businessman. He supported environmental initiatives that protected America's natural resources while his company deployed electrolytic chemistry to help solve the nation's urban pollution problems.[43] Like TR, Elon Hooker believed that he was an agent of change—a visionary in environmental as well as business matters.

4. Hooker and Toxic Knowledge at the Niagara Plant and Beyond

But that very sensibility also inured him to the deeper concerns about the Chemical Century unleashed at Niagara Falls. Hooker officials were well aware of the caustic nature of their early production processes. For one thing, they knew that fire hazards lurked in nearly every corner of their Niagara plant. In an era when factories often locked their doors to keep workers in, Hooker buildings offered easy "exits in case of fire," as one insider put it. Pictures of Hooker's picric acid facilities, which poured out "tons" of the chemical for the U.S. Army, show just that: a series of steep planks jutting out of buildings to get workers out fast.[44]

Workers faced other potential hazards from chemicals themselves. J. H. Babcock, who headed the picric acid plant, offered a seemingly benign example of the physical effects associated with massive chemical production. He once attended a baseball game flushed in "a vivid yellow." As he explained to alarmed onlookers (who thought he had liver disease), picric acid could be used as a dye as well as in explosives, and it occasionally gave Hookerites a jaundiced appearance.[45] Though a humorous part of Hooker lore, Babcock's story illuminates the visible bodily impact of chemicals. More ominous testimony came from those who plied the bleach chambers. "Working conditions [in the bleach house] were unbelievable when judged by today's standards," even the company historian conceded in the 1950s. "The plant operated with two 12-hour shifts, day and night, seven days a week, 365 days a year, with no holidays and no vacations. Turnover was tremendous." Some newly hired people, working for 15 cents an hour around 1907, quit before the end of the first day. Yet "it was not a lack of concern that caused these conditions in the company's first plant," he noted. Rather, it was "a lack of suitable equipment." Turn-of-the-century "gas masks, and other protective devices, [were] then in a primitive developmental stage." Workers improvised their own protective gear—wet rags and flannel clothing—to bolster meager company offerings. According to Hooker officials, improved workplace safety "came only through the costly process of trial and error."[46]

Workplace safety was one area that Elon Hooker wanted to seal off from Progressive environmentalism. Indeed, Hooker believed that the gospel of corporate efficiency, not the Progressive mantra of government intervention, must reign supreme inside his plant. Workplaces like Hooker Electrochemical were the province of industrial titans, not environmental reformers. The divide between corporate power and environmental health could not be breached. Elon was not the only one espousing such views. Even Progressive doctors and health officials saw invasive governmental action in industrial settings as problematic. "At a time when notions of conflict of interest remained underdeveloped and less reified throughout the medical profession," one scholar of the era has observed, industrial doctors often folded their "medical skills and practices" into "corporate economic imperatives." Thus, many doctors scientifically studied workplace safety as a byproduct of industrial efficiency, not as a human health concern in and of itself. As a result, many industrial physicians had divided loyalty between "patients and the employer who paid [their] salary."[47] At Hooker as elsewhere in industrial America, worker safety remained a fraught topic.

Well beyond the workplace, however, Hooker officials registered alarm over the potentially harmful impact of chemicals. On the battlefields of war-torn Europe, newly developed chemical weapons inspired fears among the Allied powers that reverberated all the way back to Niagara Falls. Indeed, no sooner had Americans joined the Great War in 1917 than Elon Hooker himself contacted high-ranking government officials about the hazards of the chemical front. If anyone could prepare Doughboys for the threats of chemical warfare, Elon declared, it was the company that had mastered electrolytic chemical production. Yet this very claim illuminated the potential troubles confronting Hooker's bleach workers.

Elon's concerns about the chemical front emerged well before American entry in the Great War. Theodore Roosevelt told Elon that his specialized chemical knowledge would be an important factor in looming global conflicts. TR even promised to elevate Elon to the head of a newly formed

"U.S. Gas Service" if Bull Moose Progressives won the 1912 presidential campaign. TR's loss did not end Elon's interest in military affairs, for Hooker remained a key supplier of chlorobenzol, which was used in the manufacture of explosives, to French and eventually American forces. But Elon's attention turned from offensive to defensive matters when German forces initiated the first major gas attacks of World War I on April 22, 1915 at the Belgian town of Ypres. On that day, German forces launched more than 5,000 gas cylinders laced with explosives at French and British troops. Allied forces stumbled through the gaseous haze, gasping for breath and searching for a way to get beyond the nauseating stench permeating the air. "Germans gain," the *New York Times* announced two days later, adding that "charges of poison bombs" soon flowed from the front. Field Marshal Sir John French, commander-in-chief of the British forces, accused the Germans of "making use of a large number of appliances for the production of asphyxiating gas." The French argued that these new weapons of war violated the 1899 Hague Convention against chemical bombs and condemned the Germans for falsely accusing the British of inaugurating poison gas attacks weeks before Ypres.[48] Though they waited several months, the British launched their first gas attack on September 24 at German troops gathered at Loos, Belgium.

With chemical warfare a reality, both sides scrambled for an edge. As one physician observed in 1917, "very little is known" about the composition of the much used toxic bombs.[49] But people did know that the poison bombs utilized by both the Germans and the British were based on the very product Hooker Electrochemical had produced in increasing quantities: chlorine.[50] "Elemental chlorine" ordnance played a major part in the Ypres attack in the spring of 1915. In subsequent years, phosgene and mustard gases were used in more sophisticated chlorinated "poison bombs."[51] "Chlorinated chemicals were particularly effective … weapons," biologist and environmentalist Joe Thornton has written, "because they were highly toxic and oil soluble, so they could cross cell membranes and destroy the tissues of lungs, eyes, and skin, incapacitating soldiers and causing extreme pain." By 1918, "more than a quarter of all munitions contained chemical agents."[52]

Chemical deaths in the Great War numbered in the tens of thousands (reaching around 5 percent of those killed). Yet the symbolic power of gas attacks assumed greater importance, with soldiers recalling the bewildered conditions of the chemical front. Adolf Hitler, who served in the German army during World War I, remains perhaps the most famous gas victim of the war, having been exposed to a British mustard gas attack. But the impact on Allied infantrymen was just as powerful. A British medical text from 1917, among the first to examine the subject of "gas poisoning" in wartime, described the average soldier's traumatic experience of a chlorinated gas attack in poignant terms: "After recovery from the bronchitis and pneumonia, the patient remains weak and exhausted for a considerable time. He gets tired very rapidly and is unable to walk quickly or uphill without getting short of breath, even after the last signs of bronchitis have disappeared.... The frightful experience he has passed through often affects his nervous system, and some of the attacks are doubtless aggravated by apprehension. Headache, vertigo and dyspepsia may continue for several weeks."[53]

As a chemical insider, Elon Hooker approached U.S. military officials in the hope that his knowledge would save Americans from the hazards of gas attacks. "Chlorine is the foundation product of which all the deadly gases are made," he explained. And as "the largest chlorine gas manufacturing concern in the country," Elon told the Army, Hooker could not only supply gases for offensive purposes but help soldiers prepare for enemy gas attacks. "We know the peculiarities of chlorine gas. We know how to handle noxious gases, how to work with them," he told army brass. For instance, the Army used antiquated British gas masks; Hooker officials noted that they had already innovated far superior protective technology that could save American lives during the war.[54] Though some members of the Army expressed interest, military officials would not accept Elon's offer. He was furious.

Elon's emotions flowed from a direct connection to the chemical front. His nephew, Albert Huntington Hooker Jr., son of brother Albert, was one the earliest gas officers in the U.S. Army. Born in 1895 in Chicago, Albert Jr. followed in his father's footsteps by studying chemical engineering at Cornell University. Athletic and handsome, Albert Jr. had a bright future in the industrial world. Instead he enlisted in the Army, where his family name and expertise quickly led Albert Jr. to the rank of Second Lieutenant in the U.S. Gas Service. Albert Jr. was part of a chemical vanguard. Established in 1917, the Gas Service grew out of Army research into the potential needs of its personnel in Europe. With chemical warfare now a fact of military life, Army officials projected that they would need over a million gas masks by 1918. Army officers also called for the creation of a gas service. A committee on noxious gases, formed by the National Defense Council, wired the secretary of defense on July 2, 1917, that it had formed the outlines of just such a body. Then, on August 31, the surgeon general officially formed the "Gas Defense Service." In June 1918, thinking about offensive as well as defensive needs, the Army created the "Chemical Warfare Service." Like its counterparts in Western Europe, the United States had now entered the age of chemical weaponry. And Albert Jr. was on its front lines.[55]

Indeed, by December 1917, he was on his way to France with the 27th division of the American Expeditionary Forces. He would eventually earn both the Silver Star and Purple Heart. Albert Jr. also forwarded a host of information about the chemical front to family members. One major example: A chilling note to Albert Jr. and other gas officers in May 1917 declaring that "the attention of all ranks is called to the increasing importance of gas warfare." Known as General Order 79, this command stressed the dire nature of gas preparedness. "Failure to understand the modes of employment of gas and the necessary measures for protection against it will have the most serious consequences." Gas officers like Albert Jr. would have special responsibilities, including not only the training of American soldiers in gas defense but the "collecting and transmitting to the proper laboratory...all [chemical] material of enemy origin...."[56] Throughout 1918, Albert Jr. could be found moving from labs in Paris to the front and back again. He drilled troops in what was known as "defensive gas maneuvers," researched the types of chemical explosives and gases utilized by the Germans, and explained to both soldiers and his superior officers the effects various chemical weapons might have on the body.[57]

The last year of the war was a particularly nervous time for Albert Jr. Worried that the Germans would attempt to use poison bombs in a last-ditch effort at victory, U.S. officials drafted a set of "special instructions to commanding officers." "Regimental commanders," the Army declared on August 1, 1918, "will take up the matter of gas defense in their command." They were "required to give short, clear talks, quizzes and demonstrations until all officers and men have a clear understanding of indications of the different forms of enemy gas attack, mustard gas, fires in the dugout, orders for gas entries, [and] use of the [gas] mask."[58] Although no major gas attack happened, Albert Jr. and other gas officers remained on high alert.

After coming home, Albert Jr. told family and friends about his chemical warfare experiences, noting that he had more specialized knowledge about noxious gases than most Army officials. These stories fueled uncle Elon's criticisms of the military, which he unleashed publicly in a 1920 run for governor of New York State. As Albert Jr. settled into the family business, moving to a major Hooker production facility in Tacoma, Elon blasted Army men for not knowing how dangerous chemical warfare was and for not exploiting Hooker expertise earlier. As for Albert, he never forgot the importance of his insider knowledge, later serving as a chemical officer (who advised the Air Force on incendiary bombs) during World War II. After serving as a company executive for several years, he died in 1971.

Both Albert Jr.'s and Elon's willingness to talk openly about the deadly gases soldiers encountered illuminates the underside of the Chemical Century at the moment of its birth. Yet it was a momentary glimpse of the matter. Indeed, while Hooker officials understood that chemical production carried with it certain risks as well as rewards, they did not turn their toxic knowledge into an extended analysis of workplace or environmental safety. During the Great War, Elon Hooker spoke out as a patriot with special knowledge about chemical production, not as a captain of industry who wanted to inform the public about the potential trade-offs of the rising chemical age. Elon's perspective assumed a dividing line between private and public knowledge about chemicals. That line would not be crossed until a new era of environmentalism emerged much later at Love Canal.

5. Master of the Chemical Machine

As he aged, Elon Huntington Hooker continued to celebrate the power, not the pitfalls, of chemical innovation. With a Wall Street address and bicoastal production facilities at Niagara Falls and Tacoma, Elon envisioned himself as a captain of industry who had remade the world around him. In 1934, a confident Elon commissioned noted Depression-era artist Francis Scott Bradford to produce a tableau of murals marking nearly

VIII FROM THE MURALS IN THE NEW YORK OFFICE.

Figure 7a/b The Hooker Company's Bradford Murals: These twin images, part of a mural series imagined by Elon Hooker and executed by Scott Bradford, illuminate Hooker's visionary views of chemical science and technology. By mastering the chemical age, Hooker hoped to emancipate humanity from the chains of antiquity and superstition. The murals were originally placed in Hooker Chemical's Wall Street office. (Source: Elon Huntington Hooker, 1938)

three decades of Hooker ingenuity and success. Unlike Diego Rivera, who celebrated the productive power of the masses, Bradford's murals honored the industrial titans reshaping the globe. The ten murals, which hung in Hooker's corporate offices, featured dreamy scenes of American industrial prowess. Unsurprisingly, chemical production loomed large: there were "tank cars," "storage vats," "weighing tanks," and "electric cells"—all the things that made Hooker Electrochemical go.[59]

The murals also featured words of wisdom from Elon Huntington Hooker himself. "Through human energy controlling natural force," the caption below one of Hooker's favorite murals declared, "man becomes master of the machine." It was a revealing sentiment. Like the men in his murals, Hooker had mastered nature and conjured into being a whole new era of chemical production. At Niagara Falls, Hooker became a "constructive dreamer," in his own words. He not only envisioned a new world but built it.[60] [Figs. 7a, 7b]

Another mural pictured a more ambivalent scene: a man desperately trying to break free from the known world. "Man," the caption next to the striking image reads, "though chained to earth, looks across time and space toward an unknown perfection which he may never reach but will forever seek." These were certainly appropriate words for Elon Hooker, a man born of a pioneer American family who wanted to break free from the past and create a new industrial order. Yet, perhaps unconsciously, the mural also captured the lingering human doubts about chemical and industrial creation. Could a master of the machine truly escape the limits of the known world?

The final lines of the mural's caption suggest that Elon Hooker might well have been aware of the way that epic visions contain the seeds of their own demise: "The imagination of man, trammeled by ignorance and lack of vision, struggles to free itself, and strains to glimpse the future, through the fog of the vast world of the still unknown."[61]

4

Worlds Collide at Love's Canal

In 1938, Hooker Electrochemical confronted a future without its founder when Elon died in a tragic automobile accident.[2] The longtime patriarch was just 68 years old. Hosannas to his leadership piled up in a moving tribute album, which was quickly published as a special edition of the company newsletter, "Hooker Gas."[3] "Engineer, Industrialist, Patriot, Public Servant, Author, Humanitarian": Elon Huntington Hooker was all of these things, the tribute declared, and would be sorely missed.

Yet while Elon's passing hit family and friends hard, it did not slow the firm's extraordinary growth. Indeed, over the next thirty years, Hooker Chemical (as it soon became known) grew at an even more impressive rate than during Elon's time. By midcentury, the company was a global leader in the production of an astonishing array of chemicals beyond bleaching powder and caustic soda—degreasers, rubbers, explosives, defoliants, plastics, and much more. One measure of its far-reaching reputation came in the late 1940s, when Hooker executive Bjarne Klaussen traveled from Niagara Falls to the South Pacific to watch a new round of atomic bomb tests at Bikini Atoll. Cleared of its native inhabitants, the tiny island served as Ground Zero for a weapon far more powerful than the bombs dropped on Hiroshima and

Nagasaki at the close of World War II. Klaussen was part of a small delegation from American corporations and universities that had made "special
contributions" to the nation's atomic development. "Hooker played an important role in the Manhattan Project," the company historian bragged
just a few years later (without providing further details, though they probably revolved around chemical igniters and explosives). The company would
remain a key player on the Cold War chemical front for years to come.[4]

Hooker's explosive growth during the 1940s and 1950s had a palpable
impact on the Love Canal landscape too. For booming production overwhelmed the firm's on-site disposal capacity. Searching for new ways to
deal with this growing problem, Hooker resorted to "inground disposal"
at sites beyond the Niagara plant.[5] The first disposal space was none other
than William Love's abandoned waterway in nearby Lasalle. Hooker began
a massive burial operation in 1942 that, over the course of a decade, deposited roughly 22,000 tons of chemical sludge into the landscape. Sealed
away in what Hooker thought was a secure clay vault, the chemicals became
part of a toxic mausoleum.

The operation was perfectly legal. In fact, Hooker had a city permit for
its dumping operations. Moreover, no state or federal regulations yet governed hazardous waste disposal. Only common-law concerns about the
potential public nuisance of industrial waste mitigated abusive disposal
practices such as the flushing of huge amounts of waste into rivers and
lakes that people used for boating, fishing, and swimming. More generally,
few Americans paused to consider the future impact of a chemical burial
ground, either for the environment or for the people who inhabited it. In
no small way, the environmental costs of hazardous waste were rendered
invisible and gone. Only years later would Americans rediscover this lost
history of toxic trash at Love Canal. Ironically, Hooker would become even
more famous for its disposal history in western New York than almost anything else the company did, including helping to launch the Atomic Age.

1. Hooker's Chemical Expansion

Hooker's burial operations at Love Canal flowed from the company's breakthrough production years during and after World War II. Between 1939

and 1950, company sales increased 390 percent, while net income rose an astounding 850 percent.[6] That ascension began in the early 1940s, when Hooker met the American war machine's surging needs by supplying explosives, disinfectants, rubber materials, defoliants, and a range of other goods to the Army. By 1943, net sales soared over $17 million—an 80 percent increase from the previous year.[7] Here, Hooker joined the American chemical industry's broader effort to put a swagger in the U.S. war machine. "How much chemistry per soldier," a telling Monsanto ad asked in 1943?[8] From head to toe, the average G.I. was literally draped in chemical material: plastics lined his protective helmets and insulated his walkie-talkies to ensure smooth communication on the battlefield; phosphoric acid created rustproofing material in his guns and weaponry; rubber made his dangerous life more tolerable, cushioning the soles of his boots, securing bandages on his injured feet and hands, and insulating his gas masks; carbonized textiles made his pants and shirts durable in even the worst conditions; finally, a bevy of acids served as the building blocks for the explosives he and other grunts relied on day after day. Though Monsanto's competitor, the always patriotic Hooker Chemical readily agreed that chemical products were an integral part of America's global military prowess.

After the war, Hooker broke production records almost annually by innovating new products for consumer and industrial markets. In 1947, it surpassed the $20 million sales mark for the first time in corporate history. New products helped lead the way. "DDT and Hexachlorocyclohexane, production of which commenced in a small way in 1946, reached substantial volumes in 1947," one Hooker report noted. Combined with "substantial increases" in sales of Hooker's basic chemical products—chlorine and caustic soda—the company's fortunes appeared rosier than ever.[9] Indeed, while it still produced bleaching powder, disinfectants, and explosive materials, Hooker became a company of constant innovation. "Unlike many of its ... competitors," an industry consultant reported in 1952, "Hooker's growth has been based in large part on new product developments ... rather than by company acquisitions or merger." "Year after year," the consultant continued, Hooker's "research and engineering teams weaved more threads [i.e., chemical products] into our daily lives." Even a brief history of Hooker's product line illustrated this point. Diversified (or new) products, which during the 1930s had comprised less than 10 percent of Hooker's sales, accounted for roughly 70 percent of the company's output after the war.[10] And "some 15 new major products have been developed since the end of World War II, which directly accounted for over 20% of the company sales and earnings in 1953."[11] Hooker's own annual reports touted these new products to shareholders: DDT, polyvinyl chloride (PVC), polyester resins, lindane, C-56, and on and on. As new products kept rolling out of Hooker labs during the 1940s and 1950s, the entire company surged with confidence.

That fact could be seen in the company's gleaming production facilities. According to a progress report in 1951, "the bulk of Hooker's plant is virtually new."[12] Since World War II, Hooker had invested $22 million in infrastructure.[13] And it was still building new facilities. Hooker's build-out was just part of a national trend, as chemical companies created a staggering $1.6 billion in infrastructure by the mid-1950s (the equivalent of tens of billions of dollars in the early 21st century). "Among the manufacturing industries," the 1951 progress report on Hooker chemical informed Wall Street investors, "the chemical group stands head and shoulders above all others in the amount of money it intends to invest in plant expansion."[14] Hooker had grown by ten percent a year and it was not nearly done.[15] With new chemical plants and subsidiaries established in Michigan, Ohio, and Washington, not to mention millions of dollars' worth of sparkling new machinery at its Niagara plant, Hooker's fortunes impressed everyone. "Few companies of its size in the chemical industry have expanded...at as rapid a rate since the end of the war as Hooker," a consultant cooed.[16] At the company's golden anniversary in 1955, Hooker officials beamed with pride. "As this book is readied for the press," the editor of the celebratory history *Salt, Water, Power and People* declared, "there is mounting evidence that Hooker's second half-century is underway at an accelerated pace."[17]

2. "Chemagination": Hooker Ads and Second Nature

With postwar sales booming, Hooker hoped to burnish its public image in a series of national advertising campaigns. A familiar sight in popular magazines ranging from *Newsweek* to *Fortune* (not to mention industry journals like *Chemical & Engineering News*), Hooker ads pictured a world completely remade by chemicals. Part of an industry-wide campaign that had its roots in DuPont's famous Depression-era slogan "Better Living Through Chemistry," Hooker's media blitz pushed its chemicals and plastics into mainstream consumer culture for the first time. In doing so, it spun magical tales about the American Chemical Century that it helped launch.[18]

Although it cycled through various slogans, Hooker's most famous campaign was "Chemagination." Like "Kodak" (another famous artificial word), Chemagination symbolized Hooker's ambitions as a corporate dream-maker, particularly its ability to produce visionary chemical products. Instead of film, Hooker used chemicals to reorient the world. Smitten with its linguistic creation, Hooker trademarked the term in 1965.[19] But it had been using Chemagination since the late 1950s. As one ad in *Newsweek* put it in July 1959, Hooker's "New Chemagination Center"—located across the Niagara River on Grand Island—had already unleashed a bevy of products allowing both companies and consumers "to do things that couldn't be done ten years ago." Thanks to Hooker's innovations, Americans could now "preserve foods or drugs" longer via a "sodium benzoate" product that dissolved immediately "in water"; "set a new pace in building, with a plastic foam light as a biscuit"; "make an insecticide, germicide, dye, drug, [or] non-flammable plastic—starting with one chlorinated compound"; and "power a rocket with high energy solid oxidants." These breakthroughs came from the new "chemistry of chlorine, fluorine, phosphorus, sulfur, phenolics, polyesters, foams, and high polymers" that Hooker's technicians had mastered. The results, as the tableau of practical uses in the ad showed, transformed consumer, industrial and military life in equal measure.[20]

Drawing on the medieval seductions of alchemy, Hooker ads celebrated "chemaginative people" and processes that improved Americans' daily lives.[21] [Figs. 8a, 8b, 8c] "This is Chemagination," a representative 1961 Hooker ad declared above three parallel images.[22] The first picture showed a "tough, fire-retardant, corrosion resistant" plastic mould that one company developed with Hooker's "Durez Plastics Division" to link subway cars more effectively and thus cheaply; the second image displayed a brush cutting through a row of flames via the magic of a "safety

RUBBER and the world of Mr. Jones

Stretch it, ration it, risk your life for it—and still the story of rubber was "never enough" —until chemicals came along.

Today, bubbling from Hooker electrolytic cells in three U. S. plants, come tons and tons of chemicals to help rubber-cushion and rubber-carpet the modern world of Mr. Jones.

Because of chemicals, Mr. Jones—just as you do—walks on rubber, stalks duck in

rubber, rides on rubber. In his car he's protected by 530-odd rubber parts that cradle the engine, pad the floor, ease the pedals, seal out drafts, wipe the windshield. His tires roll thousands of safe miles farther than those on the family bus in 1930—and they cost less per mile.

Hooker chemicals help make synthetic rubbers to fight heat, conquer cold, shed oil, control electricity. Hooker chemicals help

make new rubber out of old—to give America the extra rubber Nature can't supply.

Durez phenolic resins from Hooker improve properties of natural and synthetic rubbers, expanding their usefulness.

These resins, and Hooker chemicals—sulfur chlorides, lauryl mercaptan, muriatic acid, caustic soda, and many others—provide makings for most of the good things in Mr. Jones' life—and yours.

HOOKER ELECTROCHEMICAL COMPANY
207 Forty-seventh St., Niagara Falls, N. Y.
NIAGARA FALLS TACOMA MONTAGUE, MICH. NEW YORK CHICAGO LOS ANGELES

HOOKER CHEMICALS PLASTICS

DUREZ *Phenolic Plastics that fit the job*

Figure 8a–c The Golden Age of Chemical Advertising. This collection of Hooker ads displays the company's space-age understanding of itself. Still dedicated to Elon's ideals, Hooker at midcentury sought to burnish its reputation as a cutting-edge chemical maker that was almost literally out of this world. [Source: Tear Sheet Collection, Library Company)

ingredient" developed by Hooker; the third picture showed the ancient "skeleton of a tiny animal" that Hooker used to "create a cleaner world" via a new generation of cutting-edge phosphate detergents.[23] In each case, "Chemagination" symbolized Hooker's ability to produce better and cheaper goods.

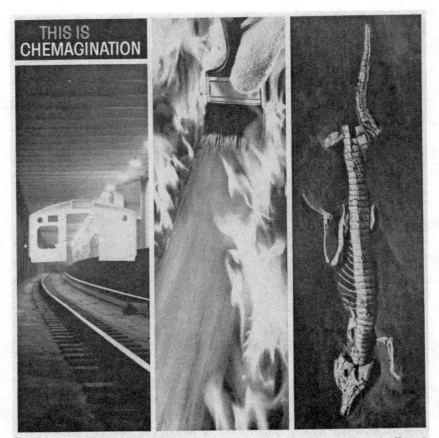

DREAM BIG   The plastic shape of things to come grows larger. One company, working with Hetron®
—a *Durez Plastics Division* polyester resin—molds ends of subway cars in single units. Tough, fire re-
tardant, corrosion resistant, these ends are part of a design that is expected to save $6 million in costs
over the fleet's life.   FOIL FIRE WITH A PAINTBRUSH   How? By painting walls,
ceilings, stairs, woodwork with paint that fights a delaying action against fire. The safety ingredient in
these paints is Het® acid—one of several Hooker fire-retardant materials. Among them may be just the one
that could help you build more safety into a product of yours.   CREATE A CLEANER WORLD
from the bones that lie within it. Phosphate rock, the three-hundred-million-year-old skeletons of tiny animals, is the beginning. Dried, heated to fiery temperatures, reacted, it finally becomes compounds that stop
minerals in hard water from retarding cleaning action. They're used in many detergents.   *If you want
to apply chemagination in your industry, write us.*

HOOKER CHEMICAL CORPORATION
102 FORTY-SEVENTH STREET, NIAGARA FALLS, NEW YORK

Figure 8a–c Continued

Hooker even claimed that its chemicals were out of this world. In the
"World of Mr. Jones" ads, which it unleashed just before Chemagination,
Hooker pictured a square-jawed businessman decked out in a series of
spacey contexts born of the company's potent chemicals. In one ad, Mr.
Jones bounced through space on a rocket-sized pencil whose eraser-like

LEATHER and the world of Mr. Jones

Riding valiantly out of the past are ancient Warrior Jones, shield covered with leather ... buckskin-clad Long-Rifle Jones slipping silently through the forests . . . Pioneer Jones, hoarding precious water across the sun-baked desert in a leather bucket.

Today it's Mr. Jones. Leather is a shield and comfort in his world, too. Perhaps you've noticed—more leather is used for more things today.

That's because it's *better* leather. Chemicals made by Hooker help make it better. Hooker chemicals remove coarse hair, soften hides, go into rich colors for leather chairs and shoes and sportswear. Other Hooker chemicals add durability and toughness to leather for industrial use.

Sodium sulfide, sodium sulfhydrate, sodium tetrasulfide, caustic soda, benzoic acid, muriatic acid—these and many other chemicals made by Hooker help nearly every industry provide Mr. Jones and you with the good things in life.

Delivered around the world by Hooker barge and tank car, this dependable supply of chemicals for industry finds new usefulness almost every day, as Hooker research develops new chemicals for new uses, and new uses for existing chemicals.

HOOKER ELECTROCHEMICAL COMPANY
210 Forty-seventh Street, Niagara Falls, N. Y.
NIAGARA FALLS • TACOMA • MONTAGUE, MICH. • NEW YORK • CHICAGO • LOS ANGELES

HOOKER
CHEMICALS
PLASTICS

DUREZ PLASTICS   HRALX CHEMICALS

Figure 8a–c Continued

base epitomized the tons of rubber "bubbling from Hooker electrolytic cells in three U.S. plants." These chemicals provided a cushy "rubber carpet" to the modern world—one that "nature can't supply."[24] In another ad, Mr. Jones sat comfortably in a bubble made by "the electrolysis of brine inside the famed Hooker cell." "From morning until night, almost everything he touches, eats, or wears," the ad declared, "is dependent... on one or more of... the hundred Hooker Chemicals" now on the market.

According to the ad, the "bubbling birth of new products" emanating from Hooker's global supply chain had transformed "the world of Mr. Jones"—and thereby all humanity—almost completely.[25]

In this manner, Hooker ads none-too-subtly alluded to the rise of second nature: a synthetic realm that now surrounded Americans, becoming the "natural" counterpart to water, wind, mountains and trees. Without the life-sustaining products emanating from the chemical industry, this second nature—inseparable from modern culture itself—was unthinkable. Yet, Hooker worried, Americans often took their second nature for granted. Chemagination ads reminded consumers that the essential elements of modern American society—plastics, insecticides, drugs, and degreasers—resulted from chemicals. As another Hooker campaign would put it rather baldly in the late 1960s, whatever product or device Americans used, "there must be a Hooker somewhere."[26]

Like Chemagination and the "World of Mr. Jones" ads, Hooker's earliest campaign touted the company's ability to conjure second nature into being. Indeed, its "Salt of the Earth" ads from the mid-1950s illuminated Hooker's ability to turn even the most basic natural element like sodium into more than a preservative or spice. "What does salt buy today?" one 1955 magazine ad wondered. Where Native Americans used salt to "purchase food, lodging and even land," the text explained, Hooker chemists utilized it to bring "us thousands of the miracle products we live by." (Images showed a scantily clad "American Indian" holding two bags of the precious white mineral.) From "chlorine that purifies water" to magical drugs that cured the sick to "strong new plastic materials that can be shaped to today's needs," Hookerized salt helped build a new world of chemical superiority.[27] As Hooker explained in another ad, its newest plant in Montague, Michigan, was situated on a massive salt mine, allowing the company to "convert the salt of the earth into chlorine and caustic soda and their myriad by-products" that would facilitate the American Dream. Montague was thus the "city that started to grow a million years ago," when a salt marsh formed along the Great Lakes. Thanks to Hooker, a "new day dawned for Montague," which would soon be a "thriving chemical center."[28]

Hooker's midcentury ad campaigns brought Elon Hooker's corporate murals to life in ways that the longtime patriarch only imagined. In the ads, as in the murals, techno-scientists mastered the world, emancipating humans from the physical restraints of nature itself. Yet the ads also removed the realities of chemical production from public view, celebrating wondrous ends over complex means. Was there any possible underside to the synthetic world of polymers, resins, and rubbers catalyzed by Hooker? The company's ads said no, but the novelist John Dos Passos certainly thought about the Chemical Century's underside. His book *Midcentury* surveyed the machine-like transformation of 20th-century American society, offering a skeptical perspective on the brand of techno-dynamism espoused by industrial titans like Hooker. Though impressed by scientific and technical innovation, Dos Passos nonetheless worried that second nature threatened the environment humans would always need. Using Hooker's Chemagination campaign as an epigraph, Dos Passos wondered if humans had finally become inebriated by the scientific machine. "This is Chemagination," Dos Passos abruptly quoted from a Hooker ad midway through his book: "combine rubber's elasticity with phenolic resin's hardness—and you get a long wearing shoe-sole material or an adhesive that seals the metal skin of a jet plane with a giant grip[....]" His words trailed off into other stories but their meaning was unmistakable: by personifying chemical products with anthropomorphic metaphors ("skins" and "grips"), Dos Passos's words suggested that humanity might lose its soul in the near future.[29]

Still, the powerful narrative deployed by Chemagination ads prevailed: there seemed to be no downside to chemicals.

3. Love Canal's Second Nature

The hazardous remnants of Hooker's midcentury rise did not simply vanish. They could be found at Love Canal and several other toxic waste sites appearing in midcentury Niagara Falls. Love Canal was not even Hooker's biggest hazardous waste dump (subsequent ones would be up to four times larger); it would, however, be the company's first major off-site disposal pit. With production booming in the 1940s, Hooker had to find a dumping ground. The old Love Canal area, company officials thought, was nearly ideal. The landscape had already been excavated, of course, creating a big bowl that contained only water. Moreover, the area was close enough to the Niagara plant—about four miles—that Hooker trucks and workers could make consistent runs without much hassle or worry. Though a wartime housing development would rise nearby in 1942, and neighborhoods existed several blocks away, the abandoned canal proper was not densely populated when Hooker first surveyed it; roughly a dozen homes stood around the old waterway. And the canal zone had a beautiful bed of clay. Indeed, company officials believed that the area's clay foundation would prevent any waste from escaping. By adding a clay cap, Hooker thought it could forever seal away the dangerous chemical residue accumulating at its factories.[30]

For these reasons, Hooker was thrilled with the Love Canal site. After surveying the landscape at the end of 1941, it began inground disposal operations the following year.[31] Hooker eventually purchased Love Canal property. The company dumped waste there until roughly 1953. Hooker began dumping operations at the northern end of the canal, near present-day Colvin Boulevard. Draining and damming two sections of the waterway, technicians sculpted large disposal pits out of the canal—30 to 50 feet in diameter, and 20 to 30 feet deep. Between 1942 and 1946, workers then unloaded thousands of 55-gallon drums into the earth. After these pits had been filled, workers moved to the canal's southern end, just a few hundred yards away from the Niagara River. Damming and draining this portion of the canal as well, they unloaded thousands more barrels. They then moved to the canal's center, dumping chemicals and ash. Overall, most of the dumping occurred in the southern and central portions of Love Canal, and probably peaked in the late 1940s, years when Hooker consistently broke production records. Company records indicate that Hooker scaled back disposal operations after 1950.[32]

According to one worker, Hooker's "general practice" was to gather hundreds of chemical drums each month at the plant before transporting them to the dump. During peak periods, however, dumping might occur on a weekly basis. Technicians estimated that they could dispose of anywhere from 600 to 1,000 drums a day at Love Canal, if need be. Made of either metal or fiberboard, the drums were often recycled or reconditioned from previous use; some were already corroding when workers placed them in the canal bed. And they were very heavy, weighing as much as 500 pounds. Some barrels broke (though no more than four or five per delivery, a technician recalled) and some chemical waste was spewed directly into the ground. Local residents told tales of disposal workers dashing to nearby homes desperately in search of a garden hose that would flush off chemical waste that had splashed onto their bodies.[33] But the dumping always continued.

Other than basic protective measures, Hooker officials did not register much concern about worker health or environmental liability. One disposal worker recalled a system of dots that separated the most hazardous chemical barrels from others. But with no laws governing toxic disposal, especially worker safety, Hooker did not do much more than that. Most workers knew that the waste was dangerous. One disposal worker recalled that his boots were eaten through by chemicals.[34] As for the land itself, neither the company nor government officials worried about environmental impacts at Love Canal. According to one person, even the prospect of future negligence did not raise much concern, "so long as the property is either owned or leased by the party doing the dumping."[35] Visiting the disposal site in 1948, Hooker engineer Jerome Wilkinfeld commented that the dump appeared to be a perfectly "reasonable" solution to Hooker's ever-expanding collection of toxic wastes.[36] And in many ways he was right: this was the status quo of the chemical industry at midcentury. Hooker believed that its disposal operations had been well planned and executed. Nature, in the form of a seemingly sponge-like clay pit, would take care of the rest. With little fanfare, the Love Canal dump was officially sealed in 1953.

Although company officials planned to place a clay cap on top of the entire dump to prevent surface migration of chemical waste, there was little evidence of it. Hooker later claimed that developers removed the cap when building new homes and streets. But subsequent investigations doubted that the company had actually capped the entire dump (perhaps only parts of it). Similarly, only a small portion of the northern section was fenced off, despite claims that the entire Love Canal site would be closed. In short, the Love Canal dump may never have been completely contained. One former resident of the new government housing project recalled that he could swim in one section of the canal while dumping occurred in another area. "It smelled just like the Hooker plant," he said.[37] There were other problems too. A disposal technician remembered that, soon after dumping had ended, Love Canal's topsoil showed signs of settling, with depressions and sinkholes forming, indicating the possibility of future leakage. A local hunter and trapper asserted that the original canal bed had underground springs, which would exert steady pressure against the thousands of chemical barrels clustered underground.[38]

But who would know about these problems? Because Hooker's own narrative of disposal at Love Canal remained buried for decades, many of these details emerged much later in court. Even then, as the federal case file put it, Hooker's "written record is quite sparse."[39] This lack of documentation about toxic dumping practices reflected a bygone era of waste disposal. Well into to the 1960s, companies either disposed of their waste on site or hired contractors to dump hazardous materials in undisclosed locations. In Massachusetts, the Riley Tannery, which was absorbed by Beatrice Foods, used its 15-acre site along the Aberjona River as a dumping ground for waste materials during the 1950s. When the case (made famous in Jonathan Harr's thrilling book, *A Civil Action*) came to trial in the 1980s, lawyers and investigators found frustratingly little archival information about old dumping procedures that had compromised area aquifers. Closer to Niagara Falls, the Pfohl Brothers Landfill in Cheektowaga, just beyond the Buffalo-Niagara International Airport, accepted all manner of hazardous and municipal waste between 1932 and 1971.[40] Though this 120-acre patch of land seemed to be nothing more than a private landscaping operation, it became the clandestine resting ground for tons of toxic sludge. And yet, details about the industrial polluters who used the Pfohl Brothers site remain hazy in the 21st century.

Interestingly, some guidelines existed for the landfilling of nonhazardous waste. A few years before Hooker began disposal operations at Love Canal, the Fresno Municipal Landfill in northern California opened as a so-called sanitary dump. Inaugurated in 1937, Fresno was the "oldest 'true' sanitary landfill in the United States," in the words of environmental scholar Martin Melosi. As he notes, "it was the first to layer refuse and dirt in trenches, compact them, and cover the filled areas daily to minimize rodent and debris problems."[41] The Fresno site was also marked. Part of a municipal reform movement dating back to the 19th century that aimed to protect the public from trash hazards, the Fresno site operated for over fifty years under the premise that there was a science to waste disposal.

Yet even Fresno encountered problems. As testing in the 1980s revealed, toxic substances had infiltrated the dump. It was eventually closed. After much debate, it became the first dump listed on the National Register of Historic Places.[42]

At Love Canal, Hooker officials did not think that they had created a chemical hazard or even a dump worthy of special note. As far as the company was concerned, Hooker's chemical mausoleum was sound because it locked toxic trash into the ground. And that allowed it to keep producing miracle chemicals without worry.

4. Suburbanization at Love Canal

Love Canal's chemical nature resurfaced briefly because of the Baby Boom. As its population surged, Niagara Falls needed new housing, schools, and neighborhood infrastructure, which pointed politicians' attention towards the same plot of land Hooker had spied earlier: the relatively undeveloped canal zone at the southeastern edge of the county. By the 1950s, the population of greater Niagara Falls topped 100,000, more than double the number when Elon Huntington Hooker created his chemical company five decades before. The shape of the city changed too. With hydroelectric power companies, industrial manufacturers, and chemical concerns choking the industrial flats along the Niagara River, the Falls moved inland. With a large military base nearby and a hulking new industrial plant, the Bell Aerospace complex, towering in the distance, the Lasalle section of the city was poised for development.[43]

Niagara Falls city planners had been moving towards Love Canal since the 1920s, when Niagara Falls annexed the town of Lasalle. Flipping through the blue carbon copies of land surveys affixed to an old city atlas, one sees subdivisions relentlessly taking shape in Lasalle neighborhoods that formerly had "some of the most valuable and productive farms" in Niagara County.[44] These surveys pointed towards a final parcel of farms awaiting development: Lot 60. Comprising William Love's old waterway and a smattering of homes with pear orchards and livestock, Lot 60 remained largely rural. By the 1950s, city engineers saw it as an essential part of the Falls' future.

But first, the city had to acquire the property from Hooker. This occurred in April 1953, when the Niagara Falls School Board purchased the
Love Canal dumping grounds from Hooker for a single dollar. Not since
the Dutch gained Manhattan for a few guilders would a New York land
transaction inspire so much subsequent scrutiny. Why? According to the
property deed drawn by Hooker, Niagara Falls was "advised...that the
premises...had been filled, in whole or in part, to the present grade level
thereof with waste products resulting from the manufacturing of chemicals by the grantor [Hooker chemical] at its plant in the city of Niagara
Falls, New York, and the grantee [Niagara Falls] assumes all risk and liability incident to the use thereof."[45]

This legalese illuminated Love Canal's toxic nature. It also highlighted the
city's culpability should anything go wrong in new developments (whatever
they might be). When Board of Education members initially approached
Hooker in early 1952 about buying the property—which would anchor a
new subdivision and elementary school—some company officials laudably
registered concern. In March, Bjarne Klaussen, now Hooker's executive vice
president, took high-ranking school board members on a tour of the Love
Canal dump, "showing where wastes were deposited, how they were covered, and the results of testing that had recently been completed." In a letter
to the school board later that fall, Klaussen re-emphasized the potentially
hazardous "nature of the property." The company wanted to make sure that
mention of the chemical dump, including potential liability for any future
harm it might cause, would be included in all subsequent transactions between the city and developers, and then between developers and homeowners. The School Board agreed to these stipulations, feeling that they would
not prevent development of the Love Canal area. At least one school board
representative, deputy corporation counsel Ralph Boniello, tried to pierce
his colleagues' overconfident attitude about acquiring the fouled landscape.
The Love Canal deed, he warned, transferred "the risk and possible liability"
of chemical injury to Niagara Falls. And that might not be worth it.[46]

Nevertheless, the board pressed on. After floating the possibility of con-
demning the property (and then claiming it), the city struck a deal with
Hooker for the dumping grounds.[47] Once it gained title, Niagara Falls
wasted little time developing Love Canal. The city ran into problems immediately. The foundation of the new 99th Street School, located in the central

part of the old dump, sank into a pit of chemicals. Construction workers had to move the building 30 yards north to avoid "this particular hazard."[48] Even this did not deter school officials. The school opened in 1955. At roughly the same time, new streets and homes began taking shape in the area, as the city spun out land to developers. By the middle of the decade, a row of nearly 70 houses on 99th Street stood near the school, their backyards jutting into the old dumping grounds. Through the logic of city development, the neighborhood was slowly but surely turning into "Love Canal": a shiny subdivision with affordable homes, nearby schools, and fine playgrounds.

Politicians and business leaders continued to discuss Love Canal's toxic nature before burying it again. When the school board sold land to private developers in 1957, the chemical company warned that "due to chemical waste having been dumped [here] ... the land was not suitable for construction." The *Niagara Falls Gazette* reported that a Hooker representative came to a school board meeting in November to remind city officials that the company had used "a section of the old Love Canal to bury chemical waste," making it a poor choice for private homes. A few weeks later, the paper quoted another Hooker representative, A. W. Chambers, as saying that "there are dangerous chemicals buried there in drums, in loose form, in solids and liquids. It was understood the land would be used for a park or some surface activity" and not "digging" underground to create new home foundations. Hooker corporate lawyer Ansley Wilcox admitted that "the residues which had been buried [at Love Canal] ... might well have a serious deleterious effect on foundations, water lines and sewer lines....." Wilcox opposed the property transfer in the first place. Even after it had been executed, he "felt it quite possible that personal injuries could result from contact" with the hazardous materials housed in the landscape.[49] Still, these and other warnings went unheeded.

Interestingly, when the city pestered Hooker about acquiring another dumping ground, the company pushed back, asserting that such landscapes should not be redeployed for people. In September 1963, Niagara Falls officials approached Hooker about purchasing some seemingly desirable property along the Niagara River. Comprising 28 acres of waterfront land situated between Hooker's chemical plants and the Love Canal dump, the city's proposed boat launch was also an active disposal site. Hooker officials argued that "there is an estimated eight years more useful life ... for [chemical] fill" at this location. "We pointed out," one official noted, "the necessity of having available to industries such as ours property located in a close proximity to our operations for this use. Our experience has been that it is most difficult to acquire land suitable for this purpose...." As the company adamantly concluded, "we are most reluctant to part with" those dumping grounds "which we have."[50] Betraying a fear of the chemical hazards it might unleash, Hooker also "pointed out that it was very questionable whether lands which have been developed through the years by burying chemical fill are suitable for recreation purposes."[51] The boat launch was nixed.

Back at Love Canal in the mid-1950s, doubts about the city's plans were not enough to curb development. As Hooker officials conceded, they "could not prevent the Board from selling the land or from doing anything they wanted... with it."[52] Niagara Falls now owned Love Canal. And their developers were building up the toxic landscape as if it were part of a Chemagination ad.

5. Living with Altered Environments, Locally and Nationally

Did nature reformers register concern over toxic dumping and/or the creative redeployment of chemical-laden landscapes? With Niagara Falls growing at such a rapid pace, and the Love Canal landscape going through so rapid a transformation, this remains a key question. American environmentalism during this transformative era for both Hooker Chemical and Love Canal constitutes a missing link between the Age of Conservation and the Era of Earth Day. Gone were legendary preservationists like John Muir and Thomas Welch, leaving a void in activist circles. And Rachel Carson had not yet published *Silent Spring*, her seminal work on chemical threats to nature and humans. Yet some environmentalists pushed Americans to re-examine their relationship to the industrialized landscape that was taking shape at midcentury.

Nationally, environmentalism became less of an elitist initiative between the 1930s and 1950s.[53] In these years, more Americans than ever examined issues ranging from soil degradation and nature study to wilderness preservation and water quality. They came to see not only industrialization but consumerism as an environmental peril. Environmental disasters fomented by human agency, particularly overdevelopment of prairie landscapes in the nation's heartland (the dreaded "Dust Bowl"), first sensitized many people to such ecological concerns. The New Deal picked up the story from there. Between 1933 and 1942, the Civilian Conservation Corps (CCC), one of Franklin Delano Roosevelt's signature work programs, marshaled an army of young men to protect America's natural resources. Stamping out nature trails, planting billions of trees, and replenishing exhausted soils, the CCC provided more than work to young Americans in the Great Depression than almost any other sector of the economy. It also offered a new environmental ethic to young people: nature could be saved, and not destroyed, by the masses.[54]

Nature study programs took off too. William Gould Vinal, former president of the American Nature Study Society and a longtime professor at the University of Massachusetts in Amherst, asked Americans to return to nature whenever they could. As the country's "foremost nature educator," Vinal argued that industrialization, commercialization and urbanization had dulled Americans' ecological sensibilities.[55] During the Depression, he challenged the nation to make nature study "a way of life." "Today we are witnessing a shift in economic and social life patterns of enough gravity to merit the thought of scientists as a whole and of nature leaders in particular," Vinal wrote in his 1940 book, *Nature Recreation, Group Guidance for the Out of Doors*. Vinal pushed "nature friends," as he called them, to educate the masses about the environmental perils of rampant consumerism and runaway technology. Until people went back to nature on a consistent basis—through camps, nature study schools, and conservation classes—they would see the landscape itself as a mutable and nearly inexhaustible resource.[56]

Vinal had many fans in Western New York. At the well-respected Buffalo Museum of Science, nature lovers, wildlife enthusiasts, and scientists coalesced into a series of interlocking organizations interested in environmental education. Ostensibly dedicated to understanding the rise of science in modern society, the Buffalo Museum had long hosted nature study groups ranging from "The Roosevelt Field Club" to the "The Geographical Hobby Club." "There is no end of interesting phases of Nature which these progressive clubs investigate and they are anxious to have you join them in their work," the Museum's popular monthly magazine, *Hobbies*, declared in 1921.[57]

From its inception at the Buffalo Academy of Natural Sciences (which then became the Museum of Science), *Hobbies* was dedicated to the idea that nature, industry, and science could coexist peaceably in American society. Yet a steady undercurrent of environmental critique also ran through the magazine's pages. *Hobbies* heralded the creation of a new state park south of the Buffalo-Niagara metroplex: Allegany State Park, which was founded in the summer of 1921. The park took back 7,000 acres of woodland threatened by timber production. Its formation was critical and "timely," according to *Hobbies*, for Western New Yorkers choked by indus-trialization's grip had fewer opportunities to enjoy nature than their coun-terparts on the other side of the state (where the Catskills, Adirondack and Palisades Park Preserves offered respite to frazzled city dwellers). "Only Buffalo, Rochester and the surrounding communities, comprising a population of over a million and a half people, have no conveniently accessible state park," one article put it.[58]

To remedy this situation, the Buffalo Academy joined forces with the Erie County Society for the Protection of Birds, Fish and Game to compel the state to purchase as much as 50,000 acres of bucolic land along the New York–Pennsylvania border. After its formation, Allegany State Park anchored many of the revamped Science Museum's nature study pro-grams. Tours, summer camps and seminars brought thousands of citizens into the great outdoors. The Allegany School of Natural History, which opened in 1926, offered instruction "in the forest" each summer.[59] By the 1930s, the Allegany School had become the model for smaller nature sanctuaries throughout Western New York, bringing professional biolo-gists, anthropologists, and geographers in contact with a varied cohort of nature lovers.

But the Science Museum's interest in environmental matters ran deeper still. By the 1930s and 1940s, agricultural depletion in the nation's heartland compelled museum officials to discuss conservation as more than a passing fancy. Holding seminars at its hulking new headquarters on Buffalo's east side, the Science Museum examined soil erosion along the Niagara Frontier as part of a national trend. Moreover, conservation groups held quarterly and monthly meetings at the museum. And "Conservation

Forums" publicly considered issues ranging from the impact of dams on wildlife to the growing menace of water pollution.

This last issue was increasingly important in Buffalo and Niagara Falls. Industrial runoff from steel plans, chemical companies, and other industries had fouled the fabled Niagara River. During the Great Depression and World War II, Buffalo papers consistently reported increasing fish kills and foul odors along the Niagara River. While some stories noted that fishermen registered concern about their bounty, others focused on the way that industry itself seemed to be a nuisance to nature. (A study later showed that industrial and chemical pollutants increasingly saturated the Niagara River by the 1940s and 1950s).[60] Local officials even held hearings on water pollution—a big step for an industrial region like Buffalo-Niagara Falls.[61] Still, the Niagara River did not improve much during the postwar era. By 1950, the *Buffalo Evening News* reported, the Niagara River's pollution problem was so disconcerting that the Army Corps of Engineers—and thus the federal government—would now try to prosecute industrial polluters.[62]

At the Buffalo Museum of Science, some *Hobbies* contributors began wondering about the supremacy of industry and technology in American society. In a stunning editorial, *Hobbies* editor Edmere Cabana Barcelona decried humans' "skinning of the earth." Barcelona worried that "the balance of nature" had been "disturbed by man heedlessly and greedily." "The writing on the earth—bearing through deforestation, uncontrolled streams, and the destruction of the support of living creatures—is vivid," he proclaimed, "so vivid" that people could no longer ignore it. "If we skinned mother Earth of her natural resources," he concluded, nature would wilt, and Americans "must die" with her." Scientific achievement would not necessarily "substitute for irreplaceable soil, for … water, for creeping, running and flying creatures." But what could Western New Yorkers do to solve this national problem? "Well, here's one answer," Barcelona replied. "First [they] can join an organization that has a broad program of conservation." Moreover, a concerned person could "put conservation on his reading list, and, when he has become informed, he can talk conservation every chance he gets." Only by making conservation a daily part of people's lives, Barcelona continued, would Americans "collectively and individually" stop "skinning the earth."[63]

Barcelona's worries about the destruction of natural resources paralleled the more famous ecological outcry by Aldo Leopold. Where Barcelona asked Americans to think *about* nature, Leopold challenged them to think *like* nature—to assume the consciousness of wild spaces threatened by industrial development. Only by "thinking like a mountain," as he famously put it in *A Sand County Almanac* (published in 1949), would Americans realize that they were a part of nature, not apart from it.[64] Working variously as a forester, western game warden, and educator, the Yale-trained Leopold saw firsthand the erosion of mountains, streams and rivers, and wilderness. By getting people back in touch with nature, Leopold hoped to create a new "land ethic" that might stand up to, and even neutralize, the gains of consumer and industrial culture. Indeed, as he saw it, environmental ethics—and not dreams of transcending nature through consumerism, industry and/or technology—should govern human views of the natural world. Yet to do this, Leopold argued, American environmentalists must become public prophets, not lab-minded professionals. "Much of the damage inflicted on land is quite invisible to laymen," he wrote in a private journal. Ecologically minded citizens thus needed to have the courage to tell Americans that the land was sick and in need of special care.[65]

Like Barcelona's notion that humans had "skinned the earth," Leopold's arresting image of the American landscape as a wounded patient at mid-century updated environmentalism by arguing that conservation was about much more than the efficient use of natural resources. Their critique of industrial society and consumer values subverted the prevailing mindset that technology and development improved nature—or that Americans could create anything like a second nature that transcended the original environment. Chemical and industrial development had limits, both Barcelona and Leopold vigorously asserted. Postwar American society must pay heed to this notion or it would ruin the natural world altogether.

And yet, for Barcelona, Leopold, and other environmental writers locally and nationally, the American landscape was still essentially "out there": a place where people hiked and hunted, farmed and fished. It was threatened, to be sure, but still somehow disconnected from the average American neighborhood. If postwar Americans were thinking more about environmental matters, they nevertheless understood "the environment" as a place to escape to, not a place where everybody lived.

And that meant that Love Canal was not necessarily worthy of consideration. As a landscape, it was banal, not beautiful. It could be used, and even abused, without much worry, as long as nearby Niagara Falls flowed freely. If environmentalism was to expand further, it needed to incorporate places like Love Canal into the movement. That would take years—and a chemical crisis in this rising Niagara Falls subdivision—to accomplish.

6. The Industrial Beat Goes On

Indeed, when Barcelona, Leopold, and Vinal began forecasting the death of nature by a thousand tiny cuts, Hooker Chemical was still in major growth mode. The company's products continued to sell, which meant it needed even more chemical burial space. When the 99th Street School opened, Hooker had already created a toxic dump on the other side of town: the Hyde Park Landfill. As for Love Canal, its chemical past would get buried again; by the 1960s and early 1970s, in fact, the toxic dump was almost completely forgotten.

The new Love Canal neighborhood became a boomlet within Niagara Falls. Young families poured into the area. Few, if any, considered themselves environmentalists. Like Barcelona, Leopold, and Vinal, Love Canal's husbands and wives believed that nature was "out there" in the Great Outdoors and environmentalism did not—could not—include them. How surprising, then, that these unheralded people with little environmental knowledge would soon be at the forefront of a movement that challenged both Hooker and American environmentalism to finally come to terms with a toxic past.

PART TWO

LOVE CANAL IN THE ERA OF ENVIRONMENTALISM

A Toxic Subdivision

The Problem at Love Canal

Leach-ate: Noun: A solution resulting from leaching, as of soluble constituents from soil, landfill, etc., by downward percolating ground water: Leachates in the town's water supply have been traced to a chemical-waste dump.

— Dictionary.com

Leachate: The term Leachate refers to any liquid or semi-liquid material which is formed when a subsurface or surface water mixes with chemicals disposed of in a landfill.

— Love Canal Homeowners Association,
Glossary of Chemical Terms, 1980

For most Love Canal residents in the mid-1970s, owning a house in a relatively new subdivision offered tangible proof that they had achieved the American Dream. The pretty tree-lined streets bisecting the ten-block neighborhood colloquially known for the old canal that once ran through the area contained rows of attractive and affordable housing stock. Kids walked to schools located only blocks away while their parents talked to one another like longtime friends. Many area fathers had secure, well-paying jobs in Niagara Falls' thriving industrial and chemical sectors, lending an aura of confidence to Love Canal life. While many American communities were still reeling from the tumultuous politics of the Vietnam War, the Love Canal neighborhood appeared to be a quiet, family-friendly oasis. Who wouldn't want to live there?

Lois Gibbs, a young housewife and mother of two who moved into the area in 1974, certainly felt blessed. "If you drove down my street *before Love Canal*," she would later write (referring to the crisis that redefined the place), "you might have thought it looked like a typical American small town that you would see in a movie—neat bungalows, many painted white, with neatly clipped hedges or freshly painted fences." It was, she continued, a "lovely neighborhood in a quiet residential area, with lots of trees and lots of children playing outside." So powerful was the sense of paradise that Gibbs did not pay much attention to early news reports about a leaking toxic dump somewhere in Niagara Falls. *Those poor people,* she thought. *Wherever they are, I hope they will get the help they need.* Thankfully, it was not her neighborhood. Like many of her friends, Gibbs focused on family and home, not the looming tragedy of hazardous waste—and certainly not the global cause of environmental justice.[1]

A snapshot of the Love Canal area during the tumultuous summer of 1978 offered a completely different picture. Gone were the peaceful images of home life; in their place, illness, uncertainty, and rage reigned supreme. Over the next few years, as residents organized themselves into a powerful lobbying group, Love Canal came to symbolize, as one resident put it, an American environmental "nightmare."[2] Trapped in a poisoned landscape, Love Canal residents felt "powerlessness," "confusion," and "mental, physical and psychological" torment.[3] "Love Canal is a chemical dump site," resident Grace McCoulf bluntly told members of the U.S. Senate, a place where a new type of "tragedy has occurred."[4] Anne Hillis, who had lived in Love Canal for nearly a decade before she began keeping a journal of her physical and mental anguish, wrote that her neighborhood seemed like "hell." Every time she came home, Hillis observed, she wanted "to scream out." But "you open your mouth and nothing comes out... you look up and down the street once again, your house is noxious, their houses are noxious... the whole outside is noxious. I don't want to be a Love Canal victim—but, oh God, I am!"[5]

The transformation of Love Canal from a cradle of the American dream to the grave of residents' belief in safe home environments took place swiftly. But it did not happen overnight. Since the area's buildup during the late 1950s, signs of chemical decay had appeared often enough that they formed a steady undercurrent of neighborhood conversation. Yet by the late 1970s, problems that had once been assigned to the realm of urban legend—rocks laced with phosphate that exploded like firecrackers when kids threw them to the ground, manhole covers that seemed to spontaneously combust, chemical burns from baseballs rolling across chemically laden outfield grass—appeared more real and ominous as a range of maladies emerged. Residents tracked rising rates of miscarriage, inexplicable clusters of birth defects, and a series of debilitating illnesses, from asthma to cancer, that appeared anything but ordinary. By the summer of '78, residents' concerns turned into anger; that anger fueled activism. Their lovely lives had been turned upside down.

While Love Canal's new image as a poster child of toxic waste tragedies included a large cast of characters—from politicians and lawyers to reporters and environmental engineers—it revolved chiefly around the residents themselves who sought to address not only their own perilous circumstances but a looming environmental crisis across the American landscape: the nation's hazardous waste zone. As one Love Canal group declared in 1980, area residents had revealed to the world the many problems associated with "man-made disasters." Now it was up to residents and their allies to mobilize for the "complete neutralization of toxic wastes" in American culture. Such a movement would not only end the tragedy at Love Canal but create a moral revolution that would also redefine American environmental values.[6]

So successful were residents and their allies in recasting Love Canal's image as a symbol of environmental ruin that they often remain a footnote in the stirring historical transformations they inspired. But there was no magic rescue at Love Canal, no speedy political solution to the problem of unregulated hazardous waste, no angels in the whirlwind. Love Canal residents themselves remained the architects of their own redemption. And in the process of becoming environmental activists, they brought Niagara's long history of dreamy development into critical focus. Indeed, if the main storyline of the Love Canal landscape from the launching of the *Griffon* to Hooker's build-up had been commercialized land use and mega-industrial development, now that storyline would revolve around citizen environmentalism. In the eyes of the people who lived in a neighborhood known as Love Canal, the area's industrial past could no longer be buried and ignored.

1. Building Love Canal

The Love Canal neighborhood of the late 1970s was the product of more than two decades of steady development. After Hooker transferred Love

Canal property to Niagara Falls in the early 1950s, developers began building on and around the old dumping grounds. By 1960, over 100 homes
stood adjacent to the Canal; a few years later, roughly 150 more houses
had been built. From there, developers completed streets and homes in
rings around the neighborhood. At the southern end of the development,
the LaSalle Expressway took shape during the 1960s, offering commuters
speedy connections to the city's chemical complex, shopping centers, and
the natural wonder of Niagara Falls itself. The rise of a few churches and
stores—including the creation of Summit Park Mall—completed the
neighborhood's appealing profile.[7]

The subdivision's appeal cannot be underestimated, especially in the
heyday of American suburbanization.[8] Though located within just a few
miles of both the industrial and urban heart of Niagara Falls, the new neighborhood offered enough distance from older and more congested developments closer to the city to feel like a new suburb. It also provided easy access
to Niagara's working and leisure environments. Moreover, Love Canal was
bounded by the "Little Niagara River" to the south and Black Creek to the
north—bucolic features that shielded the neighborhood from urban life in
Niagara Falls proper. Love Canal was a suburban oasis within city limits.

In fact, developers were planning to build more homes in the area
before the Love Canal crisis blew up in 1978. According to one report,
Love Canal was part of "the third most populous [census] tract in the
city," as well as "the fourth in income of its inhabitants[,] with a median
[income] of $10,628, which was slightly higher than the median for the
Buffalo standard Metropolitan statistical area, and...higher than the
median income for Niagara Falls as a whole." Better still, the Love Canal
neighborhood had a "household income index" a few points above the
national average. Young families loved it. There were, on average, fewer
retired persons in Love Canal, and the majority of households had young
children. With nearly four people per household, it ranked first in household size. And with most of its housing stock built after 1950, Love Canal
had an incredibly low vacancy rate—less than 3 percent of its housing
units went unoccupied. "People liked living there and seldom move," the
report noted. "You couldn't buy a home [there] because none were on the
market." For these reasons, in 1976 a consulting report ranked Love Canal
fourth best in Niagara Falls in terms of "social well-being."[9]

New schools, new housing stock, new shopping malls, new express-ways, new families—no wonder Love Canal presented "a bright picture" to businessmen, developers, and politicians alike. It really did seem like a lovely place.[10]

2. The Love Canal "Problem"

Despite this "bright picture," the Love Canal build-out was accompanied by a steady undercurrent of complaints about the area's wacky environment. In fact, the constancy of residents' complaints about odd odors and various health concerns turned the Love Canal neighborhood into Niagara's version of Area 51. *What the hell was going on there*, people wondered about the strange things they saw and smelled? A local fire chief, inspecting the Lasalle Expressway rising at the southern edge of the Love Canal neighborhood in late 1964, recalled being nearly overcome by piercing winds "permeated by the odors of chemicals and fumes." He found the stench "emanating from a pile of chemical waste" on the other side of Love Canal (in another Hooker dump at 102nd St.). The fire chief contacted the Niagara Falls city manager about possibly remediating the area. Nothing happened. The Love Canal legend continued to grow.[11]

By the mid-1970s, Love Canalers had registered such consistent concerns that local, state, and federal officials felt compelled to investigate the landscape. Between 1976 and 1978, a bevy of technicians, consulting firms, and politicians came to see the "old Love Canal" (as some people took to calling the buried dump) as a definite problem, albeit one that could be addressed on an ad hoc basis.[12] "A chemical landfill...used by Hooker," the *Niagara Gazette* reported in early October 1976, "has been seeping into the basements of homes" around the canal zone. When some residents expressed particular concerns about chemical burns their children suffered after playing on fields covering the dump, state health officials began testing the area. They found over a dozen chemical compounds, including Mirex and polychlorinated biphenyls (PCBs).[13] Nevertheless, not until 1977—when New York environmental officials worried that chemical toxins had escaped into area sewers and then into Niagara's waterways—would state authorities urge local officials to create a "corrective" plan for the leaking dump.[14] Even then, the size and scope of the chemical brew percolating underground was largely unknown. How big and how bad was it? No one knew.

"Rising constituent concern," as one politician put it, compelled still more investigations of the neighborhood.[15] Indeed, when city officials proved apathetic, state and federal politicians intervened, urging Niagara Falls to more forcefully examine the problem at Love Canal. A young Congressman named John J. LaFalce, a Democrat from nearby Tonawanda, pressed for scientific studies of the buried dump. Was it secure? If not, what steps could local and state officials take to reassure neighborhood residents that all would be well? Despite the passage of the Resource Conservation and Recovery Act of 1976 (RCRA), which, as we shall soon see, sought to deal with hazardous waste disposal from cradle to grave, few politicians had any real sense about the dangers posed by buried toxic tombs. Heeding residents' concerns, LaFalce asked for more detailed studies about the true nature of Love Canal.

Examination of the dump remained confined to the realm of technical reports, some of which were top secret. The first, conducted by the Calspan Corporation, a respected Buffalo-based technology company with roots in aviation during World War II, was undertaken in January 1977 at the behest of the state Department of Environmental Conservation (DEC). Believing that a "hydrological investigation" of the dump would lead to the creation of a "pollution abatement" plan, state officials hoped that such action would quell citizens' concern about Love Canal. City officials agreed, hoping that any report would suggest minimal clean-up measures.[16] After studying Love Canal for several months, Calspan delivered its findings—marked "Confidential"—in the late summer of 1977 (its details were not revealed until a year later). Rather blandly entitled "Calspan Technical Report: Characterization and Abatement of Groundwater Pollution of Love Canal Chemical Landfill, Niagara Falls, N.Y.," the survey delivered a firm verdict about the problem area: chemical leachate, notably PCBs and hexochlorobenzene, had migrated from the dump, posing a clear environmental hazard. But the "Love Canal leachate problem," as Calspan technicians called it, could probably be contained by a better clay cover and other remedial measures (including the use of submersible pumps to reduce groundwater runoff). Calspan researchers did not even broach the subject of evacuating residents.[17]

Nevertheless, by merely identifying specific hazardous chemicals emanating from the dump, Calspan unearthed important information. For Hooker would not disclose what the company had dumped at Love Canal for several years. Those were trade secrets. Moreover, Calspan gave politicians a glimpse of the area's future identity: Love Canal was a leaking dump and perhaps a more serious environmental problem than anyone had ever thought. Indeed, over the next year, as local, state and federal officials engaged in a series of more intensive investigations of the Love Canal problem (sometimes separately, often in concert), they always confirmed Calspan's initial findings. By the summer of 1978, in fact, no fewer than four major reports on Love Canal confirmed the presence of chemicals in homes ringing the old dump. People were talking about what to do at the dump—including undertaking a $400,000 abatement plan—but not much more than that, the *Niagara Gazette* commented in the summer of 1977.[18]

One person thought the Love Canal problem warranted bigger and better solutions. Lawrence R. Moriarty, an Environmental Protection Agency regional officer who headed a federal study of groundwater runoff from the dump in the Fall of 1977, wrote to the EPA's toxic substances coordinator in Washington, D.C. that chemical waste was not just a technical "problem" but potentially a major health hazard. "There is no easy or quick solution to this problem," he explained, "because if you go about it in a temporary way it will continue to pop up." Of course, he recognized the opposite side of the problem too, for "[if] you go full out, a cleanup will cost a considerable amount"—and it might not fully solve the problem. "[Moreover,] what to do with or how to treat the wastewater after it is removed [from Love Canal homes and sewers] may present a major problem." Translation: the toxic landfill was bleeding chemical leachate and lives might soon be threatened. But a clean-up was no simple thing.[19]

In fact, because "unhealthy and hazardous conditions exist at the landfill and in some of the homes adjoining the site," Moriarty believed that "temporary measures to clean up the area will only result in a continuing recurrence of the problem." Officials must think long-term, always bearing in mind local residents' health. "Serious thought should be given to the purchase of some or all of the homes affected," he advised, "or at least to those willing to sell." Purchased homes should be torn down and serious consideration given to a "maximum cleanup method" in which "all chemical fill, contaminated earth and debris in the area" be completely removed and the resulting gap refilled with "clean earth." At the very least, he wrote, a "minimal cleanup method" would require the placement of drainage systems around the canal and a monthly maintenance program that ensured containment of chemical waste at Love Canal. But because determining appropriate remediation plans (and culpability) could take years, some Love Canal residents' health was at stake. "The problem will not be corrected unless the fill in the surrounding earth around the private property are totally removed," he concluded. And so, Moriarty noted ominously, state officials should think hard and fast about "buying [some Love Canal residents'] homes or placing them in other facilities until the problem is corrected."[20]

While one of the first to broach buyout of area homes, Moriarty thought that such a plan would be limited, encompassing residents who lived around the canal proper (or a group of roughly 40 to 50 families). Despite the relatively low number of potential evacuees, Niagara Falls' officials would not heed Moriarty's advice; nor did they support his vision of long-term clean-up plans. Instead, they chose minimal containment measures, including the creation of onsite drainage systems aimed at collecting any chemical leachate. For many local officials, the negative press associated with even limited buyout strategies would hurt area tourism. Others simply did not see the old dump as a threat to human health. And so, after hiring the respected Canadian firm of Conestoga-Rovers to install a tile drainage system, local authorities felt they were done with the relatively minor Love Canal problem.

The problem would not go away. Responding to more "constituent concerns," state and federal officials launched an "intensive air, soil, groundwater sampling and analysis program" of nearly a dozen homes in the spring of 1978. After again confirming that chemicals had infiltrated the neighborhood immediately surrounding the buried dump, the state Department of Health undertook even more detailed examinations of the area. By June of 1978, New York State Health Commissioner Robert P. Whalen had dispatched a series of teams to Love Canal to begin "house to house health survey[s] of 97 families immediately adjacent to the landfill." By August, state authorities had put in an exhausting "13,000 manhours...on detailed health histories" of Love Canal and its people. It was already one of the largest state health studies of its kind.[21]

In just this way, the geographical size and symbolic meaning of Love Canal expanded in the late 1970s: citizens complained to politicians about their polluted environment; scientists, engineers, and health officials issued ever more detailed reports about the Love Canal problem; citizens complained some more when the problem persisted; and then more studies were done. That process repeated itself several times until, as a famous report by the New York State legislature later put it, Love Canal finally exploded like a "Ticking Time Bomb" in the late Summer of 1978.[22]

3. Boiling Points: Love Canal Residents

Given that by the summer of 1978, local, state, and federal officials had studied the Love Canal problem for over two years—only rarely discussing emergency actions like evacuation—just how could it suddenly explode? The state report conjuring that stark imagery referred not to the literal combustion of chemicals underground but to residents' overwhelming sense of alarm about Love Canal life in the wake of the latest state health study, which was made public in August 1978. Noting that chemical leachate posed a demonstrable public health threat, the state's head health official at last recommended evacuation of residents closest to the canal. As we shall see, at that very moment, Love Canal ceased to be an ad hoc technical problem associated with one subdivision in Niagara Falls, becoming instead an emblem of toxic waste nightmares regionally, nationally, and even globally. "From Moscow to Malibu, the world is learning of the Love Canal," a local reporter observed, perfectly summing up Love Canal's newfound celebrity status.[23]

But that status as Ground Zero of a new type of disaster flowed very much from residents' themselves, whose anxieties boiled over in the course of just a few summer weeks. They had watched for months and years as state and federal agencies drilled monitoring wells along the old dumpsite, entered their homes with all manner of sophisticated technical equipment to measure chemical leachate, and learned of various reports about plans to contain (not remove) the toxic stew bubbling beneath them. The more discoveries piled up—the Love Canal dump was not secured; its waste migrated beyond into area land, water, and air; a public health threat existed for certain parts of the neighborhood—the more un-satisfied residents became with official explanations about the nature of the Love Canal dump. That disconnect between official understanding of a "problem" to be contained and grassroots understanding of a looming public health crisis framed everything that followed.

Yet many residents arrived at a boiling point only slowly. When they did finally confront politicians and health officials during the sweltering summer of 1978, their anger was fueled by a deep reservoir of stories about chemical contamination. Like the dump itself, citizens' emotions lay buried for a while, as mothers and fathers, friends and neighbors believed that they suffered from some malady all by themselves. Yet during the mid- to-late 1970s, residents also began forming powerful narratives of their own suffering—narratives that pointed to deeper problems within the Love Canal landscape. Only when residents banded together in 1978, and began comparing experiences, did they realize that they spoke a common language about toxic times at Love Canal. Far from a technical problem about haz-ardous waste containment, Love Canal was for them a chemical disaster.

Niagara's environment played a key role in pushing these chemical con-cerns to the surface. Hard winters accompanied by strong spring thaws, particularly in 1977 (year of the famous blizzard that gripped Buffalo and Western New York), pushed more chemical leachate into sewers, back-yards, and basements around Love Canal, prompting residents to com-plain more forcefully about their toxic environment. Niagara's complex geology played a hand too, as the clayey subsoils that Hooker had once relied on to absorb any chemical leachate proved to be more diverse and less spongy than previously thought. "A cross-section of soils at the site shows that the top 4 to 6 feet of soil is moderately permeable," one 1978 report would note of the subterranean landscape at Love Canal; "beneath that is 30 to 40 feet of highly impermeable clay; and 40 feet below [that] the surface is limestone bedrock. The pollutants move easily through the top layer of soil, which has allowed the contamination to infiltrate the basements. Although the pollutants probably don't move in the lower tight clay soils, the pollutants may be leaking to the bedrock, which con-tains a supply of groundwater."[24] Far from a vault, Love Canal's under-ground environment allowed chemical waste to exit the dump via a variety of pathways.

With chemicals more insistently assaulting residents' senses, Love Canalers began talking openly about the ill health born of hazardous living conditions, not only in the wake of recent thaws but over the course of a decade or more. *Did your son or daughter ever get chemical burns playing in the backyard or the fields around the school? How many miscarriages have occurred on our street? Have you had severe migraines, horrible skin rashes, and/or nosebleeds?* Connecting these health dots raised another question: If the area was chemically contaminated, did government have a moral responsibility to remove Love Canal residents from their homes?

Aggrieved residents received a critical boost from Michael Brown, a *Niagara Gazette* reporter who began covering the Love Canal saga as a human interest story in 1978.[25] As Chapter 7 illustrates in more detail, Brown and a bevy of other reporters' deeply personal stories about Love Canal helped change perception of the neighborhood's problematic nature. He himself was introduced to the surreal living conditions at Love Canal through a series of gripping interviews with two related families living on the same street. One family, the Vorheeses, had lived in its 99th street home since the late 1950s; the other, the Schroeder family, lived just a few doors away. Joined by marriage after daughter Karen Vorhees met Tim Schroeder, who worked as a cement contractor in Niagara Falls, the newlyweds moved to Love Canal to raise their children near their families. Both families had nice backyards that abutted open fields, where children and grandchildren might play and old grass clippings could be placed. Better still, a school stood just a few hundred yards away. Yet this dream scenario turned foul after both families experienced the hazards of Love Canal life. The Vorheeses often found chemical leachate in their basement, its sour smell permeating the entire house. The Schroeders discovered a more visible sign of chemical infiltration one morning in 1976 when they noticed that their aboveground pool had risen several feet. Further investigation revealed that protruding chemicals had penetrated their backyard, which now became a hazard to be avoided. Like the Vorheeses, the Schroeders felt trapped in their own home. Even if they wanted to move, they knew that no one would buy houses that looked and smelled contaminated![26]

Toxic troubles hounded other families too. In April 1978, Anne Hillis, a 39-year-old mother who lived several blocks away from the Vorhees and Schroeder clans, received an alarming phone call from her son's elementary school. "Mrs. Hillis, your son is not feeling very well," the voice on the other line said. "Will you come for him?" An ordinary if unpleasant fact of parental life, the sick call soon conjured darker images for Hillis. Testing had already occurred around the 99th Street School, which her son attended, and rumors circulated among parents that the witches' brew of chemicals percolating beneath its surface was spreading toxicity. The air around the school usually reeked of chemicals as well, Hillis recalled, serving as an unofficial confirmation that something was very wrong in the neighborhood. Frayed nerves became further strained as Hillis connected the dots of sick neighbors. A family on her street had recently lost a father and son to cancer. Was her family next? As teams of state and federal officials continued to study the canal, Hillis and other residents began to dread the results even as they hoped that more specific information about what lay in the dump would lead to a firm governmental policy protecting citizens' health. "People of the area are on the verge of hysteria," Hillis wrote in an unpublished journal she began keeping. Written to process her own swirling emotions, the journal testified to the fear, paranoia, and physical torment overtaking many Love Canal residents.[27]

Hillis had moved to 102nd Street, in the extreme southeast of the neighborhood, in 1965. Though several blocks away from a dump she did not know much about, Hillis soon became familiar with the chemical sights and smells that defined Love Canal. When she and her husband Ralph, a furnace repairman, bought their home, they thought the neighborhood was a nice place to raise a family. In 1967, however, she suffered a miscarriage. A few years later, she delivered a baby boy who, as he grew older, began experiencing migraines and severe diarrhea, among other ailments. Hillis herself had a hysterectomy while still in her thirties. By the late 1970s, she became a close observer of the neighborhood's creepy nature. The spring thaws she had once anticipated as a harbinger of summer now brought a nauseating chemical stench and the weird sight of exposed barrels on the canal's surface. Dogs had bald patches from playing in creeks and puddles formed by flooding sewers. Trees leafed out from the top down during summers. "Chemical contamination surrounds us," Hills commented, wondering by the late 1970s if her family would ever escape their loony landscape.[28]

Luella Kenny lived on the other side of the Love Canal subdivision. In 1969, Kenny and her husband Norman moved into their 96th Street home, located north of the buried dump. The next decade brought much joy but ended with unspeakable sadness. With their three sons, the Kennys enjoyed playing in a spacious backyard where Black Creek meandered pleasantly nearby. Even when the creek flooded in spring and summer, Kenny's sons loved to splash around in the water-logged grass with their dog. In June of 1978, the fun stopped when Kenny's youngest son, Jon, developed a severe illness that could not be accurately diagnosed. At first, doctors thought he had allergies. The family returned to the doctor regularly, insisting that Jon had more than a seasonal malady. Jon was eventually diagnosed with nephrosis, a serious liver condition. Visits to Buffalo's acclaimed Children's Hospital eased Jon's condition somewhat, but he took a turn for the worse in the fall. He experienced "convulsions, visual hallucinations," and eventually a "massive pulmonary embolism." Jon died in October 1978. Doctors remained puzzled, for not only was nephrosis treatable in children but Jon exhibited some atypical symptoms, such as convulsions. What had caused his baffling illness?[29]

Born in 1937, Luella Kenny worked as a researcher at Buffalo's famed Roswell Park Memorial Cancer Institute. She knew about scientific rhetoric and about chemicals' potentially harmful impact on the body. Still, she had never imagined that her own home might become a toxic swamp capable of killing family members. Kenny came to think about these matters more seriously during the mid- to late 1970s, when she noticed foul odors and slimy residues emanating from the creek. But she knew a scientist needs hard evidence to draw firm conclusions. Until local, state or federal officials told residents that the Love Canal area was a health hazard, she would do nothing.[30]

Only later would Kenny learn that a storm sewer discharged dioxins from Love Canal into Black Creek—and thus right into her backyard. A medical professional with access to scientific colleagues at Roswell Park, Luella and her husband began doing their own research on Jon's condition. "We were shocked to find that during the past 10 years there have been countless reports of people developing nephrosis when they were exposed to chemicals," she later observed. While many medical and governmental officials refused to link chemical contamination to Jon's death, Luella had a private autopsy performed on her son, which showed the presence of chemicals in his system. Yet even when she and other parents complained about the potentially dire health impact of Love Canal, few officials supported a complete evacuation of the neighborhood, particularly those homes (like the Kennys') beyond the old dumping zone proper. As they continually put it, state officials would need better proof before moving anyone out of Love Canal—words that chilled Kenny to the core. But with a rash of health concerns piling up, she argued, officials should have moved more quickly to protect people who had no idea they lived in a leaking chemical zone.[31]

Several streets away from Kenny in the neighborhood's eastern section, Lois Gibbs lived on 101st Street. Gibbs worked part-time but was otherwise a devoted mother of two young children, one of whom, Michael, seemed to get sicker when he came home from the 99th Street School. Gibbs and her husband had bought their Love Canal house in 1972 when Michael was just a toddler; their daughter, Melissa, arrived in 1975. Though Gibbs did not know that she lived near a former toxic waste dump—like others, she thought the areas around the school were just old fields—she understood the vital importance of chemicals in the lives of Niagara Falls residents. Her husband, Harry, worked at one of the many chemical plants located at the other end of the Lasalle Expressway. With a husband in a secure industrial job and her kids just a short walk from school, Gibbs loved her life.

In the spring of 1978, she found out that her son's school was actually built on a chemical foundation. As she recalled, Michael had been "constantly ill," with maladies ranging from rashes to epilepsy.[32] Fearing for her son's health, Gibbs researched the dump's history and visited her brother-in-law, a man named Wayne Hadley who was a scientist at SUNY–Buffalo. Were chemicals harmful to humans, she asked? "I was really alarmed by his answer," she recalled when Hadley said that chemicals could impact the nervous system, the brain, and the immune system. "I still couldn't believe it, but if it were true, I wanted to get Michael out of the 99th St. School." On one frightening occasion, Gibbs rushed Michael to the hospital when he was desperately ill; doctors found that his white blood cell count had plummeted, indicating that his body would not be able to fight off infections and disease. Gibbs believed that the Love Canal environment had caused her son's illnesses. Yet when she asked the school superintendent to transfer Michael, Gibbs was rebuffed. If chemical seepage had made him sick, she was informed, then it probably endangered all the school's students. But who could prove that? No, the school official declared, Gibbs' son would have to remain at the school. "Like many people," Gibbs later wrote, "I can be stubborn when I get angry." By denying her request for a transfer, the superintendent had unwittingly denied that Love Canal posed a toxic problem to area residents. That attitude enraged Gibbs. "I decided to go door to door to see if other parents in the neighborhood felt this way," she remembered. "Maybe something could be done."[33]

Each of these stories about Love Canal's toxic underside developed on its own; they converged in 1978 when aggrieved residents started talking to one another more frequently about what they had endured over the past few years. When they started talking, countless tales of woe came to light. Found in newspaper accounts, TV reports, magazine articles, personal reminiscences, and congressional testimony, these toxic tales illuminated patterns of experience that, even as they remained distinct and personal, pointed to a common culprit: the chemical landscape around them. Although varying in detail—age, background, employment—residents' narratives shared a sense that Love Canal had become a poisoned environment. Most Love Canal dwellers knew about the sickening smells and disturbing sights pervading their neighborhood, from protruding chemical barrels in the fields behind the 99th Street School to leachate in sump pumps. Now they knew that many of their neighbors had experienced illnesses too. That fact of Love Canal life was uncovered just as surely as the area's chemical realities came to the surface in the late 1970s.

This led to a breakthrough in perception about the problem at Love Canal. For, as residents now argued, only by looking at the Love Canal landscape through the prism of family and environmental health—rather than the abstract lens of technical discourses about chemical leachate—would politicians and health officials understand the deep sense of dread that pervaded the sick neighborhood in the summer of 1978. That, they hoped, would allow governmental and health authorities to act decisively for the public good.

But what happened when government action still fell short of residents' expectations?

4. Summer of '78 Decrees, Part 1: State Action

The decree that symbolized Love Canal's new standing as a toxic tragedy, and not simply an ad hoc technical problem about waste containment, came on August 2, 1978. On that day, Commissioner Whalen declared a health emergency at Love Canal. For one thing, as health officials would note, testing revealed the presence of 82 chemicals—including TCE and benzene, among other known carcinogens—in locations beyond the dump itself, from basement sump pumps to monitoring wells located in residents' yards to ambient air samples collected in the neighborhood. For another thing, state officials, who had been studying the matter intensively since June, documented a rise in birth defects, miscarriages, and other ailments. Together, these discoveries mandated strong government action. In fact, after officials had interviewed virtually every family on the two streets surrounding the canal (over 200 in all) and had family members fill out a 29-page questionnaire, Whalen was stunned to find out just how many people suffered some major health problem at Love Canal. For instance, state health officials found that miscarriages in Love Canal families were 1.5 times higher than in the general population. (In the southern section of the canal zone proper, where some of the most potent chemical waste lay, a staggering 35 percent of women reported a miscarriage.) They also documented a larger-than-expected number of birth defects, from cleft palates to clubbed feet—13 percent in one section of the canal zone as opposed to an expected average in the low single digits.[34] While the absolute numbers were relatively small, Whalen had seen enough to issue his famous edict. "There is a great and imminent peril to health of the general public at or near" the dump, he declared in what became the equivalent of Love Canal's shot heard round the world.[35] As the *Niagara Gazette* commented the following day, Love Canal was "now infamous."[36] Like one of the phosphate-laced rocks children threw at the ground, the Love Canal problem had now exploded before the public's eyes.

Far from being satisfied with the state declaration, however, Love Canal residents demanded more action. Despite his dire words, Whalen's edict called for the evacuation of pregnant women and children under age 2 who lived in homes immediately surrounding the canal—a decision that impacted roughly 20 families. If there was truly an "imminent peril," other residents argued, the state must issue a broader evacuation decree. Even those affected by Whalen's order had questions. Who would pay for evacuation? Would it be permanent? What follow-up studies would be done to address residents' long-term health concerns? The school board's announcement that it would delay opening the 99th Street School did little to quell residents' concerns, either. How long would the school year be delayed and what assurances could officials give that school grounds would ever be safe?

With these questions swirling during the first week of August, the Love Canal neighborhood became a battle zone, as reporters, politicians, health officials, and citizens struggled to control the narrative emanating from the formerly peaceful subdivision. Clearly more than a technical problem, and perhaps more than a state health peril, Love Canal became a watchword for some sort of broader crisis, though whether this was political, economic, or environmental remained unclear. At the same time, the Love Canal saga interested national and international news outlets. It was a story oozing with intriguing plotlines: a residential neighborhood in world-famous Niagara Falls built on top of a leaking dump; a seemingly perfect suburban landscape haunted by a buried past; young families in turmoil over looming health threats. This wasn't news for a slow day, but a human interest story with great potential. "Events turned quickly last week as Love Canal residents began a mass exodus from their contaminated neighborhood," the *Niagara Gazette* announced in a fairly typical headline, this one referring to residents who needed no more encouragement to leave Love Canal.[37] Over the next month, a horde of reporters descended on the neighborhood to follow potential leads. Talking to citizens, health officials, and politicians, the press issued hundreds of stories on Love Canal, listening as threats, denials, charges, and countercharges flew with great ferocity. There was always a terrific story around the corner. One day residents threatened to stop paying taxes on their mortgages if evacuation orders did not expand to other parts of the ten-block area; a few days later Hooker asserted that it had no legal responsibility for the leaking dump; in between, school officials fretted about where to send hundreds of displaced students during the upcoming school year.

The physical appearance of the Love Canal environment began changing too. State officials announced that they would cordon off the fields surrounding the schoolyard with an orange snow fence—a visible sign of the chemical menace lurking beneath the playgrounds children once used. They also planned to install an imposing eight-foot-high chain-link fence around inner-ring homes, thus cutting them off from the rest of the neighborhood during remediation. (The fence was completed in October.) Residents responded to these developments by posting a series of signs throughout the neighborhood. "Wanted: healthy home for toddler less than two years old; inquire within." "Dangerous area—Love Canal." More than mere expressions of anger, these signs, as one correspondent noted, sought to capture the attention of "public officials and passersby." Children got into the act too: "evacuate us all, not just little kids!," proclaimed one sign in the hands of a little girl. Some signs used biting sarcasm to illuminate their hazardous life: "Love Canal recipe: 1. Mix 82 chemicals; 2. Place in Canal for 25 years. Yield: sickness plus death." Others used dark allusions to Love Canal's broader meaning: "If it can kill me, it can kill you."[38]

Truth be told, state environmental and political officials were in a difficult position. They had never worked on a problem like Love Canal before and had never been asked to deal with such a plethora of health and environmental concerns all at once. There were no state or federal laws detailing how to address a chemical disaster like Love Canal. Indeed, the very definition of "disaster" still revolved around natural events like hurricanes, floods, tornadoes, and earthquakes. But leaking chemical waste into nearby homes? That issue was simply not on the political radar. Moreover, while there had been various studies loosely linking chemicals and disease, there was still no model for running a health testing program on such a large (and fearful) population. The International Society for Environmental Epidemiology, dedicated to systematically studying the relationship between "environmental exposure" of toxic pollutants and public health around the world, was not even formed until 1987![39] Thus, protocols of all sorts were being formed essentially on the spot and at the same time that officials envisioned a radical redesign of a now notorious chemical dump. There was no gap between theory and practice, no pilot study, no serious literature on dealing with anxious and ornery grassroots residents.

More than twenty years after working there, Alice Stark, a longtime state health official, vividly remembered residents' protests. "That was certainly a lesson to take citizens seriously," she observed in the year 2000—ironically, at an annual meeting of the International Society of Environmental Epidemiology convening in Buffalo. Back in 1978, she recalled, state health protocols simply did not exist for a situation like Love Canal. Gone were the days when politicians and scientific authorities could simply tell people that all was safe in their world and everyone would believe it. At Love Canal, health workers had to explain everything in a way that not only convinced but soothed residents. And that was an almost impossible task.[40]

5. The Beginning of Love Canal Protest: The LCHA & CRGM

With the health commissioner's announcement prompting such turmoil, it is perhaps unsurprising that Love Canal residents began organizing protest groups. The first and most important was known as the Love Canal Homeowners Association (LCHA). Gathering angry residents into a unified body that could more effectively pressure government and health officials, the LCHA announced itself with a bang in early August of 1978 when it hired a lawyer to file suit against Hooker Chemical, the city of Niagara Falls, and/or the federal government for gross negligence at Love Canal.[41] From there, the LCHA grew in size and scope, embodying the citizens' struggle—and citizen environmentalism writ large—over the next several years. Like all protest movements, the group's vociferous presence prompted a fair share of criticism. Not only did some local governing officials blast homeowners as ornery and self-interested, but other residents within the greater Love Canal neighborhood expressed concern about the organization's focus and strategies. And though the LCHA remained a remarkably durable organization, it also faced a series of internal disputes that added further challenges to Love Canal life.

The LCHA ostensibly was born with its inaugural meeting on August 4, two days after the state declaration of a health emergency. But area residents had discussed the formation of just such a group earlier. Reporters covering the Love Canal saga noted the organization's existence in late July. *The Niagara Gazette* reported on July 26 that forty residents had already signed up for a "homeowners association" that would send delegates to meet with state officials in Albany about potential remediation and evacuation plans.[42] By the following week, the LCHA became a permanent fixture of the Love Canal crisis. Pictures of residents anxiously meeting with, and often vigorously challenging, state and federal officials soon competed with images of the polluted Love Canal landscape itself as the emblem of the crisis. Clearly, people—and not merely environmental poison—would define events at Love Canal.

The LCHA's president was a young mother who had already complained loudly about the possible link between the chemical environment and her son's various illnesses: Lois Marie Gibbs. A telegenic twenty-something, Gibbs morphed rather quickly from a housewife into a formidable environmental activist, as news outlets and others delighted in reporting. But she was far from alone in shaping, and steering, grassroots mobilization at Love Canal. As Gibbs herself recalled, the homeowners association took shape on the streets, outside of meeting halls, and in homes, as area residents struggled to find their collective voice. Yet, though she had no experience as a political organizer, Gibbs did have a commonsense approach to collective action that facilitated group action at Love Canal. As she quickly realized, no one person could stand up to local, state or federal authorities on any matter. That was clear after the first meeting between residents and health officials in June, a tense affair at which state workers and Love Canalers talked completely past each other. When residents asked if there was a true health crisis, officials responded that they were still studying the problem. When residents asked if this or that malady could be caused by something toxic underground, health officials could not—or would not yet—answer definitively. "When the audience realized that [state officials] didn't have *any* answers," Gibbs observed, "the meeting become emotional."[43]

Gibbs and others realized that by presenting a common front, Love Canal residents might achieve their goals. Perhaps that would mean evacuation; perhaps it would mean that their children would no longer have to attend "that school," as Gibbs derisively referred to the building that sat atop the dump.[44] This was in fact Gibbs' first objective as a nascent organizer in the neighborhood. In June, she began going door-to-door to gain support for a petition to have children removed from the 99th Street

School. Eventually joined by Debbie Cerrillo, a mother who lived on 97th Street, Gibbs gathered over a hundred signatures. She also had searching conversations with many neighbors about the dump. It was a particularly hot summer, Gibbs recalled, with the putrid air shrouding the area like a wet rag. The smell of chemicals seemed to stick to you, she observed. The hot summer stench underscored the common reality residents faced: a polluted and potentially toxic environment that they could not escape. In July, after state health officials met again with residents to discuss potential health findings—and again not doing a very good job of explaining whether or not Love Canal was "safe"—Gibbs and fellow residents saw the wisdom of organizing a protest group to protect their interests.[45]

The LCHA became the driving force of two key ideas that would re-shape Love Canal's public image during the late 1970s and early 1980s: first, the notion that the entire neighborhood, and not merely homes immediately around the dump, should be evacuated at government expense; second, and equally significant, the idea that Love Canal was a public health crisis. Over and over again, through months and then years of activism, the LCHA returned to these twin topics. What did Love Canal mean?, a handbill distributed among the media in 1979, wondered. "Ask those who really know! Ask the victims of Love Canal why they need immediate[,] permanent relocation...Ask the innocent victims of corporate profits." Alluding to the prospect of regaining "life, liberty and the pursuit of happiness," the flier noted that Love Canal residents desired something called environmental "justice."[46]

While they would expand on the meaning of these matters over time, in the summer of 1978 the LCHA focused on more specific concerns. One of its first official acts was to represent residents at the state capital. On August 2, Gibbs, Marie Pozniak and a few others made a mad dash to Albany (five hours away by car), where they had a preview of the health department's looming announcement about a health peril at Love Canal. Gibbs called it a "bombshell" and, judging by the reaction of her neighbors when the LCHA delegation returned, her words were quite accurate.[47] Entering Love Canal, Gibbs saw a group of homeowners in the middle of 99th Street furiously reacting to news that the leaking dump constituted a health threat—albeit one that required just the evacuation of pregnant mothers and children under age 2 near the dump. Amid angry speeches and the burning of tax statements, area homeowners expressed rage to anyone who would listen.[48]

After the announcement, a phalanx of state officials came to Niagara Falls to meet with concerned residents. Gathering in an auditorium at the 99th Street School, nearly five hundred people screamed at the experts gathered onstage for what seemed like an eternity. What did the health emergency mean? How would family members survive if they couldn't sell their homes? If the situation was so dire, why did the state evacuate so few people? Where was the governor? Standing firm in the face of such outbursts, state officials tried to explain their plan to remediate the canal and thereby contain any future health threats. Residents wanted much more than that. In fact, Gibbs and other homeowners had not come to listen politely but to interrogate health officials. Sending around a flier (produced gratis by "Mr. Copy") the day before imploring people to crowd the auditorium, Gibbs made sure that Love Canalers would, in a very real sense, drive the meeting. The plan worked almost too well. As Gibbs described it, the more officials urged calm, "the angrier the crowd got." "Everyone was emotional, myself included," she remembered. "Everywhere you looked someone was crying, or hysterical, or near panic." There may not have been much light but, for the residents at least, the emotional heat generated by the meeting was revelatory and cathartic. *Look at the potential power we have!*[49]

That power remained inchoate and subject to much internal debate over the ensuing weeks and even months. People establish organizations to solve specific problems; they become involved in social movements to change societal values. During the earliest phase of citizen mobilization, even some Love Canal residents wondered just how far their activism would go. Was the LCHA dedicated to relocation of all residents (solving a specific problem about family health and home values) or new environmental values (compelling society to reckon with the devastating nature of toxic waste)? And just who would, or could, represent the interests of Love Canal families, which ranged from renters to homeowners, before the public at large?

This last matter would become particularly troublesome, for it pitted issues of class (mostly white working-class homeowners) against race (African-American families who rented apartments at Lasalle Development—known colloquially as Griffon Manor—a few streets over from the Love Canal dump). Comprising roughly 1,200 residents, Griffon (or, in some sources, Griffin) Manor was the second of two federal housing facilities built in the Love Canal neighborhood since World War II. The first, constructed in the 1942, housed workers and their families streaming to the Falls' flourishing industrial base; the second, built in 1971 after the previous housing project became dilapidated, housed largely African-American families (roughly 60 percent of its tenants were black). By the crisis summer of 1978, renters felt slighted by both homeowners and state health officials. Indeed, though stories of foul odors and chemical sludge shadowed their lives too, Griffon Manor residents felt that few people cared about their health. By September, they formed a group of their own: the Concerned Love Canal Renters Association (CLCRA). Led by a strong neighborhood advocate named Elene Thornton (and supported by the local chapter of the NAACP), the CLCRA criticized state health officials for ignoring renters. "We're told there's no health hazard in our area," Thornton declared, but "how can they say that if there's only been random tests?"[50] When state officials replied that most renters chose not to participate in early blood testing programs—perhaps haunted by the infamous Tuskegee syphilis experiments in Alabama, in which doctors, to observe the progress of the disease, allowed African-American patients to continue untreated even after penicillin was shown to cure it—CLCRA representatives characterized the state as insincere if not outright dishonest. Noting that health officials privileged health tests from homeowners nearest the dump, the CLCRA argued that African-Americans had been pushed to the side in almost every way. But their concerns about everything from asthma to pregnancy risks should be a state priority, they proclaimed. For her part, Thornton hinted that there was more than foul odors in the Love Canal air.

Renters' concerns grew from a broader environment of discrimination and neglect. Though they had participated in the post-war population surge in Niagara Falls, African-Americans were often given the toughest, dirtiest jobs in area industries. They were also marginalized political and economic actors, no matter how much African-American populations expanded. During the 1930s, roughly 1,000 African-Americans called Niagara Falls home. By the 1960s, that number had shot up to over 8,000. But not until that decade did a black person get elected to public office in the Falls. Political marginalization was part and parcel of deeper concerns, including employment and housing discrimination. Prior to the 1970s, blacks were not often hired in the service sector, nor were they represented proportionally in white-collar jobs. And real estate agents often steered them away from many Niagara neighborhoods. In response, some folks decided to move to Buffalo, commuting over 40 miles round-trip to and from work. What housing there was for blacks in the Falls—public and otherwise—remained inadequate. In 1960, the *Niagara Falls Gazette* noted that the housing situation for many blacks was "intolerable"; four years later, another headline proclaimed (in the parlance of the day): "Negroes Find It Difficult to Find Housing at Falls."[51]

Of course, black civil rights activism aimed at correcting these problems conjured images of radicalism for many whites. Whether it was the Nation of Islam coming to town in the 1960s, or pickets in front of local department stores that did not hire many blacks, African-Americans had been fingered as public radicals. During the 1970s, nearby Buffalo divided over school busing plans, with white parents angrily denouncing desegregation initiatives that took their children to largely African-American neighborhoods. That image of "uppity" black folks complaining (again!) about their lot in life spread to Love Canal proper. Michael Cuddy, the Love Canal Task Force Coordinator, even told Gibbs that some Griffon Manor residents had criminal backgrounds and were "dangerous."[52] They should be avoided in future protest endeavors. A few LCHA members made matters worse, according to Lasalle residents, by using racial slurs in heated meetings over just who should speak for and about the Love Canal tragedy. Even if they did not go this far, other members of the LCHA's rank and file thought that renters complained about a very different problem. As more than one homeowner would say, renters had no mortgage to worry about and could therefore leave whenever they wanted.

Stung by accusations that the LCHA was less interested in the plight of renters, Gibbs tried to build bridges to the CLCRA. She also sought to represent Lasalle residents' interests when talking to state and federal officials. Later, on one trip to Washington, Gibbs met with Housing and Urban Development officials to discuss the evacuation of renters.[53] Still, for some Griffon Manor residents, racism would be a consistent problem, whether from above at the state level, or below in the community.[54]

Ironically, while Griffon Manor was far from ideal, it *seemed* like an improvement over some local housing options. Though other public housing facilities were built during the 1960s and 1970s in Niagara Falls, Griffon Manor was outside the city core on quiet streets near the Niagara River, and close to good schools.[55] But did slightly improved living conditions matter if it they were part of a chemical wasteland? By the end of the crisis summer, Griffon Manor residents demanded answers to that question too. And they looked for allies who might trumpet their health concerns without muffling their voices. While it would work with the LCHA on various initiatives, the CLCRA remained wary enough of the homeowners group that it reached out to other allies as time passed.

For its part, the LCHA struggled to keep a united front among homeowners. As Lois Gibbs described the early goals of the LCHA, homeowners hoped to "get all the residents within the Love Canal area who wanted to be evacuated, evacuated and relocated ... to do something about propping up property values ... [getting] the canal fixed properly ... and [having] air sampling and soil and water testing done throughout the whole area, so we can tell how far the contamination had spread."[56] Yet some residents did not favor such neighborhood-wide goals. Tom Heisner, who lived adjacent to the canal and had run street meetings briefly before becoming LCHA vice president, argued vehemently against expanding potential government purchases of homes to more distant parts of the area. Fearing it would diminish political support for immediate removal of residents closest to the dump, Heisner and his allies, including LCHA secretary Karen Schroeder, formed a much smaller and separate group, which focused on getting fair market prices for inner-ring homes.

Believing that a strictly economic approach would fail to win public support (especially in any long campaign to remove residents located further away from the canal), the LCHA expanded its strategic focus during the late summer and fall. In doing this, it learned one of the basic lessons of social activism: narrow visions often fail to galvanize broad support. Accordingly, over the next year, the LCHA began referring to Love Canal residents as "concerned citizens and environmentalists worried about the effects of toxic wastes in our area and across the country."[57] Though novices in movement politics, Love Canal activists were soon talking openly about environmental ethics, national hazardous waste policies, and environmental stewardship of vernacular American landscapes where most Americans lived, worked, played, and died. In these vernacular environments, the LCHA argued, Americans deserved clean and healthy air, water, and land. In fact, as more and more Love Canal activists (both in the LCHA and the CLCRA) would assert in the ensuing struggle, environmental health was very nearly an American right. And that made environmentalism much more than an abstract issue concerned with Big Nature. At Love Canal, environmentalism would focus on people's daily experiences with altered vernacular landscapes—the day-to-day environment most Americans knew and experienced.

In this key sense, differences among Love Canal groups might be less important than that which they collectively created: a new identity for themselves and their community—one that reframed the very nature of American environmentalism. For by the fall of 1978, Love Canal was no longer viewed as just a neighborhood but as an endangered landscape.

6. Summer of '78 Decrees, Part 2: A Federal Disaster Declaration

Citizen mobilization certainly changed state and federal officials' understanding of the problem at Love Canal. Indeed, they realized that the Love Canal crisis represented a public relations nightmare of enraged residents screaming about the lack of government oversight, of chemicals flushing into sewers, basements, drinking supplies, and riverways, and of mounting health claims born of industrial carelessness. Though they fumbled for responses, state and federal leaders thus became much more concerned with grassroots outreach. From Washington as well as Albany, they traveled to Niagara Falls to tour Love Canal with area residents, conduct more public meetings, and meet with nascent citizens' groups about possible next steps. Behind the scenes, politicians pushed for concrete funding of evacuation and cleanup programs. But it was in the public realm that Love Canal continued to unfold as a social and political drama. Congressman John LaFalce's August announcement that federal help, in the form of a multimillion-dollar clean-up package, had been secured for Love Canal underscored this important fact. In an effort to transcend visions of sterile decrees made from afar, LaFalce held his Love Canal press conference outdoors in the late-summer sun. This action made residents highly visible. "Love Canal Parley," a *Niagara Gazette* photo caption proclaimed. The accompanying image showed LCHA officer Debbie Cerrillo standing watch over LaFalce. The point? Citizen activism now framed every action at Love Canal.[58]

LaFalce's announcement was important in its own right, for it marked the first time federal clean-up funds had been earmarked for a chemical emergency. This in and of itself indicated that there was a major gap in federal hazardous waste laws. Undeterred, LaFalce and his staff urgently combed through various statutes, searching for possible ways to deal with the Love Canal problem. His colleagues in the Senate, the famed New York duo of Jacob Javits and Daniel Patrick Moynihan, had also researched possible federal responses. At one point they, like LaFalce, thought that Section 504 of the Clean Water Act would cover the Love Canal clean-up under the aegis of providing federal support to localities following "environmental disasters." Even sympathetic congressmen did not initially favor federal intervention of this kind, feeling that Love Canal was a local and state matter—certainly not a national disaster. In the wake of such opposition, LaFalce focused on the Resource Conservation and Recovery Act of 1976, which, though it did not deal with old toxic sites, did contain provisions for the potential funding of demonstration projects deemed appropriate to environmental clean-up and well-being. That translated into $4 million for remediation programs at Love Canal. "Now my heart is happy," one Love Canal resident exclaimed.[59]

But major questions still loomed: What would "clean-up" entail? How many more Love Canal residents, if any, would be evacuated? And who would ultimately fund the buyout of any evacuated homes, the state or federal government? As residents peppered state and federal officials with these questions, it became clear that LaFalce's clean-up announcement would not solve the riddle of Love Canal. For residents, Love Canal came to epitomize a "man-made" disaster—something relatively new in policy and relief circles. Born of human agency, its effects revolved not around physical destruction but public health. In the decade after Love Canal, a succession of these tragedies would occur in the United States and around the world, from the near-meltdown at Pennsylvania's Three Mile Island nuclear plant in 1979 to the deadly chlorine gas release in Bhopal, India, in 1984. Though accidental, none of these disasters could be classified as an "Act of God," the traditional way of interpreting an environmental calamity. But if humans caused these environmental messes—especially ones years in the making—then a key question remained: Who should clean them up?

By the summer of 1978, Love Canal residents focused on federal action. Disillusioned with local officials who had allowed Love Canal to be re-engineered as a toxic neighborhood, and dissatisfied with state responses that left many homeowners and renters out of the initial evacuation decree, residents turned to the federal government. Indeed, with continued unrest at Love Canal in the days following the state declaration of a health peril, the arrival of the nation's leading disaster officials was not a surprising event. Residents argued that they had been victimized by a man-made disaster and federal officials should intervene just as quickly as if a tornado or hurricane had blown through Niagara Falls. William Wilcox, head of the Federal Disaster Aid Administration (the precursor of FEMA) visited Love Canal immediately following the state declaration of emergency. Though officially on site to prepare a report on the use of federal funds at Love Canal, Wilcox became a key link in the chain of events leading to more expansive federal action. In a now familiar routine, residents took Wilcox on a tour of Love Canal, making sure that he visited basements and backyards saturated with chemical leachate.[60] "Stir, Joe, stir!," Lois Gibbs lectured an engineer who claimed that he could make "everyone in the room...deathly sick" by mixing the contents at the bottom of a sump pump in a Love Canal home.[61] "My personal impression is that this is a very troublesome site from the public health standpoint," the bespectacled and balding Wilcox told reporters at the end of his toxic tour. Clearly concerned, he made a prediction. "I feel confident that some federal aid will be made available."[62]

On the basis of his alarming report about the spread of toxic waste to homes around the old dump, Wilcox (and others) helped persuade President Jimmy Carter to declare Love Canal "a national emergency" on August 7, 1978. As one disaster relief official noted a bit too optimistically, Carter's order allowed local, state and federal officials "to meet the emergency needs of the Niagara Falls situation" in one fell swoop. By providing funds without restrictions, Carter's declaration was aimed not only at the technical aspects of Love Canal remediation but at protecting "the lives and safety of the people there."[63] While one step below the ultimate federal designation of a national "disaster" declaration (which also allowed the federal government to provide loans to small businesses and reimburse states for unemployment funds), the emergency order initially cheered many Love Canal residents. It also satisfied politicians desperately trying to find a solution to their constituents' ills. "This gives us the power to do everything we have to do," LaFalce, who had been lobbying the Carter administration too, proclaimed.[64] The emergency declaration enabled the federal government to mobilize financial resources for citizens' well-being and recovery as well as to plan infrastructure improvement. Just as important, it compelled the state to offer matching clean-up and recovery funds, which Governor Carey quickly pledged. That meant there was now over $8 million available—split evenly between state and federal agencies—for Love Canal relief.

Like so many things at Love Canal, Carter's emergency declaration would soon come under fire. Carter's order did not apply to the entire Love Canal neighborhood, but only to homes on the two blocks surrounding the former dump. Nevertheless, the presidential emergency declaration was a milestone. It was the first time that a human-made disaster qualified for federal emergency status under the Federal Disaster Relief Act. Though Carter issued his directive under the 1974 Disaster Relief Act, the law had its roots in a 1950 law that allowed the federal government to provide aid to localities overwhelmed by natural disasters. Though amended several times, the statute had never been utilized for anything but tornadoes, hurricanes, floods, or fires. In fact, of the roughly 600 disaster designations since 1950, none had applied to anything but weather-related emergencies. With a stroke of the presidential pen, disaster history changed. Now Love Canal would be defined as a two-block emergency zone. If nothing else, this meant that the roughly 240 families living on 97th and 99th Streets would be removed at government expense.[65]

Pat Brown was one of those evacuees. For the rest of her life, she remembered the day the president declared Love Canal a federal emergency. He did it, Brown later wrote, "to save lives." One of those lives, she believed, was her own. Brown had resided at her 99th Street home since the early 1960s. Well versed in the neighborhood's odd nature, she also experienced its tragic underside years before Love Canal became a national spectacle. Brown had two miscarriages before giving birth to a daughter, though even that happy occurrence was laced with major health concerns: doctors later found a series of baffling tumors on her daughter's knee. Though just a teenager, her daughter was given a diagnosis of rheumatoid arthritis. Brown's family was evacuated in 1978, but the sense of panic accompanying any minor illness followed her the rest of her life. There is, she later told a reporter, a panic "every time one of our children comes down with a swollen gland, a cough, anything. That fear never goes away."[66]

But Carter's emergency declaration offered validation to those like Brown who had long tried to convey the sense of hardship, dismay, and outright fear that accompanied Love Canal life. To most outsiders, Brown explained, Love Canal seemed like a textbook case of hysteria, as once happy and unsuspecting residents let the bogeyman of chemicals invade their mind. With no visual narrative of disaster—no flattened homes or debris field, no twisted fences or buckled roads, no cars submerged in flooded streets or fields cut down to mere stubble—skeptical observers could well wonder, just what were the Love Canalers marching for and yelling at? No longer, she proudly declared. "This was a new type of catastrophe not born of wind, water or fire," Brown subsequently commented. "It was mostly hidden beneath the ground," requiring citizen protest to unveil the not-so-unique health and environmental threats posed by hazardous waste.[67]

Soon after signing evacuation papers and moving out of her longtime home, Brown became part of the activist ranks at Love Canal, using her troubling experiences to aid others. And she always did the same thing when someone called out of nowhere to talk about life near a chemical dump or old incinerator or some other polluted locale. "I receive calls from other toxic waste victims across the United States and Canada," Brown would tell people wondering what she did after leaving Love Canal, "and I listen."[68]

7. The Feminine Mystique at Love Canal

Pat Brown's evolution from resident to activist was repeated hundreds of times over, particularly as remaining residents beyond the dump pushed for total evacuation. By the summer of 1979, Love Canal activists were such a common neighborhood sight that they seemed almost to be springing up from the environment itself. Hadn't they always been there protecting their interests? Not necessarily. Indeed, the intensification of activist commitments in the neighborhood was so impressive between 1978 and the early 1980s that it nearly overshadowed a corresponding shift in the area's social values. For in the space of a very short period of time, men and women who had known little besides family, work, and home got a crash course in activist politics. For many men in the neighborhood, this transformation challenged, and in some cases shattered, ingrained notions of appropriate public behavior and political comportment. Because the neighborhood comprised working- and middle-class families who often viewed themselves as bearers of traditional community values, patriotism and respect for political officials developed rather naturally in men. Becoming stereotypical hippie environmentalists or rabble-rousing activists did not appeal to the furnace repairmen, concrete mixers, and chemical workers who left home dutifully each morning and returned each evening to enjoy the fruits of their labor: a dip in the pool, a beer on the porch, a round of catch with the kids. Yet when faced with the prospect of a public health crisis in their own backyard, and revelations that political authorities had long known of the neighborhood's potentially toxic nature, many Love Canal men had to reimagine themselves as both activists and dissidents. One of the sadder, though still little known, facts of Love Canal life was that depression and suicide rose markedly among neighborhood men who felt that they had failed to protect their families. "We just had another one [a suicide] the other day," resident James Clark ruefully told congressmen in March 1979.[69]

For other neighborhood men, however, Love Canal activism provided an outlet for concerns and frustrations. It may not have been the most comfortable identity to assume—skip work for a protest meeting?—but it was a necessary one. Indeed, in an odd twist on the usual tale of historical relevancy, many working-class Love Canal men took to reminding reporters that they, too, had been activists in the heady days since August of 1978!

But no change proved more decisive than the upsurge of activism among Love Canal women, who quickly formed the nucleus of the almost every protest group, from the LCHA to the CLCRA. Dubbed "house-wives turned activists," local women staffed LCHA offices; executed the most mundane of day-to-day operations (including facilitating meetings between concerned homeowners and local, state, and federal officials); picketed, protested, and petitioned at venues stretching from Niagara Falls and Albany and New York City and Washington, D.C.; and corresponded with media figures and political officials to keep Love Canal constantly in the spotlight. [Figs. 9a, 9b] Although Lois Gibbs became perhaps the most prominent face of the Love Canal protest brigade, a host of other women enjoyed moments in the spotlight. Debbie Cerrillo, a young mother whose backyard literally pushed against the old covered dump, remained one of the more prominent Love Canal activists during the summer of 1978. Cerrillo had lived in Love Canal since 1969. Before helping launch the LCHA, and then becoming its vice president after Heisner departed, she had a few miscarriages but didn't connect them to the hazardous environment around her. But now, her environment was

Figure 9a "Protest March by Love Canal Families," c. 1978. Love Canal residents constantly engaged in marches, rallies, and public demonstrations to gain public attention. This march shows that men, women and even children participated, often with props. Note the sign on the right: "Dioxin Kills." (Love Canal Images, Courtesy University Archives, State University of New York at Buffalo)

Figure 9b "New York Governor Hugh Carey Discusses Love Canal Problems with Lois Gibbs," Spring 1978: As this classic image shows, women like Lois Gibbs dominated protest activities at Love Canal. As the head of the Love Canal Homeowners Association, Gibbs often met with state and federal officials, including Governor Carey. (Love Canal Images, Courtesy University Archives, State University of New York at Buffalo)

defined by "gunk" and "goop," as she and Gibbs put it: leaching chemicals that made homegrown vegetables look like science experiments, "black holes" beyond her fence where oily ooze bubbled to the surface, barrels pushing up near (and in some cases in) her backyard.[70] In the week between state and federal emergency declarations, Cerrillo was pictured flanking federal officials touring the neighborhood.[71] Though she was evacuated, Gibbs recalled that Cerrillo was at the LCHA offices with her "99 percent of the time."[72]

Like Cerrillo, other women found ways to keep protest fires burning. LCHA members Marie Pozniak, Luella Kenny, Anne Hillis, and Grace McCoulf would later offer moving testimony about life in the Love Canal crisis zone. Hillis wrote letters to the editor and corresponded with residents located near hazardous waste dumps in other parts of the country. Kenny spoke to Hooker Chemical shareholders and medical officials about Love Canal horrors. And waves of women showed up at nonviolent rallies, marches, vigils, and other, more theatrical displays of anger and rage. Nothing simply happened at Love Canal—these women made it happen.

Area demographics help explain women's key role in Love Canal protest. For one thing, the neighborhood contained a large proportion of households with young mothers and children (61 percent, according to one study). For another, Love Canal women were also much more likely to remain stay-at-home mothers than work even part-time (though some did work outside the home as well). As mothers and housewives, then, women remained at the center of Love Canal's domestic life. Women were there when chemical fumes pervaded homes throughout the day, there when children came home with a variety of ailments from coughs to chemical burns, there when friends and neighbors talked about corroded chemical barrels popping through the grass in area backyards or chemical leachate dripped down basement walls while someone was doing laundry, there to pick up children at the fetid landscape around the 99th Street School. In short, Love Canal had a high percentage of young women who saw things from a water-torture perspective: drip by drip, chemicals invaded parts of their domestic life. Whatever these women did in response would frame Love Canal's future.[73]

Many neighborhood women became activists. Indeed, if Love Canal women initially stood out as homemakers, a completely different picture emerged after the summer of 1978. David Shribman, a Pulitzer prize–winning reporter and now editor of the respected *Pittsburgh Post-Gazette*, vividly recalls the impression Love Canal women made on him. He was a cub reporter cutting his teeth for the *Buffalo Evening News*, and Love Canal was Shribman's first major story, which he often covered with a veteran environmental journalist named Paul MacClennan. In that time and place, Shribman remembers, Love Canal women were a revelation. With no college education (for the most part), no public relations experience, and little in the way of administrative background, Love Canal women formed the backbone of a formidable grassroots movement. Indeed, he notes, though they had the proverbial weight of the world on their shoulders,

Love Canal women refused to give in to the stress, anxiety, and outright disappointment that often accompany activist struggles. "They were some of the bravest people I've ever met," he declared flatly almost thirty years later.[74]

Ironically, women's path to prominence initially went through the prism of motherhood and domestic life. In fact, most neighborhood women became activists in the first place precisely because they felt that their sphere of influence—the *home*—was under siege. Faced with increasing occurrences of miscarriage, birth defects, and illness, Love Canal women argued that the leaking chemical dump threatened the very foundations of the modern nuclear family. State and federal intervention would thus help women protect their families and homes, physically, emotionally, and psychologically.

Yet these maternalist conceptions of activism proved to be only a stepping stone. Realizing that consciousness-raising—talking about and defining the problem of environmental illnesses—would not bring relief to the majority of families in the area, women embraced social movement politics with a vengeance. It is hard not to see the influence of Betty Friedan's *The Feminine Mystique* percolating through Love Canal women's evolving notions of protest. (Lois Gibbs' autobiography begins allusively with a chapter entitled "The Problem at Love Canal," perhaps a nod to Friedan's iconic chapter about the need to define postwar American women's sense of malaise, "The Problem That Has No Name"). Like Friedan, Love Canal women were hard pressed to define a problem that had no name in 1970s America. A chemical disaster? Phooey. Male authority figures made more than a few derogatory comments about Love Canal women's activism to suggest that area activists faced a double bind: they had to overcome gender bias as well as environmental naysayers—those who believed that there was no great health threat beyond the dumping zone proper. Love Canal? Governor Hugh Carey once quipped that that was a cute name for women's sexuality! A less notorious but no less illuminating example came from a lower-ranking state official who sought to calm women's frayed nerves by recommending that they should not stay in fetid basements too long washing clothes. "Throw the laundry in and come right back up," he warned. That was the way to avoid pesky chemical fumes.[75]

This manner of advice betrayed a none-too-subtle sexism and implied strongly that Love Canal women were overreacting—indeed, that they reacted "hysterically" to the environmental conditions in their midst. Often employing discourses of science and rationality to frame discussions of Love Canal, state officials downplayed the broader hazards posed by the toxic situation. Problems were small, technical, contained. "Life is a chancy thing, you know," David Axelrod, Whalen's successor as state health Commissioner, would tell residents. Anne Hillis responded incredulously that she and others wanted better chances "for my family and my neighborhood."[76]

Local as well as national reporters took note of the neighborhood women who drove Love Canal activism. "Two years ago they were housewives and mothers coping with illnesses and tensions that they did not realize were extraordinary," Dudley Clendinen, the latest in a string of reporters covering Love Canal for the *New York Times*, wrote from the neighborhood in May of 1980. "Now they are the leaders of the Love Canal Homeowners Association—which is, in fact, a grassroots political force—and they are so skilled at speaking to classes, confronting politicians, feeding reporters and dramatizing for the cameras that sociologists come by to observe." Though some women joked that they might still answer the phone of the LCHA offices with the greeting, "Love Canal *homemakers*," the *Times* reporter did not hesitate to call them "political leaders."[77]

Although most men were supportive, some found women's activism unnerving. More than a few interviews with reporters betrayed the sense that women's protest threatened to overrun the original LCHA goals of protecting traditional nuclear families. "Sure, it's messing up my love life," one sympathetic husband, who remained an activist himself, remarked humorously. "But for the women, it's about time they did something besides cut the grass. The hell with all the equal rights stuff—they're fighting for their families."[78] Such words honored women's new identity as activists even as they suggested that some men were a bit uncomfortable with the broader implications of Love Canal activism. Men were quite happy to have activist-housewives in the family—so long as activism produced housewives again when relocation occurred and the protest dust had settled. Many women did not see things that way. Love Canal was becoming a national cause, not simply a local concern. Women wanted to remain activists. As a result, several marriages broke apart in the wake of the prolonged crisis (including Gibbs' marriage). But for local women, activism proved to be liberating precisely because it became linked to a broader reform sensibility and sense of mission.

8. The New Love Canal Environment

As the summer came to a close, and the months passed in rapid succession, Love Canal no longer resembled a classic American neighborhood of quaint streets accented by the sounds of family life. The exodus of inner ring residents combined with the clamor of other homeowners' calls for evacuation put the entire area in a state of "organized chaos," as one reporter put it in August.[79] Trying to reestablish the rhythms of day-to-day life became difficult. "Tension is always with us," a headline blared above a letter to the editor from a woman named Madeline Boddy, who worked at the 93rd Street School. Located just a few blocks from the canal, the school was then at the edge of the crisis but still too close for comfort. Boddy wrote to the *Niagara Gazette* about the sick feeling she got when driving to school each morning. As she passed through the neighborhood, she saw evacuation buses lined up in case of an emergency caused by remediation work. The buses—ranging from six to a dozen—were always idling and ready to go. "Ready for what?" Boddy wondered. Gas explosions? Chemical plumes? How could an area be habitable if the state kept evacuation buses ready for almost anything? "The tension of living and working in the Love Canal area is always with us," she commented. And it was almost too much to bear.[80]

For some, the will to leave surpassed every other concern. Almost immediately after state officials declared an emergency on August 2, several families around the Canal proper began packing up their belongings. After the federal emergency declaration of August 7, the trickle of evacuees became a flood. No one slated for evacuation wished to spend any more time in the presence of potentially harmful chemicals than necessary. Some family members stayed with relatives, while others lodged temporarily in hotels (where they often relied on donated food from local businesses because state funds did not, at first, reimburse for it). Even then, there were anxious moments. Would evacuated homeowners be responsible for their property? According to one agent, there was "no physical loss here," only "a change in the condition of the land" under and around homes.[81] Indeed, vacancies further complicated matters, for most insurance policies required owners to maintain their dwellings, even if they left temporarily. Until the state or federal government finalized all home purchases in the inner ring, these homeowners had to worry about that problem too.

Such matters made little difference to other people. Charles and Barbara Arbotsky, parents of four children with another one on the way, moved out of their home on 99th Street in a matter of days. They ended up at Falconer Manor, a military barracks at a nearby Air Force base. Charles took a week off from work without pay, he told one local reporter, to make sure that the move occurred swiftly. "If this baby is all right," he said, pointing to his pregnant wife's bulging belly, "and the tests for my kids and my wife, negative, I'll be the happiest man in the world. I won't bother anybody. But if something goes wrong, somebody's going to have a lawsuit on their hands."[82]

Although they lived in Love Canal for less than a year and had recently redecorated their home, the Arbotskys had only been renting and could move rather easily. They knew of others who had recently purchased Love Canal homes but didn't think to look at the fine print on their mortgage agreements, which declared that, if anything went wrong, Hooker Chemical would *not* be responsible. All the same, the Arbotskys were happy to get out of Love Canal and have their kids play on "chemical free dirt." Like other evacuees, however, they remained haunted by their old neighborhood. What would be the long-term impact of chemical exposure at Love Canal? "I just don't know," Charles Arbotsky somberly concluded.[83]

Within a month, over two hundred other families followed the Arbotskys out of Love Canal. The two blocks of homes ringing the 99th Street School were now empty; they would eventually be demolished, their remains bulldozed into the remediated landscape already taking shape. After the chain link security fence was erected around 97th and 99th Streets—letting remediation workers in and keeping others out—Love Canal seemed like a border zone: a chemical Checkpoint Charlie. "*Admittance By Permit Only*," a sign warned darkly.[84] Armed guards and a mobile security unit patrolled the forlorn streets. Garbage and detritus from speedy evacuations piled up. Save for doghouses, swing sets, and other things left behind in the haste to leave, the inner ring was barren. There was simply no way to bring back the Norman Rockwell images of Love Canal's glory days.

For the remaining 700-plus families, from homeowners to renters, life became a mixture of the mundane and surreal, with a dose of the macabre liberally spread around. Unable to attend the 99th Street School, roughly 400 neighborhood kids took buses across town to Cleveland Street Elementary, which had been shuttered but was hastily reopened for the year. When they passed Hooker headquarters, where some of their fathers worked, the kids yelled epithets out the window—an alarming display of anger suggesting early-onset PTSD, according to some doctors. The surreal atmosphere was completed by lines of families gathering at the 99th Street School itself, which served as the command center of state health testing and relocation efforts even though it was officially closed. A photographer for the (Buffalo) *Courier Express* captured a memorable triptych of images depicting young children who endured blood tests at the school "to determine if [they] suffered any ill effects from the toxic chemicals that have been buried in the area and which are now leaking out of the ground."[85] Registering anguish, sadness, and fear, the children were ciphers of their parents' anxiety.

As Boddy's letter to the editor had shown, the remaining residents' anxiety was intensified by remediation plans for the leaking dump. The state DEC's remediation strategy sought to contain wastes via a system including, among other things, a new clay cap and trenching system that would capture chemical leachate. Though it would eventually surround the entire dump, the trenching system initially comprised two earthen grooves nearly ten feet deep around the southern end of the old canal. Clay piping inserted into the trenches would channel leaking wastes out to a 30,000-gallon tank located on site (near abandoned homes), which would separate waste into solid and liquid components. The giant half-dome structure looked like a mammoth iron lung that had been dropped onto the canal. "Newco Chemical Waste Systems," a white sign on the blue-grey edifice announced, "Special Services Division."[86] There was no mistaking just what it treated. The filtered leachate would then be sent through the Niagara Falls sewer system, which, after passing through a regular water treatment plant, would be released into the Niagara River. A second, portable tank, with activated carbon filters, would treat the remaining hazardous waste material, which would be landfilled either at Love Canal or elsewhere. That second unit, promised by the EPA, would also be placed on site, though if it did not arrive (or did not work) state officials planned to send the leachate to Ohio by truck—meaning that thousands of gallons of still toxic liquid waste might ride on area highways before arriving at its final destination.[87]

As technicians moved industrial machinery into the remediation zone and began working on the dump, many residents feared that they had become part of a giant science experiment. Though engineers and technicians assured them otherwise, Love Canal families worried that remedial work itself, by excavating and exposing parts of the dump, would make matters worse in the short term. Chemically laden dusts might be kicked up in the warmer months; contaminated mud could be tracked through the streets and even private homes in winter.

Despite assurances that remediation work was entirely safe, state engineers and technicians nevertheless planned emergency evacuation measures for themselves in case volatile chemical wastes exploded, caught fire, or shot dangerous gas clouds into the atmosphere. "Ambulances, gas masks, sealed air suits and fire trucks standing by were among the safety precautions recently recommended before any holes were bored into the chemical soup of the Love Canal in Niagara Falls," Michael Desmond reported in a Buffalo paper. Citing the Calspan study of 1977, which warned that "direct drilling into the landfill material with power equipment could puncture drums with release of possibly toxic or flammable liquids and gases," Desmond's article showed that remediation had inherent risks. Further evidence came in the form of a $1 million insurance policy New York secured for its Love Canal workers.[88]

At first, state officials did not take similar steps for residents. When they revealed the safety plan to Lois Gibbs, the LCHA's president nearly screamed—there was no evacuation plan for area residents. "I explained to the state people that if they showed the safety plan to the residents, they might demonstrate and burn things down, or worse. Our men had guns, and some had been in Vietnam ... They knew about explosives, either from the military or because of their jobs." Shocked that residents had been overlooked, Gibbs pushed state officials to include specific evacuation plans for them; thus, the buses on standby during remedial work. The buses even had a route through the neighborhood, stopping at sights marked "Emergency Evacuation Pick Up." (Former residents of Griffon Manor still have pictures of buses parked near evacuation sites).[89]

The buses did little to calm people down. When state officials held a public meeting on safety plans, things again turned confrontational. Would remediation work stir up hazardous material? one woman asked. "What will it be like? Is anything there that will hurt my children playing outdoors?" "It will smell like hell," the official replied, "it will smell like Hooker. But it won't hurt you." Residents shifted in their seats uneasily. "Wait a minute," the woman shot back. "If there is an odor here, and it's going to smell like Hooker, something must be causing it. How do you know it won't hurt my child?" Similar questions followed. When another resident asked state health officer Dr. Nicholas Vianna if he would wait for buses to load up after an alarm sounded, he did not hesitate to answer. "No," he told the audience forthrightly, "I would run like hell."[90]

As Gibbs had warned, debates over safety initiatives for canal workers and residents illustrated just how problematic remediation would be at Love Canal. If the local landscape was so damaged that merely digging into it could cause an explosion, however unlikely that might be, then most people would not feel safe living beside those same chemicals. Gibbs did not say that Love Canalers would resort to violence—"but," she made clear, "I heard talk." Push people to the brink of despair, she continued, and "something could happen."[91]

As these words indicate, Love Canal had also become a case study in how communities respond to what they perceive to be an extreme environment. With thousands of people living next to a massive chemical dump that had just been declared a state and federal emergency, Love Canal was essentially a ready-made lab of mass psychological distress. Adeline Levine, a sociologist at the University at Buffalo, recognized this powerful fact in the summer of 1978. As she watched the drama unfold up the road, she decided to drive out to the Love Canal neighborhood soon after the state declaration of a health peril was made public. When she got there, and began chatting with residents, Levine was not really prepared for the extreme set of responses she encountered. "The situation was very chaotic," she recalled nearly thirty years later. "I saw people moving out of their well-kept homes, met a pregnant woman convinced that she was carrying a monster, spoke to another woman afraid that her daughter would be unable to bear children [and] saw worried men and women lined up to get information from newly established government offices."

Love Canal had all the appearances of a disaster zone, yet little of the physical damage associated with a hurricane, tornado, or flood. Levine returned home knowing that she had a unique opportunity to study a new disaster typology. Over the next few years, she worked diligently with Love Canal residents and a stable of researchers to understand how people responded to human-made disasters. Indeed, though her case study method flowed from a "classic sociological tradition" of community analysis, she also wanted to understand how residents mobilized "to secure the resources they needed to escape homes poisoned by chemical wastes."

Through painstaking work, she and a bevy of graduate students logged hundreds of interview hours with Love Canal residents, collecting tens of thousands of pages of documents relating to the science and politics of the disaster. Levine eventually donated her personal archives to two different institutions in the Buffalo area, allowing subsequent generations of scholars to re-examine the Love Canal saga from a rich documentary perspective. As her intense interviews revealed, Love Canal's hard-working, family-centered, and normally very patriotic residents felt betrayed by industry and government officials who, in their eyes, responded less than vigorously to continued complaints about the toxic neighborhood. The joys of life—home and family—turned into hazards as terrified residents endured outbreaks of illnesses. Meanwhile fears of a future compromised by exposure to hazardous wastes constantly haunted residents' minds. Without question, Levine showed that Love Canal was a community under siege.[92]

Meeting in various locations, from residents' homes to temporary dwellings for evacuated people to offices of the LCHA's headquarters, Levine and her students tracked Love Canalers' feelings on a weekly, monthly, and eventually yearly basis. Levine's interview forms illustrated the complex matrix of emotions she had to catalog. On one form from the spring of 1979, Levine asked a staggering 67 questions. The queries on the four-page form piled up, appearing very much like the SAT; just filling it out would seem a daunting proposition. Levine labeled this a "feeling inventory," a way to examine the stresses of Love Canal life. In her interviews, Levine sought to gauge not only residents concern about health impacts but their sense of economic dislocation, psychological trauma, and outright anger at political and health officials. The first question related to residents' emotions at the very start of the interview. After that, questions ranged over individual, neighborhood, and societal matters:

- Has anything happened to your health and to your family's health since last time we spoke?
- Do you want to be relocated?
- Do you feel safe in your home now?
- How much do you think the Love Canal situation costs you?
- Specifically, what efforts have you made to leave the area?
- Are you arguing with [members of your family] much?
- What are your feelings about going back to your old home?
- Do the children talk about chemicals?
- What do you think your government's goals have been in the situation?
- Do you think the publicity has had an effect on the situation? Positive or negative? Has the press been accurate?
- How has Hooker responded to this whole crisis?
- During this crisis, who or what was most helpful to you?
- Do you think there is a long-term deep impact on your life from all this?

Many answers were unsurprising in their basic form: *Yes, we're scared now and concerned about the future health of our family.* What shocked Levine was the depth of anxiety and the sense of fear in many residents' minds. Indeed, well before she produced the book that came out of these interviews, Levine offered a preview of her findings at a meeting of sociologists in 1979. Arguing that residents suffered from acute psychological distress, she indicated that many Love Canalers felt a sense of "powerlessness." With little or no control over key aspects of their lives, particularly those relating to health and economics, residents felt marginalized and alienated.[93]

But Levine's research uncovered another side of Love Canal residents' collective personality—one that was durable, resilient, and highly capable.

After spending time with people struggling to make sense of lives turned upside down, she found that many Love Canal residents turned to activism as balm. By overcoming both chaotic environmental circumstances and societal norms (women as environmental activists?), Love Canal residents-turned-reformers created a formidable social movement centering on the little-known problem of hazardous waste. In the introduction to her well-regarded book, which was published in 1982, Levine emphasized that while she "initially planned to study the Love Canal families' responses to stress," she soon discovered that themes of resiliency and creativity predominated. In fact, after years of field research, hundreds of interviews and re-interviews with residents, health officials and politicians, and the archiving of laws, histories, and scholarly commentary, she remained most struck by citizen mobilization. While others doubted or delayed, tried to manage the problem in technical and/or scientific terms, or simply tried to keep the story hidebound, Love Canal residents "wanted the world to know everything."[94]

Like the chemicals beneath the ground, citizen activism was now a central fact of Love Canal life.

9. Love Canal Promises

For years, Love Canal had been defined as an idyllic, if environmentally quirky, neighborhood beyond the urban core. By the mid-1970s, however, residents' consistent complaints about the Love Canal landscape changed that picture, compelling political and health officials to examine the area's problematic environment. Over the course of one week in August of 1978, Love Canal suddenly morphed into a state and then federal emergency zone—a notorious neighborhood from hell (for many residents), a still-containable problem (for many politicians, technicians, and health officials), a conundrum (for many others). In many histories of the crisis, this is where the story climaxes and resolves itself: with the quick burst of populist rage compelling government authorities to act swiftly on behalf of the public health and civic good; the drama soon ends with mass evacuation of the neighborhood and lessons about hazardous waste well learned.

But that is not how the story actually went. Hundreds of families were left in Love Canal as remediation work continued. For many remaining residents, anxieties unleashed in the summer of 1978 continued to grow. Such was the terror inspired by hazardous waste at the time that even some residents protected by state and federal emergency declarations felt that they had been sacrificed to the hazards of chemical modernity. "Many feared the future," Lois Gibbs poignantly recalled. Indeed, though she still had a faith in government and believed that health studies would prove the efficacy of total evacuation, she could still be shaken by the sights and sounds associated with a neighborhood boiling with rage. After Governor Carey promised to buy toxic homes, Gibbs saw a man crying. "It was strange to see a man cry. I'd never seen a man cry before then. He had one child with a birth defect. He kept on saying, 'they're buying my house but it's too late. She's already pregnant.'"[95] Worried that a toxic conception would eventually harm his new child, the man stood in front of all his neighbors and openly wept for the future.

Sights like that became all too familiar for remaining Love Canal residents. Indeed, for all their sense of accomplishment in putting the neighborhood on local, national, and even international radar, Gibbs and other residents realized that the transformation of Love Canal had only just begun. To make it into an icon of modern grassroots environmentalism, area activists had to intensify their efforts. "Sometimes you have to shout to be heard," an old saying goes. At Love Canal, the shouting would continue for a couple more years.

6

Growing Protest at Love Canal

The current political unrest that exists all over the world have left us in fear of another world war....[But] we don't need sophisticated nuclear weapons [to harm us]; all we need are the multitude of dumps strategically placed all over the country that will insidiously destroy everything and everyone in its path.
—Love Canal Resident Luella Kenny to Occidental
Petroleum Shareholders, May 1980[1]

As the seasons turned and a new year passed, Love Canal remained a whirlwind of remediation activity. "A plan is being set in motion now to implement technical procedures designed to meet the seemingly impossible job of detoxifying the Canal area," EPA administrator Eckardt C. Beck declared in January 1979. Though a cold Western New York winter had set in, Beck explained that everything remained on track. "The plan calls for a trench system to drain chemicals from the Canal. It is a difficult procedure, and we are keeping our fingers crossed that it will yield some degree of success." Beck reiterated that securing Love Canal's poisons, rather than evacuating all area residents, remained the key to the neighborhood's future. While conceding that no "one has paid more dearly already than the residents," Beck commented that the Love Canal "tragedy" was well on its way to a successful resolution.[2]

Beck was wrong. In February, New York declared homes beyond the inner ring potential health hazards to pregnant women and children under age 2. Health officials recommended temporary evacuation but no more home buyouts. While roughly two dozen families exited, remaining residents exploded.[3] If the broader neighborhood was deemed unsafe, they clamored, then everyone should be evacuated.[4] The LCHA, several of whose members had been arrested in December for blocking remediation vehicles, intensified its protests but to no avail. Most Love Canal residents remained in a toxic environment. As one person put it dimly, the neighborhood itself had become a chemical "prison."[5] A local punk band called the Vores captured the area's dark mood. "Contaminated. We're all contaminated. Don't get near us, or you'll turn blue," the band growled in a tune entitled simply "The Love Canal." "Contaminated. We're all contaminated. Don't let us move in or you'll get it too."[6]

The troubling tenor of the times notwithstanding, Love Canal residents refused to give up. Throughout 1979, as Michael Brown observed in *The Atlantic*, "Love Canal people [had] chanted and cursed at meetings with state officials, cried on the telephone, burned an effigy of the health commissioner, traveled to Albany with a makeshift child's coffin, threatened to hold officials hostage, sent letters and telegrams to the White House, [and] held days of mourning and nights of prayer."[7] Expanding their definition of environmental justice, area activists also called for a greening of the nation's urban and industrial core, where an untold number of abandoned toxic sites threatened people's health. As a newly formed activist group, the Ecumenical Task Force, put it in 1980, "Love Canal is not only a local problem, but a global problem"[8] If politicians, business leaders and citizens did not confront America's toxic waste archipelago, Love Canal would not be the last toxic tragedy.

As they entered a new decade, then, Love Canal activists saw themselves not only as a band of aggrieved citizens but an environmental vanguard. Whether testifying before congressional committees about the impact of toxic chemicals on public health, or advocating for national hazardous waste clean-up laws, residents claimed Love Canal as both a polluted site and powerful symbol. The LCHA's Marie Pozniak put it best when she told federal politicians that Love Canal protestors aimed at much more than change in one American subdivision. Rather, they "fought for clear air, water and most important clean and safe homes" throughout the nation.[9]

1. Love Canal and American Environmentalism

When Love Canal activists first organized, grassroots environmentalism was still in its infancy. The inaugural Earth Day, which mobilized an estimated 22 million Americans at rallies, teach-ins, and demonstrations, was observed on April 22, 1970. Faced with a nation of polluted rivers and skies, Earth Day organizers channeled the spirit of earlier eco-critics to warn about the postwar environmental dystopia taking shape under the twin mantras of industrial progress and mass consumption. "You simply can't live an ecologically sound life in America," Denis Hayes, a leader of Earth Day activities, declared. "The people of America are still coughing, our eyes are running, our lungs are blackening... our property is corroding and we're getting angry."[10]

The guiding spirit of this new brand of environmentalism was Rachel Carson, the acclaimed author of Silent Spring. Published in 1962, Carson's book argued that the nation's neighborhoods, parks, and roadways were under siege by the postwar petro-chemical complex. In her book's famous opening chapter, "A Fable For Tomorrow," Carson imagined a town denuded of its songbirds by chemical despoliation. "No witchcraft, no enemy action had silenced the rebirth of new life in this stricken world," she wrote. "The people had done it themselves." Through an unquestioning reliance on chemicals (especially pesticides), she warned, human populations might seal their own fate too.[11] By casting her work in moral as well as technical terms, Carson hoped to stir the type of mass outrage that would wash over both politics and society at large.

Carson died of cancer in 1964, but her ideas continued to shape environmental activism over the next several years. Indeed, throughout the decade a variety of writers conjured images of what became known as "Ecocide": the human "murder" of nature.[12] Part of what the political scientist Charles O. Jones labeled the "eco-scare" genre, Ecocide writers asserted that Americans had created an "ecosystem depression" (as one observer put it) that would "make 1929 like a shower at a garden party."[13] Such heated rhetoric appealed to Baby Boomers who believed passionately in reform causes. Membership in environmental organizations tripled between the publication of Silent Spring and Love Canal. Perhaps as important, concern about environmental degradation spread to mainstream politics. Between the late 1960s and early 1970s, the nation's lawmakers created a federal regulatory machine aimed at greening American society. From the Environmental Protection Agency, created in 1969, to the Clean Air and Clean Water Acts, passed in 1970 and 1972, respectively, the federal government became an environmental guardian with more expansive powers than ever before.[14] Eco-reform had never seemed more certain.

As Love Canal residents would soon discover, however, there were key gaps in postwar American environmentalism. Indeed, toxic waste issues did not receive nearly as much attention from federal lawmakers as other concerns. Thus, while the Resource Conservation and Recovery Act of 1976 (RCRA) offered guidelines for the handling of waste streams in both the present and future, it did not address the cleanup of discarded hazardous waste dumps. "There are a lot of difficulties with that law," Congressman John LaFalce testified in 1979. Though Congress had wisely "attempted, through that act, to deal with the problem of hazardous wastes from cradle to grave," he continued, "RCRA does not now deal with . . . Love Canal situations."[15]

In addition, leading environmental organizations often expressed more interest in "Big Nature" issues—forest preservation, wildlife protection, resource conservation—than hazardous waste remediation. To gain federal support for these signature environmental concerns, a new generation of green lobbyists emerged in the 1970s. The scruffy Earth Day activist who once appeared poised to join a counterculture commune now donned a suit and tie to appeal to federal politicians. By 1978, over 70 environmental organizations had lobbyists working in Washington, up from just two in the early 1960s.[16] Although they added immeasurably to environmental policy, green lobbyists often eschewed unpopular political causes like hazardous waste remediation in the American Rust Belt.

Lois Gibbs still remembers the mixed blessing of mainstream environmentalists. On the one hand, major environmental organizations seemed little interested in supporting Love Canal activists. On the other, regional branches of certain groups, including the Sierra Club, offered key aid and support.[17] But even that would not be enough to liberate residents from their chemical environment. As Love Canalers learned, they had to do much more than scream about leachate in their backyards and basements. They had to organize more effectively.

2. Making the Toxic Environment Visible

Indeed, activists had to expose and explain the area's hazardous environment. "Chemical waste" was a potent but abstract term. By taking politicians, health officials, and dignitaries on "toxic tours" of the neighborhood, LCHA members could illuminate the day-to-day reality of chemical infiltration. Going to contaminated backyards and into poisoned cellars, residents gave outsiders a glimpse into the realities of the toxic zone. LCHA members usually flanked political officials, reporters and dignitaries on these tours, providing constant commentary about the impact of chemicals on their health. When movie star and activist Jane Fonda visited Love Canal in October 1979, she and Gibbs went inside the remediation area, which was usually off-limits. "We showed Jane the boarded up houses, the dead vegetation, the remedial construction," Gibbs remembered. "By the time we finished, it was an emotional scene. Jane was crying."[18] Gibbs never let anyone forget a toxic tour. On one occasion, New York Senator Daniel Patrick Moynihan tried to remember precisely when Gibbs had paraded him around Love Canal. Without missing a beat, Gibbs alertly responded that their 1978 toxic tour occurred on "October 27, at 3:30."[19] Though Moynihan chuckled at Gibbs' precise memory, her quick-witted response flowed from much experience: she and other residents had given a multitude of such tours, keeping track of who came when and why. [Fig. 10a]

Residents also made sure that photographers captured haunting images of the neighborhood. From the marshy areas around the 99th Street School (where oily black leachate pooled) to chemical barrels protruding through the soil, Love Canal offered a powerful portrait of an American landscape under siege. For residents, these images had an unrivaled explanatory power. "I'm part of this environment too," Irene Walker, who resided several blocks away from the dump on 101st street, told one local reporter exploring the area's chemical sights and smells. "If there's anything in the air [or ground], we've been exposed to it too." Standing near her children, Walker remembered her daughter saying that she was told not to go to the school playground on certain days because of chemical "seepage." Back home, Walker continued, family members noticed that newly painted walls would quickly yellow from powerful chemical fumes. For her, chemicals were no abstraction—they pervaded her family life and home. Walker wanted others to know these facts of her daily life and environment.[20]

Remediation work further uncovered the area's chemical nature. From pictures of hazmat workers spreading new soil on the old dump to images

Figure 10a "No Trespassing/Dangerous Area": One of the many signs warning people away from the Love Canal landscape in 1978, this image shows the temporary snow fence placed around the fields of the 99th Street School. Zones like this became part of residents' toxic tours for reporters and politicians. (Photo by Penelope Ploughman, copyright, August 1978, All Rights Reserved. Use courtesy University Archives, State University of New York at Buffalo)

Figure 10b "Barrels of Toxic Waste Removed From Love Canal": Images like this showed the world the chemical reality lurking beneath the surface of Love Canal: thousands of barrels of toxic waste. Such photographs helped create the visual narrative of disaster that verified residents' claims that their neighborhood was built on a hazardous foundation. (Courtesy, University Archives, State Universtiy of New York at Buffalo)

of chemical barrels unearthed by the clean-up operation, remediation altered the visual narrative of the Love Canal disaster by showing the world the fouled environment residents inhabited. Suddenly, activists did not have to explain chemicals hazards; pictures of the toxic landscape circulated widely. This disaster iconography would remain a powerful part of the Love Canal story for years to come.[21] One of the most famous photos, taken in 1985 by the Associated Press's Mary Esch, made Love Canal's subterranean world of chemical flow visible via a chilling maze of excavated barrels. Entitled "Deadly Drums," the picture showed nearly five hundred 55-gallon barrels gathered neatly in a field near Love Canal.[22] The photo turned Love Canal's chemical landscape into a geometry lesson, ominously suggesting that thousands more deadly drums remained buried in the ground. Even if the chemicals weren't seen, Esch's photo—and many more like it—exposed Love Canal's subterranean reality. In fact, images of

Figure 10c "Remediation Work (Clay Capping) at Love Canal": Workers ply the old dump, smoothing over the new clay cap placed on Love Canal. While officials claimed that this would help resolve the Love Canal problem for good, a new state health order that same month—evacuating pregnant women and children under age 2 from the neighborhood—sent residents into a fury. New groups, like the Ecumenical Task Force of the Niagara Frontier, soon took shape to bolster area activism. (Photo by Penelope Ploughman, copyright, February 1979, All Rights Reserved. Courtesy University Archives, State University of New York at Buffalo)

Love Canal detritus (waste barrels, corroded drums, and loose chemical sludge) circulated constantly, making the dump's toxic contents nearly as famous as the people protesting to get out of Love Canal. [Figs. *10b, 10c*]

3. Citizen Science and Public Health at Love Canal

Making the toxic environment visible was one thing; linking it to public health concerns another. As head of the LCHA, the indefatigable Gibbs pleaded with everyone from congressmen to United Nations representatives to see Love Canal as a public health crisis. Gibbs' most consistent target was state health commissioner David Axelrod, who replaced Robert Whalen in January of 1979. Gibbs wrote so many missives to Axelrod that she began thinking of them generically as her "Dear David letters." On some occasions, she wrote to him several times a day. "Dear David," she began in the first of several missives on May 24, 1979, "this memo is to confirm our phone conversation last week," in which Axelrod promised to send Gibbs health information on toxic waste sites throughout New York State. A second letter proposed "the creation [of] a central file or library of copies of all information gathered through the Love Canal study"—a public health clearinghouse for residents as well as public officials. In other notes, Gibbs grilled Axelrod about ongoing state health tests at Love Canal. "Dear David," she began a detailed letter on August 20, 1979, "I have received a copy of your interim report on [the] New York Department of Health, environmental and epidemiological studies done at Love Canal." In the interim report

> you outlined the various studies done by New York State...including soil, storm sewers, effects on pregnant rats, residence health, etc. Although I realize that this report is only a summary of your ongoing studies, I found many problems with the way the studies were done and the conclusions you arrived at when completing each one. Enclosed you will find a memo addressing some of the [expert] comments I have questions [about] which need to be answered. Many of the questions have been asked many times before and I am hopeful that you will be willing to answer them now.

The accompanying report, spread out over several pages, offered an extended analysis of state tests conducted during the previous six months and their relationship to government policies limiting evacuation of residents to those living closest to the canal. Gibbs criticized the testing protocols in one study that left pregnant rats in Love Canal homes for roughly three weeks. The tests found that rat fetuses had no unusual characteristics when compared to the control group in Albany. "Although I am not a scientist, I find many problems with the way the study was conducted," she commented. Why, she asked, were the rats impregnated away from the contaminated area and then placed in Love Canal homes? To approximate true conditions at Love Canal, she argued, officials should have exposed rats to chemicals prior to pregnancy.[23]

Gibbs disputed other test results and asked why she sometimes received conflicting information about what scientists actually found in her neighborhood. After one study found lower levels of dioxin in many area homes, Gibbs showed that she had received a different set of readings from state officials with higher concentrations. "Could you clear up this discrepancy?" she asked. She also pleaded with Axelrod to keep "investigating the pipes" and sewer systems at Love Canal, which could be vectors of dioxin "discharge." If Axelrod was not going to do this, she demanded, "please explain why."[24]

As her letter-writing campaigns showed, Gibbs had grown significantly as an activist. The daughter of a Niagara Falls brick mason, she had no college education or organizing experience; it would have been hard to predict her speedy rise to activist prominence. Almost too terrified to speak when she began protesting in the summer of 1978—she had a nervous "habit of saying 'okay' after everything"[25]—Gibbs soon became a powerful presence at meetings, rallies, and political events. "She was like a hurricane and we just kept going," friend and fellow activist Luella Kenny said of Gibbs decades later. "She did not have all of this, shall we say, Wall Street and Washington know-how," Kenny continued, but she had this "hidden talent she wasn't even aware of": an ability to fight, organize, and remain active in the face of dogged opposition.[26] Gibbs personified the gritty yet savvy grassroots campaign residents developed. When she first approached school officials about her son's ailments, they told her to "stop worrying and accept the fact that Michael was a sickly child." Like others, Gibbs was unsatisfied with such responses, choosing to redouble her efforts to find out about the leaking dump in her midst. Meeting with political and health officials, connecting with scientific advisors, and doing her own research, Gibbs "began organizing and educating her community" about the potential health impact of the toxic landscape. She also crafted a David-and-Goliath narrative, arguing forcefully, as one missive recounted, that Love Canal residents had to "fight the authorities and force them to address the needs and concerns of the residents."[27] "If we hadn't assembled this large citizen organization," Gibbs observed years later, "we would still be living at Love Canal, with authorities still maintaining that there are no health problems."[28] For years, Gibbs wielded this underdog story as a sharp and effective rhetorical weapon.

Other residents-turned-activists shared Gibbs' commitment to ongoing grassroots struggle. It was not easy to maintain the residents' movement after the initial burst of energy in the summer of 1978. But working full days and long nights, LCHA members managed to keep the struggle in the public and political spotlight. Working out of various offices, from Lois Gibbs' home-turned-headquarters on 101st Street to the 99th Street School, where state officials provided a room and phone, LCHA officers met almost daily. Anne Hillis' son Ralphie told one reporter that his parents were always attending environmental meetings of one sort or another (implying that they were rarely home).[29] If this perseverance did not result in the speedy evacuation of everyone, it did allow a critical mass of residents to retain a sense of unity.

And that allowed them to focus on the myriad health threats they faced. As they gathered, talked and continued to protest in 1979, Love Canal activists realized that they had unique insight on the psychological, physiological, and public health dimensions of chemical contamination. They now had to translate that information to the public. Indeed, just as they had shown people the way chemicals affected their local environment of schools, yards, and homes, residents realized they also had to discuss what chemicals did to their bodies and minds. Anne Hillis began this process in her journal, where she compared Love Canal to a chemical fortress. As she put it, her home was a "cesspool [that] we could not sell, rent or even give away." "I was supposed to be free," she continued, from the type of toxic pollution that might define "some backwoods country." But the state and federal evacuation orders had stopped well short of her street and it seemed as if time itself would bury her at Love Canal. "Where is my freedom now?" Hillis wondered, as she struggled to cope with the mounting psychological stress of the situation.[30]

Like Gibbs, Hillis turned to activism as a way forward. "I may be sick from chemicals but I'm not *dead* yet!" she observed. By illuminating the perils of chemical waste, discussing her health problems with politicians, and writing letters to the editor about Love Canal health concerns, Hillis experienced the thrill of fighting back. She took particular satisfaction from picketing in front of the muddy construction entrance to the Love Canal remediation site on a cold December day, soon after state officials announced that they had found dioxin—one of the deadliest chemical byproducts—seeping out of Love Canal. Though a police officer pleaded with Hillis to move on, she refused, distributing activist literature to workers and contractors about the toxic perils they now faced. Even after being arrested, Hillis returned to the worksite to protest again and inform others about the public health threat of toxic waste.[31]

The LCHA's "Chronological Report" showed that this brand of activism had increasingly re-defined Love Canal as a local, state, and national problem. A compendium of grassroots protest activity from 1978 onward, the report documented 22 straight months of protest on a range of issues.[32] From demonstrations outside of the Hooker plant along the Niagara River to a massive "walk of concern" focusing attention on hazardous waste in American culture, LCHA activists remained busy in the service of their cause. (Indeed, as the report humorously noted, Gibbs had become such a familiar face to state officials that Governor Carey himself quipped, "I've spent more time with you than anyone else outside my own family.)"[33] Health concerns often lay at the center of residents' activist universe. Dating the advent of the residents' struggle to a state health department declaration that a "health hazard" might well exist at Love Canal, the Chronological Report followed residents as they organized a movement, protested limited evacuation decrees, opposed remediation plans, and pestered health officials about chemicals' short- and long-term impact on the human mind and body.

As the LCHA timeline indicated, Love Canal activists made perhaps their biggest splash by conducting grassroots health studies that linked disease data to chemical waste flow patterns throughout the neighborhood. Among the first "citizen science" efforts in the nation, these health censuses charted residents' illnesses, miscarriages, and birth defects (among other things) over and against Love Canal's adverse environmental conditions. The effort began in the summer of 1978. After state tests showed that a chemical threat existed for pregnant women and children under age 2, Love Canal residents expressed grave concern about the chemical landscape surrounding them. But they could not get meaningful information from even the most well-intentioned state official. "At Love Canal," toxicologist and environmental health expert Stephen Lester commented, "people were given slips of paper listing levels of six or seven chemicals found in their basements." But there was nothing more. "People wanted to know, 'What does this mean? Does this mean I'm going to get cancer, or will my kids get sick?'" Lester knew the situation well, for in October 1978 he began serving as a liaison between health workers and residents. "I remember one woman in particular—I told her, 'I can't say what this means for you as an individual, I can only tell you in general what the risks are.' She said to me, 'We can put a man on the moon, and you're telling me that we don't know what these chemicals are going to do to us?'"[34]

Lester helped convince state officials to let residents gather health information too, an effort that fit well with the LCHA's organizing and outreach activities. Creating a neighborhood health registry was daunting for local activists, but it allowed residents themselves to learn more about the poisons at Love Canal. Indeed, as the LCHA conducted research, its members tried to educate residents about toxic waste. The LCHA's Chronological Report created a glossary of chemical "definitions" that allowed residents, reporters, and others to understand the potential connection between human health and environmental hazards. The glossary defined "ambient levels," "exposure," "carcinogen," "dioxin," "trichloroethylene" and dozens of other words in the chemical lexicon. "The term Migration," the LCHA explained, "refers to the movement of chemicals or leachate away from a landfill, whether by runoff, seepage through the soil, or through the air." "Lindane," the glossary noted, has "been shown to cause adverse effects in the reproductive capacity of exposed animals... including convulsions and epileptic seizures."[35] The glossary's lessons continued through a whole alphabet soup of toxic terms.

The LCHA moved into more divisive terrain by mapping disease clusters at Love Canal. Working with Dr. Beverly Paigen, a geneticist and cancer researcher at Roswell Park (who told Gibbs to refine her analysis of chemical impacts), the LCHA devised the "swale theory" of chemical contamination in outer ring homes.[36] According to Gibbs and Paigen, Love Canal's worst health impacts occurred in historically wet areas of the subdivision, where buried streams, called drainage swales, conducted chemicals to homes well beyond the dump. "We took out our health survey notebook and started to put squares, triangles, and stars on a street map, with a different symbol for each disease," Gibbs recalled. When they transposed a swale map on the grid, "suddenly a pattern emerged!"[37] The map became famous after it was made public in October 1978.

Residents thought the swale map might convince state and federal politicians to evacuate the entire subdivision. Instead, state health officials dismissed it as "useless housewife data."[38] This opened a new front at Love Canal: the battle over scientific legitimacy. Indeed, if previously residents and politicians debated policy—who should be evacuated from an area where chemical waste had been shown to exist, and how evacuation and remediation would be paid for—now they argued about the very definition of health impacts. Were citizens themselves allowed to claim authority over Love Canal's toxic trouble, or were health authorities the only ones who could and should define adverse health impacts? Though residents experienced backlash from officials on this question, Paigen came under particularly intense fire for her work, which some medical authorities dismissed as mere advocacy. In one meeting, an inflamed Governor Carey flung Paigen's Love Canal health report into the air; as the pages scattered, he accused her of acting emotionally and unscientifically—gendered code words aimed at undercutting her scientific authority. Paigen quietly picked up the papers, reassembled them, and handed the report back to the governor. She then explained her methodology.[39] It was an interesting role-reversal: the emotionally wrought governor getting a lesson in professionalism from Paigen. But that did not stop Carey and others from attacking Paigen's work as unsound and unwelcome.

Patient, organized, and thorough, Paigen argued that public health officials should put human safety before industry demands.[40] Her work at Love Canal showed that something was amiss and that the toxic environment could not be ruled out as a factor in increased miscarriages, birth defects, and a range of other maladies. As a scientist working at the cutting edge of toxic epidemiology, she was soon cited as a scientific authority in other toxic places and studies. In fact, once the swale theory hit the news, citizens' groups around the country contacted her for help.[41] Paigen's credentials, methodology, and public health experience, however, mattered little to many critics who continued to dispute her findings.[42] Paigen eventually had to get pre-approval from Roswell Park for any Love Canal appearances. By the early 1980s, the entire saga had taken a toll on her own health and well-being.

Still, Paigen's (and Gibbs') broad analytical perspective influenced subsequent studies of area health. Indeed, New York health officials validated residents' claims that historically wet areas of the old dumping zone were linked to an inordinate number of ailments, including low birth weights, seizures, eye problems, hyperactivity, and abdominal troubles.[43] As an insightful article in *Chemical Engineering and News* would observe, Gibbs and Paigen's "idea about swales carrying chemicals was refuted publicly" in 1978 and 1979, "only to be partly vindicated in later comparisons by the department that found higher illness rates in 'wet' versus 'dry' locations." In another interesting role-reversal, the article explained that the state "health department...maintained that they were doing their best with the scientific tools they had."[44] Like Paigen and Gibbs, health officials were still feeling their way through Love Canal health impacts in the late 1970s and early 1980s—though they would not dare admit that at the time.

Little wonder that both Paigen and Gibbs reported their health findings to Congress as a way to reframe debates over Love Canal health concerns. Hoping to emphasize the authority of residents and their allies who had documented Love Canal's adverse impact on public health, a host of activists spoke before congressional committees in the winter and spring of 1979. Much as before, their sense of grassroots authenticity and homespun righteousness impressed federal officials. Among the first residents to testify was Anne Hillis, who spoke movingly about the invasive nature of chemicals in her life. "I am a wife and a mother," she told the Senate Subcommittee on Hazardous Waste in March. "I also live close to a dump, a dump called Love Canal. I don't want to live there anymore. I hate Love Canal. I hate my life at Love Canal. The strange life that I lead now is filled with disruptions and frustrations and sleepless nights and a grip of fear that only those in similar situations could understand." In a crisp and moving presentation, Hillis explained her family's struggles with various illnesses. She also discussed constant battles with state health officials over expanded evacuation programs. "I believe most Americans assume that the government will be there when they need help," she concluded. "Is this belief wrong[?]" Since the state response was still lacking, Hillis pleaded for federal intervention. "If our federal government does not help us, we are all doomed at Love Canal. May God help us and our country, for we need it. We need help desperately."[45]

A train of others followed, both in Washington and at field hearings in Niagara Falls. On Capitol Hill, Jim Clark, a Green Beret and self-described "disabled American veteran" whose family "suffered many serious health problems," called for the total evacuation of Love Canal. Disputing the idea that Love Canal was a false crisis born of hysteria, he noted that the dump contained "over 200-something" toxic chemicals that had seeped into the environment. Leachate had already prompted a variety of "adverse health effects," he continued, making evacuation a just and wise policy. Like others, Clark also called for "a national program" of hazardous waste re-mediation. Without such a plan, he said, other Love Canals might endanger the health and safety of untold numbers of people around the country.[46]

When her turn came, LCHA member Grace McCoulf compared Love Canal life to a hazardous worksite. Explaining that state tests had revealed elevated levels of benzene inside her house, McCoulf learned that no state or federal guidelines existed for residential air quality in homes. Yet there were guidelines for the workplace, and she discovered that her home environment approached the actionable limits for safety. Given these conditions, McCoulf challenged congressmen to think more deeply about that: she lived in a place that might not pass muster as a worksite.[47] Marie Pozniak, who lived down the street from "the last boarded-up house" in the inner ring, told senators that her Love Canal life was a constant mix of "confusion and stress." With an asthmatic daughter, she worried constantly about elevated levels of airborne contaminants, especially during remediation work. With the psychological and physical toll mounting, she was not sure what to do to protect her family. She asked Congress to act decisively by moving residents from such an unhealthy landscape.[48]

Congressmen were visibly moved. "I believe your tragic experience and the experiences of your neighbors are certainly very grim and frightening proof that old waste dumps can be nothing but environmental time bombs that can spew forth human suffering and tragedy," Senator Chet Culver, Republican of Iowa, said.[49] In a speech introducing Love Canal residents, Culver went further, noting that direct testimony from people in the toxic zone would highlight the "alarming problems that have developed because we, as a nation, have for too long paid little attention to the generation, distribution, and disposal of toxic and hazardous materials." Culver's colleague, Republican John Chafee of Rhode Island, agreed, adding that Love Canalers' moving tales would "contribute greatly" to a "national response to a problem that is growing."[50]

Yet, despite their strong words of support, neither Culver nor Chafee guaranteed that Love Canal residents would be evacuated anytime soon. While activists had made public health a key part of the entire Love Canal saga, that would still not be enough to escape their toxic neighborhood.

4. Second Wave Environmentalism at Love Canal: The Ecumenical Task Force

The charged atmosphere of congressional hearings had much to do with New York's February 8, 1979 health declaration. Issued by new health Commissioner David Axelrod, the decree was "[b]ased on continuing evaluation of environmental and health data" suggesting that more Love Canal sections had elevated rates of miscarriage, among other maladies. After reviewing the evidence, Axelrod recommended evacuation of pregnant women and children under age 2 residing between 97th and 103rd Streets.[51] But Axelrod's order brought as much confusion as clarification. Not only would evacuation be temporary—removing pregnant women and infants only during the remediation process, which was partly completed— but it threatened to divide families: husbands, brothers, and sons had to pay their own relocation expenses if they wanted to follow wives, sisters, and daughters. Moreover, despite the state's concerns about public health, the new order affected only 49 families out of more than 700 remaining in the ten-block neighborhood. Residents challenged Axelrod's limited edict, peppering him and other state workers with a new round of hard questions: Was a child who had just turned two safer than an 18-month-old? Were other family members safe in Love Canal? Should women even considering pregnancy leave the area too? Residents screamed at Axelrod in yet another tense public meeting.[52] In an eerie version of Love Canal déjà vu, residents flew into a panic, vowing to protest even more vociferously for mass evacuation. As the LCHA noted with utter contempt, Love Canal women must "interpret the state's response [to pregnancy risks] as... [a form of] birth control."[53]

The uproar spurred the formation of another activist group at Love Canal: The Ecumenical Task Force of the Niagara Frontier (or the ETF, as it became known). Officially founded on March 13, 1979 at the Wesley

Methodist United Church—across from the Love Canal dump—the ETF boasted a membership of over 200 religious figures ready to mobilize on behalf of residents. Several Love Canal families joined the ETF as well. Despite its religious foundation, the ETF included a range of people with social reform expertise. ETF board member John Lynch was the Director of Catholic Charities in Niagara County, while his colleague Roger Cook worked in antiwar and anti-nuclear groups.[54] Donna Ogg engaged in outreach activities for the Presbytery of Western New York; Roberta Grimm headed New York State Church Women United, an ecumenical group dedicated to social justice initiatives and women's rights. And no one had more disaster relief experience than the ETF's Executive Director, Sister Margeen Hoffman. A Franciscan nun, Hoffman had master's degrees in social work and community organization. She arrived in the spring of 1979, fresh from coordinating flood relief efforts in Rochester, Minnesota.

ETF members blended pragmatism with prophetic beliefs in social justice. As Hoffman herself put it, "[w]here the needs of the people are not being met, it is unchristian not to be political."[55] Like other ETF figures, Hoffman vowed to aid all Love Canal residents while also ministering to their spiritual needs. Her background as spiritual advisor and disaster-relief worker prepared her well for these twin tasks. On the one hand, she sought to work with politicians to get people out of harm's way. "I know the jargon, the red tape, the bureaucratese and the governmentese" she told one reporter during her first year in Niagara Falls. On the other, she knew that Love Canal families, particularly children, were suffering from "fear and confusion." "We're being gassed here," an outraged Hoffman declared on one occasion, emphasizing that reformers needed to pay attention to residents' spiritual needs as the crisis evolved.[56]

The ETF made Love Canal much more than a public health concern or a matter of residential relocation. Rather, it defined the disaster as part and parcel of an American spiritual crisis. With technology and consumerism ascendant, Americans paid little attention to toxic pollution. Now Love Canalers would pay the price. People of faith, the group argued, must therefore respond to the crisis as a moral matter. Indeed, ministry remained an important part of the ETF's disaster relief agenda. Pastoral activities such as "active listening," the group asserted, allowed residents to talk about their deepest concerns without fear of offending family members or neighbors.[57] Pastors, priests, and rabbis were encouraged to join hands with spurned residents, giving them spiritual succor as well as material support. "The churches have to do something," Joann Brietsman, a founding member of the ETF who worshipped at a Presbyterian church in nearby Lewiston, declared after seeing frightened Love Canalers respond to the state's February 1979 temporary evacuation order. Brietsman lived in Lewiston and queried her own minister, the Rev. Paul Moore, about pastoral responses to the evolving crisis in her backyard.[58] Moore, who had been involved in other social justice initiatives, responded that the faithful must not stand by while the Love Canal siege continued. Soon after, Briettsman, Moore, and roughly two dozen religious leaders— Baptists, Methodists, Catholics—created the ETF.

The ETF's formation came at a propitious moment for religious environmentalism. Challenging long-held Judeo-Christian notions that the Old Testament enshrined earthly dominion over natural resources (Genesis 26:1 declares that humanity should control "... every creeping thing... "),[59] mid–twentieth century Christian environmentalists began exploring notions of faith-based environmental stewardship. Using the Bible and other religious traditions as a guide, this evangelical vanguard argued that an almighty power commanded nothing less than the protection of Earth's beauty and bounty (Genesis 1:28 tells humans to "replenish the earth"). The ETF saw Love Canal as an environmental wake-up call—a divine admonition to replenish nature after polluting it. According to the ETF, humanity was on the edge of an ecological catastrophe. "This is God's good earth, not ours," Moore observed in one pamphlet, and humans had the "eternal" task of preserving it. But at Love Canal, "God's law has been broken." Unless humankind reformed its ways, damnation might follow.[60]

Like the LCHA, the ETF saw Love Canal as much more than a standalone catastrophe. It was, the group argued, a metaphor of technological arrogance and human-made disaster. The group found its iconic image of an American Garden of Eden destroyed by chemicals in a snapshot of a young boy standing before a Love Canal warning sign. "Hazardous Chemicals—Unauthorized Entry Prohibited," the sign proclaimed, as the naïve youngster reflects, trance-like, on a tiny handful of flowers in his hand.[61] The image, affixed to the ETF's first annual report in 1980, artfully played up the idea of Love Canal as the place where Americans had fallen from environmental grace. This gentle Love Canal lad represented both a timeless innocence and an arresting maturity—someone whose elemental regard for the beauty of nature stood in striking contrast to the polluted environment around him. "The Land is Cursed," the ETF announced boldly in 1980, further underscoring the point. At Love Canal, as elsewhere, humans were losing touch with their environmental soul. Only a new brand of environmental stewardship aimed at the protecting people as well places from future Love Canals could revive the great American landscape.[62]

In making such claims, ETF visionaries tried not to exploit Love Canal to gain converts. Rather, the group sought to create a nondenominational but faith-based approach to chemical disasters. Like the LCHA, the ETF would soon argue for environmental justice: the notion that urban dwellers, minorities, and working-class communities had a right to clean and safe living environments. Indeed, while the ETF would "provide direct aid to Love Canal residents... [and] inform religious communities of the issues [at Love Canal]," the group hoped to work "toward[s] long-range solutions to the chemical waste problems locally and throughout the country."[63] As it argued, "inadequate government response to human needs" in "human-made" disaster settings like Love Canal were an abomination. The ETF mobilized to guarantee "the rights of each citizen," no matter their race, class, or creed, to safety and security, and to provide "caring stewardship of the earth" so that hazardous waste catastrophes would not occur again.[64]

Still, faith informed nearly every aspect of ETF life. No sooner had it been formed than the group addressed the theological meaning of inadequate government responses to the Love Canal crisis. Using scripture to underscore its central point that both government and society must confront the nation's past mishandling of hazardous waste, the ETF punctuated its literature with Biblical wisdom. "The earth lies polluted under its inhabitants" (Isaiah 24:5) became the group's mantra, serving as an epigraph for essays, position papers, and annual reports urging political officials to broaden their concept of environmental stewardship by including America's hazardous waste zones. "Where There Is No Vision, The People Perish" (Proverbs 29:18) similarly framed the group's agenda. Noting that government inaction had left hundreds of families stranded in

Love Canal many months after President Carter's initial emergency declaration, the ETF promulgated a "theological rationale" for government intervention. To restore the earth and the people who inhabited it, government leaders must intervene in human-made disasters such as Love Canal.[65]

In this way, the group contributed to an emerging Love Canal jeremiad, preaching that hazardous waste menaced the American people and offended a just God. Activists who joined the ETF could regard themselves as linked in a sacred chain of environmental reform sanctified by a higher power. "As a creature made in the image of God and charged with responsibility for the protection of the earth," a group pledge went, an ETF member would not "pollute its water... [nor] defile the land...." "[A]nd when I find others corrupting our common environment, I am commanded by God to challenge the injustice of such cruel, irresponsible and arrogant behavior."[66] Using theological insight to legitimize citizen protest further shielded Love Canal activists from claims that they were hysterical and self-aggrandizing loonies.[67] When state officials argued that they would not only remediate the Love Canal landscape but perhaps attempt to spur future growth in the area, the ETF replied that such policy views were not only wrongheaded but immoral. The group vowed to fight back against what it saw as corrupt environmental values at Love Canal and elsewhere. Indeed, the ETF saw Love Canal as much more than a narrow dumpsite disaster; rather, it was a national environmental call to arms. "The practices of the past are our poisons of the present," Margeen Hoffman declared.[68]

To realize its ambitious agenda, the ETF soon created a bevy of action committees, including those dedicated to "direct aid," "funding," "public policy" and "educational response." To help ETF officers and Love Canal citizens better understand the medical science behind public health testing, the group assembled a technical/scientific advisory board of over 20 doctors, chemists and lab scientists. "But maybe our biggest accomplishment," ETF Board Member Terri Mudd, explained in a second "progress report," "is that the Love Canal situation is called a *disaster* by the world now."[69] Working alongside, and sometimes competing with, members of the LCHA, the ETF helped spread the word that local, state, and federal governments were dragging their feet while Love Canal residents suffered.

With access to the vast institutional networks of American churches, synagogues, and interfaith groups, the ETF put impressive strength behind broader evacuation campaigns. Within a year of its formation, ETF members convinced various regional, national and international religious bodies to produce no fewer than six appeals to New York for mass evacuation at Love Canal. These appeals came from near and far. In September 1979, the Niagara Council of Churches demanded a more effective state response to "the man-made disaster at Love Canal," including "voluntary evacuation of all affected residents" as well as "compensation" for their harm and suffering. In May 1980, representatives from the World Council of Churches signed a similar memorandum to Governor Carey. "Be it resolved," the missive began, "that the following persons from 17 different countries on all five continents—through our commitment and involvement in church groups, people's movements, and social organizations, which have a responsibility to confront injustice and serve as advocate for those caught in conflict—request the honorable Hugh Carey to immediately . . . buy Love Canal homes." The ETF also raised over $50,000 in its first year of operations, more than one-fifth of which was expended on "direct aid" to residents in the form of food, medical assistance, help in paying bills, and other expenditures. From "Mennonite Disaster Services," which provided a $350 donation, to the "American Baptist Church," whose $12,700 donation was the largest of the year, subventions large and small came down the ETF pipeline. In a short time, the group made a big difference.[70]

5. Environmental Discord and Environmental Justice at Love Canal

With both the ETF and the LCHA on the scene, Love Canal was clearly a hotbed of environmental activism by the middle of 1979. But an LCHA and ETF alliance was not preordained; in fact, with foundations in different activist movements, these two groups often diverged. They had to figure out how to play with, and off, each other. That was not always easy. Steeped in a tradition of religious reform, the ETF was a classic advocacy group that forged intimate ties to various Love Canal residents. It sought to imbue modern environmentalism with a theological foundation and thereby provide further insight on the perils of toxic waste in both marginalized communities and post-industrial locales. As the group rather elegantly put it, Love Canal was now "a symbol not just a site." Unless and until both governments and environmentalists assumed responsibility for the dilapidated parts of God's creation, environmental reform itself would lag.

For the LCHA, an archetypal grassroots group that had already struggled to earn respect both within and beyond the neighborhood, Love Canal was a life-and-death matter. While there always seemed to be some dissent within the LCHA (a vocal minority pushing for different strategies, different leadership, different committee structures) the group had unified around its identity as an authentic voice of outraged residents. Though the LCHA recognized that its cause revolved around something ominously new in American society, the hazards of toxic waste, the group's first priority remained residents' health and well-being—and that meant mass evacuation. LCHA members had been arrested, cajoled, threatened, and ridiculed in their attempt to be heard. For them, Love Canal was about people stuck in an unhealthy and possibly deadly place: the toxic zone.

The differences between the two groups were real. Gibbs worried that the ETF was not truly a residents' organization and thus might siphon support from the LCHA; indeed, she later claimed that the ETF—though well-meaning—may have unwittingly delayed mass evacuation by reducing residents' unity and bargaining power. As for the ETF, its members plugged Love Canal into a range of broader issues, from anti-nuclear concerns to spiritual reawakening in industrial society, believing in some way that the LCHA was too narrowly focused and perhaps a bit too territorial. Finally, the LCHA and the ETF did not always agree about tactics; many members of the former group favored confrontational behavior, while members of the latter organization often counseled nonviolent appeals to morality and conscience.

Yet the two groups found common ground. Gibbs had an at-large voting membership in the ETF in its first year and the LCHA collaborated with religious figures on various protest activities. There was more: both organizations fought in the political and legal realm; both were media savvy; both had galvanizing leaders and committed members. Perhaps most important, both groups saw the chemical disaster as a launching pad for environmental justice struggles nationally. In adopting this approach, they ingeniously turned what Lois Gibbs had called the "problem of being first" on its head.[71] Skeptics continued to accuse Love Canal protesters of exploiting this first-ever chemical emergency for personal gain (by seeking government payouts for poisoned homes). With the purchase of inner-ring houses as a precedent, critics feared an expensive future of government buyouts across the nation. But when LCHA and ETF activists began referring to Love Canal as a proving ground of environmental justice, democracy, and the American way, then their cause stood for something larger and more compelling.

In fact, by the spring of 1979, members of the both LCHA and ETF had made much broader claims about their struggle. In essays, pamphlets, speeches, and congressional testimony, residents and their allies made searing comments about the poisoning of the American landscape, industrial greed and neglect, and government apathy. In the words of LCHA member Grace McCoulf, Love Canal residents had "grown from a tattered neighborhood group to a real national power." Though they wanted "safe and healthy homes to raise our families," McCoulf continued, Love Canal residents also hoped to become a vanguard of citizen environmentalism. Just as they were now "pushing politicians" to prevent future Love Canals from happening, so too would other citizens use Love Canal protest as a model for rallying against environmental pollution in their midst.[72] As the ETF's Jim Clark told Senators, activists wanted a "clean up[,] not a cover up" at Love Canal. By greening their own toxic landscape, Love Canal protestors sought to inspire national laws protecting everyone from the hazards of chemical waste.[73]

As these views indicate, Love Canal activists engaged in more rigorous modes of environmental reflection by 1979 and 1980. Both residents and their allies worked more closely with members of the Sierra Club and Environmental Defense Fund; they read more books and essays about environmentalism; they met in study groups to discuss the religious/philosophical meanings of environmental stewardship, conservation, and natural resource protection; and they formed tighter relationships with labor and social reform groups. Several residents read *Silent Spring* for the first time, believing that Rachel Carson's fable had predicted Love Canal's dystopian reality. Adopting Carson's poetically dark tone, Anne Hillis (who moved between the LCHA and ETF) wrote of the fear she now associated with the change of seasons in Niagara Falls. "Spring will be here soon," she commented in a 1979 *Niagara Gazette* article, "and trees will bloom, grass pop out of the ground, a new surge of life for survival." But "spring... [had] a new meaning" for Love Canal residents, she continued, as melting snow and the onset of a rainy season meant the flushing of toxic leachate into area sewers, rivers and perhaps even homes. Hillis felt a strong connection to Carson, referring to *Silent Spring* as a touchstone of her own activism.[74]

The ETF agreed with Hillis' assessment, reading Carson's words ("I know of no community that has experienced all the misfortunes I describe") as an omen of Love Canal. *Silent Spring* was no "fable of tomorrow," the group proclaimed. "The community in Carson's fable does exist," And that "community has experienced all the misfortunes she describes. The imagined tragedy has become a stark reality. That community is the Love Canal neighborhood of Niagara Falls." Quoting Carson directly, the ETF asserted that "a strange blight crept over the [Love Canal] area and everything began to change." "First, trucks from the city of Niagara Falls came to dump their garbage" in the old canal, and "then chemical corporation trucks came to dump the drums filled with chemical waste products." When Baby Boomers settled here, they could not have known about "the creeping, underground menace" percolating below their yards, schools, and streets. But, the ETF emphasized, an ominous chemical presence was soon confirmed in a series of serious health effects—miscarriages, birth defects, and more—that would have made Carson cry.[75]

According to the ETF's Margeen Hoffman, Love Canal was no accident. "The age of technological man-made disasters had to happen," she asserted. With Americans' increasing reliance on chemicals during the 20th century, Love Canal was preordained. "The practices of the past are our poisons of the present." That meant that "sooner or later... the poisons [would] leach to the surface, migrate through underground streams to our municipal drinking water plants and rivers, enter and infiltrate basements of homes, schools and eventually penetrate not only the air but the bodies of man, woman, children and the children yet-to-be-born." There were thousands of other chemical dump sites in the United States. Collectively, they could spew unknown quantities of poison into the atmosphere, onto various landscapes, and into the water. Turning again to Biblical analogies, the ETF proclaimed: "the bitter harvest of that which has been planted is now being reaped—ecological disaster and human tragedy."[76]

For both the ETF and LCHA, the rise of environmental justice movements mitigated the impact of these human-made disasters. Concerned with protecting everyday environments—not just Big Nature—proponents of environmental justice gained more traction in American public life at the same moment that Love Canal protest matured. Moving from basic arguments in behalf of everyone's rights, environmental justice advocates now argued that socioeconomically marginalized populations suffered disproportionately from the toxic threats of modern industrial society. Like the vernacular landscapes they inhabited, from city grids saturated with hazardous waste facilities to Indian reservations beset by uranium mining refuse, residents of the toxic zone faced environmental perils that others did not. And that happened on a daily basis. Yet neither government nor industry seemed to care. With little political or economic power, residents of the hazardous waste archipelago were in a real sense stuck.

Though environmental justice became a more familiar term in the wake of a 1987 United Church of Christ report linking environmental pollution and racial discrimination, the concept had its roots in a series of community struggles in the late 1970s. Love Canal was perhaps the first movement to gain national and international attention.[77] But it was far from the only community to mobilize around the principles of environmental justice. In St. Louis, Missouri, in 1978, for instance, a federal judge declared that a hazardous waste company had to pay about 700 citizens for the environmental contamination of their landscape. Noting that their environmental rights had been abrogated, the judge declared that justice required compensation to local residents. A year later, Houston researchers and activists launched a discrimination lawsuit, *Dean v. Southwestern Bell*, against the famously un-zoned city for consistently placing hazardous waste facilities in minority neighborhoods. Soon after, a group of North Carolina residents charged county officials with storing hazardous waste in their community, which was largely African-American, without their approval. Over the next several years, similar cases took shape in California and Massachusetts.[78]

Still, Love Canal provided an initial platform for the nascent environmental justice movement. The notoriety born of the crisis made local residents into national celebrities. As Gibbs would put it, Love Canal residents' refusal to accept their toxic conditions redefined not only the place they inhabited but the troubling conditions they and countless others confronted. Love Canalers had "jolted" awake the nation to the twin problems of hazardous waste and the neglect by government and industry of marginalized people threatened by the chemical past. "Eyes were opened to the way our democracy works—and doesn't work," she explained. Indeed, the "residents of this blue-collar community have come to see that corporate power and influence are what dictated the actions at Love Canal, not the health and welfare of citizens." Only by fighting back, she continued, could activists reverse that trend and secure the "public's right to live, work, and play in safety." It was an environmental struggle but a "political fight."[79] Members of the ETF agreed (even if they saw it as an ethical battle too). In no small way, then, both the LCHA and the ETF viewed Love Canal as the environmental justice ur-moment. As Gibbs would tell Congress in 1979, "[w]e are the first but not likely to be the last" toxic crisis. And that meant that more citizens would soon be arguing that their rights had been violated.[80]

By moving from extreme localism to the national level, Gibbs invited people across the country to join the battle for environmental justice. As one scholar put it, Gibbs and the LCHA created a powerful narrative that others could use: that "little people" around the country were "unwitting victims of industrial carelessness."[81] The LCHA used almost that exact phrase in an October 1979 poster, stating that Love Canalers were "the innocent victims of corporate profits." "We cannot lead a normal life," the handbill continued, listing the various reasons that citizens had mobilized. "We cannot go in our basements because of contamination from the Canal; cannot eat anything from our gardens because of soil contamination; cannot allow our children to play in our yards because of contaminated soils...cannot breathe the outside air because of air contamination...cannot have normal children because of the 56% risk of birth defects...cannot sell our homes...cannot have our pregnant daughters, or grandchildren visit [because] it's unsafe for them." Invoking the famous last words of the Pledge of Allegiance —"with liberty and justice for all"— the flyer ended with a lament: despite guarantees to the contrary, there was no "Justice for all Love Canal victims."[82]

As the flyer showed, trust in government—or lack thereof—remained a major concern for Love Canal residents. Eileen Matsulavage, who lived on Greenwald Street, north of the dump, testified that her faith in "government of, for, and by the people" was nearly shattered after experiencing a Star Chamber of bureaucratic horrors. Though air tests would reveal the presence of benzene and toluene in her house, and various medical authorities recommended that she leave, Matsulavage's family remained ineligible for state evacuation funds because it lived a few blocks from the official evacuation zone. The family could not sell its house, either.[83] Not only would it be difficult to find a buyer, but the state would not provide a note certifying the house as "safe." (State officials claimed they could not do so.) "Life at home was hell," she told congressmen in 1979. One state health representative suggested that Matsulavage deal with chemical infiltration by sealing off her basement door with wet rags. In the face of all this, she and her husband refused to believe "that the state would leave us there to rot if there was a health threat." Matsulavage finally moved when her daughter was diagnosed with leukemia. "It was hard enough for us to face the fact that our home is contaminated and that our work and investment was for nothing," she observed. But "what is impossible to accept is the state's denial of what they must surely know to be factual": that the entire Love Canal neighborhood was a contaminated environment...." Matsulavage accused New York (and even federal) officials of "misleading the people by giving them false hope." "We know our health has been affected," she stated. "Why can't we get anybody to believe us?" In a separate letter to the state health commissioner, she challenged Axelrod to issue a broader evacuation order. That, she stated firmly, would "restore my faith in our public officials."[84]

Many residents saw federal intervention as the only way to get people out of the contaminated environment—and to restore trust in government. "Too many people have turned their backs on us," the LCHA's Loretta Gambino told senators in April 1979. "We have been victims of greed in today's society without the least concern for human lives." She blamed not only "Hooker for not telling us the seriousness of the chemicals" that industry produced but "the government...for not having any type of control of these plants" or their disposal operations. The federal government must intervene to establish equity at Love Canal.[85] Anne Hillis agreed, noting that "most Americans assume that the government would be there when they need help." After their collective experience with government officials, however, "the people of the Love Canal are now very disillusioned." Without federal aid to residents, or federal oversight of the chemical industry, Hillis asserted, Love Canalers would become more alienated. And what message would that then send to other communities suffering from chemical threats? As she told the congressmen, her home registered airborne chemical matter but her family remained ineligible for relocation. Little wonder that she remained in "the grip of fear that only those in similar situations can understand."[86]

It all came back to the concept of justice, for Love Canal families felt that they had been sacrificed on the altar of profit and power. Fearful of upsetting the chemical industry and/or bloating government budgets, state and federal officials refused to evacuate people whose homes showed evidence of chemical contamination. Activists wondered: Would the government be so apathetic about hazardous waste in an affluent area? Further research on the nation's toxic grid added ammunition to this argument. As more toxic waste sites were discovered after 1978, and more hazardous waste facilities were planned for the future, they fell into a familiar geographic pattern: certain places—particularly blue-collar locales and communities of color—faced greater toxic threats. Speaking to the World Council of Churches in Austria in May 1980, the ETF's Margeen Hoffman declared that "people of poverty and the people of pollution are one people."[87] Working with Love Canal families and fielding questions about hazardous waste problems in other socioeconomically challenged communities had led Hoffman to see environmental pollution as a potent form of social discrimination with global reach. "No longer can we merely divide into the rich nations and poor nations. While one group may be dying from economic starvation, the other is dying from ecological pollution and companies from the developed world began to make plans to ship their toxic wastes in third world countries, no longer can we remain silent."[88] As Hoffman saw it, polluted lands would always yield sick populations. Until Americans adopted broader programs of environmental stewardship that protected endangered people as well as endangered places, there would be many more Love Canals.

6. Exposing Toxic Waste From Love Canal to Maine

East Gray, a small town off the rugged coast of Maine, seemed like an unlikely place to feel the ripple effects from Love Canal. The town provides easy access to Big Nature and recreational relief from various northeastern cities. Even today, East Gray seems like the antithesis of an industrial place ripe for environmental justice struggles. Yet in 1979, a woman named Cathy Hinds discovered that East Gray's aquifers had been polluted by hazardous waste, especially benzene.[89] The death of her newborn son compelled Hinds to become an environmental activist. When she first mobilized, Hinds knew that few Mainers had experience with toxic waste. But she did what an increasing number of people were doing: Hinds corresponded with Lois Gibbs. Following Gibbs' advice, she began telling neighbors about the potential health impacts of toxic waste. After gathering support, Hinds testified before Maine legislators about the need for a law "monitoring... toxic chemicals[,] beginning with manufacturing all the way through waste disposal." Though speaking publicly of her family life was wrenching—she almost fled the legislature in tears—Hinds' testimony helped secure Maine's first anti-toxic law. "No bill had ever been pushed through committee so quickly," she was told.[90] Like many others, Hinds was now drawn into the Love Canal drama.

She was not alone. From the wilds of Maine to the halls of Congress, "Love Canal" symbolized the perils of a buried toxic past as well as the hope of regenerating the toxic landscape in the future. That development certainly cheered activists, who wanted their hazardous experiences to spur environmental change both locally and nationally.

But Love Canal residents most wanted out of their neighborhood. And by 1980, they worried that this was an increasingly distant possibility.

Widening the Circle of Influence

[W]e are discovering almost every day, in almost every day's newspaper, new hazards that have been released into the atmosphere over the period of our industrial revolution. [They] suddenly crop up in Love Canal, up in New York State... to create enormous hazards to public health, property values, to people.
—Senator Edmund S. Muskie (D-Maine), interview circa 1979[1]

Although known as "Mr. Clean" for his longtime environmental advocacy, Edmund Muskie had little knowledge of the American hazardous waste grid until 1978. A congressional sponsor of the landmark Clean Air and Clean Water Acts, the senator from Maine epitomized environmental politics. In fact, a few months before the Love Canal crisis unfolded, Muskie proposed yet another federal environmental law: a "comprehensive scheme to assure full protection of our national resources" in the wake of oil drilling disasters, tanker spills and toxic train derailments. Yet Muskie soon realized that his plan omitted something important: hazardous waste dumps. Love Canal had illuminated the toxic perils many Americans faced in their own neighborhoods. With an EPA study showing that tens of thousands of old toxic sites had yet to be contained, it was clear that the everyday landscape of homes, playgrounds, and schools needed environmental protection too. "In our society," Muskie told an interviewer in the late 1970s,

we are discovering almost every day, in almost every day's newspaper, new hazards that have been released into the atmosphere over the period of our industrial revolution. [They] suddenly crop up in Love Canal, up in New York State... to create enormous hazards to public health, property values, to people. So we

are constantly dealing with problems that [we] were not antici-
pating, which suddenly create almost insoluble problems for people
and communities... [A]ll of these poisons and toxic materials
were buried in landfill sites here, there, and elsewhere and sadly
begin leaking in underground water, or into lakes and rivers,
streams[,] only to rise up to hit people in the face with disease,
with cancer, declining property values so on.[2]

For Muskie, Love Canal was revelatory. It showed that federal law
lagged behind the mounting problem of hazardous waste. After hearing
Love Canal residents' testimony, he believed that the time had come for a
national statute governing toxic waste remediation—what he would refer
to as a "clean land" law.[3] As Muskie's shifting understanding of hazardous
waste revealed, Love Canal touched an ever-widening circle of politicians,
reporters, and citizens. In this way, Love Canal transcended itself. No
longer just a toxic place, or even a powerful symbol, Love Canal became a
metaphor for new modes of environmental thinking and new ways of environmental organizing. Even if people had no idea where Love Canal
was, they understood that it represented a newfound determination to
uncover, and then solve, the problem of toxic trash.

1. Clean Landscapes Beyond Love Canal

Love Canal spawned a new round of environmental assessment locally and
nationally. After families mobilized in Lasalle, residents in nearby Lewiston
began complaining about their toxic environment as well. Lasalle and
Lewiston had been the bookends of William Love's power canal. Now they
shared a toxic past. After Lewiston residents read about Love Canal waste,
they began researching their own landscape's history. They learned that a
chemical company (not Hooker) had utilized this end of Love's abandoned waterway to deposit hazardous waste during the 1950s. Residents'
complaints prompted local officials to test area soils.[4] The scope of inquiry
soon expanded beyond the old canal zone. By Fall 1978, Niagara County
officials had tested "38 chemical dump sites" scattered across the region,
especially those that flowed into the Niagara River and "could possibly

affect people and homes." "The problem is," a state Department of Environmental Conservation official said, "we don't actually know what went into any of those dumps."[5] With Love Canal constantly in the news, citizens throughout Western New York demanded answers.[6]

That meant creating a toxic waste dump inventory, something that did not exist before Love Canal became a public issue. Although several "chemical waste calamities" had occurred in the state, as Michael Desmond reported in the Buffalo *Courier Express* in September, New York had "no record of how many waste dumps" existed.[7] State officials scrambled to "determine where present sites might become future disasters."[8] The following summer, state Senator Thomas Bartosiewicz began surveying toxic waste sites across the Empire State. Released in March 1980, his report bore an ominous title: "609 . . . and Counting[:] Hazardous Wastes and the Public's Health in New York State." Documenting the hundreds of toxic sites that littered the landscape from Long Island to Lewiston, the report shocked Empire State politicians. Although heavily industrialized locales like Erie and Niagara counties contained over 200 toxic dumps, rural areas seemingly untouched by the 20th century chemical revolution also registered an alarming number of hazardous waste sites as well. Allegany County, located on the Pennsylvania border and home to the beloved state park created with the support of luminaries like Elon Huntington Hooker, had five; Oswego, along the scenic shores of Lake Ontario, had twenty-two. The list went on: St. Lawrence, thirteen; Saratoga, thirteen; Rensselaer, eight; Steuben, four; and even tiny Yates, five, all registered on New York's toxic grid. In fact, of the more than sixty counties surveyed (including all five boroughs of New York City), only eight had no hazardous-waste dumps. Unsurprisingly, few toxic sites sat in the affluent areas. But the bigger story was that New York's toxic grid was still expanding. Only by monitoring these sites—and creating an "early warning" system about their potential health effects—would New York prevent the next generation of Love Canal–style disasters from occurring.[9] Armed with Bartosiewicz's report, state politicians planned tougher laws on hazardous waste disposal.

Federal officials scrutinized the nation's hazardous grid too. Estimating that there were well over 30,000 uncontained dump sites across the United States—and perhaps as many as 2,000 that could be termed lethal—EPA representatives began talking openly about the need for a national toxic remediation law. In Congress, John LaFalce moved from mobilizing disaster relief funds to advocating for a national hazardous waste remediation law.[10] In 1979, LaFalce wearily recalled that he had testified before congressional committees "no less than a dozen times over the last year on the need for new laws and regulations which would authorize the federal government to clean up, contain, and monitor abandoned sites as well as compensate victims for personal injury and property damage."[11]

LaFalce called this a "super fund approach" to toxic waste. At joint Senate-House field hearings in Niagara Falls in May 1979, LaFalce explained that Americans needed a comprehensive national law "to better handle not only Love Canal but future Love Canal problems."[12] While noting that the spate of environmental laws passed during the 1970s helped improve national environmental quality, LaFalce reminded his colleagues that the Clean Water Act, RCRA, and other federal statutes had provided only limited aid to Love Canal families. For example, section 504 of the Clean Water Act, according to LaFalce, allowed the EPA to offer "immediate assistance... to cope with imminent hazards that exist in areas such as the Love Canal." And yet, he continued, Congress dedicated only $10 million to this provision of the law—hardly enough to deal with the single case of Love Canal, much less "the thousands or so abandoned hazardous waste sites that exist across this country."[13]

As his ardent support of stronger toxic waste legislation indicated, LaFalce was a genuine convert to the Love Canal cause. Indeed, few people better exemplified Love Canal's widening circle of influence than the man who had been concerned with the matter since he first called for tests at the old dump. As a freshman congressman in 1976, LaFalce was not concerned with toxic waste. And before 1978, as he recalled in an interview thirty years later, LaFalce had "never even heard" of Lois Gibbs or any of the other women who would soon turn Love Canal into a *cause célèbre*.[14] But they were "my constituents," he said firmly, and he felt obligated to address their concerns about a potentially hazardous environment. LaFalce, who hailed from nearby Tonawanda, came to understand the "human dimensions" of the crisis, especially the frustration and fear associated with Love Canal life.[15] He was involved in many memorable events in the Love Canal neighborhood, from confrontational public meetings in the summer of 1978 to a bevy of toxic tours with various health and political officials in the ensuing years. "I represented Love Canal," he shrugged when asked about dealing with the fiery band of residents in the embattled neighborhood. "I was dealing with human beings... and the instinct for self-survival... is a natural one."[16]

LaFalce came to believe that he had to wring greater meaning out of the crisis in his congressional district. By 1979, he was committed not only to aiding Love Canal families but securing comprehensive federal laws aimed at future hazardous waste cleanup. "Love Canal is only the first of what may prove to be many exploding ticking time bombs," he testified. "Yet the federal government has been remiss in its responsibility to the public to act in this case and formulate an approach for handling future Love Canals."[17] A superb legislator, LaFalce roamed congressional halls to win friends for his "super fund." As LaFalce told anyone who would listen, he believed that such a law would protect people and places on the nation's hazardous waste grid.[18] "What I saw in [Love Canal] basements and backyards frightened me," he remembered of his own toxic tours.[19] And so no matter the opposition, LaFalce vowed to keep fighting.

2. The Green Beat: Love Canal and Environmental News Coverage

Citizens and politicians were not the only ones re-examining hazardous landscapes beyond Love Canal. An increasing number of journalists also investigated the national dimensions of toxic waste. Reporters were, of course, essential to Love Canal's emergence as a public issue. *Niagara Gazette* reporter Michael Brown's early and sustained coverage gave Love Canal "legs," making it a compelling human-interest drama as well as environmental crisis. From there, a multitude of regional and national scribes covered the story. From the *Buffalo Evening News* to the *New York Times*, Love Canal was routinely in the media spotlight.

While many reporters came to Niagara Falls, others went around the country to discern Love Canal's impact. Michael Desmond, who worked for the now defunct Buffalo *Courier Express*, logged thousands of miles and produced a dozen stories on "the health and safety threat posed by the mishandling of toxic chemical wastes" across the United States. Desmond's series "Bury Now, Pay Later" showed that neither state nor federal governments were prepared to deal with Love Canals brewing elsewhere. "Since hazardous waste isn't going to go away or stop coming, something has to be done, and done quickly," he wrote. "That may seem obvious to some, but it is apparently not obvious to a wide array of bureaucrats in various levels of government."[20] Having visited sites in Louisiana and California, Desmond realized that Love Canal was *the* rule of the hazardous waste road. He referred to RCRA—the federal statute that many people thought would deal with the generation of toxic waste moving forward—as a "dead letter" law for old dump sites. He also wrote of apathetic federal officials who had only recently begun to study uncontained hazardous waste sites, arguing that "taxpayers are being hit for [the] massive cleanup bills" at dumps around the country. "Perhaps if some of the bureaucrats wandering through the problem were forced to live along the Love Canal in Niagara Falls," he pointedly observed, "they might do something."[21] For his vigorous efforts, Desmond won awards from both the EPA and the National Association of Journalists.

As Desmond's series indicated, Love Canal was anything but an isolated story. It had inspired people around the country to investigate their landscape's potentially toxic past. Little wonder that Love Canal remained big news. From *Time* and *Newsweek* to "The Phil Donahue Show" and NBC's "Today," more and more media outlets covered the residents' saga as a potent symbol of the times. Love Canal even hit primetime with an ABC News documentary: "The Killing Ground." Premiering on March 28, 1979, the show examined Love Canal against the backdrop of toxic troubles in New Jersey, Louisiana, and Michigan. Hosted by Brit Hume (now better known as a Fox News host), "The Killing Ground" showed unforgettable pictures of tarred landscapes and angry citizens screaming at local, state, and federal officials to do something about the polluted environment. Premiering during congressional hearings on Love Canal, "The Killing Ground" helped crystallize national concern about hazardous waste. By its encore showing on August 21, 1980—with Hume updating the toxic plight of various communities—America's toxic past was no longer a novel issue. "It is getting to be a familiar spectacle," Richard

Shepard wrote in the "Home" section of the *New York Times*, "the television views of chemical dumps, of citizens enraged and hurting, of disclaimers by officials that lethal waste problems do not belong on their desks."[22]

Yet media coverage did not manufacture environmental discontent at Love Canal; it reflected it. Indeed, "The Killing Ground," like most reporting on the toxic grid, covered issues citizens, politicians, and health scientists deemed increasingly important. John Dowling Jr.'s review in *The Bulletin of the Atomic Scientists* hailed "The Killing Ground" for its "careful examination of the problem of hazardous chemical wastes." "Perhaps [chemical] companies...will face up to the problems and try to do things right," Dowling wrote, concluding that government agencies must act with increased vigilance on the matter.[23] With no major state or national law governing toxic waste remediation, press vigilance became a critical means of uncovering the buried and potentially harmful nature of the nation's chemical past.

This is a critical point, for traditions of environmental reportage going into, and coming out of, Love Canal show that hazardous waste was not deemed an important topic until citizens mobilized in Niagara Falls. The Green Beat, as environmental coverage became known, emerged only after World War II when a new generation of reporters examined environmental issues on a daily basis. *The New York Times*, which sent a stream of reporters to Love Canal, was one of the first major newspapers to make the environment weekly news at midcentury. John B. Oakes, the influential *Times* editor who also created the modern "Op-Ed" page, launched a "Conservation" column in the 1950s. Written in a lively style, Oakes' columns looked at endangered species, polluted rivers, threatened parkland, and soil conservation efforts, among other concerns. Oakes even offered one of the earliest journalistic examinations of chemical hazards. "The indiscriminate use of chemical sprays to eliminate ragweed and other noxious plants is condemned as harmful, shortsighted and self-defeating," he began his "Conservation" column on November 7, 1954, referring to new studies of the matter.[24] Like Rachel Carson, who began to consider the issue at about the same time, he argued that DDT and other pesticides had been overused. The Audubon Society, the National Wildlife Federation, and the Natural Resources Defense Council (NRDC) all subsequently hailed Oakes as a pioneer environmental journalist.[25]

Despite his powerful example, Oakes did not engender a wave of followers in environmental reporting. In fact, prior to 1980, fewer than 100 environmental journalists worked at American newspapers. After Love Canal, however, the Green Beat exploded, with roughly 1,400 environmental journalists working at the dawn of the 21st century.[26] Love Canal did not cause this shift by itself. But it was a critical part of a new journalistic sensibility that allowed reporters to turn environmental coverage into something completely different. No longer was the Green Beat essentially about nature "out there," where hermits and prophets brought back transcendent news about the wilderness, or the philosophical meaning of nature itself, which, since Thoreau, had been a key strain of environmental literature; rather, Love Canal coverage made people a key part of the environmental story. In short, Love Canal allowed reporters to picture the environment with a human face.

Interestingly, the Buffalo-Niagara region already had one of the nation's earliest Green Beat reporters: Paul MacClennan of *The Buffalo Evening News*. By the time he arrived at Love Canal, MacClennan had covered Western New York's Rust Belt environment for roughly a decade. One of his early environmental beats was the brawny town of Lackawanna, south of Buffalo, where the hulking Bethlehem Steel plant employed over 20,000 people. Although the plant remained the lifeblood of the town, residents registered increasing concern over the soot that rained down on their cars and homes, making summer look like winter and winter even more grey and grim. MacClennan covered investigations of Bethlehem Steel, including EPA lawsuits that charged the company with violating new clean air standards.[27]

As the dean of the local Green Beat, it was not surprising that MacClennan covered Love Canal. But he stayed with the story longer than anyone else, filing a staggering 300-plus articles between the late 1970s and the early 1990s. He covered other concerns too, often using his own environment column in the *Buffalo Evening News* as a clearinghouse for a variety of pressing issues: the near-death of Lake Erie via phosphate pollution, the health of New York State's canal system, the rise of citizen environmentalism. Just as important, MacClennan assisted other reporters at Love Canal, making sure that they mastered the story. "Oh, he was great," David Shribman, who as a young scribe was often paired with

MacClennan, recalled of his tough but lovable colleague. "I learned so much from Paul."[28]

On MacClennan's Rust Belt beat, one could see the transformation of environmental news coverage: where before he and other local reporters examined places (polluted cityscapes, for example), by the 1980s they focused much more on people. Indeed, MacClennan often emphasized the way that Love Canal engendered new modes of environmentalism. "The Love Canal situation has riveted national and international attention on the problem of toxic, cancer-causing chemicals seeping into the [home] environment," he and Shribman wrote in one early Love Canal story.[29] Here and elsewhere, MacClennan (and Shribman) emphasized the ultimate lesson of Love Canal: people were a critical part of the environment, whether as actors or reactors, and they must always be inserted into the story.

Despite MacClennan's environmental expertise, no reporter better exemplified the new journalistic sensibility coming out of Love Canal than Michael Brown. A Baby Boomer who was roughly the same age as many of the young families he followed at Love Canal, Brown had not been trained as an environmental journalist. A Niagara Falls native, he worked as a city reporter and then columnist for the *Niagara Falls Gazette* (later shortened to the *Niagara Gazette*). Curious about Love Canal, he covered the engineers probing the buried dump. The more he followed the story, the more disturbing it became, especially when tests revealed potential health threats to area residents. By the summer of 1978, his articles on the problematic nature of the buried dump epitomized media coverage of the Love Canal saga. His visceral reporting style—influenced by the so-called New Journalism of the 1960s, where investigative correspondents inserted themselves into the story—brought toxic landscapes alive for readers. Brown went inside people's homes, where chemical waste oozed down basement walls, and out to their backyards, where corroded barrels erupted through the soil. Inhaling the foul odors that had long defined industrial progress in Niagara Falls, Brown observed that Love Canal residents had it worse than some chemical workers. "When you sit down with Aileen Vorhees in her kitchen," he wrote of the 99th Street family whose property abutted the canal and helped inspire Brown's earliest stories on the neighborhood, "you get the noxious odor of Love

Canal chemicals that have vaporized throughout her home." Brown was not sure if even a visitor would be safe there for an hour at such a place.[30]

Populated by anxious and fearful residents who had experienced miscarriages, cancers, and a host of other troubling ailments, Brown's Love Canal was not the suburban idyll its residents once thought they inhabited. Driven by an old-fashioned sense of justice, he became a voice for aggrieved Love Canalers. "The System Flounders While Residents Fume," a typical headline above one of his stories proclaimed on July 30, 1978, only a few days before the blockbuster state report noted that Love Canal families faced a clear and present health "peril." "You're killing our children by not ordering all families out," he quoted Lois Gibbs as shouting at state officials a bit later, after a partial evacuation was ordered. He interviewed another woman who said ruefully, "I don't want my children to die before they're forty."[31]

Though Brown's sympathy for residents was a vital aspect of his stories, his reporting expressed a broader concern with government and industrial accountability. In the post-Watergate era, where politicians struggled against a gnawing suspicion that they did not act in the public interest, it is unsurprising that Brown meditated on these matters. As much as he relied on citizens for insight, he regularly quoted political and administrative sources as well, making sure that they had a chance to explain (or impugn) themselves. Readers thus had a chance to decide whether or not government and industry acted wisely. Appearing on the ABC show "Nightline" in 1981, for instance, he refuted Hooker's claim that in the 1940s the Love Canal area was a barren countryside far from any human populations. "There are pictures of a neighborhood just a few blocks away," he said with exasperation.[32] As Brown showed again and again, the concerns of government and industry officials often did not align with those of residents. Until that gap narrowed, the social and political costs of Love Canal would continue to rise.

Brown filed more than a hundred stories on Love Canal. He also traveled through America's toxic waste archipelago. His articles appeared in *The Atlantic Monthly* and *The New York Times*; his two books, *Laying Waste* and *Toxic Cloud*, were best-sellers. No matter the venue, Brown's message remained the same: Americans had only begun to confront the Chemical Century's impact on the landscape. In New Jersey, he noted, coverage of leaching hazardous waste dumpsites dominated the local news, prompting deep concerns among both politicians and citizens, about the effect of chemicals on regional drinking water supplies. In Michigan, he examined polluted wells near a Dow Chemical plant that blighted family farms and harmed wildlife. In Pennsylvania, Texas, and Missouri, he showed that industrial lubricants were spilling into the landscape at an alarming rate despite technologies to recycle them.[33] For Brown, many Americans now lived in "Love Canal, USA": a nation saturated with toxic waste.[34]

By the early 1980s, Brown's searing portraits of the toxic zone were merely the vanguard of a growing roster of articles and books re-examining the nation's hazardous-waste problem. Writers emphasized the human impact of hazardous waste and the raw emotions experienced by communities mired in toxic trash. Ominous titles, like Irene Kiefer's *Poisoned Land* (1982), predicted that toxic "time bombs" were "waiting to explode" across the United States as more and more citizens studied their local landscape histories. "The episode at Love Canal is one of the worst environmental disasters ever," Kiefer, a former chemical industry insider, observed. "But it is only part of the story." The real saga lay in the thousands of uncontained hazardous waste sites across the United States. Though she struck a positive note about the possibility of regulating hazardous waste in the future, Kiefer stated bluntly that "cleansing our poisoned land of its lethal burden will take many years and billions of dollars."[35] But it could be done, she optimistically predicted, if government and industry faced the reality of Love Canal.

David Morell and Christopher Magorian, academics who moved between university and policy-making worlds, were not so sure. Believing that hazardous waste disposal had reached a crisis point in America—with more communities rising in protest over the siting of hazardous materials—they called for more open policies guiding the placement of toxic dumping grounds, incinerators, and dumps. Failing that, they argued in *Siting Hazardous Waste Facilities* (1982), the nation's toxic problem would grow worse, with more communities exploding like Love Canal.[36]

3. Just the Facts: Hooker and Love Canal

As the company whose toxic byproducts sat at the center of controversy, Hooker had an obvious stake in the Love Canal saga. While some

commentators characterized Hooker's response as apathetic, the company responded to the crisis in a variety of ways.[37] Initially, Hooker tried
to contain the disaster narrative by supporting remediation plans. In early
August of 1978, the company announced that it would provide $200,000
"towards cleaning up the Love Canal"—as long as government entities
supplied the rest of the remediation funds (which might total roughly a
half-million dollars, according to early—and, as it turned out, very low—
estimates).[38] But Hooker maintained that the company "is not liable for
any claims of damage or harm that may result from this unfortunate situation," in the words of vice-president Bruce Davis. [39] Like other Hooker
officials, Davis emphasized this point again and again: the company was
no longer legally responsible for the dump. As Davis informed a congressional subcommittee on hazardous-waste, from "1953 to 1978, Hooker
Chemical had no connection with this property, no ownership of the
property. It was owned by the school board." And because Niagara Falls,
through its contractors and housing developers, had breached the dump
by building streets, sewers, and school foundations, it was the responsible
party.[40]

    Though it repeated this claim many times, Hooker learned that it had
to respond more creatively and vigorously to Love Canal activism. As one
resident lectured Congress in 1979, Hooker should not have been allowed
to turn "the scenic wonder" of Niagara Falls "into a chemical dump."[41]
With comments like that circulating through political venues and the
media, Hooker had a major public relations problem on its hands. It had
to do more than claim that other parties were responsible for the disaster.

    In fact, Hooker soon sought to neutralize some of the essential claims
born of Love Canal, from the idea that the company was morally—if not
legally—culpable for the chemical crisis to the notion that its chemicals
had poisoned the world. Indeed, the company even created a newsletter
that rebutted any and all claims made by area activists. Known as "Factline,"
the newsletter was launched in April 1979, soon after Love Canal residents began testifying in Congress. Factline featured monthly and bi-
monthly brochures that addressed various aspects of the Love Canal
problem from the company's standpoint. Distributed to media outlets
around the country, the sturdy three-paneled foldouts were the antithesis
of the space-age advertising campaigns unleashed by Hooker. But that

was precisely the point, for Factline's no-frills style allowed the company to claim that it was an honest and even caring corporate neighbor trying to cut through the hype of Love Canal. Hoping to convey "a more accurate perspective" on "the emotional and highly controversial Love Canal situation," Hooker distributed roughly 10,000 copies of Factline between 1979 and 1982.[42]

With attention-grabbing titles—"A Hard Look at the Love Canal," the first issue declared—Factline echoed corporate critiques of environmentalism dating back to *Silent Spring*. Not only was the Love Canal crisis overblown, Factline claimed, it had been guided by emotionalism. For that reason, "we have been updating employees, their families and friends, and Hooker's neighbors in the Niagara area regarding the *facts* of the Love Canal problem. . . ." And the facts, Hooker proclaimed, would reveal that the company had acted responsibly.[43]

Hooker also claimed that it always followed best practices when dealing with chemical waste. At Love Canal, Hooker asserted, dumping proceeded openly and via city permit in the 1940s and 1950s.[44] As corporate president Donald Baeder told members of the banking community worried about Hooker's ability to withstand the crisis, "a task force of the American Institute of Chemical Engineers recently concluded that the canal site would conform to most provisions of present pending federal legislation," including RCRA requirements that toxic waste be monitored and properly disposed of in closed landfills, among other things (critics would take issue with this point).[45] And when Hooker deeded the dump to Niagara Falls, the company told city representatives that chemicals sat below the landscape. Making sure its perspective got out to the public, Factline reprinted *Wall Street Journal* stories showing that company officials had made this clear in the 1950s and, further, that both Hooker and the city had "an unwritten understanding at the time of the gift that the [school] board would not dispose of the land in any way that might lead to . . . construction work" at the canal. Hooker stipulated that only surface activity, such as the building of a park or playground, would be appropriate for the site.[46]

By conjuring a history of open corporate practices, Hooker tried to turn the tide of public opinion and even picture itself as an aggrieved party. As "a good company" that had "been around 75 years," as Baeder claimed, Hooker tried to follow local, state, and national rules on toxic waste disposal and oversight. But now it was in "the national spotlight" because Americans were reconsidering chemical wastes in their midst.[47] As Baeder saw it, Americans loved Hooker's products but had chosen to ignore their environmental underside. That was unfair to both Hooker and the chemical industry, for it meant judging past actions by present-day standards.

But Hooker did not simply attack local environmentalists. Rather strikingly, some company officials conceded that Hooker was in a business that produced dangerous byproducts, including highly toxic materials that were ultimately disposed in the earth. This stunning admission departed from chemical company protocol. But this turn towards realism allowed Hooker to claim that it understood the grave realities of chemical production and disposal—and that it would never sacrifice either workers' or the public's health. "How [is] Hooker…meeting the challenge of environmental pollution problems [at its Niagara Falls plant]?" one edition of Factline asked. Before answering that question, the pamphlet inserted a telling quote from a Hooker production employee who "recently told a newspaper reporter: 'the Niagara plant ain't no chocolate factory.'" According to Factline, the employee "was simply stating a fact of life": chemical culture produced "rather dangerous but necessary substances— substances important to the welfare and economy of our nation." But the public should not be concerned, Factline continued, for Hooker trained workers in the proper "handling and manufacturing of chemicals," always taking "steps to ensure that conditions both inside and outside the plant are as safe as current technology allows."[48]

In this way, Hooker acknowledged its products' dangerous but necessary nature. Some officials went one step further by also conceding the importance of environmentalism writ large in modern American society. Bruce Davis even offered backhanded praise to Rachel Carson. "Many people date the nation's first general awareness of the environmental movement to the publication in 1962 of Rachel Carson's 'Silent Spring,'" he observed. Though Davis underscored Carson's importance as an environmental prophet, he ultimately agreed with Baeder: chemical companies still needed time to adjust to the shifting environmental landscape left in her wake.[49]

The same held true on the public health front. While Hooker officials slammed Love Canal protest as emotional and overhyped, they also realized that a revolution in public health had made Americans more sensitive to the topic than ever before. No longer could chemical companies simply ignore public concerns. Yet, as Davis told Congress, this was a mixed blessing. New technical instrumentation had made it "possible to detect trace quantities of chemicals in the range of parts per billion and even parts per trillion." These microscopic measurements were "mind-boggling," for "one part per billion is akin to locating one bad apple among 2 million barrels of apples." As Davis put it, the problem of hazardous waste appeared to be getting worse in part because new technologies made it seem more prevalent.[50]

The reality was more complex, Davis stated. On the one hand, as he explained, "in the manufacture of all of [our] chemical products, wastes or residues are inherently generated," some of which are "potentially harmful to human health or the environment." On the other hand, he said, the public health risk associated with chemical production remained low. To back his point, Davis compared chemicals to "carbon monoxide," a "substance that may be classified as toxic." "But," he continued, "this doesn't necessarily mean its sheer presence in the atmosphere creates a hazardous situation. If you did, automobiles would have been banned long ago. By the same token, Hooker makes products intrinsically toxic, but they are beneficial to mankind when used properly. We attempt to make absolutely sure that all of our plant practices in handling in disposing of toxic materials do not present a hazard to our people or to the surrounding communities."[51]

Here and elsewhere, Hooker officials paid homage to the formidable nature of Love Canal protest even as they critiqued it. In a very short period of time, local residents had compelled a major chemical company to admit publicly—and in Congress!—that its own products were hazardous to the environment. This admission forced Hooker to recalibrate its Love Canal strategy. Once again, Hooker got creative, picturing itself as a caring corporate partner in Western New York. Bruce Davis became perhaps Hooker's most visible bearer of this message. Before being transferred to Texas in the early 1980s, Davis was a whirlwind of activity. He testified before state and federal officials, met often with business leaders in Western New York, constantly fielded questions from reporters, and even appeared opposite Lois Gibbs on the radio. Davis also became the literal poster boy for Hooker print ads in 1979. "Bruce Cares," the ads proclaimed. "And don't let anybody tell you differently." Flanked by a diverse and working-class crew of citizens worried that anti-Hooker action might destroy the local chemical industry (and thus jobs), Davis projected an air of concern. Indeed, though his position as vice president of the allied chemicals group made him an expert in certain technical areas of production, Davis' stint as Hooker's point-man played to the idea that the company valued not just profits but community and family as well. Through him, Hooker felt confident about declaring (as it did in another print ad) that "Hooker Cares. And we want you to know it."[52]

4. Hooker's Reframing of Love Canal

Hooker's attempt to reframe perception of the Love Canal crisis was more than a PR stunt.[53] By 1979, Hooker was the subject of increasing environmental scrutiny both regionally and nationally. On the other side of Niagara Falls, the company's Hyde Park dump drew the interest of federal officials. Opened after the Love Canal dump was closed, Hyde Park took in four times as much waste as the Love Canal site between 1953 and 1974. Comprising 16 acres, it also sat near a neighborhood with hundreds of residents and a university (though no homes or schools sat on the dump proper). Part of the dump drained into Bloody Run Creek, which discharged into the Niagara River Gorge, potentially spreading toxic leachate—including C-56 and dioxin—throughout the region.[54] In December 1979, the U.S. Department of Justice filed interconnected lawsuits against Hooker and its parent company, Occidental Petroleum (which purchased Hooker in 1968), to "clean up [Love Canal, Hyde Park and other] chemical waste dump sites in Niagara Falls...posing substantial danger to residents of the area." The nearly $120 million lawsuit, as one EPA administrator declared, "should serve notice to those who generate or handle hazardous wastes that these kinds of dangers will no longer will be tolerated by the American public."[55]

At the state level, Hooker was under increasing scrutiny from New York's Department of Environmental Conservation. According to the *New York Times*, the company "had committed 400 violations of state law by dumping toxic chemical wastes into landfills on Long Island." As a local Republican official declared after releasing internal company memos illuminating the extent of such dumping, Hooker had buried a "whole delicatessen of chemicals" in the eastern part of the state, including "millions of pounds of such substances as vinyl chloride, trichloroethylene, and perchloroethylene." While Hooker conceded the accuracy of these reports, it claimed not to have violated any laws. Indeed, a corporate spokesman argued that the uncovered memos illustrated Hooker's concern with environmental impacts. Like others in the wake of Love Canal, the official said, Hooker wanted "to determine whether there were any possible problems from [its] past practices" at other dumps and had thus opened its records for examination. New York officials replied that the company ignored recent regulations preventing the dumping of hazardous waste into municipal landfills. At the Syosset dump, near Oyster Bay, state DEC representatives worried that leachate from Hooker's plastic waste might contaminate area drinking water. But years of negotiations over a clean-up settlement with the company had not produced any agreement on getting the dump remediated. "After going around and around with them," an exasperated Long Island official noted, "I'm convinced they deal in rhetoric."[56] Hooker held off settlement talks a bit longer but the negative publicity from Long Island was not welcome at all.

On the national front, the news was not any better, as Hooker faced nearly 20 investigations of its disposal sites beyond New York. At the plant in Montague, Michigan, opened in the 1950s and located roughly 200 miles northwest of Detroit, state health investigators found chemical leachate emanating from an 880-acre dump located behind the company's main production facility. National media outlets told tales of Michigan's pristine wilds—and some community drinking wells—being fouled by C-56 and other toxic compounds from the Montague dump. "There's no doubt about it," John Shauver in the Department of Natural Resources declared in September 1979, "that's the worst environmental contamination problem in the state of Michigan—in size and in scope and in the company's unwillingness to, over the years, take care of their own mess."[57] By 1980, Occidental had to negotiate a multiyear, multimillion-dollar clean-up settlement with Michigan that averted an even more costly lawsuit. The deal provided a "sound environmental solution to the problem at Montague," in the words of the state attorney general, and allowed Hooker/Occidental to bask in the aura of "responsible corporate action."[58] But

Love Canal left its mark here too. Had the Montague dump been discovered in another time—and not in the late '70s against the backdrop of rising citizen protest hundreds of miles away in Niagara Falls—the company would likely have defended itself more vigorously in court.[59] Occidental founder Armand Hammer was known to be a fierce negotiator and he counted legendary lawyer Louis Nizer among his advisors. But, with the Love Canal spotlight shining brightly all the way to Michigan, Hammer and Nizer thought the better of it; reaching an environmental deal at Montague made the most sense for these two hard-nosed men accustomed to getting their way.

In fact, Hooker conceded the toxic nature of its Michigan dump as well. As Bruce Davis told reporters, the Montague facility did not represent "the [company's] best practice." "What we did in Michigan was not the worst practice of the industry. It was fairly common."[60] And yet, the Montague example was bad. As Davis' comments revealed, Hooker was far from the swaggering company that helped launch chemicals into the jet age. Though its midcentury ad campaigns had spun magical fables of a chemically altered world with no underside, by the late 1970s Hooker realized that it had to admit that it was in a compromised position. "For some time," Harry Boyte's book, *The Backyard Revolution* (1981), declared, "the American public seemed unconcerned and passive when it came to political affairs—whether local or national in scope." No longer, for since the mid-1970s "an identifiable citizen movement was beginning to grow out of spaces as personal and immediate as one's own backyard or block."[61] Though it did not focus on the crisis in Niagara Falls, Boyte's book illuminated the gritty style of grassroots protest launched at Love Canal and in no small way framing Hooker's future. As Boyte showed, citizen-oriented protest was here to stay. And Hooker had to take stock of that in and beyond Western New York.

This became clear in the summer of 1980, when Hooker/Occidental issued a special report on the Love Canal crisis to the nation's financial community. (Hooker's name was removed from the company in 1982.) Ostensibly aimed at building confidence in recently shaken energy and chemical markets—on top of Love Canal, the OPEC embargo cut oil supplies and raised fuel prices to alarming levels—the report turned into another public defense of Hooker in the age of grassroots environmentalism. Entitled "The Other Side of Love Canal: Facts vs. Fallacies," the pamphlet-sized document repeated many of Factline's assertions (that Hooker had adequately warned the school board about the chemical nature of Love Canal, that the neighborhood was not as hazardous as residents claimed, that Hooker/Occidental was a caring corporate entity) while also emphasizing the company's ability to withstand the financial turmoil of environmental challenges nationally. Yet the company also emphasized its newfound concern with the "public's health and safety." "Hooker has been developing and implementing remedial programs at the waste site properties it presently owns," Armand Hammer himself told financial representatives gathered in New York City's Waldorf Astoria hotel. And, he continued, it was engaging in "cooperative efforts" with officials in New York and California to reach remediation agreements like those made in Michigan—clean-up covenants based not on fear and hysteria but sound science, environmental concern and "responsible corporate action."[62] Hammer's words were designed to soothe anyone concerned about Hooker/Occidental's post–Love Canal standing, environmental, financial, or otherwise. Yet Hammer's stand also underscored residents' broader impact on corporate environmental practices. As Hammer now vigorously asserted, "public health and safety" would ever be a part of his corporate mantra.[63]

Back in Niagara Falls, the Love Canal crisis certainly took a toll on Hooker personnel. Already reeling from several corporate shakeups after Occidental had purchased the company, Hooker (which remained a subsidiary) was not ready for the onslaught of media attention and citizen activism fomented by the crisis. "What a mess that was," recalled John W. Johnstone, a former Hooker sales representative. Having worked at Hooker for over two decades after arriving in 1954, Johnstone lived through the company's midcentury boom.[64] It was, he said, "the real go-go time of the [chemical] industry" as a whole, an era of almost "incomprehensible" growth.[65] As far as he could recall, no one ever mentioned the Love Canal dump or any other disposal site. Johnstone left Hooker in 1975 to pursue other opportunities in the industry, but he saw former colleagues "just destroyed" by Love Canal. Well into the 1990s, he believed that "hysteria ruled the waves, not good science." In his eyes, the whole saga was "a disaster" for Hooker too. "That would've probably destroyed me" as well, Johnstone bluntly commented.[66]

Over time, Johnstone realized that Hooker was not alone in facing new scrutiny of its hazardous waste practices. Working elsewhere, he saw that few if any chemical companies had sophisticated environmental disposal and/or monitoring programs before Love Canal. "If you look at the environmental side of it," Johnstone observed, midcentury hazardous waste management "was almost sort of a hobby of plant managers. They just sort of had it as a tag-on responsibility if it happened to be on site." As he put it, "abandoned or closed sites [were] scattered all over the place, and nobody had any responsibility for them. They just sort of sat out there." Love Canal was not a singular event, then, but a warning sign for the entire chemical industry. To be sure, he believed that citizens, government, and media outlets alike overreacted to the problem. Yet even Johnstone conceded that Love Canal had prompted sober—and perhaps necessary—reflection among chemical insiders.[67]

He saw this firsthand in Niagara Falls, where Johnstone remained off and on during the Love Canal crisis. He became the senior vice president of the chemical group at Olin Corporation, which had a production facility in the area. Though Olin had already faced scrutiny over its production of DDT, the company's broader disposal practices did not attract much attention until the Love Canal crisis. In 1979, a federal judge subpoenaed Olin's dumping records to better understand the scope of toxic waste troubles in Niagara Falls. As more communities worried about abandoned hazardous waste sites in their midst, Johnstone realized that corporate hazardous waste policy had not kept pace with the times. "There really was a focus on getting our hands around this environmental issue," he recalled, especially in light of potential litigation. Add to that the liability concerns of the insurance industry and it was clear to Johnstone and others that environmental compliance must now become a more formal part of good corporate citizenship.[68]

At Olin, Johnstone helped transform chemical production and disposal practices. Hazardous waste monitoring and oversight was so new that he ended up moving people from "engineering [and] R&D... [and] even sales and marketing" over to "community affairs and the whole thing." Though he remained critical of citizen environmentalism, Johnstone offered a backhanded compliment to activists by noting that they compelled chemical companies to revolutionize their operational and public relations approaches to hazardous waste disposal. And that produced tangible and long-lasting results.[69]

The industry-wide impact of environmental scrutiny notwithstanding, no company faced more criticism than Hooker. Surprisingly, some chemical industry figures viewed Hooker itself as toxic. J. Roger Hirl, who spent nearly three decades at Olin before becoming president of Occidental (and thus Hooker) in 1983, noted that "people had an arm's length attitude toward" the company following Love Canal—in essence, blaming Hooker for a new era of federal intervention in chemical affairs. Other executives, he recalled, wondered, "what kind of a company is this?" Like Johnstone, Hirl would champion new environmental initiatives for the chemical industry while also remaining skeptical of citizen environmentalism. But Hirl admitted that when he came to Hooker in the early 1980s, he did not know much about environmental matters, save for ongoing investigations of Olin's DDT production in Alabama. Love Canal compelled him to get up to speed quickly.[70]

At Hooker, interestingly, some officials thought that the Love Canal crisis pointed toward the cessation of toxic landfilling altogether. As Bruce Davis told Congress in 1979, "the life of a steel drum is limited."[71] Hooker was therefore distancing itself from the antiquated model of dump-and-cover and embracing incineration technology. "We incinerate all chemicals that we can," Davis continued, pointing out that in the roughly decade and a half since it embraced incineration technology, "we have disposed of over 200,000 pounds of chlorinated hydrocarbon materials that would otherwise have gone to a landfill site." And in the past five years alone, he claimed, Hooker had "reduced the volume of material that we are sending to fill sites by 50 percent." Davis confidently predicted that Hooker had "programs moving forward . . . to eliminate almost entirely the materials we send to the landfill sites."[72]

When Senator John Chafee, Republican of Rhode Island peppered Davis with questions about just how far incineration technology could go, he got the Hooker executive to admit flatly that "there is no way we can get to zero. There is no way all chemical residue materials can be completely eliminated from going to landfill sites. There will always be some materials that cannot be incinerated." For example, asbestos disposal would require "a secure landfill area," Davis said. "I thought you were saying you are getting this down," Chafee interrupted. "We are working to get it down as low as we can," Davis retorted. "We are trying to approach zero and become completely independent from having to use a landfill site, but we can never reach that point."[73] As Davis told reporters in September of 1979, "I think Hooker is the cutting edge of the sword in the field of solid waste disposal that the entire industry is going to have to go ahead and face up to."[74] Incineration was an important part of the industry's bold new future, but it too had limits.

No matter how hard it tried, then, Hooker could not make toxic waste disappear.

5. Toxic Tipping Points

Hooker's caring PR strategy brought snickers from some politicians and angry responses from residents still stuck in their homes. Not only did the company fight back against many lawsuits, but it acted capriciously when confronted by activists. Luella Kenny recalled that company officials shut off her microphone at a shareholder meeting, the theme of which was corporate responsibility.[75]

But Hooker could not silence the citizens' struggle, whose cultural influence had only increased since the summer of 1978. Indeed, not since the first Earth Day observances had an environmental movement fomented such expansive media coverage, political scrutiny, or industry reflection. Commentators conjured a plethora of reasons for this development, from Americans' post-Watergate distrust of industrial and political leaders to Love Canal residents' apotheosis as American underdogs. Perhaps the best analysis came from a *New York Times* review of Michael Brown's *Laying Waste: The Poisoning of American by Toxic Chemicals.* "Every now and then an incident occurs in one of those places on the map," Yale Professor Kai Erikson explained, that "allow[s] a story to be told" in the most captivating and ramifying "human" terms. Like "volcanoes" and other sudden "eruptions," these stories shake people from the complacency of their daily lives and force them to confront basic questions about their community, values, and society. Love Canal was just such a story, for it became a marker of environmental degradation at the local level that simultaneously raised questions about industrial waste at the national and even global levels.[76] As he explained, Love Canal was a chemical disaster with a very human face. After reading about residents' struggles in a toxic zone, Americans not only sympathized with their plight but wanted to emulate their movement to discover what potential poisons lurked in their midst.[77] As Erikson perceptively argued, Love Canal's ripple effects would continue to be felt for years precisely because residents had successfully linked the safety of the American home to the safety of the American environment.

And that meant practicing a brand of environmentalism that flowed not from trips to the great outdoors but little ventures into one's backyard, playground, or school. As Love Canal residents proved, anyone could become an environmental activist. And they could make a big difference too.

PART THREE

LEARNING FROM LOVE CANAL

In the End Is the Beginning

Love Canal Lessons

> *Love Canal… The fenced 70-acre superfund site consists of the original 16-acre hazardous waste landfill and a 40-acre cap, as well as a drainage system and leachate collection and treatment system that are in place and operating… Approximately 950 families were evacuated from a ten-block area surrounding the landfill. The contamination at the site ultimately led to the passage of Federal Superfund legislation.*
>
> —EPA website[1]

As yet another summer approached with little prospect of change, Love Canal residents took more risks to get out of their toxic environment. On May 19, 1980, the LCHA detained two EPA representatives visiting the group's headquarters.[2] Residents were angered by the results of a much debated genetic test showing that roughly one-third of the thirty-six people sampled may have suffered chromosome damage (a possible indicator of future illness).[3] Angry and confused, residents gathered en masse at the group's headquarters. Spilling fuel on the lawn, they lit a fire that read "EPA." Hoping to quell rising discontent, the EPA officials drove over to meet with Love Canal families. When they arrived, however, the two men were told "they couldn't leave." While Gibbs explained that she was protecting the men from the chaos outside, others proclaimed that they would be held until the federal government vowed to evacuate all area residents. "If we won't be relocated, keep them here," one activist remembered someone shouting. The scene grew increasingly tense. A crowd of residents, some holding two-by-fours, stood guard as police officers arrived. On the phone, Gibbs explained residents' demands to politicians in Washington. "We'll keep them fed, we'll keep them happy," she also told reporters. But the LCHA would not release the men.[4] The drama ended a few hours later when the FBI phoned LCHA headquarters, darkly warning that agents would storm the home if the hostages were not freed in "six minutes." The EPA representatives were let go—one thanked residents for serving delicious oatmeal cookies—while LCHA activists were put inside a police car, driven around the corner, and then released.[5]

That same month, LCHA figures engaged in a sit-in at the county legislature. The demonstration came after county politicians vetoed a novel plan to "revitalize" parts of Love Canal, including the possible purchase of outer-ring homes. The proposal, which lost by a single vote, would have created a public authority that might use state matching funds to "restore" the toxic neighborhood (and buy out homes from people who didn't want to live there). Some local politicians worried that this would put county government at considerable risk of future lawsuits. "What it does is impose a moral obligation" on the county to solve the Love Canal problem, one attorney told the *New York Times*. And, he wondered, how do you dispense of a moral obligation?[6] Gibbs was furious. "I hate you—I hate all of you murderers!" the usually unflappable leader of the LCHA shouted as politicians left the legislative chambers. Gibbs hopped onto a chair near a podium and refused to leave "until satisfied." Other residents tried to support Gibbs' demonstration of activist resolve. But the sit-in fizzled when "a wave of sheriff's deputies" swept in and removed Gibbs. A parade of Love Canal families followed somberly, heading home to an uncertain future.[7]

Yet May also brought a stunning change of fortune when President Carter issued an unprecedented second emergency declaration at Love Canal. The edict, announced on May 21, provided up to a year of federal evacuation funds for remaining residents. Behind the scenes, John LaFalce pushed White House officials to understand the emotional anguish of Love Canal life; Carter's new announcement, which cited residents' acute psychological distress, proved that they had finally listened (a looming presidential campaign did not hurt matters, either). And so began a fast-moving train of events that eventually led to the permanent evacuation of the area. "There must never in this country be another Love Canal," Carter declared upon signing the final buyout bill in October 1980.[8] "I couldn't believe it," Lois Gibbs would later write, "we had actually won our major goal—permanent relocation."[9] Residents celebrated and cried. Once they departed, residents assumed, Love Canal would be no more.

As with so much else in the toxic neighborhood, the reality was more complex. For starters, permanent evacuation remained a tough sell all the way through the summer and fall of 1980, as state and federal officials clashed over just who would fund the buyout of roughly 550 private homes, as well as relocation funds for renters. Next came battles over the toxic landscape itself. Would a "superfund" be created to remediate Love Canal, a host of state and federal politicians wondered, thereby offering a new way of dealing with America's hazardous waste archipelago? Finally, there was the legacy of grassroots protest at Love Canal. As activists fled their homes, they learned that they were environmental icons for people around the country worried about toxic trash. Looking for advice on forming grassroots movements capable of changing their environment too, would-be reformers from near and far contacted Love Canalers, seeking support for their own struggles. As former residents learned, they could not simply leave behind the toxic town they had once occupied. Love Canal now stood as an enduring monument to their grassroots struggle.

1. Leaving Love Canal, Redux

Leaving Love Canal was not so easy. The giddiness accompanying President Carter's second emergency declaration soon gave way to the realization that significant details needed to be addressed. Evacuation was slated to be temporary, not permanent, creating a familiar sense of dread in many residents. "It's the same thing all over again," declared one woman who refused to move until permanent buyout funds had been secured.[10] As the LCHA constantly reminded both politicians and the media, Love Canal families sweated out every last detail of relocation while state and federal figures bickered over funding schemes. Since May, New York Governor Hugh Carey had "rejected one federal proposal after another for housing relocation assistance" to Love Canal families, the *New York Times* reported.[11] Believing that lawsuits against Hooker—which amounted

to hundreds of millions of dollars—would repay any state monies dedicated to evacuation, federal officials offered loans to New York State for
residential relocation. But Carey wanted outright grants from the national
government. Worried that they would still be stuck when temporary removal funds expired, activists confronted both state and federal politicians at the Democratic Party convention in New York City in August
1980.[12] "President Carter is a liar! We're going to set his ass on fire!" they
chanted as delegates politely tried to bypass them.[13] Needing Carey's support for re-election, however, Carter soon gave in. Yet even then, some
Love Canal residents remained wary of a proposed deal. "I'm just leery
that tomorrow the red tape will come out," the LCHA's Barbara Quimby
commented. Until permanent evacuation was signed and sealed by lawmakers, she and others would not pop any champagne bottles.[14]

But the novel state-federal buyout plan became a reality in the fall. It
created a $20 million fund, with the federal government providing $7.5
million in outright grants to New York for Love Canal home purchases
and another $7.5 in loans (which the state would try to recoup via lawsuits
against Hooker); New York would provide an additional $5 million to fa-
cilitate both relocating the residents and cleaning up the area. The state,
through the Love Canal Area Revitalization Authority (LCARA), which
was created by Carey on June 18, would be responsible for purchasing
area homes at fair market value. LCARA would also be tasked with developing a master plan for Love Canal's future—including the possibility of
resettling parts of the neighborhood. Yet that sticky matter would have to
wait. For the moment, relocation remained the state's priority. With
federal support, New York officials could now buy all Love Canal homes
and provide relocation funds to renters, thus letting hundreds of dis-
tressed people move on from their toxic life. On October 1, President
Carter made it official by traveling to Niagara Falls to sign the permanent
evacuation order into law. Even then, the LCHA was not done. At the
signing ceremony, the ever-vigilant Gibbs whispered to Carter that Love
Canal families needed 3 percent mortgages to rebuild their lives elsewhere (rates then hovered near 9 percent).[15]

Buyouts began soon after. The first family to go—a young mother and
father with a son at home and another on the way—sold their house to
LCARA on November 15, 1980. By May of the following year, the agency

had contracted for nearly half the homes in the ten-block Emergency Declaration Area (EDA), which stretched from 93rd to 102nd Streets.[16] The LCARA purchase contracts became an emblem of change. Health tests, public meetings, rallies—these things drove Love Canalers' lives for over two years. Now residents confronted a new reality: home buyouts, housing leases elsewhere, and moving vans. A town meeting on November 21 detailed the dizzying range of home-related issues confronting evacuees. "If you're concerned about the high cost of replacing your home," a handbill posted around the area declared, "then join your neighbors in finding answers to these questions: how can I afford a home in today's market? What financing alternatives are available? Can I save money by building my own home? Where can I find a new home?" These were not rhetorical questions. With the exception of the roughly six dozen families who for various reasons decided against departure, most people wanted out of Love Canal forever.[17]

Realizing this, LCHA officials and their lawyers urged patience. LCHA legal counsel Richard Lippes advised anxious sellers to wait for amendments to the buyout bill that would clarify ambiguities in the LCARA purchase contracts (for instance, it was unclear whether or not evacuees could be held liable for any future contamination found in their Love Canal homes). Such concerns mattered little to most families. By May 1981, hundreds of people were long gone. A local reporter touring the EDA noted that Love Canal had an "eerie" quality, with most of the homes empty and lifeless.[18] Some houses had been vandalized, others torched; nearly every lot had overgrown lawns and a field of debris, suggesting hasty exits. The sense of abandonment was all but complete by 1982, when most families had left the area. Where activists' shouts once defined Love Canal's soundscape, now silence reigned supreme. "Let me tell you," one resident who waited several months before moving said of the area's stillness, "that really got to me."[19]

The Love Canal exodus carried people to a variety of locales. Many wanted to stay close to family in Western New York. The LCHA's Luella Kenny surveyed parts of New York State for a metropolitan area without hazardous waste landfills before deciding on Grand Island, which, though located just across the Niagara River, contained no major dump. Her colleague Joann Hale moved there too. Other residents wanted to get as far away from Love Canal as possible. After examining "nationwide survey maps of chemical dumpsites," the Torcasio family settled in Las Vegas. "It was one of the clean areas on the map," Eleanor Torcasio told a reporter.[20] Back in Niagara Falls, the LCHA offices moved to various locales. Though the group was in limbo while its leaders tended to home sales, moving trucks, and getting their kids set in new schools, activists vowed to keep it alive. LCHA president Lois Gibbs, who moved to Arlington, Virginia, to launch a new grassroots environmental organization, wrote in the early 1980s: "The Love Canal Homeowners Association Will Go On!" Many of her colleagues agreed. But the harried nature of evacuation took some of the steam out of the group.[21]

2. Learning From Love Canal, Part 1: Superfund

The details of Superfund's passage were not nearly as exciting as the drama of evacuation. But many reporters linked the two issues, noting that Love Canal activism had shaped impending federal legislation on old toxic waste dumps. "The drive for legislation to clean up abandoned toxic waste sites was spurred by the discovery of such sites as Love Canal," Philip Shabecoff wrote in the *New York Times* in September 1980.[22] For Shabecoff, as for others, the nation's new Superfund law was part and parcel of the entire activist saga. It remained one of Love Canal's great legacies.

Superfund came to fruition in December 1980, nearly two years after initial versions of the law had been discussed in Congress. The statute had a rather uninspiring official name: the Comprehensive Environmental Response, Compensation and Liability Act (CERCLA). For that reason, most people refer to the law as "Superfund." In doing so, they acknowledge the seminal law's Love Canal beginnings: John LaFalce's "super fund" concept for national hazardous waste clean-up. Many Americans also know Superfund by its axiom: "the polluter pays." But this adage is only partly accurate. According to the original provisions of CERCLA, the federal government lists the nation's worst hazardous waste landfills, which it then plans to remediate via a fund built largely from taxes on chemical companies, oil refiners, and other hazardous waste producers. Congressional appropriations initially supplemented the program. To defray the costs associated with Superfund operations—to really make the polluter pay—the government vowed to pursue toxic scofflaws in federal court. In this sense, CERCLA became a liability law. Unlike the Clean Air Act, a regulatory statute designed to enforce compliance with environmental quality standards, Superfund works both retroactively and proactively to clean toxic landscapes. By suing "Potentially Responsible Parties"—i.e., old and new polluters—for federal clean-up costs, Superfund makes everyone consider the price of toxic liabilities. Put another way, Superfund compels companies to worry not only about their own disposal practices but those of others, too. "Potentially Responsible Parties" to hazardous waste pollution could include individual companies, multiple parties, or firms who had only recently—and even unknowingly—purchased property with old toxic dumps buried on site.[23]

The legal concept behind this capacious definition of hazardous waste responsibility is known as "strict, joint, and several liability." Translation: toxic landscapes are no longer "someone else's problem" but "everyone's problem," in the well-chosen words of one legal scholar. Indeed, "what made...[this concept of] liability so transformative of the law...was its potential scope of application." By saying that toxic waste sites were the responsibility of a single person or company (strict liability), a combination of people or corporate entities (joint), or anyone who came into contact with and/or possession of them over time (several), Superfund compelled businesses, real estate agents, transportation companies, and others to think about what had been done to the landscape they inhabited—and what they might do to protect themselves from future liability.[24] Needless to say, chemical industry officials disliked this provision of the law. John Johnstone of Olin Corporation, who saw the Love Canal crisis as a clarion call to clean up the chemical industry from within, viewed "strict, joint, and several liability" as unconstitutional.[25] Yet Superfund had industry supporters as well; Irving Shapiro, chairman of DuPont, called the law "rational legislation dictated by the facts." At last, the nation would take responsibility for its toxic past—a past first unearthed at Love Canal.[26]

Little wonder that John LaFalce remained Superfund's most ardent advocate in Congress. In January 1979, the Western New Yorker introduced twin bills in the House of Representatives on hazardous waste reform:

H.R. 1048, titled the Hazardous Waste Control Act, which sought to create a national program "to identify and monitor abandoned hazardous waste sites" throughout the United States; and H.R. 1049, the Toxic Tort Act, which would have allowed citizens to sue for damages arising from the dumping of hazardous waste. In both cases, LaFalce believed that the lesson of Love Canal was simple: the federal government must pass strong toxic remediation laws, as the text of the Hazardous Waste Control Act stated, to "protect the public health, safety, and environment." Though he had abundant friends on both sides of the aisle, LaFalce's draft laws were not universally popular. Indeed, the Toxic Tort Act, which allowed people to sue for "damages ... [caused] by the negligent manufacture of a toxic pollutant" and proposed a new division of the EPA called the "Toxic Pollutant Compensation Agency," alienated many potential supporters. Where his draft law establishing federal oversight of hazardous waste sites attracted nearly 40 co-sponsors (including many Western New York Republicans), the tort law had roughly a dozen co-sponsors (and no Western New York Republicans). Nevertheless, LaFalce's idea of creating a national toxic remediation law spurred consideration of many other "super fund" proposals.[27]

By the spring of 1979, in fact, LaFalce had joined forces with Senator Daniel Patrick Moynihan to offer a joint House-Senate bill that would pour $300 million into a federal clean-up fund, one that would still compensate citizens affected by hazardous waste. Moynihan, a savvy politician who meditated much on the meaning of civil society and governmental ethics in postwar America, knew that Love Canal was no passing problem. Though not the assiduous advocate that LaFalce was, Moynihan soon argued that Love Canal represented a fundamental reckoning with American industrialization's hidden costs. It was, he came to see, a major societal issue only recently unearthed in a corner of his home state. But more such discoveries loomed elsewhere. Like LaFalce, Moynihan believed that the federal government must be ready to respond when these toxic tragedies took shape. Moynihan, like LaFalce, had already heard much from his constituents about the chemical crisis; by the early 1980s, Gibbs and the LCHA were on a first-name basis with both Moynihan and LaFalce. The senator recognized that area residents had long since shaped the essential narrative of Love Canal; he called them "victims of a technological assault" who had now vividly demonstrated the nature of America's toxic waste problem.[28]

Indeed, Moynihan even came to Niagara Falls in 1979 to co-chair field hearings on toxic waste that might bolster the creation of a superfund law. With his flair for dramatic rhetoric, he opened the special investigative session by placing Love Canal in the broadest possible context. "We are here today to investigate one of the most serious environmental problems confronting us today," he told those assembling before him on a crisp May morning, noting that Love Canal had now "stirred fear and concern throughout the nation."[29] His aim was not to lay blame, nor was it an attempt to score points for the Democratic Party—the super fund legislation had bipartisan support, he coolly asserted. Rather, Moynihan, LaFalce, and New York's entire congressional delegation hoped to create a roadmap for solving a problem Love Canal protesters had forced them to face. As he put it in downtown Niagara Falls, there was "no better place to begin learning about this situation [of old toxic dumps] than here, for it was here that the initial discovery was made." Sitting beside him, LaFalce nodded his approval.[30]

The LaFalce-Moynihan duo symbolized Love Canal's resonance throughout the hallowed halls of Congress. Though they were both members of the Democratic Party, these men moved in different political circles. LaFalce was a tireless political worker, Moynihan a statesman. That they agreed to work closely on a superfund bill said that the stakes of Love Canal had been raised well beyond local or regional politics. Discussing matters with their colleagues in the House and Senate, they discovered that others favored a national hazardous waste clean-up law; across the country, they learned, citizens complained to their representatives about toxic problems in their neighborhood. By 1980, both the House and Senate had done more than talk about the matter; each house had passed separate superfund proposals. These congressional bills offered a much larger cleanup fund than either LaFalce or Moynihan had envisioned, with the Senate bill appropriating $4.6 billion and the House $1.2 billion for toxic remediation (interestingly, the victims' compensation fund was also much stronger in the Senate bill). In addition, both versions of the law would be funded via a direct tax on chemical and oil producers—the House bill stipulated that 50 percent of the money come from such a tax, while the corresponding figure in the Senate version was 75 percent. This, too, departed somewhat from LaFalce's original idea of creating an indirect tax to back a superfund law. These differences aside, the final version of the law ("Superfund") was still charged with the spirit LaFalce had originally conjured at Love Canal. He called for a significant national response to toxic waste hazards and he seemed to have it as the 96th Congress readied for recess in November of 1980.[31]

Yet intense lobbying by some members of the chemical industry created a near impasse. The key issue was victims' compensation—something near and dear to LaFalce's heart but not to most chemical companies or many congressional representatives. The Chemical Manufacturers Association (CMA) had pledged support for some sort of national remediation law but wanted it to be much smaller in size and scope than either of the congressional bills; the CMA also wanted to reduce the chemical industry's contribution to Superfund. When the CMA pushed for further delays in the passage of the bill, Moynihan got so angry that he publicly accused the industry of bad faith. (Moynihan believed the CMA was waiting for a Republican victory in the 1980 elections that would bring a more industry-friendly group of politicians to Washington).[32]

This last-minute showdown over Superfund pushed debate into the lame-duck session of Congress before Christmas. "Save the Superfund," a *New York Times* editorial trumpeted,[33] After a series of intense negotiations, the statute was signed into law on December 11, 1980. With a $1.6 billion budget (far below the Senate figure) being generated over the course of five years (and 89 percent of the funds coming from a tax on oil and gas producers, which was more than earlier House and Senate proposals), CERCLA established the first federal protocols for hazardous waste cleanup. The EPA would create a National Priorities List (NPL) of the nation's most problematic toxic sites; the federal government would then work with state entities to clean them out. Of the roughly 1,200 sites initially deemed most hazardous, Love Canal became cleanup site number one.

While pleased with this outcome, LaFalce did not stop there. Like others embroiled in Love Canal protest and politics, he believed that Superfund was only the start of a broader effort to deal with nation's hazardous waste past—and future. As much as LaFalce wanted strong statutes spurring the cleanup of old toxic waste sites, he also favored proactive measures aimed at cutting hazardous waste streams moving forward. Now concerned with preventing "other Love Canals," as he put it, LaFalce submitted a new bill in March of 1982 seeking an outright ban on certain hazardous waste disposal practices. The press release announcing the proposed law noted that LaFalce's "district contains Love Canal," a rhetorical shot indicating that few politicians knew more about the perils of unchecked toxic landfills than the congressman from Western New York.[34]

LaFalce's proposed law, the "Hazardous Waste Management Act of 1982," would have put "an immediate and permanent ban on the landfill disposal of liquid waste." As he noted in newsletters, congressional speeches, and memos, Love Canal had created a teachable moment. Recognizing this fact, politicians must attack toxic troubles from a bold new perspective. Rather than look at the issue from the position of efficiency—what is the cheapest yet most effective way to store mounting waste streams?— LaFalce wanted federal lawmakers to ask a more basic question: "how safe are hazardous waste landfills?" Needless to say, LaFalce continued, this is "a question that we in Western New York can never afford to stop asking, for Love Canal clearly demonstrates the potential for severe health and environmental damage from the landfill of hazardous waste." But, he worried, many politicians already seemed to be forgetting the lessons of Love Canal. Under President Ronald Reagan's leadership, he argued, the EPA would allow up to 25 percent of a landfill's contents to be composed of liquid wastes—loose liquid material that could leach out of an uncontained site. Moreover, LaFalce warned, the EPA had announced that it would reduce oversight of industrial landfilling itself. As many as "20 million gallons of [new] hazardous liquids" could end up in landfills before the EPA stiffened its regulatory muscle, he said. Despite the presence of Superfund laws, LaFalce believed that future hazardous waste generation threatened to kill the American environment.[35]

With this troubling thought in mind, LaFalce asked a slightly more philosophical question: how should Americans "dispose of hazardous waste" in the post–Love Canal era? His new bill represented "the opportunity to move the nation away from the landfill disposal option and toward the application of alternative technologies for the treatment, recovery and disposal of hazardous waste." By preventing the disposal of liquid hazardous waste, which could most easily move from corroded steel drums and mushy soils into water systems, parks and playgrounds, and even homes, LaFalce envisioned a world in which landfilling was "a method of last resort." "I do not believe that we have any real choice," he claimed, desperately hoping that Americans would agree.[36]

Not everyone agreed with LaFalce's visionary ideas. Several environmental activists worried that alternative technologies—including hazardous waste incinerators—might flood the atmosphere with deadly particulate matter. Moreover, many congressmen did not view landfilling as a thing of the past; too much chemical waste was still being generated. More ominously, even Superfund came under attack, making LaFalce's visionary ideas about the future less important than guarding the nation's new remediation law from assault. After Reagan swept into the White House in 1980, "small government" philosophies came to dominate federal government. Among other goals, Reagan sought to ease regulatory oversight of heavy industry (including oil and chemical producers). He also reduced federal support for Superfund itself (to the tune of a 20 percent cut in federal expenditures by 1982).[37] This upset environmentalists and worried congressmen like LaFalce. The "[e]nvironmental protection program will be a central target of the Reagan administration's regulatory reform effort," he wrote in a missive to constituents on "The American Environment" in the summer of 1981.[38] Even Superfund expenditures so recently hammered out faced a budgetary ax. LaFalce blasted EPA plans "to *suspend* [the] requirement that manufacturers of hazardous wastes report [their] quantity...and disposal practices annually" as "conceding defeat in the government's effort to protect the public and the environment from the historic abuses in this field."[39]

With anti-regulatory currents circulating through Washington, LaFalce's proposed 1982 law was destined for defeat. Nevertheless, LaFalce's idea that Americans needed to shore up support for Superfund did gain advocates in and beyond Congress. Indeed, the cultural tenor of the times—that American landscapes remained in peril from an avalanche of hazardous waste—still seemed to be on LaFalce's side. Congress passed the Hazardous and Solid Waste Amendments of 1984, the first major update of RCRA since that law's passage in 1976. These provisions established national rules minimizing the landfilling of many hazardous wastes, particularly "non-containerized" liquids and the byproducts of certain solvents deemed especially problematic.[40] Among other stipulations, the law required landfill operators with underground storage tanks to categorize their contents. The reauthorization of Superfund in 1986—which included mandates that chemical companies publicly list emissions for public consumption—further expanded federal hazardous waste policy. Nearly a decade after he had first heard about Love Canal, then, LaFalce's concerns about hazardous waste generation and storage did help create meaningful change. Indeed, one authority reports that even the Reagan administration backed down from a showdown over these measures, fearful that Americans would slam Republicans at election time.[41]

Support for stronger action on hazardous waste came not only from federal figures like LaFalce but state officials as well. During the 1980s, a variety of state lawmakers began considering new limits on hazardous waste streams. In 1989, Massachusetts passed the Toxic Use Reduction Act (TURA), which sought to reduce hazardous waste generation by half in less than a decade.[42] Other states—including Oregon, New Jersey, California and Illinois—debated similar measures. Still, industry pushback softened the blow of many such laws. In Massachusetts, for instance, the 1989 law had "non-enforceable" provisions—i.e., there would be no drastic crackdown on hazardous waste generators that were not in compliance with prevailing statutes. Rather, the state utilized incentives to encourage industry acquiescence. Bay State businesses had access to government funds and "innovation waivers" that allowed experimentation with new remediation technologies. By bringing chemical companies and hazardous waste operators into the equation, Massachusetts hoped to initiate an era of environmental reconciliation—a way to learn from Love Canal while also moving beyond it.[43]

3. Learning From Love Canal, Part 2: Citizen Environmentalism in the 1980s

Even after the passage of Superfund and various state laws dealing with hazardous waste, activists learned that grassroots environmental protest was still necessary. Anne Hillis and her family showed why. Following

Carter's second emergency declaration, Hillis decamped to New Port Richey, on the western coast of Florida. "We just started a new life," Hillis explained to a journalist eager for news about her post–Love Canal experiences. She was happy to raise livestock and plant a garden without fear of chemical contamination. But even here Love Canal stayed with Hillis. "I don't even use chemicals on the garden," she stated flatly. Like others, she remained active in her new environment by talking to neighbors about the potential hazards of chemicals and hazardous waste.[44] No matter what the government did, Hillis believed, citizens must remain their own best anti-toxics advocates.

Hillis' story of carrying her newfound environmental sensibility to neighborhoods far beyond Love Canal was repeated dozens of times over.[45] Luella Kenny continued to work with both the Love Canal Homeowners Association and other activist groups after she moved, while Pat Brown eventually became director of the ETF. Whether giving tours of the old dump or speaking to high school and university classes about toxic waste, former residents felt compelled to share the Love Canal story with new generations of people. Indeed, like myriad others, Brown and Kenny testified to Love Canal's enduring symbol as an environmental movement and not merely a polluted place. As the Chemical Century closed, an increasing number of people wanted to know about toxic troubles in their own neighborhood. Wherever they were—from small towns in the Pacific Northwest to big cities on the East Coast—people threatened by toxic landscapes felt that they could and should reach out to Love Canal activists for insight and inspiration.

No one understood this better than Lois Gibbs, who called Love Canal a part of "everyone's backyard."[46] From her new home in Virginia, Gibbs established the Citizens' Clearinghouse for Hazardous Wastes (CCHW) in 1981. Drawing on Love Canal residents' experiences as novice activists, the CCHW created a "one-stop shopping" center for grassroots reformers struggling to make sense of toxic troubles in their midst—exactly the type of agency or institution she needed during the Love Canal crisis. As "Everyone's Backyard," the group's newsletter, announced in its inaugural edition in 1982, the CCHW was thoroughly dedicated to grassroots activism. In the opening issue alone, local reformers could find legal advice, organizing tips, and a glossary of key environmental terms for nascent reformers ("dumps are exactly what the name implies," the CCHW explained, while "secured landfills" ensured "that no wastes or leachates came into contact with natural waters").[47] In the days before the Internet, the CCHW's attempt to bring local environmental "groups together in a centrally organized information exchange" was revelatory. So, too, was its overarching emphasis on eco-justice as a binding force for activists scattered across the country. As the CCHW later noted, the group remained "a clearinghouse of information, a networking resource, a training and technical assistance center, and a dynamic initiator of [environmental] campaigns of its own." By 1990, the CCHW claimed a subscription list of 8,000 people and/or organizations.[48]

As the CCHW's growth illustrated, grassroots environmentalism flourished in the 1980s. Superfund sensitized many local communities to hazardous waste concerns, while Reagan-era retrenchment convinced grassroots environmentalists to redouble their organizing efforts. But Love Canal itself remained a touchstone for aspiring environmentalists nationally. If before many Americans had sympathized with Love Canal activists, now they wanted to become them. The CCHW told them how. "I think there's a dump in my backyard—what do I do next?" the group's newsletter asked rhetorically in 1982. While suspicion about toxic waste dumps in one's area was a starting point for concern, the group advised, "you need two more things: research and documentation." Yet, the newsletter continued, whether contacting political and business representatives for waste disposal information or monitoring area health concerns, the key person in the activist equation "is 'you.'"[49] Would-be reformers should never forget this axiom, the CCHW declared.

Responding to this challenge, local activists wrote masses of letters to the CCHW. In Villanueva, New Mexico, a group named "Save Our Planet," launched in 1981 to focus on "environmental problems" in the Southwest, sent the CCHW its own newsletter, which announced the formation of a research library dedicated to eco-reform movements aimed at land, air, and water quality improvements. Thousands of miles to the east in Oak Ridge, New Jersey, Theresa Pisano wrote to the CCHW about "Informed Citizens for a Safe Environment," whose 350 members fought against a solid waste transfer station sited near the community's main drinking water source. "Our legal battle lasted 18 months and I couldn't begin to write of all the heartache we experienced," she observed. But she reported that the group's protest thwarted the station, instilling a sense of pride and confidence in local activists.[50] Like myriad others, Pisano became a corresponding member of the CCHW, an act that imbued her local exertions with a sense of national purpose. "Your newsletter," she told Gibbs and the CCHW, "is refreshing to me because I at least can take heart that other areas of the country are experiencing success." Pisano let Gibbs know that she understood the toil associated with grassroots activism; she also understood its necessity. "We all worked very hard [to stop the transfer station,]" she recalled, which is what "I feel...our politicians are supposed to be doing." When political figures balk, she proudly reported, local citizens "become the crusaders for clear air and clean water."[51]

Similar letters came from grassroots activists across the nation. Largely comprising lower-middle and lower-class residents of communities that bore the brunt of industrial and chemical production, CCHW correspondents felt marginalized from political decision-making processes that settled the location of hazardous waste dumps, chose the routes for the transportation of toxic waste, and determined appropriate levels of air quality associated with the incineration of hazardous materials. Some correspondents merely wanted a benediction from one of the world's most famous environmental activists: Lois Gibbs. Others wanted to know that they were not alone in the struggle for environmental justice.

Significantly, women dominated grassroots environmentalism in the 1980s. No longer "housewives turned activists," as they had been at Love Canal, female environmentalists became known as "women movers" (a label doubtless reflecting the imprint of second wave feminism). Still, such commanding phraseology belied the lonely reality of grassroots environmentalism, as women still had to rationalize their activism to skeptical husbands, family members, and politicians/business leaders. In response, the CCHW tried to cultivate a sense of women's collectivism—a movement culture—that mitigated the alienation expressed by female environmentalists. "There are always times when you feel alone, isolated in your local fight," one CCHW article noted. "How do you know, during those times, that you are truly part of a larger movement?" As one Pennsylvania activist answered in 1989, you knew because "women movers" connected local problems to national and international concerns, proving that "the problem with toxics isn't just in my backyard. It's a global problem." In this way, the CCHW put women "in contact with hundreds of other people who have problems like mine," making clear that "we're all trying to make a difference."[52] As a Wyoming woman wrote, "it feels good to be part of a change [in environmental consciousness]. A change that is necessary in order to preserve the world... And it's fun."[53]

In one exemplary case from Coffeyville, Kansas, a woman named Lynn Hill wrote to the CCHW in 1987 about worrisome incineration operations in her neck of the woods. Before moving to Kansas, Hill had lived in Houston, where she reported on midnight dumping operations. But, as she put it, she gave up after a while. "I figured there were more grumpy people than people like us—and against the odds, I couldn't make a difference." But in Coffeyville she discovered that local officials were about to approve a hazardous waste incineration plant without community knowledge or support. "I wish you'd take a look at this article!," she wrote to Gibbs, enclosing a clipping from the *Coffeyville Journal* outlining the incineration plan. "What can be done here in Coffeyville? Could you please send some information? I don't know that I'm the person to organize anything but... help. Oh help! Please." Hill finished with a plea that really hit Gibbs and her colleagues. "When you focus on the children and what they are going to inherit, you've done something."[54]

Though bombarded with such letters, Gibbs and the CCHW often replied personally to people like Hill. After the frustrating experience of Love Canal—where residents felt that few people in any position of power actually heard their pleas—individual contact established credibility with grassroots reformers. "Dear Lynn," Gibbs wrote back to Hill a few weeks later, "we got your letter.... We can be of some help. Please send us your phone number so we can get in touch with you." Gibbs also forwarded "a couple of our publications," including those on "incinerators" and "community organizing," as well as a series of personal contacts in the region. These people, Gibbs emphasized, "know a lot about the company [in your region] and how to beat them."[55]

The idea that the CCHW represented all manner of American underdogs was reified in the saga of Love Canal. In CCHW literature, handbooks, and correspondence, the residents' struggle to overcome governmental and industry apathy stood as a grand totem of grassroots environmentalism.

Gibbs herself cultivated Love Canal's sense of timelessness in books, speeches and letters. The CCHW's "Leadership Handbook on Hazardous Waste" noted that Gibbs was the "founder of the Love Canal Homeowners Association in Niagara Falls," where she "organized a small blue-collar community and successfully took on City Hall, the state and the White House to achieve their major goal—evacuation of 500 families with their homes purchased at fair market value and [the bringing of] the improper disposal of hazardous wastes to national prominence." Now Gibbs and the CCHW published booklets and pamphlets for people "who want to start or strengthen organizations addressing [their own] hazardous waste issues."[56]

To show that grassroots struggle worked, the CCHW touted success stories from around the country. "History shows us," the group argued vehemently, "that the only effective way to resolve hazardous waste problems is for citizens to join together. By doing this, they create enough pressure on government and corporations to ensure that the needs and concerns of people are dressed. Organized groups are the most effective way to solve problems." The CCHW's point was always the same: unheralded citizens could redefine their community's environmental priorities by banding together.[57]

In making such pronouncements, Gibbs relied on a brand of activist authenticity matched by few others in the environmental community. People gravitated to her leadership precisely because of her powerful example as the "housewife who took on Washington." Gibbs solidified her reputation by publishing an autobiography in 1982, *Love Canal: My Story*. Perhaps the most important environmental narrative of its time, Gibbs' book had special appeal to the grassroots community. Written in a basic and direct style that allowed people with little formal education beyond high school to follow her example, the book illustrated how average citizens mired in hazardous circumstances could confront both governmental and corporate powers. "Almost everyone has heard about Love Canal," she began, "but not many people know what it is all about." Her autobiography took readers behind the scenes and inside the hearts and minds of local activists fearful of Love Canal life. Tellingly, the original paperback edition of *Love Canal: My Story* featured a cover with an epigraph that evoked Gibbs' central purpose: "Love Canal: Ask Those Who

Really Know." Using the line from a LCHA handout, Gibbs indicated that Love Canal remained a story defined by residents' experiences, not (eventual) government action. "The most powerful thing you have is your story," Gibbs would tell grassroots reformers.[58] By crafting her own story out of the shards of a jagged Love Canal experience, Gibbs created the first grassroots environmental memoir of life in a toxic zone.

Though written in a plain style, Gibbs' tale hewed to some of the classic conventions of American autobiography, particularly themes of enlightenment and uplift. Punctuated by folk wisdom (she lectured her brother-in-law to "translate some of that jibber-jabber" of science "into English"), Gibbs' narrative guided readers through her education as an activist. Emphasizing the ups and downs of grassroots reform, from the thrill of planning rallies to the disappointment of returning to a polluted neighborhood, Gibbs made clear that it was worthwhile. For Love Canal now endured as a symbol of grassroots environmentalism.[59]

Gibbs' story was also made for the movies. Unsurprisingly, there were murmurs about turning her Love Canal saga into a *Rocky*-style blockbuster. While that never happened, a TV movie did get made: "Lois Gibbs and The Love Canal." The CBS docudrama aired in prime time and made Gibbs synonymous with the movement itself. Needless to say, the film put Gibbs in a tough spot, for while she demurred from suggestions that she was a singular presence at Love Canal, she (and other activists) were nonetheless happy to get their message out to a much broader audience. Debuting in February 1982, just as American politicians debated whether or not Superfund had overextended government regulation of hazardous waste, the movie featured Hollywood star Marsha Mason as Gibbs. Even more than Gibbs' autobiography, the movie centered on a mother's love for her children rather than on growing environmental commitments. Nevertheless, as one reviewer summarized the plot, Gibbs learned that she had to become a political player to save her family, for partial government action at Love Canal "just isn't enough" to avert a health crisis in the toxic neighborhood. As a result, Gibbs "begins a loud and aggressive movement to force the United States Government to relocate the residents of Love Canal, and to reimburse them for the loss of their property."[60]

The CCHW picked up where the movie left off: by building grassroots activism nationally. With the spotlight again on her Love Canal experiences, Gibbs needed to show that the toxic waste problem remained much larger and more serious than a lone polluted dump in Niagara Falls. As the CCHW showed, toxic troubles still haunted marginalized communities everywhere. For Gibbs and the CCHW, then, leaving Love Canal meant constantly learning from its activist example.

4. More Love Canal Shadows: NIMBY

Not everyone was thrilled with citizen mobilization in the post-Love Canal world, however. Pro-growth politicians and business leaders argued that Love Canal had generated a runaway "Not In My Backyard" (NIMBY, for short) movement. Indeed, critics worried that grassroots activists had enshrined their local environments as de facto national parks—precious landscapes where development itself would be prevented. "Not here, not now, not ever," one famous NIMBY sign declared.[61] "We are totally deadlocked," one observer who examined the impact of NIMBYs on local decision-making processes declared on Love Canal's tenth anniversary. "We're losing facilities faster than they're being replaced, whether it's prisons, power plants or hazardous-waste treatment facilities. We're rapidly getting to the point where we're going to be at a crisis in many of these areas."[62]

References to Love Canal as the problematic source of the NIMBY phenomenon became commonplace. "Many say the NIMBY syndrome started to become a sharp challenge to American business with events that unfolded in a small suburb of Niagara Falls, N.Y.," William Glaberson wrote in the *New York Times* in the summer of 1988. "The name of the community was Love Canal and it became an immediate symbol of the dangers modern industry can bring with it—and of the power communities can summon when they decide to fight back." Yet a decade of grassroots protest had also created a sense of crisis in many communities, he continued, as thousands of Lois Gibbs–style reformers took on both city hall and the business community, "provoking questions that had no easy answers: Why should that plant be here? Will it affect the water? How will you get rid of the waste? Can you be certain those prisoners will stay behind the walls? What about the traffic, the noise?" For these reasons,

Glaberson noted, the NIMBY movement was "extensive and growing"—and (as he saw it) really problematic.[63]

While business and political figures often criticized post–Love Canal NIMBYs as refuseniks, the CCHW argued that they formed the last line of defense against potentially new polluters. Citing a 1984 report that argued for citing hazardous waste facilities in communities least likely to combat them—because they lacked economic and political clout—the CCHW encouraged grassroots activists to fight back with all their might.[64]

But the NIMBY phenomenon also provoked criticisms from members of the political left who believed that the advent of Green Politics in Europe and America trumped the rise of grassroots environmentalism. For these commentators, Love Canal–style activism was superficial, for it improved only a small part of the American landscape rather than fomenting calls for structural economic change. Where Green Parties criticized capitalist production itself, fusing socialist notions of political economy to traditional environmental thought, some activists worried that grassroots environmentalism offered relatively limited critiques of consumerism.[65]

This critique also misses the mark, for Love Canal activism spawned important changes in environmental policy and democratic politics, from the advent of "community right-to-know" laws in the 1980s to the growth of environmental epidemiology as a robust public health field. Prior to the Love Canal crisis, for instance, chemical companies were not required to disclose their toxic releases. But the 1986 Superfund Amendment and Reauthorization Act created the first federal right-to-know law. As the EPA puts it, the "Community Right-to-Know provisions help[ed] increase the public's knowledge and access to information on chemicals at individual facilities, their uses, and releases into the environment. States and communities, working with facilities, can use the information to improve chemical safety and protect public health and the environment."[66] Had it not been for Love Canal activists, who first pushed for public disclosures of toxic information, right-to-know laws might not have taken shape when they did—if ever.

This is far from a minor point, as a host of grassroots activists learned in the post–Love Canal world. In 1984, Diane Heminway, who lived about thirty miles from Niagara Falls in a highly rural community, discovered the importance of toxic knowledge when her two children were exposed to methyl isocyanate, a chemical used by an area pesticide manufacturer. After an accidental release of 50 gallons, a chemical vapor cloud sailed over her son's school, where it filtered into the ventilation system. Roughly a hundred children endured emergency treatment at a local fire hall. Yet residents had no idea that the chemical was being produced in their community, nor did they know where or how its wastes were being stored. Heminway eventually joined the "Citizens' Environmental Coalition (CEC)," a grassroots group formed in 1983. As Heminway noted at a conference on the legacy of Love Canal for "environmental social movements," "beneficial" right-to-know laws made it much easier for citizens in her community to research potential health hazards.[67]

NIMBY-style activism thus enhanced many citizens' understanding of environmentalism itself. At the CCHW, Gibbs and her colleagues received a constant stream of letters underscoring grassroots reformers' concerns with local and regional land-use policies. "I was NIMBY...to begin with," a woman from Emelle, Alabama, wrote to the CCHW. "But I've realized that I don't want them to dig it up and move it somewhere else." As she explained, local activists wanted to share information on landfills, toxic exposures, and chemical manufacturing processes "with people all over the United States," creating a dedicated network of eco-reformers that would keep entire swaths of the country safe from toxic threats.[68]

The CCHW was not the only group preaching Love Canal lessons in the 1980s. The ETF continued to highlight toxic tragedies, both in and beyond Western New York. Like the CCHW, the ETF hoped to foster broader dialogues about post-Love Canal environmentalism, though again with the group's signature focus on the spiritual dimensions of eco-reform. For the ETF "rediscovering and reclaiming our fundamental connectedness to the earth and one another" remained an important goal. As Margeen Hoffman put it, Love Canal taught everyone that nature resided in urban locales no less than in the Great Outdoors; heeding this lesson, mainstream environmentalists should talk more about the "stewardship of humans in the environment."[69] As its annual reports showed, ETF members constantly busied themselves on a wide variety of environmental initiatives in the wake of Love Canal. Take the busy year of 1985, when ETF members helped launch the "Niagara Environmental Coalition," which brought together twenty groups to discuss regional environmental priorities. In addition to that endeavor, ETF members traveled to an "Environment 2000" conference convened by New York Governor Mario Cuomo on future ecological concerns in the Empire State; mobilized in support of a law limiting the discharge of nearly a hundred types of chemicals into area waters; participated in a national conference on "Toxic Substances and Public Health"; worked with grassroots environmentalists in upstate New York to prevent a landfill from being built near a local water supply facility; served on the Hazardous Materials Advisory Council for Niagara Falls; and sat on the New York State Superfund Management Board. The ETF had also spoken to, or worked with, some three dozen schools, groups, and churches on issues ranging from toxic waste storage and remediation to the broader meaning of environmental stewardship in late 20th century America.[70]

Little wonder that the ETF also found itself fielding numerous calls for help during the 1980s. "Over the past year," the group reported in 1986, "requests for information and referral [about toxic waste] have been received from individuals and organizations... [in] Alabama, California, Connecticut, Florida, Illinois Iowa, Maine, Maryland...." The list went on. And the ETF still received requests for "site-seeing" tours" of toxic dumps "on average of six a month."[71] Like the CCHW—with which it worked on several occasions—the ETF discovered that Love Canal's symbolic power remained strong for many years.

Indeed, for both the ETF and CCHW, post–Love Canal activism served as the coda to a new era of environmentalism. Locally centered yet nationally and even globally conscious, grassroots reformers believed that unless they carried the Love Canal struggle forward to communities large and small, environmentalism itself would remain an important but distant movement about nature preservation.

5. "The Tip of the Iceberg": Love Canal a Decade Later

The tenth anniversary of the Love Canal crisis prompted a flurry of reflections on the legacy of the nation's first toxic waste tragedy. Heavy-hitting journalists re-examined Love Canal's place in environmental history;

activists gave tours of their former neighborhood. Everyone agreed that Love Canal was still big news. "The discoveries of toxic waste at Love Canal in 1978 traumatized the neighborhood and alarmed the nation," the *New York Times* reported in August 1988. While Love Canal now looked like a ghost town, it remained a potent symbol of environmental neglect and grassroots mobilization. After all, the story continued, in Love Canal's wake "Congress established a multibillion-dollar program, known as the Superfund, to clean up hazardous waste sites" around the country. For this reason alone, Love Canal was legendary.[72]

Yet there was no denying the haunting quality of the Love Canal landscape itself. Years after the crisis began, many women remained traumatized by their experiences in the toxic neighborhood. David Shribman, who initially covered the Love Canal saga for the *Buffalo Evening News*, wrote a moving anniversary article in the *Wall Street Journal* (subsequently republished in *Family Circle*) about the place and people who helped launch his journalistic career. "Even after 10 years, victims of Love Canal can't quite escape it," the headline above his article declared. To be sure, Shribman remained impressed by the activist women he had met years before. Indeed, Shribman captured perhaps better than anyone else the idea that Love Canal was not simply a place, or even an enduring symbol, but a movement of unheralded citizens (led by women) who believed that they could change the world. Still, Love Canal would not let go of their psyche. Shribman wrote of one woman who had recurring nightmares that someone would make her move back to the toxic subdivision. Other women worried about their kids' lifelong health. All knew that Love Canal would never really end. But that was the point: the entire experience was a rude awakening for the nation no less than Love Canal residents. And no one should ever forget it.[73]

9

Creative Destruction

Resettling Love Canal and Its Discontents

> 1. *The Love Canal Resettlement plans and planning process should serve as a model for redeveloping superfund sites, as measured by content, vision and implementation success.*
>
> 2. *The Love Canal area will be redeveloped in* an environmentally responsible manner...*[Emphasis in original].*
> —"Goals and Objectives," *Love Canal Area Master Plan, 1990*

Although the tenth anniversary of the crisis pictured Love Canal as a thing of the past, the area still inspired dreams of development in the future. That became clear in September 1988, when Health Commissioner David Axelrod returned to Niagara Falls to announce that the state would back Love Canal resettlement. The longtime mayor of Niagara Falls, Michael O'Loughlin, beamed at the news. This was the first "positive statement about Love Canal" in years, he said.[1] Axelrod's resettlement recommendation was the result of a five-year, $14 million study. Using massive amounts of test data, the study drilled down into Love Canal's new nature to see if the monumental remediation plan had worked. The study determined that parts of the ten-block Emergency Declaration Area (EDA) had acceptable chemical levels and only slightly higher contamination risks than comparison areas hard by landfills, steel plants, and old manufacturing facilities in the American Rust Belt. While no one could certify the neighborhood's absolute safety, Axelrod proposed that people might soon move into sections of the nearly empty subdivision.[2]

Former residents again fumed at Axelrod. Joann Hale called Axelrod's decision "piece meal," at best, and dangerous at worst. Anything but a

223

"black and white" answer about the safety of resettlement was wrong. The ETF's Roger Cook said that resettlement posed "unacceptable risks" to future residents.[3] Janet Ecker, a former resident not known for screaming and shouting, told a reporter that Axelrod's announcement was "very sad." "I don't agree it is a safe place. The chemicals don't know that they're supposed to stop" at certain places. The mere mention of Love Canal brought back unhappy memories to Ecker, who left in 1980 for Florida and was still "glad to be as far away as I can get from that place."[4] Lois Gibbs went even further: it was morally wrong for the state to resettle the area.[5]

As these divergent perspectives on Axelrod's announcement indicated, Love Canal remained a hotly contested environment well after final evacuation had occurred. Whether the issue was residential resettlement, the evolving implications of state and federal health studies, or the memory of area activism itself, Love Canal's many stakeholders continued to skirmish over the area's past, present, and future. But they did agree on one thing: Love Canal remained a precedent-setting place. Whatever happened here would exert a ripple effect well beyond Niagara Falls. As Gibbs angrily put it, Love Canal resettlement would prove that other toxic sites around the country could be repopulated too. A landscape design firm hired to create a new "Master Plan" for the revitalized neighborhood actually agreed, noting that the new Love Canal would "serve as a model for redeveloping Superfund sites" everywhere. Though on opposite sides of the matter, both Gibbs and the design firm saw Love Canal as more than just a place, toxic or otherwise. They saw it as a paradigm of future dealings with hazardous waste.

And so once again the Love Canal landscape served as a symbol of broader forces, bigger movements, and deeper desires. It was still an environmental hotspot and a (potentially) working neighborhood whose tax coffers could boost the local economy; still a toxic waste battle zone and a seemingly normal patch of American suburbia where kids and parents might again live, work and play in affordable homes; still a proving ground for the ideals of grassroots environmentalism, which sought to make Love Canal a lesson in toxic trouble, and a test site for the wonders of American "hazmat" technology, which might overcome any problem, including a notorious chemical disaster.

1. Resettling Love Canal

City officials had dreamed of bringing people back to Love Canal from the moment angry residents departed. The area's shifting demographics help explain why. By 1990, 64,500 people lived in Niagara Falls, roughly half of the city's midcentury high. Declining populations meant a declining tax base. Love Canal's relatively new housing stock and favorable location next to area suburbs and near highways made it attractive to city planners looking for ways to get bodies (and dollars) back into the Falls. But the massive dump warned developers away. For any resettlement to occur, state and federal authorities needed to show that Love Canal had been remediated and thus posed little health risk to the public. Love Canal Area Revitalization Agency (or once again, LCARA) officers who would sell area property also had to deal with the powerful image of Love Canal as America's Ground Zero of toxic waste. Though daunting, neither task deterred local or state figures eyeing a repopulated Love Canal. City officials disliked the idea of mothballing the subdivision or turning it into a "sanctuary," in the words of one consultant.[6] And state representatives believed that remediation had worked, making Love Canal an attractive investment for many families. Even before evacuation had been completed, in fact, LCARA officers expressed support for neighborhood revitalization.[7]

Nevertheless, it would take nearly a decade for Love Canal resettlement to occur. Throughout the 1980s, experts drew vastly different conclusions about the area's environmental health and potentially habitability. A 1982 EPA report served as the first shot in the battle over Love Canal's future. Based on an analysis of massive amounts of chemical data gathered between August and October of 1980, the report was the most comprehensive environmental study of its kind. With well over 6,000 air, soil, water, and biotic samples, the study was a technical tour de force. Its three volumes stretched to nearly 3,000 pages, mostly in the form of complex scientific tables, graphs, and appendices. The report also reflected the latest in computing technology and multimedia analyses of the environment. EPA officials utilized mainframe computers to crunch meta-data, and technicians used cutting-edge radar technology to peer into Love Canal's subterranean chemical world. With the latest tools of science and technology at its disposal, the EPA hoped to definitively determine the success or failure of remediation work at the dump.[8]

But the EPA report was more than a technical analysis. As project coordinator John Deegan Jr., a respected mathematician and academic administrator with a flair for dramatic pronouncements, later recalled, the EPA team was directed not only "to integrate, interpret and report the data" on potential environmental contamination, but "to assess, from an environmental perspective, the habitability of the area...." From the start, in other words, testing of the dump was linked to the possibility of neighborhood redevelopment. The study subdivided the ten-block emergency declaration area into ten sample zones (eleven, including the Love Canal dump itself). Field agents probed both "intentional" sites (wet areas known to contain chemical contaminants) and random ones (various yards and homes whose chemical fate was unknown) in order to get the full measure of pollution at Love Canal. They paid particular attention to contamination "pathways"—sewers, rivers, creeks, streets and swales that served as vectors of Love Canal chemicals—in order to determine whether or not hazardous waste had migrated beyond the dump.[9]

After months of analysis, the EPA monitoring program "revealed a limited pattern of environmental contamination restricted mainly to the immediate vicinity of the inactive hazardous waste landfill." While there was certainly evidence of "localized and highly selective migration of toxic chemicals through soils in...homes near the old landfill," and "substantial residual contamination in those local storm sewer lines originating near the former Canal" (as well as "in the surface water and sediment of area creeks and rivers"), the EPA study did not find massive chemical contamination. The remediation system seemed to be working. As Deegan explained in a technical review article in 1987, "the reasonable conclusion was that there was no environmental basis in which to find the...area uninhabitable."[10]

The EPA report inspired LCARA officials, who began touting the virtues of Love Canal life. A story running across AP wires in February 1983 noted that several prospective buyers had already toured area property. Though Love Canal "conjures up images of buried industrial poisons [and]...a homeowner's nightmare," the article declared, there were now "people who wanted to move back in—to buy vacated homes in what once was a quiet, middle-class section of this upstate New York community." Soon, LCARA had a list of roughly 250 people interested in Love Canal. "I don't think there's anything wrong with the place," said one person who claimed to have lived there as a child. With a discount of as much as 10 to 15 percent off the assessed price—LCARA had paid $35,000, on average, for evacuated homes—Love Canal property seemed like a steal.[11]

To further demonstrate its desirability, LCARA leader Richard Morris moved into a Love Canal home. The bearded, often smiling Morris had been in the real estate division of the New York State Department of Transportation before taking the job. On the very day he moved into Love Canal, Morris recalled, someone asked about buying a house across the street. For Morris, this indicated that many people simply wanted a decent home at a good price—even if the home was part of an infamous area. "They drive in here and…say, 'Gee whiz, I don't see anything wrong with this place. I don't see any dead bodies.' They see dogs and kids and they're still alive and breathing."[12]

As it turned out, Morris's plan for a speedy resettlement of Love Canal was premature. New York State Attorney General Robert Abrams, acting in the public interest, threatened a lawsuit against the resettlement agency if it moved too quickly. And both former citizens and environmental activists argued that Love Canal remained unfit for habitation. The ETF's John Lynch, who actually served on the LCARA board to monitor area redevelopment efforts, called resettlement "a farce." "The evidence we have suggests it is a risk to live in that neighborhood," he said. Lynch told a *New York Times* reporter that he feared the EPA report would "whitewash" Love Canal hazards. Even Morris' decision to move into Love Canal drew the ire of some local residents. He did not purchase his home, they discovered; he merely rented it from LCARA, minimizing his financial risk. Others worried that he put his family at risk to make a point that didn't need to be made.[13] Either way, Morris was one of the few people to move into Love Canal during the 1980s.

2. Resettling Love Canal, Redux

Doubt about resettlement resurfaced in June 1983, when a second federal study on Love Canal's environment came out. Presented by the federal

Office of Technology Assessment (OTA), it was downright short (less than a hundred pages) when compared to the mammoth EPA study. Prompted by Congressman John LaFalce's concerns about the 1982 report, the OTA study challenged the EPA's conclusions. "The OTA has reviewed and analyzed the EPA monitoring study," in addition to nearly every other federal and/or state analysis of Love Canal, the new report proclaimed. And the OTA found that it was "not [yet] possible to conclude either that unsafe levels of toxic contamination exist or that they do not exist" at Love Canal. With that in mind, the OTA could not support "immediate and complete habitation" of the neighborhood.[14] "There remains a need to demonstrate more unequivocally that the [area] is safe immediately and over the long term for human habitation," the study declared. "If that cannot be done, it may be necessary to accept the original presumption that the area is not habitable."[15]

The OTA found fault with the EPA study on several fronts.[16] For example, the EPA's sampling methodology may not have accurately accounted for the "true level" of chemical contamination throughout the ten-block area. Moreover, in determining risk, the EPA did not acknowledge the "uncertainties over possible synergistic human health effects of multiple toxic chemicals present at low levels."[17] But overall, the OTA criticized the EPA for not asking what Love Canal would look like in a century. Without paying attention to the "very long term," the 1983 study asserted, even the best science and technology would be useless. Here the OTA used Love Canal's powerful symbolism to urge further study of the effects of hazardous waste on both environments and people. While the report did not say it was unthinkable Love Canal would again be habitable, it called for more thoughtful examination of the matter. With so many people out of Love Canal, why rush to move others back in?

The OTA-EPA debate over Love Canal's future reflected increasing doubts about scientific objectivity as the Chemical Century drew to a close. From the 1970s onward, science, technology, and the environmental policies that flowed from them were scrutinized as never before. As science became more closely associated with industry and commerce, it lost some of its moral authority. While many Americans still trusted scientific institutions (and thus such things as technical analyses of environmental conditions), others wondered openly about the social, political, and economic pressures shaping science-based policy decisions. The fallout from industry-backed studies claiming that smoking did not harm human health (when internal results showed that it did) further undermined public faith in science.[18]

By the 1980s, Love Canal had become a popular framing device for public doubts about scientific authority and trustworthiness. Syndicated columnist Art Buchwald offered a hilarious send-up of Reagan-era EPA administrator Rita Lavelle, who came under public scrutiny for meeting privately with chemical companies being investigated for glaring violations of environmental policy. Imagining one such dinner between Lavelle—a supposed representative of government autonomy and scientific integrity—and a chemical insider, Buchwald pictured the EPA administrator as a naïf. As Lavelle tries to find an entrée that is not contaminated, her dinner partner quizzes her about Love Canal: "How do you feel about Love, Miss Lavelle?" "That's a very personal question," she replies. "I meant Love Canal," he continues. "Do we have to talk about Love Canal while we are eating?" she wonders. With both parties stymied for pleasant topics of conversation, the dinner fizzles. But Buchwald's sarcastic point was clear: If readers thought any conversation between the EPA and chemical company executives would be this innocent, then they were the naïve ones.[19] In fact, Lavelle would soon be indicted, fined, and imprisoned for obstructing federal investigations into shoddy toxic waste disposal policies at her former place of employment in California. As G. Allen Carver Jr., the assistant United States Attorney leading the prosecution, said, Lavelle had "a high responsibility, duty and obligation to the American public and she didn't measure up."[20]

Reagan-era budget cuts further complicated debates over Love Canal habitability. Declining funds for remediation programs compromised EPA's ability to clean up America's hazardous waste zone and inspired jokes about the agency's ability to deal effectively with industry power. A famous cartoon lampooning EPA ineffectiveness featured fabled Broadway character Annie standing atop a number of chemical waste drums as she belts out the iconic phrase from the musical of the same name: "Tomorrow, tomorrow, we'll clean up. Tomorrow. We're only the EPA!"[21] With EPA's budget under attack, and public concerns about scientific integrity rising, definitive answers about Love Canal safety seemed hard to find.

3. Re-Engineering Love Canal

Scientists and policy wonks were not the only authorities debating Love Canal's future. Another group of experts soon emerged with visions of transcending the area's poisoned past: environmental engineers. And their labors did much to frame resettlement debates at Love Canal. Relying on a mixture of engineering expertise, environmental sensitivity, and high-tech tools, a new generation of remediation specialists argued that they could not only manage the toxic past at Love Canal but prevent future chemical disasters from occurring anywhere else. It was a bold declaration but one that fit perfectly with Superfund's goal of cleaning up the environment and moving on from the nightmare of Love Canal.

For environmental engineers no less than politicians and chemical industry figures, Love Canal represented a fundamental break from the nation's past. Because toxic troubles were no longer buried, few people could ignore them. Hazardous waste was now a matter of public record, not private concern. Yet regulatory enforcement of hazardous waste disposal practices remained such a new concept that many sectors of the chemical industry were simply unprepared to deal with state and federal scrutiny. "Only recently have we come to understand the complexity of the problems caused by toxic materials," a federal researcher noted in 1978, "and the methods society must use to regulate their use and limit exposures to them."[22]

In this brave new world, where antiquated disposal practices met the realities of Superfund, environmental engineers stood tall. With a grand lineage of sanitary reform as inspiration—especially the great sewer projects of the 19th century, which, ironically, had launched the career of Hooker's own founder, Elon Huntington Hooker—they hoped to lead both industry and the public out of the nation's toxic waste quagmire. The growth of environmental engineering after Love Canal was certainly impressive. Once again, the local scene illuminated national trends. Ecology and Environment, a Buffalo firm established in the late 1960s with just a few employees, grew to nearly 1,200 employees by 1990. Clearly, American society's newfound interest in environmental clean-up made remediation "a lucrative business," as one of the firm's founders observed in a story about the legacy of Love Canal remediation.²³ Who else but environmental engineers could, and should, clean up Superfund sites?

Hidebound trade journals had been saying something similar for decades: techno-science was an ally, not an enemy, of clean environments. Yet not until Love Canal would Americans understand the technical exigencies of toxic waste remediation. (Even the leading industry journal, *Environmental Science and Technology*, did not address Love Canal fully until 1980). Unsurprisingly, a splashy new monthly magazine touting the virtues of environmental engineering took the lead in reimagining a post–Love Canal future born of technical wizardry: *HazMat World* magazine. Debuting in 1987 as the brainchild of an environmental innovator named Alan John Borner, *HazMat World* argued that the public needed to know about the dazzling work of remediation experts. His magazine had impressive support: a circulation of 100,000 readers and a loyal following of environmental professionals, business managers, lawyers, and engineers/technicians. Full of colorful ads and snappy articles, it soon won awards, too.

Borner was not simply a showman. He had already founded the Environmental Hazards Management Institute (EHMI), a nonprofit organization "dedicated to resolving environmental problems through education and consensus." The Institute held a well-known 1979 conference on "the growing scandal of hazardous waste" that brought together academics, politicians, EPA figures, engineers, industry representatives, and "victims of hazardous waste contamination."²⁴ Both the EHMI and *HazMat World* flowed from Borner's hope of creating a third way of environmental action in the post–Love Canal world. Situating himself between environmentalists and industry/government officials, Borner wanted to deploy environmental "knowledge and tools" to anyone concerned with cleaning up (and moving beyond) hazardous waste crises.²⁵ Significantly, *HazMat World*—like EHMI—was nonprofit and independent (unlike the chemical industry–sponsored journal *Environmental Science and Technology*). Just as important, Borner saw eco-professionals—including engineers—as central to the project of building a new consensus on environmental health and safety in the 1980s.

In this sense, *HazMat World* owed a debt to *The Whole Earth Catalogue*, the famous environmental handbook launched by Stewart Brand in 1968. Just as Brand's catalogue became one-stop shopping for eco-pragmatists

seeking "tools" to reduce their global footprint, so too did Borner's magazine give environmental professionals access to a range of sophisticated
technologies that could speed remediation work.[26] Interested in practical
solutions to toxic threats, *HazMat World* testified to the way that Love
Canal had reshaped Americans' understanding of environmental struggles.
Indeed, Borner challenged the chemical industry to confront the realities
of toxic waste.[27] Far from a problem born of emotionalism and hysteria,
toxic waste threats were real, grave, and omnipresent. Yet Borner's magazine also offered advice on averting or overcoming a tragedy. In Borner's
eyes, anything seemed possible—so long as the chemical industry took
responsibility for its waste. If industry joined the war on toxic trash, the
magazine proclaimed, then even the most hazardous environments could
be revived, including Love Canal.

The magazine's ads underscored such beliefs. Issue after issue featured
not only stories on hazardous waste concerns, from litigation to health
testing, but a host of industry ads addressing the problems of the American
toxic grid. "Uncle Sam wants you…," a stunning full-page ad from the
Asahi/America Corporation (a leading producer of "thermoplastic" valve
systems able to withstand even the most corrosive fluid transfers) declared
in a special edition on "Emergency Response Issues," "to protect the environment with dual containment piping."[28] With the stern figure of Uncle
Sam pointing at *HazMat World* readers, Asahi/America proclaimed that
its innovative piping product "satisfies EPA requirements," thus allowing
industrial plant managers to "avoid the risk of fines and even jail sentences
for noncompliance with EPA regulation." "Rest assured," the headline of
another ad announced, by using GSX Chemical Services to manage all
your industrial waste needs. "[I]f you're continually losing sleep because
your hazardous waste management company is continually letting you
down," the ad slyly commented, "we'd like to suggest a simple cure: start
sleeping with GSX." Whether it was "regulatory compliance" or having
the "technical expertise… to develop an environmentally sound program"
of toxic waste disposal, GSX declared, "we'll be there." The company
would even "analyze, document, ship and dispose of all your hazardous
waste… [s]o [that] in the morning, you won't have any regrets about
sleeping with GSX."[29] A picture of a terrified plant manager fretting over
his hazmat failings highlighted the point: in the post–Love Canal world,

plant managers could choose whether or not to overcome the problems of toxic waste.[30] Flipping through the pages of *HazMat World*, readers found many similar ads touting the virtues of all the new remediation tools available to chemical companies in the era of Superfund.

The environmental professionals remediating Love Canal in the 1980s would have relied on the products advertised in *HazMat World* magazine. In fact, the very idea that Love Canal could be resettled depended on the work of environmental professionals. Often caught between the worlds of activism and politics, environmental engineers, consultants, and technicians worked in an unenviable climate. Concerned citizens often confronted them about the hazards of the job, while political and industrial officials wondered about the efficacy (and cost) of hazmat remediation programs. Decades later, some of Love Canal's environmental engineers still register an understandable sensitivity about their work, noting that they had been charged with cleaning up Love Canal at a time when very few models existed.

But the reengineering of Love Canal also put project engineers in a more prominent place than they otherwise would have been. Many of North America's leading environmental engineering firms worked on site: E.C. Jordan, Malcolm Pirnie, CH2M Hill, and Conestoga-Rovers, among others. Love Canal offered an unparalleled opportunity for them to show their talent—and they took advantage of it. An intriguing perspective comes from the company responsible for Love Canal remediation in the first place: Conestoga-Rovers. A Canadian firm founded just a few years before Love Canal emerged as a toxic tragedy, Conestoga-Rovers billed itself as a small but cutting-edge environmental engineering company. Although it started with roughly a dozen employees, the firm's founders thought their company would grow as deindustrialization advanced and more communities and governments confronted the various waste legacies of the industrial past. They were right: twenty-five years after the firm began working at Love Canal, Conestoga-Rovers employed more than 2,300 people throughout North America. During that time, Conestoga-Rovers remediated some of the most important Superfund sites in the United States, including nearly half of the "top ten" worst places as defined by the EPA. Yet the firm's big break—once advertised on the company's website as a milestone in environmental engineering—was Love Canal. As Don Haycock, co-founder of the firm, recalled, "[w]e did the engineering and construction supervision of the [Love Canal remediation] project and got a high profile out of that." As a matter of fact, he continued, "that led to a whole lot of opportunities to work on clean-up projects across the U.S. and Canada."[31]

Ironically, company co-founder Frank Rovers was lecturing at the University of Buffalo on "solid waste management failures in North America" when the Love Canal problem arose. As he remembered, American engineers approached him in 1977 about a leaking dump in Niagara Falls. Where potential liability concerns and/or project inexperience held other firms back, Rovers saw it as a "golden opportunity."[32] Young and bold— about the same age as many irate Love Canal residents—Haycock and Rovers implemented the remediation plan that state and federal officials hoped would put the Love Canal problem to rest. They then monitored it for several years, becoming in effect the face of the remediation project itself. During resettlement debates, for instance, Conestoga-Rovers engineers testified to Love Canal's improving health. As a 1985 engineering report put it, a remedial action plan "was initiated by [Conestoga-Rovers] to reduce the environmental and health hazard that resulted from the escape of toxic chemicals from the dump."[33] And the firm's plan seemed to be on track.

4. Landscape Life Support

As habitability experts would learn of Love Canal remediation, Conestoga-Rovers followed a "worst first" formula that tackled "the greatest environmental health hazard"—leachate—before creating a long-term vision of waste management at the dump. Accordingly, the remediation program initially sought to seal the dump off from both the elements and surrounding landscape—to dry it out and shore it up.[34] During the first phase of containment operations, which stretched from October of 1978 through November of 1979, workers created a massive barrier drain system that funneled leachate to a pumping station. Consisting of a three-foot-wide trench—made of "7000 feet of extra strength perforated vitrified clay tile"—the drain encircled much of the dump. Installed at depths of between 12 and 20 feet and gently "bedded in and covered with a minimum of one foot of crushed stone," the tile drain system funneled wandering wastes "to wet wells where the liquids were pumped out of the ground." At the treatment plant, "raw leachate" was sorted into solid and liquid components. Solid waste was then stored in on-site tanks, while liquid substances were filtered through massive "activated carbon absorbers," flushed with hydrogen peroxide, then released into storm sewers. As the 1985 report bragged, the Love Canal containment system was state-of-the-art and could process 160 gallons of leaking waste per minute. The dump needed this advanced hydraulic technology, for in roughly six years the filtration plant processed the rather unbelievable total of 22 million gallons of leachate (approximately 4 million gallons per year).[35] Engineers completed Phase I operations by installing a three-foot-thick clay cap over the dump ("final permeability...less than 1×10^{-7} centimeters per second") that prevented "volatiles and fugitive dust" from becoming airborne while also limiting the "infiltration" of rainwater inside the dump.[36]

With the basic task of securing the dump complete, engineers moved to Phase II by refining the containment system and obliterating the most contaminated homes. With the majority of the neighborhood evacuated (or soon to be out of their homes), workers began bulldozing inner-ring houses in mid-June of 1982. "Bulldozers have smashed the first of 227 bungalows to be destroyed near the old Love Canal dump," the AP reported.[37] Over the course of the summer, the rest of the homes around the canal would be plowed under, their remains covered with clay and embedded forever in the toxic landscape. Strangely, the 99th Street School was not initially slated for demolition (the city continued to battle the state over the loss of school property); it finally came down in 1983. Project managers also improved the dump's clay cover by putting a "high density polyethylene" sheet over the entire site, which they then topped with a grassy knoll. Though the Love Canal dump now had three layers of protection—clay, plastic, and grass—the polyethylene liner remained its key (if hidden) element. Functioning, in one engineer's words, like "a big umbrella" over Love Canal, the polyethylene liner more effectively pushed rainwater and snowmelt towards the filtration system surrounding the dump. A miracle of environmental technology, the liner was stitched from some of the same basic chemical elements sitting in the ground it covered—an irony lost on few experts.[38]

Throughout the 1980s, engineers worked on the third phase of Love Canal remediation: cleaning area creeks and sewers. They cut off many of the neighborhood's sewer lines from city infrastructure, further separating the dump from its natural environment. Engineers also extended treatment and monitoring programs to nearby sewers and creeks, as well as the 93rd Street School grounds, which also registered chemical contamination. By the end of the decade, project managers had dredged Black Creek and erected a new brick treatment plant at the dump.

In theory at least, the dump was contained as the 1980s came to a close. With its impressive collection of pipes, tiles, hydraulic pumps, and synthetic covers, Love Canal was shielded from rainwater, snowmelt, and floodwaters that might release the dump's dreaded waste into the world. In a way, technology had allowed the Love Canal landscape to return to its initial postwar identity as a hazardous waste dump. But it was more than that now. For the new Love Canal was a steely inorganic machine that kept the local landscape alive via the latest remediation technologies. Love Canal was not so much remediated as on life support. Project managers testified to the hydraulic sublime they created at Love Canal by conjuring one simple fact: by 1985, the treatment plant processed, on average, 31,000 gallons of leachate per day![39]

Despite this impressive containment system, even engineers emphasized the extended nature of Love Canal remediation, both in terms of costs and maintenance. That became clear when the clay cap placed on the southern part of the dump was compromised. As a 1985 report explained, leachate came to the surface, thus "contaminating parts of the clay cap" and hindering the reduction of waste flows. Engineers built "lateral drains" across the canal to solve the problem.[40] (Later, in 1993, engineers would again have to repair "a portion of the Love Canal cap").[41] But the lesson was clear: Love Canal would always need the helping hand of technology to survive. It could never be considered a natural environment again. (The 1986 Superfund Amendments would require five-year status reports, drawn from monitoring wells pervading the Emergency Declaration Area).

Why not remove toxic waste altogether? That question came up occasionally, but most remediation experts argued against removal of Love Canal waste. For one thing, the process would require intensive monitoring of waste every step of the way to its new resting place, a very costly matter. For another, the new dump would need to comply with RCRA provisions on such issues as dioxin disposal. (Now an old dump could not transfer its contents to a new dump without having to meet RCRA regulations about waste disposal!) Finally, few other dumps or communities would want Love Canal waste in their midst. For these and other reasons, environmental engineers recommended dealing with Love Canal waste on site.

Like it or not, some environmental engineers predicted, this was the future beyond Love Canal too: cleaning and reusing troubled landscapes. Knowing that a skeptical public would doubt such claims, Conestoga-Rovers took various opportunities to explain its remediation program at Love Canal. In perhaps the most famous example, Frank Rovers testified before Congress in March 1979. Put in the nearly impossible place of following the hard-hitting testimony of Love Canal residents, Rovers did quite well, explaining to wary senators who had just heard tales of environmental hell that his firm was cleaning up Love Canal. Although it would certainly cost a significant amount of money, Rovers said, remediating old hazardous sites was necessary and proper. The environmental bill for decades of industrialization had come due; he made clear that governments, industry, and even citizens must now pick up the tab. But, he emphasized, a combination of environmental vigilance and technical savvy would surely allow "North American society" (in Rovers' words) to prevent future chemical disasters and reclaim hazardous areas for productive use.[42]

Like the citizen environmentalists preceding him, Rovers set Love Canal in a much wider social and political context. Noting that industrial society had reached a crisis point, Rovers argued that the time had come for a rigorous approach to hazardous waste. Companies should do "in-house" reviews of their past practices; environmental agencies should establish remediation guidelines and programs; and politicians should implement new laws regulating toxic waste disposal. No one could avoid responsibility for the world's toxic past or future—not government; not industry; not even consumers, who devoured plastic products and new chemicals with abandon. Now that Love Canal had uncovered the problem of toxic waste disposal, politicians, consumers, and businesses could forthrightly address the problem. With environmental experts like Conestoga-Rovers leading the way, the future would be less hazardous indeed.[43]

Still, there was one issue Rovers could not confidently tackle: Love Canal habitability. That was a political question. But Rovers was sure that the Love Canal landscape could be remediated and reused in some way, shape, or form. After all, he had already staked his company's reputation on it.[44]

5. More Expert Debate at Love Canal

Divisions remained over Love Canal resettlement. As a result, state and federal officials created a Technical Review Committee (TRC) to oversee future studies of Love Canal. Working under the aegis of the EPA, the Centers for Disease Control, the Department of Health and Human Services, and both the New York Department of Environmental Conservation and Department of Health, the TRC was composed of senior officials who would try to reach consensus on Love Canal habitability. In 1984, the TRC assembled a blue-ribbon committee of nearly a dozen experts in fields ranging from toxicology and medicine to epidemiology and the sociology of disaster. With glowing dossiers, the panelists represented some of the best minds working in fields relevant to Love Canal habitability (most notably, perhaps, Dr. Devra Davis, an authority on public health and toxic pollution).[45]

TRC experts examined Love Canal from every possible angle. They toured the dump and neighborhood, met with remediation engineers as well as former residents, and pored over every study available on toxic waste (the group's bibliography of cited works stretched to 60 pages). They also conducted seven public meetings—six in Niagara Falls and one in Buffalo—each with a stenographer who dutifully recorded panelists' every word for the public record. As the panel's final report noted, "the public" had become a critical part of environmental debates at Love Canal and must therefore be included in all deliberations about the area's future. "To assure community understanding and support for government actions regarding the EDA," the document explained, "no significant changes in procedures or operations related to Love Canal remediation and management activities...should be made before community input is sought."[46] Activists, former residents, and even those who never left Love Canal took panelists at their word, attending meetings and asking difficult questions. At several meetings, the ETF's Margeen Hoffman reminded panelists that the health and well-being of future residents must remain a priority, while the indefatigable Joann Hale represented the LCHA's stand that the area should never be resettled.[47]

Though empaneled to shed light on Love Canal habitability, TRC experts decided that they would not issue a specific recommendation on that thorny matter. Rather, the review panel would establish "habitability criteria" that might allow state and federal officials to issue an authoritative decision on resettlement. Forming habitability criteria was itself a difficult and complex process. Panelists had to consider toxicological data gathered at Love Canal since remediation efforts had begun, the latest findings in modern epidemiology, and insights drawn from comparative urban and public health studies. There were no easy answers, they discovered. But panelists came to see habitability in aspirational terms: experts sought to establish goals that would have to be met in order for Love Canal (or any comparable area) to be defined as livable. If these conditions were met, then political officials could render a decision on resettlement—but not before then.

Experts considered several ways of establishing habitability criteria. One methodology involved investigating Love Canal remediation over time—in other words, judging whether or not clean-up work had successfully reduced chemical threats to the neighborhood. Another revolved around a risk assessment of Love Canal chemicals: whether or not they had been shown to affect animal and/or human health. Still another way concerned epidemiology: assessing disease patterns in the neighborhood and their relationship to chemical waste. Experts also debated the merits of comparison studies: studying a remediated Love Canal in relation to a state-of-the-art hazardous waste dump somewhere else in the United States to see if conditions in Niagara Falls were better or worse than average.

Each of these approaches offered a scientific foundation for expert analysis, though none offered an absolute habitability standard that might unlock Love Canal's future. For instance, experts noted that risk assessment data—much of which came from animal tests—was not advanced enough to determine if Love Canal chemicals definitively harmed human life (in fact, risk assessment determinations had shifted as new lab work came in). Similarly, the rising field of epidemiology could not always link specific chemicals to certain diseases (even if, as members of the public pointed out, some studies did connect chemical exposures to various cancers). Studying the abatement of chemical waste over time was also deemed inappropriate, for the simple reason that monitoring data at Love Canal proved to be disputatious (experts learned that some earlier chemical samples from area homes were not collected or stored properly). As for comparing a remediated Love Canal to a state-of-the-art dump, panelists noted that most hazardous waste facilities contained a unique toxic brew of waste, not to mention different geological conditions and disposal histories. With different toxic pasts, they contained little that might be compared to Love Canal.

Though the panelists aimed to separate the science of resettlement from the politics, they recognized the inherent difficulty of doing so at Love Canal. Merely establishing the parameters of possible resettlement might lead politicians to believe that Love Canal was habitable. Here, the voices of former residents and activists haunted expert deliberations. Indeed, they often challenged panelists to consider alternative uses for the area that avoided resettlement altogether. Some experts agreed with this line of thinking, but others believed that habitability criteria might create useful environmental benchmarks. After all, a century of industrialization, chemical production, and toxic dumping had altered environments from Chicago to Cleveland to Boston. Some experts asked : Was the remediated Love Canal categorically worse than other areas of the American Rust Belt? If not, it might make sense to create habitability criteria that, once met, would allow people to live voluntarily in a new Love Canal.[48]

The robust character of expert debate on this and other matters indicated that scientific discourse alone could not solve the riddle of habitability criteria. Indeed, as the committee proceeded, it often moved out of the realm of lab science and into the realm of social science. For instance, experts examined not only the science of remediation but the meaning of neighborhood life in a post-disaster setting like Love Canal. Assuming remediation worked and certain parts of the area were resettled, the question remained whether a true neighborhood could ever take shape again. Certain streets had been literally bulldozed out of existence, while other parts of the area had chemical hot spots. A Love Canal street with a mix of resettled homes and uninhabitable lots might look more like *Mad Max* than *Leave It To Beaver*. Who would want to live in such a pockmarked zone? Neighborhoods, as the sociologists on the panel argued, comprised much more than good houses and yards. They had a sense of social cohesion as well. Yet the social cohesion of neighborhood life had been undermined at Love Canal. With this in mind, experts concluded that area resettlement must not be done on a house-by-house basis. For the neighborhood to be "viable" again, whole streets must be declared habitable.[49]

Despite continual challenges, TRC experts eventually submitted a report defining a "multistep approach" to Love Canal habitability criteria.[50] The first step sought to apply environmental health standards to specific chemicals (a small group of Love Canal Indicator Chemicals, or LCICs) found in remediated areas of the neighborhood. Though still relatively new, environmental health standards—including the federal government's known action limits on certain chemicals, like the one-part-per-billion standard for dioxin—had the virtue of clarity. A high reading of LCICs would disqualify an area from resettlement; a lower reading would not. By examining chemical concentrations throughout the EDA, health officials could thus establish whether or not certain homes, streets, waterways, and sewers met threshold limits set by state and federal agencies.

The second step in the process compared the presence of LCICs in the remediated Love Canal landscape to those in a similar neighborhood in the Buffalo/Niagara region. Here, experts believed that they might discover where Love Canal stood in the region's post-industrial ecosystem. There was one caveat: any comparison neighborhood must be located at least a mile away from a hazardous waste dump. With roughly 200 hazardous waste dumps in Western New York, that would be difficult. But experts thought it could be done.

Its task done, the expert panel turned things over to the TRC. In doing so, panelists did not offer a road map to Love Canal resettlement. Indeed, some experts doubted the efficacy of a speedy repopulation of the area. But they hoped that by establishing criteria, they might begin a thoughtful discussion of habitability, including whether or not resettlement even made sense.

The TRC then produced a report of nearly 1,000 pages, entitled "Love Canal Emergency Declaration Area Proposed Habitability Criteria." The massive document did more than summarize panel proceedings: it rendered a positive verdict on Love Canal's future. While the TRC report certainly underscored experts' and others' reservations, it nevertheless favored Love Canal resettlement. According to the TRC document, "scientists concluded that habitability criteria could and should be established for the EDA."[51] Noting that "the process of establishing habitability criteria was open to public and community involvement was actively solicited throughout the process," the report implied that few people on or off the panel offered outright objections to habitability.[52] This meant that, if the habitability criteria were met, resettlement not only might but should begin. It was perhaps a slight modification of what some experts had said. But it was an important shift in tone and emphasis.

Indeed, the report turned doubt into decisive action, arguing that lack of adequate knowledge about chemical impacts was no reason to stop resettlement from being considered and, if habitability criteria were met, pursued. "In most situations, including that of the Love Canal EDA, judgments about suitability for human habitation rarely involve a simple 'yes/no' response," the TRC report explained. When debating habitability criteria, the report continued,

> Important considerations include the degree of certainty about the presence or absence of risks and whether these risks are immediate or delayed, serious or negligible, voluntary or involuntary and whether restricted habitability or alternative land use is intended. With regard to the Love Canal EDA, the judgment is also complicated by the fact that . . . the existing exposure and health assessment data of Love Canal have created questions in the community concerning the risks posed by re-habitation of the Love Canal EDA. To the degree that they exist, any risks would be imposed involuntarily, may cause delayed health effects, and may be related to serious health outcomes.[53]

In short, the final TRC report indicated that the available science and technological expertise extended only so far. Risk and doubt were there but they would always be an inherent part of the resettlement debate. For example, while sampling data had been extensive, it was not full proof.

And so, the very idea of creating "statistically valid comparisons of low-level environmental contamination between [Love Canal] EDA neighborhoods and comparison areas" created "certain major problems." Among other things, there was "a high percentage of reported 'non detect' results for chemicals known to have been deposited in Love Canal" (meaning that tests registered between zero and current action levels but not above them) and "little data" on LCICs in "comparable residential settings in the US."[54] Love Canal could never be certified as absolutely safe—or uncontaminated—because the science could not prove that.

Yet rather than concluding that these problems rendered even habitability criteria null—or empaneling experts again to discuss alternatives—the TRC reframed resettlement debate by stating that there was ample reason to move forward.

6. Love Canal's New Future

Between 1985 and 1989, the TRC addressed the expert panel's two main habitability questions: What chemical threats existed in the EDA, and how did certain portions of Love Canal compare to other industrialized areas of the region? On the first matter, the TRC found that several parts of the EDA had acceptable levels of chemical concentration, as test readings for the half-dozen or so (out of 200) LCICs were often— though not always—lower than known threshold limits. On the second matter, the TRC compared Love Canal's chemical nature to four regional census tracts (one each in the Erie Country towns of Cheektowaga and Tonawanda, and two in Niagara Falls), finding that the neighborhood did not have dramatically worse chemical contamination than these areas. Though no part of Love Canal was deemed safe in absolute terms, the TRC argued that habitability criteria had been met. According to one news report, no less than the head of the EPA believed that Love Canal was "safe enough from chemical contamination to permit people to move back in."[55]

With the EPA's blessing, resettlement decisions devolved down to the New York State Health department. On September 27, 1988, David Axelrod announced that several parts of Love Canal were deemed "suitable for residential use."[56] After nearly a decade of remediation activities, several years of intense scientific study, and millions of dollars of testing, Axelrod's words ratified the dreams of those who believed that even the most poisoned landscapes could be redeveloped via the artful workings of environmental engineering. Perhaps as important, almost no taxable land would be left behind in deindustrializing Niagara Falls, in this case over 200 parcels of property that would supply as much as $3 million to city coffers. Pending further remediation of the area, including the dredging of nearby Bergholtz Creek, and the approval of what Axelrod referred to as an "overall land-use plan," LCARA would soon be selling homes. The rush was on, the *New York Times* observed, as "more than 400 people have expressed interest in buying one of the abandoned Love Canal homes" at a discount.[57]

While Axelrod approved resettlement north and west of the dump (an area now known as "EDA sampling areas 4, 5, 6 and 7"), he rejected habitability on streets "East of the Canal and South," ("EDA sampling areas 1, 2 and 3"). Although several families chose to remain there through the 1980s, Axelrod noted that these sections had higher chemical readings and "are not now suitable for residential use." (Nevertheless, Axelrod would not require current residents to leave.) Despite experts' concerns about a pockmarked neighborhood, Axelrod's "split decision" turned several Love Canal areas into a No Man's Land, where homes stood empty and the landscape ran wild a few streets away from refurbished houses.[58] One empty and never-to-be-restored street near the old dump had become known as "Desolation Row." "There's nothing worse on this side of the street than on that side," one resident who had stayed in his home on 101st Street told a reporter. "It doesn't make any sense."[59] But in the new logic of Love Canal resettlement, it did.

Like the TRC, Axelrod argued that risk remained omnipresent in all resettlement decisions. "Both the criteria and the ultimate decision [to repopulate sections 4–7 of the EDA] are...bound by the limits of scientific knowledge about the impact of toxic exposures upon the health of our citizens," he observed. "Although the scientific knowledge is greater than it was in the 1940s and 1950s when the Love Canal was used as a hazardous waste disposal site, the scientific knowledge is not now and never will be complete or absolute, so that any public health judgment necessarily involves the assessment of an inherent level of uncertainty."

And yet, government was in the business of rendering such difficult "public health judgments on behalf of its citizens." The "specific case of Love Canal" was unique only insofar as it compelled government officials to make a complex decision about a highly visible place. But Axelrod remained confident that he had done the best he could with the science available to him.[60]

By turning doubt into decisive action, Axelrod invited angry rebuttals from former residents. As Lois Gibbs pointed out, Love Canal comparison areas were in industrialized zones of Western New York, not the pristine suburbs that might form an environmental control. For Gibbs, comparing Love Canal to other gritty neighborhoods was "like comparing rotten oranges with rotten oranges."[61] Gibbs argued that the "decision set a bad precedent for assuring public safety from abandoned dumps."[62] (The TRC very nearly agreed with Gibbs, noting that it could not comply with the expert panel's original recommendation of finding a comparison area at least one mile away from a toxic dump; it settled for half a mile as a gauge). A lawyer for the Natural Resources Defense Council, ready to file a lawsuit on behalf of Gibbs, agreed, calling the EPA's defense of Axelrod's habitability decree "a narrow legalistic reading of [the agency's] responsibility, which is to determine what is safe for people."[63]

More worrisome, Gibbs and others wondered why no one had conducted a risk assessment of Love Canal's new environment. After all, according to the EPA, risk is defined as "the chance of harmful effects to human health or to ecological systems resulting from exposure to an environmental stressor." A standard tool in the study of human health, risk assessments determine the possible impact of chemicals, radiation, and other "stressors" on human disease patterns. For many Love Canal activists, there could be no greater example of an "environmental stressor" than the tons of chemicals still in the ground.[64] Joined by others, activists insisted on a risk assessment for the new Love Canal.[65]

Well versed in the give-and-take of Love Canal politics, state and federal officials expressed confidence in their habitability decision. On some occasions, they even redeployed doubt as a tool for moving forward with resettlement. As EPA Administrator William K. Reilly wrote to Gibbs in May 1990 (just before the first homes went on the market), "the lack of appropriate toxicological data for the many chemicals present in the canal

and the lack of standards of acceptability for these chemicals make the...
risk assessment approach unworkable at this time."⁶⁶ In other words, science was still not up to the task of determining whether the presence of
certain chemicals, at Love Canal or elsewhere, translated into a major
health threat—but that should not stop resettlement. An incredulous
Gibbs met personally with Reilly to further press her case, arguing stren-
uously that if too much remained unknown about Love Canal chemicals,
then no one should live in the area.⁶⁷

For this reason, Gibbs and other activists saw the Love Canal habitability decision as a new call to arms. "We must stop this madness," Gibbs
announced in a CCHW missive about Love Canal resettlement. "If they
move families into Love Canal and cover up the problems, people at sites
across the country will be HURT. No longer will Love Canal be the
symbol of shame for corporate polluters or the symbol of failure by
government regulators."⁶⁸ Focusing again on the fact that no risk assessment had been done, and that comparison areas in Niagara Falls contained
some of the same pollutants as at Love Canal (meaning that they shared a
toxic ecosystem and thus provided no measure of environmental safety),
Gibbs asked the national grassroots community to stand up and be heard
by bombarding both the EPA and the governor of New York with letters
of opposition.

7. Creative Destruction: Love Canal Becomes
Black Creek Village

This time, their protest failed. On August 15, 1990, Love Canal's residential history came full circle when LCARA put ten refurbished homes in
the northern end of the sub-division on the market. Having already received hundreds of inquiries, the redevelopment agency anticipated a tide
of prospective buyers.⁶⁹ LCARA would not be disappointed. Advertised
at 10 to 20 percent below market rate (the average selling price of a middle-
sized ranch house was around $50,000), homes sold at a steady pace
during the 1990s. In just a few years, nearly 100 houses had been purchased; by 1995, roughly 70 more were under contract. LCARA officials
predicted that every one of the nearly 240 houses would soon be gone.⁷⁰

The revitalized subdivision "has all the characteristics of a terrific neighborhood," an LCARA representative told a reporter. "The street pattern is very good, the vegetation is mature, there's a mall nearby." The refurbished homes also offered people a chance to make history, for "the first people in [to the new Love Canal are]...pioneers of a sort."[71]

William Love would have been proud. Now renamed "Black Creek Village," the habitable area was also dubbed "A Model Community," as a sign proclaimed outside the LCARA sales office on 96th Street. Where was the dump? LCARA could not simply ignore that question, for a massive chain link fence remained the neighborhood's most prominent feature. But there was no signage, nor would there ever be, marking the remediated landscape. The tall fence surrounding the dump, as well as the monitoring wells and hazmat building on the grounds inside, were all that marked the area as forbidden and otherworldly.

Yet new homeowners could not totally ignore the dump, for LCARA purchase contracts included a provision that buyers acknowledge the receipt of documents relating to Love Canal's toxic past. The packet included information on the habitability decision, a fact sheet on resettlement, and an infrared photo of Love Canal wastes that had been locked inside the remediated landscape. This information was designed to underscore Love Canal's new nature. Sealed by the best environmental engineering available, the chemicals were no longer a threat. *The Niagara Gazette,* where Michael Brown had worked to uncover the problem in the 1970s, now cheered resettlement. "Let's get on with the sale of homes," the paper editorialized. With the wastes contained and several areas deemed habitable by both state and federal agencies, LCARA should "move swiftly" to get the homes spruced up and new people moved into the subdivision. "Ten years is a long time to study a problem," the editorial commented, and now that the state had rendered a verdict in favor of resettlement, everyone should move beyond the "acrimony" of days gone by and embrace the "new neighborhood" taking shape in Niagara Falls.[72]

This rosy view of things was soon challenged. When LCARA produced a promotional video of Love Canal's troubled past and golden future, its plan to use children from a nearby YMCA summer program was scuttled when a mother complained. Telling a local reporter that she opposed resettlement, a boiling "mad" Gina DiFranco refused to let her child appear in the video. DiFranco lived in Forest Glen, another city area where residents were being evacuated because of chemical contamination.[73] She derisively said that the only way her children would appear in the video was if they were "dressed in black." State Attorney General Robert Abrams also threatened to sue the agency if it did not correct misleading portions of the video, including LCARA's claim that the Love Canal landscape was geologically "well-suited for a landfill." According to Abrams, this view was "inconsistent with the well-established presence of fractured soil around the canal, the shallow sandy soil and the high water table, all of which contributed to the migration of chemicals toward surrounding homes."[74]

Such skirmishes did little to deter LCARA. The agency's job was to promote area redevelopment and it did so quite well. Indeed, well before the first refurbished home was sold, LCARA officials focused on rebranding the entire neighborhood. LCARA flirted with several new names, including "Sunrise City," before settling on "Black Creek Village" (a nod to the creek running along the neighborhood's edge).[75] But LCARA realized that a name change would be just the start of Love Canal's creative destruction. In 1989, it hired Saratoga Associates, a well-known landscape design firm, to craft a Master Plan for the changing neighborhood. Placing its strategic plan in a much wider context of urban renewal, the firm stated that "the rehabilitation and redevelopment of the Love Canal EDA presents a unique opportunity which very few large metropolitan cities can take advantage [of]." A Love Canal makeover would allow Niagara Falls to simultaneously recapture "a lost tax base and provide new residential and commercial opportunities." Of course, the new Love Canal would also be a model for reusing Superfund sites.[76] In short, there was much to commend a Love Canal makeover.

While it acknowledged the area's hazardous past, Saratoga Associates accentuated the positives of Love Canal resettlement. Agreeing with LCARA that redevelopment, rather than a no-growth or "passive greenspace" alternative, offered the most benefit to the Falls' economy, the Master Plan's "Preferred Land Use Concept" called for variegated development in the neighborhood. Sections north and west of the dump, deemed habitable, would be ideal for owner-occupied homes (with the exception the former Lasalle Development, which would become senior housing), while sections east and south, deemed uninhabitable but salvageable pending further remediation work, would be designated for light industrial use, including office parks and small manufacturing operations. The Master Plan envisioned 5,000 people living and working in Black Creek Village, with roughly half residing in habitable sections and half working in industrial/ commercial sections. To complete the mixed-use plan, the report called for several parks—about thirty acres, or enough to support up to 300 people per day. Agreeing with Frederick Law Olmsted's classic notion that parks restored urban dwellers' minds and bodies, the Master Plan made sure that Black Creek Village looked and felt green.[77]

The Master Plan also emphasized the erasure of historical memory as a vital part of the area's future.[78] In the parlance of the Master Plan, the dump would be renamed the "Containment Area" while mention of the Love Canal crisis would vanish from the sub-division's future operations. As the "Master Plan" added rather tellingly, local officials should interpret any future chemical crisis as new and unrelated to Love Canal's past.[79] To overcome physical reminders of the dump, landscaping was also deemed indispensable to the area's rebirth. The Love Canal Land Use Advisory Committee, created in the wake of Axelrod's 1988 habitability decision, made this goal explicit when it recommended that the dump be "isolated from the residential communities surrounding the site in a manner which is aesthetically pleasing and which enhances the whole EDA area."[80] While the massive chain link fence posed an obvious hurdle to that goal, consultants recommended "screening" and "buffering"—the strategic placement of shrubs and trees in front of the fence and the many monitoring wells behind it—to make the landscape appear more green.[81] Soon, the dump itself would have park-like attributes, including a lush lawn that was mowed consistently, lines of trees along the fence, and plants.

While former residents continued to protest these developments, Love Canal's metamorphosis into Black Creek Village proceeded without major interruption in the 1990s. Reporters interviewing new homeowners found that they liked the refurbished subdivision's affordability and location. But something else emerged as well: prospective homeowners thought that the neighborhood was safer than most places in Western New York precisely because it had been remediated via Superfund. As one person put it, the area is now "probably one of the safest places to live in Niagara Falls" because its toxic nature had been exposed, fixed and contained.[82]

The speed with which this new narrative of Love Canal's representative safety took shape was impressive. According to this view, the remediated portion of the neighborhood was actually better off than most other places in the region (or even the country) because it was constantly monitored. As one LCARA representative stated, "a lot of neighborhoods in the Niagara Falls area are built on sites filled in with chemical waste."[83] But few if any had the built-in environmental warning signs like those in Black Creek Village. Knowing that, LCARA officials declared, new residents could move in full of confidence about their landscape. In this sense, even redevelopment officials found it hard to ignore and forget Love Canal's past. As they discovered, it could even be used to sell new homes in the area.

7. A Toxic Monument

Beyond LCARA, activists continued to raise concerns about the new neighborhood. Indeed, the notion that Love Canal would become a model for the wonders of toxic remediation among the population at large—and not just environmental engineers or health officials—worried former residents. Lois Gibbs, Pat Brown, Luella Kenny, and others argued that Love Canal remained a touchstone of skewed environmental values precisely because politicians had again placed economic development ahead of public health. Gibbs, who in 1990 won the Goldman Prize for environmental activism, accused local, state, and federal officials of wanting to erase Love Canal from public memory altogether.[84] Gibbs again took her struggle to the White House, hoping that federal officials beyond the EPA would scuttle plans for Black Creek Village. She also told reporters that she was going to "picket" governor Mario Cuomo and meet with worldwide leaders at the United Nations about turning back Love Canal resettlement.[85] But her protest did not work. Black Creek Village was soon settled.

Far from wanting Love Canal to simply lie fallow, activists like Gibbs envisioned the neighborhood as a memorial to toxic waste victims.[86] From historic markers placed around the subdivision to a toxics education center, they wanted Love Canal to inspire global conversation about hazardous waste policies past, present, and future. "We've learned a lot from Love Canal," Brown told a reporter from the *Christian Science Monitor* in

1988. But, she suggested, Americans needed to learn much more; for instance, that it was not feasible to really "clean up toxic waste" and resettle areas like Love Canal. "If so, let's face up to it."[87] Brown and others thought that Love Canal should stand as a shrine to environmental neglect. Perhaps no one made this point more artfully than Violet Iadicicco, a former resident who argued that the area "should be turned into a public exhibit on the dangers of toxics." So shocked was she by the whitewashing of Love Canal's hazardous past that Iadicicco created "a large sign on the boarded frames of her old house" that proclaimed: "Tourists!! This is it! Love Canal!"[88] Thus, even as Black Creek Village's homes sold and Love Canal became a case study in successful remediation practices nationally, former residents kept alive a counter-narrative: that their old neighborhood was still beset by the flawed environmental values that led to the chemical crisis in the first place. For that reason, as Lois Gibbs would put, "Love Canal is not over. Love Canal will never be over!"

Epilogue

Haunted Love

> Love Canal taught us that we needed a mechanism to address abandoned
> hazardous waste sites, especially those that posed a threat to people's
> health. Decades later, Love Canal has become a symbol of our success
> under Superfund. It is once again a thriving community.
> —*EPA Regional Administrator Jane M. Kenny, 2004*[1]

At the edge of Black Creek Village, a short walkway leads to a granite
monument near a baseball diamond. Lined by flowers and shrubs, the
shiny slab sits below a tall flagpole where Old Glory soars above the
field. From a distance, visitors might guess that the monument honors a
local donor who sponsored area Little League teams, or perhaps a neighborhood hero lost in war. Closer inspection reveals a vastly different commemorative story. For the monument marks the Love Canal disaster.
Though situated about a quarter-mile away from the fenced-in dumping
grounds, it is the only public acknowledgement of the tragedy in the
area.[2] [Fig. 11]

Despite its near-hidden location (or perhaps because of it), the memorial heralds the subdivision's rebirth as a productive landscape. Placed
here after the Love Canal Area Revitalization Agency officially closed in
2003, the monument highlights key moments in the area's tumultuous
past, culminating in the advent of Black Creek Village. From the state's
declaration of a health peril at Love Canal to the resettling of the subdivision years later, the memorial—erected by LCARA representatives—
offers a tidy portrait of a toxic history that was once problematic but is
now squarely locked away.

Figure 11 Memorializing Love Canal, 2015: Situated a few blocks away from the fenced-in dump, the granite memorial provides the only official commemoration of the tragedy. It also illuminates the success story narrative of the Love Canal saga. (Courtesy Giles Holbrow)

This vision fits well with the EPA's triumphant narrative of Love Canal remediation. According to the announcement removing the dumping grounds from the National Priorities List in March 2004, the nightmare neighborhood had been transformed into "a flourishing community," as sections "to the west and north of the [old] canal have been revitalized, with more than 200 formerly boarded-up homes renovated and sold to new owners, and 10 newly-constructed apartment buildings." Heralding the prospect of further growth, the EPA noted that the "area east of the canal [once saddled with rows of empty streets] has also been sold for light industrial and commercial redevelopment."[3] Though the neighborhood's toxic trash was contained, the EPA cautioned that the "Love Canal site will continue to be monitored and remain eligible for cleanup work in the unlikely event that a change in site conditions should warrant such an action." Still, for the EPA, the main story was not Love Canal's problematic past but rather Black Creek Village's bright future. Indeed, the Love Canal landscape served as a symbol of Superfund glory. "Today," the EPA reported of hazardous waste remediation efforts in the 21st century, "Superfund sites are model airplane fields, airports, major department stores, soccer fields, golf courses, wildlife refuges and much more."[4] Love Canal now stood as a poster child of toxic remediation.

In both the physical memorial at Black Creek Village and EPA press releases touting Superfund successes, politicians, business leaders, and others tried to affix a final exclamation point to the neighborhood's toxic saga. Love Canal's problematic past, they proudly declared, was truly buried and gone.

Others disagreed with this triumphant narrative of Love Canal remediation. In fact, former residents saw the memorial itself as a flawed attempt to mark the Love Canal tragedy. By celebrating swift government action in the 1970s and 1980s, and area redevelopment in the 1990s and early 2000s, the monument emphasized progress over protest at Love Canal, leaving area visitors with a skewed version of the landscape's tumultuous past. Whether from the LCHA or ETF, activists have no place on the monument—there is no sign that they played a key role in rescuing Love Canal residents from toxic peril. Indeed, activists argued, the memorial erased grassroots protest altogether from the site's commemorative landscape.

This was an ominous sign of the times, activists claimed. With Congress refusing to reauthorize the tax on oil and gas companies, Superfund was imperiled (the original federal tax provision lapsed in 1995). By the early 2000s, even the EPA estimated that it did not have enough money to properly administer all of Superfund's needs.[5] As the *New York Times* opined, Superfund was less able than ever to work its miracles.[6] Luella Kenny put these pieces together, linking what she saw as faulty Love Canal memorialization to leaky environmental policies nationally. As she argued in March 2004, the EPA's recent removal of Love Canal from the National Priorities List seemed to say that all was fine at Superfund site number one and thus with toxic remediation throughout the land. But, as Kenny knew, Congress had just rejected another attempt to revive Superfund taxes. She saw EPA's action as an attempt to shift attention away from Superfund's financial troubles. As she put it, "environmental cleanup has decreased dramatically during the [George W.] Bush administration, and it has been suggested that the removal of Love Canal from the Superfund list was facilitated to demonstrate how the Bush administration cares for the environment."[7] If Superfund vanished, Kenny and others argued, who would pay for the future remediation of toxic sites around the country? (Like many others, Kenny supported Superfund programs but not the resettlement of neighborhoods around toxic dumps.)

Kenny's criticism flowed from years of struggle to keep Love Canal's activist memory alive. Focusing less on the site's rejuvenated nature, and more on the activists who heralded toxic peril in and beyond Niagara Falls, former residents and their allies focused again and again on the need for an updated Love Canal movement. Already by the mid-1980s, both the LCHA and the ETF used the Love Canal struggle to spur updated grassroots environmental action. After working with local, regional and national groups on toxic waste threats in the mid-1980s, the ETF produced "EarthCare: Lessons From Love Canal." Though most residents had been relocated from the infamous area, the ETF asserted that American society still had much to learn about "the transportation, storage and disposal of toxic wastes." These issues were far from buried and gone. As the group noted trenchantly, we "have learned in these nine years [since the leaking Love Canal dump was first discovered] that advocacy and vision cannot be one-time responses."[8] New generations of activists must compel American society to remember Love Canal, they said, particularly as the crisis receded from public consciousness. For the ETF, as for the LCHA, the memory of Love Canal activism and the prevention of future Love Canals went hand in hand.

Former residents often returned to their neighborhood to make just this point. For many years, Luella Kenny took students, environmental groups, and political and medical officials on Love Canal tours. Often stopping within sight of her former house—which is directly in the sightline of the LCARA monument—she recounts the way her family life fatefully intersected with Love Canal's volatile nature. "That's where my son played," she says to visitors in a whisper, pointing to the backyard that looms behind the LCARA monument. And, she continues, that's where the contaminated creek flooded its banks, creating pools of toxic water a stone's throw from her former back door. For Kenny, 1978, the year her youngest son died, is not part of some distant past; it remains palpably present. By bringing people back to the area she departed in sorrow, Kenny performs an unofficial act of memorialization. Even when local residents glare at her, or tell her to go away, Kenny stands her ground. "It's public property," she says. Stopping along the chain-link fence by the dump, walking through fields where old housing foundations still appear, and, finally, standing at the LCARA monument itself, she knows that this is a place where her family's personal tragedy became a symbol of toxic trouble everywhere. By telling her story, she hopes that others will learn to examine their own local environment—and fight back if they find problems.[9]

On that score, activists argue that the Love Canal site itself should never be deemed squeaky clean or even safe. "It's obviously not cleaned up," Gibbs argued vehemently in 2004 when the Superfund site was delisted, "because there are still 20,000 tons of chemicals buried there."[10] The LCHA's Barbara Quimby agreed, asserting that the EPA's removal of Love Canal from the active Superfund list sent the wrong message: that the area was "safe" and sound. "If it was safe, I'd [still] be living there. How much longer before what they've contained leaks back out?"[11]

With cutting comments like these, it is unsurprising that activists are not really welcome at Love Canal these days, either for official commemorations of the tragedy or unofficial tours of the neighborhood. Still, they dutifully return every few years for reunions and unofficial commemorations of the chemical crisis they endured and reshaped into an environmental movement with worldwide resonance. Visiting the area as part of a 35th anniversary reflection in 2013, Lois Gibbs told a reporter that she was still angry with the Black Creek Village success story narrative. By returning to Love Canal yet again, she hoped to raise awareness about chemical threats near and far. Using the area's physical modifications as a metaphor, she argued that Black Creek Village beautification disguised the subdivision's true (and polluted) nature as well as those who unearthed it decades beforehand. "They work so hard to cover up Love Canal that private property looks like it's some kind of gated community." But this "is not a gated community," Gibbs said; it is a toxic dump.[12]

Local, state and federal officials take these criticisms in stride. As one federal official commented in 2013, Love Canal remained "the most sampled piece of property on the planet."[13] It must be a habitable environment.

As these vignettes suggest, the Love Canal landscape still conjures powerful and powerfully conflicting views in the 21st century. Just as the EPA, LCARA officials, and Black Creek Village residents want to put Love Canal in the rearview mirror, so too do former activists seek to recall its memory by planning rallies, tours, and a variety of commemorative events. For the former group, Love Canal is now just another neighborhood on the American landscape; for the latter, it is sacred environmental ground and a shrine to toxic tragedies everywhere.

Scholars have a special term for embattled places like Love Canal: a memory site. According to historians of cultural conflict, a "memory site" is a contested environmental, historical, and/or physical space where official history collides with grassroots traditions. Even as official memory says one thing about an historic site or monument, dissenters conjure alternate interpretations.[14] The Lincoln Memorial offers the best example: Originally designed to monumentalize Lincoln's heroic memory as a Civil War statesman, it was redefined by civil rights activists (and most recently, LGBTQ reformers) as a battleground for equality.[15] At the Lincoln Memorial, like Love Canal, memory remains a rough-and-tumble sport.

Although conflicts over commemorating Love Canal began as soon as residents departed in the early 1980s, they intensified during resettlement debates, when both activists and LCARA representatives utilized the past as a way to frame area rehabilitation. Where LCARA defined Love Canal's troubles as part of a distant past—one buried by the wonders of remediation technology—activists unearthed the timeless nature of the toxic tragedy as well as the need to keep learning from it. But the terms of this battle over Love Canal's essential meaning were not always equal. While LCARA had the power of official institutions behind it (the state redevelopment agency and area politicians eager for tax revenue), activists remained on the fringes. Once again, they had to fight for legitimacy and public visibility. In fact, evacuation of the neighborhood proved to be a hurdle for activists hoping to remain relevant to Love Canal's future. If they no longer inhabited the area, critics asked, why should former residents matter?

In response to these and other challenges, activists innovated new ways of memorializing their struggle. For instance, they made sure that their archival records went to major university libraries. In 1988, Lois Gibbs bequeathed a portion of her voluminous CCHW files to Tufts University in Boston as a testament to grassroots environmentalism at Love Canal. (The entire run of "Everyone's Backyard," the CCHW's newsletter, is available free online). A dozen years later, Tufts Library purchased Gibbs' republished autobiography—strategically re-released in 1998 to mark the

20th anniversary of the Love Canal crisis and revealingly called *Love Canal: The Story Continues*—as its "one millionth book."[16] Speaking at a special reception in her honor, the now famous activist focused on present as well as past environmental struggles, bringing "the Love Canal story up to date" and "discussing the ongoing issues of grassroots environmental organization" around the country. As a reporter noted afterward, Gibbs' "visit came together with other events aimed at raising environmental awareness [in New England] and the pressing need for citizens to play a role in preserving a safe habitat."[17]

After folding in the early 1990s, the ETF donated its vast collections to the State University of New York at Buffalo as a way to "document the organizing of a unified grassroots response to Love Canal, one of the nation's most significant environmental disasters."[18] With over one million linear feet of documents, the "Love Canal Collection"—including an online link to residents' congressional testimony, resettlement debates, and maps—offers one of the most expansive portraits of environmental activism anywhere. Like the CCHW, the ETF believed that libraries and archives—dedicated as they were to preserving key parts of the nation's past—would sanctify their struggle for new generations of people.

As Gibbs and other activists knew, there was no lack of toxic trouble awaiting former residents, making Love Canal an enduring symbol of grassroots power in the 21st century. In the fall of 2014, for instance, the Missouri Coalition for the Environment invited Gibbs to speak at a "teach in" on the West Lake Landfill (located near St. Louis). A notorious radioactive dump, the landfill became double trouble when a slow-moving fire headed in its direction. Authorities claimed that the dump and fire racing toward it posed no significant health threats to area residents, but local activists remained dubious. At an event heralded as "Love Canal/West Lake with Lois Gibbs," the Missouri Coalition for the Environment asked the celebrated Niagara Falls activist for insight and inspiration on Missourians' grassroots struggle. Calling West Lake one of the worst dumps she had seen, Gibbs urged Missouri activists to keep fighting for stronger state and federal responses to the threatening situation. "West Lake Landfill is this generation's Love Canal," she told CNN.[19]

Ironically, even as they aided residents around the country in the new millennium, Gibbs and other Love Canal reformers discovered that their old neighborhood was again in the news for toxic trouble. Indeed, the 35th anniversary of the original Love Canal crisis coincided with a new round of residential complaints about chemical threats in Black Creek Village. In January 2011, area contractors removed an old sewer pipe from a street just outside the fenced-off dump (or containment area), which had "certain 'signature' Love Canal contaminants," as a report put it. Although Glenn Springs Holdings, the Occidental subsidiary responsible for monitoring the site since 1995, developed a remediation plan, local residents were not informed of any potential hazards. The state called it an isolated issue not worth much fuss. "Data from sampling over the past 25 years have demonstrated that the containment system is operating as designed and *is protective of health, safety and the environment,*" Glenn Springs Holdings reported.[20] (At that time, the dump's collection system was processing over 3 million gallons of leachate annually, more than 8,000 gallons per day). But some residents remained concerned. Indeed, several families went public with their health fears. As one story put it, a group of residents complained about "birth defects, soft and/or crumbling teeth, gastrointestinal disorders, reproductive disorders, cancer and severe heart conditions," among other maladies. Six families filed suit against various parties, including Occidental. By 2014, there were over a thousand claims pending from past and present residents of the neighborhood.[21] "History could be repeating itself," an AP reporter proclaimed. "The lawsuits, which don't specify damages sought, contend Love Canal was never properly remediated and dangerous toxins continue to leach onto residents' properties."[22] For her part, Gibbs counseled new residents to use the original Love Canal protest struggle as a guide. "The lesson we learned here is to turn up the heat," Gibbs said, noting that their fight had been a political as well as legal one. The issue remains unresolved.[23]

West Lake and Black Creek Village are only the most recent examples of next-generation toxic tales inspired by Love Canal. By the 1990s and early 2000s, "toxic literature" became a whole subgenre of environmental writing. Ruminating on the physiological and psychological impact of buried hazardous waste sites nationally and globally, these toxic tales often picked up where Love Canal left off. For instance, in *Lake Effect* (2008), former TV reporter Nancy Nichols examined the public health consequences of buried industrial waste in her beloved hometown of

Waukegan, Illinois.[24] Searching for answers after her sister is diagnosed with cancer, Nichols uncovers the bucolic town's toxic past. Once known as "Green Town"—a line taken from a story by native son Ray Bradbury about a beautiful Midwestern town modeled on Waukegan—the city's idyllic landscape turns brown when Nichols finds lurid details about its toxic foundation. Both the Johns Manville Corporation, an asbestos producer, and Outboard Marine Corporation, a manufacturer of PCBs, operated plants along the city's waterfront. Yet only much later, Nichols wrote, did any public examination of the town's industrial pollution take place.[25] The book ends with federal officials instituting a Superfund program along the waterfront. But this is no happily-ever-after saga, for, as Nichols shows, many politicians and officials sought to whitewash the area's hazardous past; some went so far as to remove stories about toxic pollution from area libraries and archives. Here, as at Love Canal, economic redevelopment remained the city's highest priority. And so, the "Waukegan story," Nichols concludes rather sadly, is "not unique." From Love Canal onward, the attempt to bury hazardous pasts has remained a problematic part of American culture.[26]

A thousand miles to the east of Waukegan, a similar story took shape on Long Island at the close of the 20th century. As Kelly McMasters' *Welcome to Shirley* (2008) illustrates, her hometown, located about an hour from New York City, had become a case study in the haunting quality of hazardous waste. For many area residents, the town of Shirley was best known as the home of the Brookhaven Atomic Laboratory. Yet scientific achievement was not what McMasters remembered most about her youth. Indeed, she grew up on fantastical tales of nuclear mistakes leaking out into the community. Later, after details of leaks surface, McMasters is stunned that no public discussion of Brookhaven's potential health hazards takes place. Town fathers react to the nuclear news by holding a name-changing contest (which doesn't work). Like the nearby nuclear facility, everything is hidden in plain sight. It is up to McMasters to uncover and remap the toxic town she loved but had to leave.[27] Indeed, she discovered that parts of her neighborhood were going through what Love Canal residents once endured. On one street bordering Brookhaven, colloquially known as "Death Row" (so named for multiple cancer fatalities), McMasters visits residents who launched a $1 billion class action lawsuit against the lab's management company. Significantly, McMasters writes, Love Canal lawyers headed the case. *Welcome to Shirley* memorializes the town she cannot forget but still dreads, as concerns about toxic consequences to her own body and to her family linger for years.

Perhaps the most famous toxic tale of the post–Love Canal era came from biologist Sandra Steingraber, who in the 1990s uncovered information about pesticides in rural Illinois. For Steingraber, the idea that Illinois— outside of Chicago, a bastion of soybeans, corn, and rural productivity— would be saturated with chemicals was far-fetched. But re-examining her local landscape indicated otherwise. As she discovered, most of the state's farmland was treated with pesticides, or over 50 million pounds per year. As she put it in *Living Downstream: A Scientist's Personal Investigation of Cancer and the Environment* (1998), since "World War II, these chemical poisons quietly familiarized themselves with the landscape."[28] Like Love Canal residents, she found that few people wanted to discuss the potential health impacts of pesticide use, partly for fear of disrupting the economy, partly for fear of the unknown. Like others, Steingraber's book followed in the footsteps of Gibbs, Paigen, Kenny, and other Love Canal residents, who decades earlier, had tried to put potentially harmful chemical pasts on the radar of both public health officials and politicians.

In fact, when Gibbs updated her autobiography for a third time in 2010, she tellingly called it *Love Canal and The Birth of the Environmental Health Movement*.[29] "Today," this version of her life story opened, "Love Canal is uttered alongside Chernobyl, Bhopal and now Deepwater Horizon as shorthand for one of the worst environmental health disasters in history." But when she first moved to Love Canal in the 1970s, Gibbs reminded readers unfamiliar with her story, "neither [her family] nor her neighbors knew anything about chemical health threats in the day-to-day American environment." Their "struggle to overcome a hazardous landscape," she proclaimed, raised "public awareness" about toxic threats across the nation. And that struggle was far from over when her most recent book was published. As Gibbs told a group of public health professors and students at the University of Maryland in the Spring of 2014, "the environmental justice movement [still] needs strong voices" to raise consciousness about the potential health impacts of chemicals, hazardous waste, and new energy initiatives like hydrofracking. Holding up a copy of the

CCHW's newsletter, "Everyone's Backyard," Gibbs argued once again that all Americans must fight for clean daily living environments.[30]

By this time, Love Canal represented not only a potent brand of grassroots activism but a new understanding of public health. According to *Generations at Risk,* a well-regarded study of toxic epidemiology, Love Canal was "one of the most significant environmental flashpoints" of the 20th century precisely because it linked concepts of public health to everyday environmental safety. More particularly, Love Canal raised questions about the meaning of toxic data in public health discourses—who gathered such data, why, and with what broader political, social, and legal significance. Love Canal also pointed to the limits of authoritative knowledge about toxic epidemiology. The "body of information we have to make informed decisions" about toxic impacts on the body "is characterized as much by what we don't know as by what we do know." Thus, "we must act boldly to correct past mistakes, replace dysfunctional [health testing] models with new ones fit to the task, and re-examine our social and public health priorities."[31] This might mean reworking the very calculus for determining toxic health threats in the American environment.

Unsurprisingly, one such calculus for understanding toxic health emerged at Love Canal. With the personal health and well-being of onetime residents a top priority, activists formed the Love Canal Medical Fund (LCMF, or the Fund) soon after evacuation occurred. Created in the wake of a legal settlement with Hooker/Occidental in 1983—one of many lawsuits against the company—the LCMF established a trust for "medical problems which *reasonably* could have been associated with exposure to toxic chemicals emanating from [the] former landfill in Niagara Falls, New York, known as the 'Love Canal.' "[32] Officially incorporated by New York State in 1985, the Fund placed nearly a million dollars in an account that could be used by the 1,328 residents involved in the lawsuit. Although governed by a board of directors and "medical officers," the Fund has remained a citizen organization through nearly three decades of operation. It still operates today. Luella Kenny has been its head officer for many years, and both Lois Gibbs and former Love Canal resident Joe Dunmire have served on the board.

Like a medical safety net, the Fund offers both preventative and supplemental care to former Love Canalers. While most former residents have some form of health insurance, they could not count on complete coverage for escalating health care costs, particularly diagnostic tests and medications associated with long-term and/or catastrophic illnesses potentially related to chemical exposures.[33] Moreover, with deindustrialization ravaging benefits plans at many large companies, the LCMF offered an additional layer of care for former residents who might otherwise avoid annual check-ups and physicals. Having access to lifelong care is vital for former residents. Studies have showed that, as Love Canalers entered their fifties and sixties, the prevalence of certain diseases increased, including diabetes and various "site specific" cancers (usually those related to internal organs that filter environmental waste, like the bladder and kidneys).[34]

For this reason—and with the sanction of the New York State Supreme Court, which has oversight of the group—the Fund has adopted a capacious definition of toxic risk. According to the LCMF's guidelines, "reasonable" risk translates into the very simple idea that a "disease *could* be related to exposure" to Love Canal chemicals. In this way, the Fund has flipped the American notion of environmental impacts on its head. The standard in epidemiology has historically been a 95 percent link between cause and effects—an extremely difficult threshold to prove. The LCMF takes its cues from popular epidemiology, which uses a lower threshold to account for potential illness links: anywhere from 50 to 80 percent certainty that a disease is related to chemical exposures. More broadly still, the Fund offers expansive coverage for prescription drugs and mental health care, very important matters for people under 65 (and Medicare/Medicaid thresholds).[35] Despite these policies, the Fund has acted prudently; there have been no "giveaways." (In the 1990s, the LCMF capped disbursements at "[$]10,000 per year per person.") At the close of 2010, the Fund was still in good financial shape, having paid out $1,157,600 in benefits since its inception (with a remaining balance of nearly $1.5 million).[36]

The Fund also worked to raise consciousness about the long-term impact of toxic waste on human health. As the Fund's managers put it in 1997, the LCMF had a much broader agenda than assisting former residents with health concerns; in no small way, the organization hoped to pick up where Love Canal activism left off. Accordingly, the LCMF sought to help "other agencies with research [on chemical threats to health];

gather health, insurance and medical information pertinent to possible policy establishment for fertility difficulties[;] and [establish] ... a newsletter to be sent to [any health study] participants on a regular basis."[37] In the 21st century, the LCMF joined the digital revolution when it launched a website providing residents and others access to the Fund's annual reports and newsletters. The website contains links to documentaries on the disaster, history lessons on Love Canal, reprinted health studies, and an image bank featuring recent as well as classic pictures of Love Canal residents. But one of the most popular features of the website is the basic information it provides to many former residents. "How do I know if my medical problem is related to having lived in Love Canal?" one of the "Frequently Asked Questions" wonders. "Whenever there is a question about coverage," the website explains in response, "you should submit a claim for reimbursement and our Claims Adjuster will let you know if it is covered."[38]

Interestingly, the LCMF initially supported and then disputed a major Love Canal study undertaken by New York State at the close of the 20th century. Launched in 1996, the study tracked the health outcomes of over 6,000 residents known to have lived at Love Canal between 1978 and 1982. Though conducted by the New York State Health Department, it was prepared under the aegis of the federal government, the U.S. Agency for Toxic Substances Database and Registry. Billed as a 20-year follow up to initial health inquiries at Love Canal, the study took over a decade to complete. Finished in 2008, it comprised four separate analytical regimes, each peer reviewed and then put together in a final report, revised and updated in 2011.[39] The study examined "death rates," "cancer incidences," "birth outcomes," and the existence of chemicals in residents' "stored blood samples."[40]

Though the report was supposed to offer a definitive portrait of Love Canal health impacts across time and space, the study actually reached a series of mixed conclusions.[41] For instance, while the mortality outcomes study showed that there was no general difference between Love Canal residents' long-term death rates and regional or state-wide death rates, it also noted that certain types of deaths occurred more often in the Love Canal population. Heart attacks, motor vehicle accidents, and suicides were more common (perhaps due to stress and/or neurological trouble prompted by chemical exposure). In addition, Love Canal residents had higher incidents of "site specific" cancers, particularly bladder and kidney cancer. On top of all this, the study indicated that there could be no last word on Love Canal health for the simple reason that its former population was still aging and might confront unforeseen hazards that were still not understood by medical science. If former residents did not agree with many of the study's findings, then they could at least agree on this final point: there was much to learn about Love Canal health in the future.

Yet before the study was even concluded, former residents raised a number of concerns. Because the study drew on older test results, incomplete disease and death registries, and possibly compromised environmental data, the LCMF publicly wondered about the conclusions. For example, blood samples stored by the state had thawed in the wake of a power outage in the 1990s and might have been damaged. Would the study forthrightly discuss such problems? In addition, the new study would draw information from cancer and birth defect registries that had the appearance of authority but were limited by design. How would the state address this matter? The birth defect registry was not created until 1983, while the cancer registry had been established in 1972. Despite these limitations, the study sought to examine Love Canal residents' health dating back to the early 1940s, when dumping began. But the health data for someone who died of cancer before 1972, say, or moved away before 1978, would not be included in the study. "This study will not give former residents vital health-based information nor will it be useful to other communities faced with serious health risks due to chemical exposures," the Fund reported flatly in 1999.[42] In many ways, Love Canal remains an open sore.[43]

Which brings us back to the residents of Love Canal. After being evacuated, after hundreds of millions of dollars in lawsuits, after $350 million dedicated to remediating the old dump, after decades of denial about the toxic legacy of industrial expansion in the Chemical Century—after all of that, the former residents of Love Canal still stand tall. For in that fateful landscape's 500-year transformation, they ended up asking the toughest questions of all: How did industrialization and chemical production affect both the human and natural environments around Niagara Falls? What were the lingering impacts of the Chemical Century? And how would medical science, political bodies, and legal institutions grapple with the legacy of Love Canal in the 21st century? In our time, no less than the 1970s and 1980s, these remain ramifying questions.

And that reminds us that the Love Canal protest movement was not merely about toxic ruin or corroded property values or even frightened residents who simply wanted out of their polluted homes. Now as then, Love Canal stands for the prospect of environmental redemption, not only in Niagara Falls but far beyond.

NOTES

Introduction

1. Dickens, excerpt from "American Notes" (1842), reprinted in Charles Mason Dow, ed., *Anthology and Bibliography of Niagara Falls* (Albany, 1921), 230.
2. On the Falls, see generally Pierre Berton, *Niagara: A History of the Falls* (New York: State University of New York, 1997).
3. See Heather Rogers, *Gone Tomorrow: The Hidden Life of Garbage* (New York: The New Press, 2006); Susan Strasser, *Waste and Want: The Social History of Trash* (New York: Henry Holt & Co., 1999).
4. See Philip Shabecoff, *A Fierce Green Fire* (New York: Island Press, 1993).
5. See Glenn Jordan's review of "Lois Gibbs and the Love Canal" (1982), in the *New York Times* movie review database at: http://www.nytimes.com/movies/movie/29840/Lois-Gibbs-and-the-Love-Canal/overview.
6. Carolyn Merchant, ed., *Major Problems in American Environmental History* (Lexington, Mass.: D.C. Heath, 1993), 511.
7. See George A. Cevasco & Richard P. Harmond, eds., *Modern American Environmentalists: A Biographical Encyclopedia* (Baltimore: Johns Hopkins University Press, 2009), 175–181.
8. "Love Canal: Public Health Time Bomb" (Albany, 1978), 6.
9. See the Edmund S. Muskie Collection, Library of Congress, Series 23A. Sound Recordings: Cassette Tapes. Event No. 1,224. CBS interview, date unknown.
10. Eckhardt C. Beck, "The Love Canal Tragedy," *EPA Journal* (January 1979), at http://www.epa.gov/aboutepa/history/topics/lovecanal/01.html.
11. See the official ATSDR website at http://www.atsdr.cdc.gov/about/congress.html.
12. On Love Canal's influence on other groups, see Richard Newman, "From Love's Canal to Love Canal: Reckoning With the Environmental Legacy of an Industrial Dream," in Jefferson Cowie & Joseph Heathcott, *Beyond the Ruins: The Meanings of Deindustrialization* (Ithaca, N.Y.: Cornell University Press, 2003).
13. See Jane S. Shaw's report for The Property and Environment Research Center (PERC), "Superfund: The Shortcut That Failed," PERC Policy Series PS-5 (May, 1996), 1.
14. On the Sydney tar ponds, see Elizabeth May & Maude Barlow, *Frederick Street: Life and Death on Canada's Love Canal* (Toronto: HarperCollins, 2000). On the

Elizabeth Street landfill, see Ashley Fishel-McFadden, "Hurricane Katrina: The Echo of Environmental Injustice," paper presented in "Legal Lessons of Katrina and Other Natural Disasters," California Western School of Law, Fall 2009 (Professor Kenneth Klein).

15. "Junior" Rodriquez of St. Bernard Parish, September 7 2005, quoted in "We've Got Another Love Canal Down Here," reported on the Global Community Monitor website, available online at http://www.gcmonitor.org/?s=junior& submit.x=0&submit.y=0.

16. Hugh Gusterson, "The Lessons of Fukushima," in *Bulletin of the Atomic Scientists*, Web Edition, Mar. 11, 2011 online at http://www.thebulletin.org/web-edition/ columnists/hugh-gusterson/the-lessons-of-fukushima.

17. *Buffalo News*, Sept. 23, 2011.

18. See posts on "Yucca Mountain Project To Be Shuttered?" available at: http:// thedragonstales.blogspot.com/2009/03/yucca-mountain-project-to-be-shut-tered.html.

19. See Lois Gibbs, *Love Canal: My Story* (Albany: State University of New York Press, 1982), 174. The EPA states that "one in every five Americans lives within three miles of a site where EPA has acted to remove immediate threats to human health." See "Superfund Success Stories," on the EPA website, available at http://pubweb.epa.gov/superfund/accomp/success/thumbs4.htm (accessed December 8, 2015).

    On Superfund today, including interactive maps of Superfund locations, see Paul Voosen, "Superfund Sites," *National Geographic* (December 2014), available online at http://ngm.nationalgeographic.com/2014/12/superfund/voosen-text.

20. See, most recently, Elizabeth D. Blum, *Love Canal Revisited: Race, Class, and Gender in Environmental Activism* (Lawrence: University Press of Kansas, 2008), which examines Love Canal from the perspective of environmental justice struggles in the 20th century. See also Thomas Hobbs Fletcher, *From Love Canal to Environmental Justice: The Politics of Hazardous Waste on the Canada–U.S. Border* (Peterborough, Ont.: Broadview Press, 2003); Craig E. Colten & Peter N. Skinner, eds., *The Road to Love Canal: Managing Industrial Waste before EPA* (Austin: University of Texas Press, 1996). The classic treatment of the Love Canal crisis proper is still Adeline Levine, *Love Canal: Science, Politics, and People* (Lexington, Mass.: D.C. Heath, 1982). Allan Mazur's *A Hazardous Inquiry: The Rashomon Effect at Love Canal* (Cambridge: Harvard University Press, 1998) offers a critical scholarly perspective on citizen activism.

21. See, for example, W. Barksdale Maynard, *Walden Pond: A History* (New York: Oxford University Press, 2004), Robert W. Righter, *The Battle over Hetch Hetchy: America's Most Controversial Dam and the Birth of Modern Environmentalism* (New York: Oxford University Press, 2005). On urban environmental history, see especially William Cronon, *Nature's Metropolis: Chicago and the Great West* (New York; W.W. Norton & Co., 1991).

22. Anne Hillis, quoted in the *Niagara Gazette*, Apr. 10, 1979.

23. For a recent distillation of the terms "wilderness" and "landscape," see Michael Lewis, ed., *American Wilderness: A New History* (New York: Oxford University Press, 2007). The classic treatment is still Roderick Nash, *Wilderness and the American Mind*, 4th ed. (New Haven: Yale University Press, 2001).

24. Landscape definition at "Answers.Com": http://www.answers.com/topic/ landscape.

25. See especially John B. Jackson's seminal *Discovering the Vernacular Landscape* (New Haven: Yale University Press, 1984).
26. See the EPA's "Terminology Services" webpage for multiple definitions of "landscape": http://iaspub.epa.gov/sor_internet/registry/termreg/searchandretrieve/termsandacronyms/search.do;jsessionid=8f3e1e4750d5b74a5157e418be1a735bedb36e85c52f149863c1c5e4a3e1dda1?search=
27. William Faulkner, *Requiem for a Nun*, Act I, Scene 3.

Chapter 1

1. Louis Hennepin, *A New Discovery of a Vast Country in America* (2 vols.: London ed., 1698), I, 90.
2. Anne Hillis, entry circa July 1978, in "Love Canal's Contamination: The Poisoning of an American Family," unpublished ms., in the Ecumenical Task Force of the Niagara Frontier Records, "The Love Canal Collection," University Archives, SUNY–Buffalo, MS 65, Box 38, Folder 9.
3. See the New York State Department of Health's report, "Love Canal: Public Health Time Bomb" (Albany, 1978), 1–2.
4. The *Niagara Gazette* Love Canal Chronology, reposted at: http://library.buffalo.edu/specialcollections/lovecanal/about/chronology.php#niagara.
5. Ecumenical Task for of the Niagara Frontier, "History of Disaster at Love Canal—Chronology of Events," ETF Progress Report, Mar. 20, 1979–Aug. 1, 1980, ETC Records, University Archives, SUNY–Buffalo, 1.
6. See Andrew C. Revkin, "Love Canal and Its Mixed Legacy," *N.Y. Times*, Nov. 25, 2013.
7. On Niagara's longstanding importance in North American history, see Pierre Berton, *Niagara: A History of the Falls* (Albany: SUNY Press, 1992). See also William Irwin, *The New Niagara: Tourism, Technology and the Landscape of Niagara Falls, 1776–1917* (University Park: Penn State University Press, 1996).
8. Hennepin, *A New Discovery*, I, 53–56.
9. On La Salle's vision, see, for example, William Foster & Johanna S. Warren, eds., *The La Salle Expedition on the Mississippi River: A Lost Manuscript of Nicolas de La Salle* (Austin: Texas State Historical Association, 2003). On the environmental and economic visions of Europeans in La Salle's era, see William Cronon, *Changes in the Land* (New York: Hill and Wang, 2003) and W. Jeffrey Bolster, *The Mortal Sea: Fishing in the Atlantic in the Age of Sail* (Cambridge: Belknap Press, 2012).
10. Ibid.
11. Hennepin, *A New Discovery*, 53–56.
12. Ibid., 53–56, 93–94.
13. Ibid., 93–94.
14. Ibid., 56.
15. Ibid., 25–95.
16. Francis Parkman, *Montcalm and Wolfe: The French and Indian War*, reprint ed. (Boston: Da Capo Press, 1995), 22.
17. René Bréhan De Galinée, "Exploration of the Great Lakes" (1669), in, Charles Mason Dow, ed., *Anthology and Bibliography of Niagara Falls* (Albany: State of New York, 1921), 21.
18. Capt. John Enys, "Visit to Niagara" (1787), in ibid., 75.
19. J. Wallsteed, "The Falls of Niagara," in ibid., v. 2, 745–746.

20. New York State General Assembly, "Report of the Commissioners... to Explore the Route of an Inland Navigation, from Hudson's River to Lake Ontario and Lake Erie" (New York 1811), 12.

21. Peter Kalm to Benjamin Franklin, Sept. 2, 1750, in the Papers of Benjamin Franklin, American Philosophical Society and Yale University, Digital Edition, Packard Humanities Institute, online at http://franklinpapers.org/franklin//.

22. On the Iroquois, see Daniel K. Richter, *The Ordeal of the Longhouse* (Chapel Hill: University of North Carolina Press, 1992). The Tuscarora migrated from the mid-Atlantic region to become the sixth member of the League in the early 1700s.

23. See Granville Ganter, ed., *The Collected Speeches of Sagoyewatha, or Red Jacket* (Syracuse: Syracuse University Press, 2006), introduction and xxi.

24. See Shepard Krech III, *The Ecological Indian: Myth and History,* paperback ed. (New York: W.W. Norton & Co., 2000). For a series of critiques of Krech, see also Michael E. Harkin & David Rich Lewis, eds., *Native Americans and the Environment: Perspectives on the Ecological Indian* (Lincoln: University of Nebraska Press, 2004).

25. See Eric Stradling, *The Nature of New York: An Environmental History of the Empire State* (Ithaca: Cornell University Press, 2010), ch. 1.

26. On Native–Colonial environmental clashes, see Cronon, *Changes in the Land.*

27. See Dean R. Snow, *The Iroquois* (Malden, Mass.: Blackwell Publishing, 1994), 1–4.

28. Ibid., 7, 24, 37.

29. Peter Jemison, ed., *The Treaty of Canandaigua* (Santa Fe: Clear Light Publishing, 2000).

30. See especially Charles E. Brooks, *Frontier Settlement and Market Revolution: The Holland Land Purchase* (Ithaca: Cornell University Press, 1996).

31. See Ganter, ed., *The Collected Speeches of Sagoyewatha,* xxi.

32. Ibid., 140–42.

33. Ibid.

34. Ibid.

35. Among other books on the Erie Canal, see especially Carol Sheriff, *The Artificial River: The Erie Canal and the Paradox of Progress, 1817–1862* (New York: Hill and Wang, 1996).

36. Gerrit Smith to N. S. Denton, Feb. 20, 1866, Syracuse University Library, Gerrit Smith Broadside and Pamphlet Collection, available online at: http://digilib.syr .edu/gerritsmith/image/168.htm.

37. Henry P. Beers, "A History of the U.S. Corps of Topographical Engineers," entry on the official U.S. Corps of Topographical Engineers historical page, online at http://www.topogs.org/History2.htm.

38. Williams died Sept. 1, 1846. See "William G Williams," entry in the U.S. Corps of Topographical Engineers biographical dictionary, online at: http://www .topogs.org/b_williams.htm.

39. See "William G. Williams, class of 1824," Vol. 1, 330, in George W. Cullum's *Biographical Register of Officers and Graduates of the United States Military Academy* (West Point, 1891). Bio No. 375.

40. Williams' stamp is still acknowledged as important in Michigan. See, for example, the U.S. Army Corps of Engineers, Detroit District, "Origins of the Detroit District, 1820–1865," in "Great Lakes Update " (July 2008), available

online at: http://www.lre.usace.army.mil/Portals/69/docs/GreatLakesInfo/docs/UpdateArticles/Update172.pdf.

41. For a good modern treatment of the Niagara Ship Canal, see William Irwin, *The New Niagara: Tourism, Technology and the Landscape of Niagara Falls, 1776–1917* (University Park: Pennsylvania State University Press., 1996), 15–16.

42. See the Hon. Henry W. Hill, "Historical Sketch of Niagara Ship Canal Projects," *Publications*, Buffalo Historical Society (Buffalo, 1918), Vol. 22, 203–269.

43. Ibid., 214–216.

44. Ibid., 208–232.

45. Irwin, *The New Niagara*, 15–16.

46. Paul E. Johnson, *Sam Patch, The Famous Jumper* (New York: Hill and Wang, 2003), 80.

47. See "Artist's Rendering of Biddle Stairs at Cave of the Winds," undated image in the Niagara Falls Public Library Digital Collection, Record ID 99079, online at http://www.nflibrary.ca/nfplindex/show.asp?id=99079&b=1.

48. See Horatio A. Parsons, *Steele's Book of Niagara Falls*, 5th ed. (Buffalo, 1838), 15.

49. "Certificate Issued or Passing Behind the Horseshoe Falls at Table Rock," Aug. 14, 1839, in ibid., Record 100500, http://www.nflibrary.ca/nfplindex/show.asp?id=100500&b=1.

50. See Hill, "Historical Sketch of Niagara Ship Canal Projects," 203–269.

51. See Mark Twain, "Extracts From Adam's Diary," in William Dean Howells, Mark Twain, and Professor Nathaniel S. Shaler and others, eds., *The Niagara Book* (Niagara Falls, 1893), available online at the Niagara University library, http://library.niagara.edu/about/special-collections/digital-collection-of-niagara-falls-guidebooks-from-the-19th-century/the-niagara-book-by-w-d-howells-mark-twain-prof-nathaniel-s-shaler-and-others-1893/.

Chapter 2

1. E. T. Williams, *Niagara Falls and the Electrical Age: Marvelous Effect of the World's Greatest Electrical Power Development Upon a Famous Region and the United States at Large* (Niagara Falls, N.Y.: Cataract Journal Co., 1914), 1–5.

2. William T. Love, "Model City: Niagara Power Doubled" (Lewiston, N.Y., 1893), 1.

3. E. T. Williams, *Niagara: Queen of Wonders* (Niagara Falls: 1916), 166.

4. William Cronon, *Nature's Metropolis: Chicago and the Great West* (New York: W.W. Norton & Co., 1992), Introduction. See also Martin Melosi, *The Sanitary City: Environmental Services in Urban America from Colonial Times to the Present*, reprint ed. (Baltimore: Johns Hopkins Press, 2008).

5. See "Model City: Niagara Power Doubled," 1–2. Love published several versions of his prospectus. See, for instance, the book produced by his Model Town Company entitled, *Description and Plan of the Model City Located at Lewiston, Niagara County, N.Y.: Chartered by Special Act of the New York Legislature. Designed to Be the Most Perfect City in Existence* (Lewiston, 1893).

6. Ibid.

7. Love, "Model City: Niagara Power Doubled," 1.

8. Ibid., 1–4; see also *Model City Power*, Apr. 4, 1897. For Love's company newspapers, look under these various names between 1894 and 1897: *The Model City Searchlight, Model City Bulletin, Model City Standard*, and *Model City Power*.

9. Love, "Model City: Niagara Power Doubled," 1.

10. Daniel T. Rodgers, *Atlantic Crossings: Social Politics in a Progressive Age* (Cambridge: Harvard University Press, 1998), 49, 112, 113–144.

11. On Chicago's great fair, see Donald L. Miller, *City of the Century: The Epic of Chicago and the Making of America* (New York: Simon and Schuster, 1996), especially 378–434. On Burnham and city planning, see Carl Smith, *The Plan of Chicago: Daniel Burnham and the Remaking of the American City* (Chicago: University of Chicago Press, 2006).

12. Henry George, *Progress and Poverty* (New York, 1879).

13. Model Town Company, *Special Act of the New York Legislature. Designed to Be the Most Perfect City in Existence*, 1–5. See also *Model City Power*, Apr. 9, 1897.

14. See Robinson and Loring's testimonial in Love, "Model City: Niagara Power Doubled," 1–5.

15. See English poet and reformer William Blake's "Jerusalem" (1804) for a searing commentary on the industrial revolution's environmental impact on a formerly "green" landscape.

16. See advertising postcard from Duane Belden, Industrial and Real Estate agent in the Falls: "Niagara Falls: The Coming Manufacturing City of North America," 1893, in the Postcard Collection, Niagara Falls Public Library.

17. George V. Davenport, *The Niagara Falls Electrical Handbook* (Niagara Falls, 1904), 4. The book was part of a ten-part series on electrical development across the nation.

18. Nikola Tesla, quoted in William Irwin, *The New Niagara: Tourism, Technology, and the Landscape of Niagara Falls, 1776–1917* (University Park: Penn State University Press, 1996), 120.

19. See the Model Town Company, *Special Act of the New York Legislature. Designed to Be the Most Perfect City in Existence*, title page.

20. Irwin, *The New Niagara*, 144–146.

21. Love, "Model City: Niagara Power Doubled," 1.

22. *Buffalo Daily Courier*, Dec. 28, 1894,

23. Ibid., July 14, 29, 1894; Dec. 28, 1894.

24. Love, "Model City: Niagara Power Doubled," 1–5.

25. Thomas V. Welch, circular letter to New York politicians, Jan. 26, 1885, *How Niagara Was Made Free: The Passage of the Niagara Reservation Act of 1885* (Buffalo: Publications of the Niagara Frontier Historical Society, 1903), 9.

26. Ibid., 10.

27. On the reservation generally, see Irwin, *The New Niagara* and Berton, *Niagara: A History of the Falls*. See also *How Niagara Was Made Free: The Passage of the Niagara Reservation Act of 1885*, and "Niagara Falls and Vicinity," map included in William Dean Howells, Mark Twain, et al., *Niagara Book* (Niagara Falls, 1923 ed.), 331.

28. On Welch and the Niagara Reservation, see the following: Williams, *Niagara County: A Concise History*, 2 Vols. (Chicago, 1921); Vol. 1, 234–235; Vol. 2, 433; *Buffalo Daily Courier*, May 9, 1896.

29. Thoreau, *Walden; or, A Life in the Woods* (Boston, 1854).

30. Muir, *The Yosemite* (1913), quoted in Daniel Payne, *Voices in the Wilderness* (Hanover, N.H.: University Press of New England, 1998), 84. On Burroughs and Muir's religious visions of nature, see particularly chs. 4–5. On Hetch Hetchy's development, see Robert Righter, *The Battle Over Hetch Hetchy: America's Most Controversial Dam and the Birth of Modern Environmentalism* (New York: Oxford University Press, 2005).

31. On the Sierra Club and Muir, see Donald Worster's wonderful book, *A Passion for Nature: The Life of John Muir* (New York: Oxford University Press, 2008), 328–355. See Muir to Theodore Roosevelt, Apr. 21, 1908, in *John Muir: His Life and Letters and Other Writings* (Seattle: Mountaineers Books, 1996), 378–379.

32. See the *Illustrated London News*, Mar. 3, 1906 on Niagara's "disfigurement."

33. McFarland, "Beautiful America: Shall We Make a Coal Pile of Niagara?" *Ladies Home Journal*, 19 (September 1905). See also Newman, "From Love's Canal to Love Canal," in Jefferson Cowie &, Joseph Heathcott, eds., *Beyond the Ruins: The Meanings of Deindustrialization*, 121.

34. See *Buffalo Daily Courier*, Apr. 28, May 8, 9, 1896.

35. Ibid., May 9, 1896; see also Feb. 14, 1895.

36. See Irwin, *The New Niagara*, Introduction, 213.

37. The *Buffalo Daily Courier* Sept. 30, 1894.

38. Ibid., Dec. 20, 22, 1894.

39. Ibid., Feb. 13, 1894.

40. Ibid., Aug. 5, 1895.

41. Ibid., Feb. 13, 1894. See also Edward Williams' later commentary on Love's failure, in *Niagara: Queen of Wonders*, (Boston, 1916), 166–171.

42. See the *Buffalo Daily Courier*, Jan. 16 and Mar. 5, 1896. See the same paper for Mar. 16 and 28.

43. As the following issues of The *Buffalo Daily Courier* illustrate, Love's Canal received positive press coverage well after the Panic of 1893: May 24, Aug. 1, Oct. 27, and Dec. 19, 1894; May 1, 1896.

44. Ibid., Mar. 28, 1896.

45. Ibid., Apr. 26 and May 13, 1896.

46. Love also provided the easiest of credit lines. All investors had to do was put down 5 percent or 10 percent on a plot of land in Model City; and in one month time, he assured them, that investment would double. Thus, a plot of land worth $500 required a $50 down payment. It would be worth $100 in 30 days. Love's investors eagerly took him up on this risky plan, which increasingly drained his finances. Moreover, Love had only a theoretical right to the over 10,000 acres in Niagara County dedicated to Model City. Love had to bargain with farmers for each acre. These contracts, or options, often lasted for one year before expiring. Love had to renegotiate with farmers year after year—and as each year passed, his new contracts with farmers called for new prices. In his last year of operation, Love created a three-year contract system to solve this problem. But he could not solve the other dilemma: the assured 100 percent return to investors within one month. See *The Buffalo Daily Courier*, "Western New York" section, on the following dates for reports on the growth and final failure of Love's Canal: Jan. 16 and 19, 1896; Mar. 16, and 30, 1896; Apr. 25, 1896; May 1, 1896. See also Edward Williams' 1916 commentary on Love's failure, in *Niagara: Queen of Wonders*, 166–171.

47. *Niagara County 1908* (Century Map Co., New York, 1908), 93.

48. *Model City Power*, February 1897.

49. See Love's essays in the *Mount Holly Herald*, June–July 1931. See also the *Niagara Falls Gazette*, Oct. 30, 1931.

Chapter 3

1. "Mural Paintings by Francis Scott Bradford in the Offices of the Hooker Electrochemical Company" (New York, 1934), caption opposite Mural VI.

2. Ibid., Mural VIII.

3. The classic formulation is by R. W. B. Lewis, *The American Adam: Tragedy, Innocence and Tradition in the Nineteenth Century* (Chicago: University of Chicago Press, 1955).

4. *Elon Huntington Hooker, 1869...1938: Engineer, Industrialist, Patriot, Public Servant, Author, Humanitarian,* a special issue of the company publication "Hooker Gas" (Niagara Falls, 1938). The pages are not numbered but counting from the dedication page, the quotation "bring things to pass" appears on page 9. The first chapter of the booklet is entitled, "The Vision." Hereinafter EHH.

5. "The Huntington Family in America: A Genealogical Memoir of the Known Descendants of Simon Huntington from 1633 to 1915, Including Those Who Have Retained the Family Name, and Many Bearing Other Surnames," published by the Huntington Family Association in Hartford, Conn/ (1915). 4-disc. digital ed. on CD-ROM © November 1999.

6. See Edward Hooker & Margaret Huntington Hooker, "The Descendants of Rev. Thomas Hooker, Hartford, Connecticut, 1586–1908: Being an Account of What is Known of Rev. Thomas Hooker's Family in England: And More Particularly Concerning Himself and His Influence upon the Early History of Our Country..." (published by Margaret Huntington Hooker, 1909), Google Books edition. Original from the University of Wisconsin–Madison, digitized Jan. 3, 2008. Horace Hooker, Sr., quote at 172.

7. On Hooker family members, see the "Hooker Family Papers" and the "Hooker-Huntington Collection," both at the University of Rochester, Department of Rare Books, Special Collections and Preservation.

8. See Kathleen Stewart Howe's entry on "Travel Photography" in John Hannavy, ed., *The Encyclopedia of Nineteenth Century Photography* (New York: Routledge, 2013), 1407.

9. Elizabeth Brayer, *George Eastman* (Baltimore: Johns Hopkins University Press, 1999).

10. See Robert Evans Thomas, *Salt, Water, Power and People: A Short History of Hooker Electrochemical Company* (Niagara Falls, 1955), 3–4. Hereinafter SWPP.

11. EHH, 1–11.

12. On Elon's work in New York, see *N.Y. Times,* May 11, 1938.

13. On the DFC, see Tom Cornell, *Establishing Research Corporation; A Case Study of Patents, Philanthropy, and Organized Research in Early Twentieth-Century America* (New York: Research Corporation Publications, 2004), 76, 113.

14. Henry Wiggleworth, "Chemical Industries," in H. T. Warshow, ed., *Representative Industries in the United States* (New York: H. Holt & Co., 1928), 130.

15. Ibid., 131. In 1925, Iron and Steel production totaled roughly $6.46 billion, while chemical production was valued at $6.43 billion.

16. Ibid., 150.

17. Ibid.

18. On the history of American chemical producers, see, for instance, Davis Dyer & David B. Sicilia, *Labors of a Modern Hercules: The Evolution of a Chemical Company* (Cambridge: Harvard Business School Press, 1991); and E. N. Brandt, *Growth Company: Dow Chemical's First Century* (East Lansing: Michigan State University Press, 1997).

19. SWPP, 1–6.

20. SWPP, 1–6.

21. EHH, 15.

22. SWPP, 21.
23. Ibid.
24. SWPP, 21–27.
25. Ibid., 27.
26. SWPP, 51.
27. See William Cronon, *Nature's Metropolis* (New York: W.W. Norton & Co., 1991), Introduction; Martin Melosi. *The Sanitary City* (Rev. edition: Pittsburgh: University of Pittsburgh Press, 2008).
28. Henry G. Stott, "The View of the Engineer," in *Proceedings of the Conference of Governors...*" (Washington, D.C., 1909), 404–05.
29. Cornell, *Establishing Research Corporation*, 76.
30. See *Chemical Abstracts*, American Chemical Society, 1916, volume 10, January through May, abstract 1–1446; Cornell, 446–7.
31. Ibid.
32. Ibid.
33. SWPP, 7.
34. Albert H. Hooker, *Chloride of Lime in Sanitation* (New York: John Wiley & Sons, 1913), 85–86.
35. See Phelps' review in the *American Journal of Public Health*, Aug. 3(8), 1913 (New York, 1913), 826.
36. A. H. Hooker, *Chloride of Lime in Sanitation*, 85–86.
37. Ibid.
38. SWPP, 6.
39. For a good summary of TR's conservationist ethic and work, see the National Park Service website, "Theodore Roosevelt and Conservation": http://www.nps.gov/thro/historyculture/theodore-roosevelt-and-conservation.htm. See also Douglas Brinkley's illuminating work, *The Wilderness Warrior* (New York: Harper Perennial, 2009).
40. Harry F. P. Hooker to Mother Hooker, Nov. 16, 1912. Hooker Family Papers, University of Rochester, Special Collections, Box 14, Folder 14.
41. For a good general summary of TR's Bull Moose days, see Edmund Morris, *Colonel Roosevelt* (New York: Random House, 2010), Bull Moose notation at 213.
42. Harry F. P. Hooker note, 11:7, and Blanche Hooker to Mother Hooker, c. 1906, both in Hooker Family Papers, University of Rochester, Special Collections.
43. SWPP, 6.
44. Ibid., 43.
45. Ibid., 42–44.
46. Ibid., 24–25.
47. Christopher Sellers, *Hazards of the Job: From Industrial Disease to Environmental Health Science* (Chapel Hill: University of North Carolina Press, 1997), 116–117.
48. *New York Times*, Apr. 24, 1915.
49. "Gas Poisoning," Ch. 10, in Arthur F. Hurst, M.A., M.D., (Oxon), F.R.C.P., *Medical Diseases of the War* (London: Edward Arnold, 1918), posted at http://www.vlib.us/medical/gaswar/chlorine.htm.
50. See the U.S. Centers for Disease Control website entry on mustard gas, http://emergency.cdc.gov/agent/sulfurmustard/basics/facts.asp.
51. Both phosgene and mustard gas have become firmly identified with modern war. According to the Centers for Disease Control, which still tracks deployment of potentially deadly chemical weapons, "Phosgene was used extensively during

World War I as a choking (pulmonary) agent" and "[was] responsible for the large majority of [chemical] deaths." Heavier than air, phosgene, or "CG" in military terminology, would saturate battlefields by actually sinking to the lowest-lying ground, including fortified trenches. After initial CG exposures, soldiers would experience blurred vision, watery eyes, and a burning sensation in the throat and lungs. Vomiting and skin lesions might follow; then perhaps pulmonary edema, or water in the lungs, followed often by death. Surviving soldiers could develop emphysema and other breathing disorders. See the U.S. Centers for Disease Control website entry on phosgene, http://emergency.cdc.gov/agent/phosgene/basics/facts.asp.

52. Joseph Thornton, *Pandora's Poison: Chlorine, Health, and a New Environmental Strategy* (Cambridge: MIT Press, 2000), 236.

53. Hurst, "Gas Poisoning," in *Medical Diseases of the War*, at http://www.vlib.us/medical/gaswar/chlorine.htm.

54. See Elon Hooker's memories of his World War I arguments, *N.Y. Times*, Oct. 20, 1920.

55. See Jonathan Tucker, *War of Nerves: Chemical Warfare From World War I to Al Qaeda* (New York: Pantheon, 2006).

56. U.S. Army General Order 79, "extract from G.O. 79," Albert Huntington Hooker, Jr. Papers, Washington State Historical Society, MS 39.2, Box 1.

57. Special Order 33, in ibid., Aug. 22, 1918.

58. "Special Instructions," in ibid., Aug. 1, 1918.

59. Some of the murals are reprinted in *Elon Huntington Hooker, 1869...1938: Engineer, Industrialist, Patriot, Public Servant, Author, Humanitarian*, including outtakes on the front and back of the book.

60. See Mural X and caption, which appears on unnumbered page 6 in ibid.

61. Mural X and caption, in ibid.

Chapter 4

1. Often referred to as the "Quit Claim Deed," the Indenture agreement between Hooker Chemical and the Niagara Falls School Board was executed on April 28, 1953. Copies of the document are located in several places, including online at: https://upload.wikimedia.org/wikipedia/commons/2/2c/Hooker_ Electrochemical_Quit_Claim_Deed_to_Board_of_Education.pdf.

2. Elon died on May 10, 1938. Rochester Review 26.2 (Nov. –Dec. 1947), 6, available online at: http://www.lib.rochester.edu/?page=3483&y=1947&v=26&i=2 &p=6

3. See *Elon Huntington Hooker, 1869...1938: Engineer, Industrialist, Patriot, Public Servant, Author, Humanitarian*, which was also a special issue of the company publication "Hooker Gas" (Niagara Falls, 1938).

4. SWPP, 88–89.

5. On inground disposal, see Newman, "From Love's Canal to Love Canal," in Cowie & Heathcott, *Beyond the Ruins*.

6. Hooker Electrochemical Company Progress Report (1951), 1, 2–11. [Hereinafter, Hooker Progress Report.] For these and other company reports below, see Albert Huntington Hooker, Jr. Papers, Washington State Historical Society, MS 39.2, Box 1.

7. Hooker Electrochemical Company Annual Report (1947), 7.

8. 1943 Monsanto ad, "How much chemistry per soldier," in the author's possession.

9. Hooker Electrochemical Company Annual Report (1947), 7. An adjustment in the government regulated price index certainly helped boost sales figures, but Hooker's production surge also remained crucial.

10. See Report of Marine Midland Investment Research Department (1952), 1–10.

11. Ibid., 10.

12. Hooker Progress Report, 1, 2–11.

13. Ibid., 1–12.

14. Ibid., 9.

15. Ibid., 3

16. Hooker Progress Report, 1–2, 8–9, 11.

17. SWPP, 1.

18. See DuPont's own website on branding: http://www.dupont.com/corporate-functions/our-company/dupont-history.html, "Our Company/History/1927–1940: Discovery/1939 Better Things," with a detailed discussion of corporate public relations and a mural depicting "Better Living Through Chemistry," similar to the Hooker series.

19. Hooker applied for trademark status for "Chemagination" in 1963; it received approval and was registered in 1965. See http://www.trademarks411.com/marks/72181141-chemagination.

20. "New Chemagination Center," ad in Newsweek, July 6, 1959.

21. Ibid.

22. "This is Chemagination" Newsweek, Dec. 12, 1960.

23. "This is Chemagination," Hooker advertising sheet, circa 1961, in the author's possession. Other examples of Hooker ads have been assembled through my own research in magazine files from Newsweek, Fortune, Time, and Life, in my possession, but which are sometimes undated.

24. "Rubber and the World of Mr. Jones," Hooker ad sheet, circa 1955, in the author's possession.

25. "The Bubble and the World of Mr. Jones," Hooker Ad sheet, 1955, in the author's possession.

26. "Just a year ago, Pascal Verna mined coal 3000 feet beneath the soil of Belgium," part of a "There must be a Hooker somewhere" ad sheet, circa 1968, in the author's possession.

27. "What does salt buy today," 1955 Hooker ad sheet, in the author's possession.

28. "The city that started to grow a million years ago," 1955 Hooker ad sheet, in the author's possession.

29. Dos Passos, MidCentury (New York, 1961), 215,

30. United States v. Hooker Chemicals and Plastics Corp. 850 F. Supp. 993 (W.D.N.Y. 1994), 1006–1008.

31. See U.S. v. Hooker, 850 F. Supp. at 1005–07.

32. Ibid. at 1007–1008

33. Ibid. at 1008–1009.

34. Ibid. at 1010.

35. Ibid. at 1008.

36. Ibid. at 1009.

37. Joe Dunmire interview Aug. 21, 2000, quoted in Newman, "From Love's Canal to Love Canal," in Cowie & Heathcott, Beyond the Ruins, 96, 107, 111.

38. See U.S. v. Hooker, 850 F. Supp. at 1004–1010.

39. See ibid. at 1004.

40. "Public Health Assessment," Pfohl Brothers Landfill, Agency for Toxic Substances and Disease Registry, http://www.atsdr.cdc.gov/hac/PHA/pfohl/pfo_p1.html

41. See Barbara Whitaker, "Its Notorious Past Unearthed, Dump Loses Landmark Status," N.Y. Times, Aug. 29, 2001. See also Martin Melosi, "The Fresno Sanitary Landfill in American Cultural Context," Public Historian, Vol. 24, no. 3 (summer 2002), 17–35.

42. See also "Fresno Sanitary Landfill," in A Guide to Historic Architecture in Fresno, California, available online at: http://historicfresno.org/nrhp/landfill.htm.

43. For information on contamination at the former Bell Aerospace site, see EPA Region II document id. #6276, "Statement of basis/final decision in response to comments summary," Sept. 11, 1992, online at: http://www.epa.gov/osw/hazard/correctiveaction/sbs2/pdfs/ny6276.pdf.

44. See the New Century Atlas, Niagara County (Philadelphia, 1908), "property of John A. Reynolds, civil engineer, Niagara Falls," in the Buffalo and Erie County Historical Society. LaSalle development maps, including subdivision plans by various land companies, appear between pages 115 and 139. "A record of some of the most valuable and productive farms" in Niagara County appears at page 129.

45. Copy of the original "Indenture...between Hooker electrochemical company and the Board of Education... of the city of Niagara Falls, April 28, 1953, located in the Adeline Levine Papers, The Buffalo and Erie County Historical Society. For all intents and purposes, the contract for the Love Canal landscape appears standard: "Witnesseth, that the party of the first part [Hooker chemical], in consideration of one dollar...paid by the party of the second part [Niagara Falls] does hereby remise, release, and quitclaim unto the party of the second part, its successors and assigns forever, all that tract or parcel of land situate[d] in the city of Niagara Falls, County of Niagara and State of New York, being part of lot number 60...of the mile reserve...."

46. U.S. v. Hooker, 850 F. Supp. at 1019–1028.

47. Occidental Chemical Factline, No. 13, September 1982, 6–8.

48. U.S. v. Hooker, 850 F. Supp. at 1029–1030.

49. Factline 13, 8–11.

50. Hooker official [Carl?] Parker to Edward Connell, Niagara Falls City Manager, Sept. 27, 1963, ETF Papers, University Archives, SUNY-Buffalo, Box 34.

51. Ibid.

52. Ibid., 9.

53. Neil M. Maher, "A New Deal Body Politic," Environmental History, July 2002, 450–451.

54. The best book remains Neil M. Maher, Nature's New Deal (New York, 2009).

55. The phrase is used in William Gould Vinal, Nature Recreation, Group Guidance for the Out of Doors (Reprint: New York: Dover Publications, 1963).

56. William Gould Vinal, Nature Recreation, Group Guidance for the Out of Doors (Original edition: Boston: American Humane Education Society, 1940), xii, ix, 15.

57. Hobbies, The Magazine of the Buffalo Science Museum, Vol. 2, No. 7 (December 1921), 5.

58. Edward F. Brown, "The Allegheny State Park," Hobbies, Vol. 1, No. 10 (March 1921), 3–4; "The Allegheny State Park," a special production of the Buffalo

Society for the Natural Sciences, Summer 1921, essay by Henry R. Francis, professor of forest recreation, New York State College of Forestry, 3, 14–16.

59. *Hobbies*, Vol. 12, No. 7 (March 1932), 143–149.

60. *Buffalo Evening News*, May 31, 1950. For historical perspectives on Niagara River pollution, see Jim Perry & Elizabeth Leigh Vanderklein, *Water Quality: Management of A Natural Resource* (Hoboken, N.J.: Wiley-Blackwell, 1996), 574.

61. See *Buffalo Evening News*, Sept. 21, 1949.

62. *Buffalo Evening News*, May 31, 1950.

63. Barcelona, "Skinning the Earth—an Editorial," *Hobbies*, Vol. 19, No. 3 (February 1939), 41.

64. See "Thinking Like A Mountain," in Leopold's classic collection of essays, *A Sand County Almanac* (New York: Oxford University Press, 1949), 137–141.

65. Daniel G. Payne, *Voices in the Wilderness* (Lebanon, N.H.: UPNE, 1996), 23–35.

Chapter 5

1. Lois Gibbs, *Love Canal, The Story Continues*, 20th anniversary edition (Poughkeepsie, N.Y.: Hudson House, 1998), 26. On Gibbs' background and early activism, see also Kevin Konrad, "Lois Gibbs: Grassroots Organizer and Environmental Health Advocate," American Journal of Public Health, 2011, available online at: www.ncbi.nlm.nih.gov/pmc/articles/pmc3154230.

2. Marie Pozniak testimony before the U.S. Senate, "Sub-Committee on Toxic Substances and Chemical Wastes," May 3, 1979. See also Luella Kenny, "Testimony submitted to the House Sub-Committee on Oversight and Investigations," Apr. 2, 1979. For these and other Love Canal resident testimonies before several congressional committees, see "Testimonies of Love Canal Residents," Love Canal Collections, available online at: http://library.buffalo .edu/specialcollections/lovecanal/collections/.

3. See Pozniak and Kenny testimony, in ibid.; see also Grace McCoulf's testimony before the U.S. Senate, "Sub-Committee on Toxic Substances and Chemical Wastes," Apr. 5, 1979.

4. Ibid.

5. Anne Hillis, "Love Canal's Contamination: The Poisoning of an American Family," unpublished manuscript, circa 1979–1980, Ecumenical Task Force of the Niagara Frontier Records, 1946–1995, University Archives, SUNY–Buffalo, MS 65, Box 38, Folder 9.

6. See the "Resolution of the Ecumenical Task Force of the Niagara Frontier," in "Progress Report of the Ecumenical Task Force of the Niagara Frontier...March 20 1979–August 1, 1980," v. See reprint on the Love Canal Collections website, SUNY–Buffalo, available at: http://library.buffalo.edu/libraries/specialcollections/ lovecanal/documents/pdfs/etf_progress1.pdf.

7. "Vetri File," LCHA survey of homes built circa 1954–1978, Center for Health, Environment and Justice Records, Tufts University, Special Collections.

8. Among the many recent and classic works on suburbanization, see Dolores Hayden, *Building Suburbia: Green Fields and Urban Growth, 1820–2000* (New York: Pantheon Books, 2003).

9. See R.C. Polk Survey quote from 1976 in "Profile of a City in Distress," in Emergency Needs Grant Application, 1980, Love Canal Area Revitalization Records, University Archives, SUNY–Buffalo, MS 74, Box 4, Folder 11, 14–18, 19–25.

10. Ibid.
11. *Niagara Gazette*, Aug. 12, 1978. Hereinafter *NG*.
12. On "Old Love Canal," see *NG*, May 20, 1978.
13. *NG*, Oct. 3, 1976; Nov 2, 4, 1976.
14. *NG*, Apr. 30, 1977.
15. John J. LaFalce interview with the author, July 27, 2009.
16. Calspan report noted in the *Buffalo CourierExpress*, Aug. 7, 1978.
17. Calspan Report—ND-6097-M1, "Calspan Technical Report: Characterization and Abatement of Groundwater Pollution of Love Canal Chemical Landfill, Niagara Falls, NY" (1977), 1–18.
18. Editorials, *NG*, Aug. 15, 1977; see also *NG* reportage on Aug. 10, and editorial on July 27, 1977. See also a summary of Love Canal *NG* reportage on Aug. 10, 1978.
19. See Lawrence Moriarty, EPA Rochester Program Support Branch, to William A. Librizzi, EPA Toxic Substances Coordinator, Oct. 18, 1977. The EPA report was filed under "Chemical Waste—Love Canal." It is available online at the SUNY–Buffalo Love Canal Collections website, http://library.buffalo.edu/libraries/specialcollections/lovecanal/documents/pdfs/epa1.pdf.
20. Ibid.
21. "Love Canal—Public Health Time Bomb, A Special Report to the Governor and Legislature" (Albany, 1978), http://www.health.state.ny.us/environmental/investigations/love_canal/lctimbmb.htm. Whalen quote in "Epidemologic Investigation."
22. Ibid.
23. *NG*, Aug. 20, 1978.
24. "Love Canal—Public Health Time Bomb, "Soils and Groundwater" section.
25. *The Niagara Gazette* succeeded *The Niagara Falls Gazette*.
26. See reprints of Michael H. Brown's accounts of the Vorhees and Schroeder families in *Laying Waste: Love Canal and the Poisoning of America* (New York: Pantheon Books, 1980).
27. Hillis, "Love Canal's Contamination."
28. Ibid.
29. See Kenny, "Statement to Occidental Petroleum Shareholders [on] Corporate Responsibility Resolution," May 21, 1980, Love Canal Collection, SUNY–Buffalo, and Kenny, "Love Canal Testimony Submitted to the House Subcommittee on Oversight and Investigation," Apr. 2, 1979, reprinted in Daniel G. Payne & Richard S. Newman, eds., *Palgrave Environmental Reader* (New York: Palgrave Macmillan, 2005), 230–231. Luella Kenny, interview with the author, May 3, 2004.
30. See sources cited in preceding note.
31. Ibid.
32. Gibbs, "Learning From Love Canal: A 20th Anniversary Retrospective," *Orion Afield* (Spring 1998), posted conveniently at http://arts.envirolink.org/arts_and_activism/LoisGibbs.html.
33. Gibbs, *Love Canal: My Story* (Albany: State University of New York Press, 1982), 12–24, 26–29. Hereinafter, Gibbs, Love Canal.
34. "Love Canal—Public Health Time Bomb, "Miscarriages and Birth Defects" section.
35. Donald G. McNeil Jr., "Health Chief Calls Waste Site a 'Peril,'" *N.Y. Times*, Aug. 3, 1978 (hereinafter *NYT*).
36. *NG*, Aug. 2, 1978
37. *NG*, Aug. 6, 1978.

38. *NG*, Aug. 7, Nov. 6, 1978; *Buffalo Courier Express*, Aug. 7, 1978; *Buffalo Evening News*, Aug. 8, 1978.
39. See the International Society for Environmental Epidemiology's website (ISEE), http://www.iseepi.org/.
40. Alice Stark, interview with the author at the 12th Annual ISEE Conference, Aug. 21, 2000, in Buffalo. Stark participated in a panel entitled, "The Continuing Impact of Love Canal."
41. *NG*, Aug. 5, 1978.
42. *NG*, July 26, 1978.
43. Gibbs, *Love Canal*, 30, 36 (emphasis added).
44. Ibid., 9, 11.
45. Ibid., *Love Canal*, 25–26.
46. Quotes from an LCHA advertisement October 1979, reprinted at the NYS Heritage, Digital Collections: http://nyheritage.nnyln.org, See also Gibbs, *Love Canal*, cover-page facsimile; 72.
47. Gibbs, *Love Canal*, 29–30.
48. Ibid., 30–42.
49. Ibid., 36–37.
50. *Buffalo Courier Express*, Sept. 27, 1978; see also Elizabeth Blum, *Love Canal Revisited* (Lawrence: University of Kansas Press, 2008), especially 73–76.
51. See "Blacks in Niagara Falls, New York: 1865 to 1965, A Survey," in *Afro-Americans in New York Life and History* 28:2 (2004), especially footnote 111.
52. See also Blum, *Love Canal Revisited*, 68, 74–75.
53. See Gibbs in "Notes From Washington Visit" Folder, circa 1980, Lois Gibbs Papers, Tufts University Special Collections.
54. See "Blacks in Niagara Falls, New York: 1865 to 1965, A Survey," footnote 111; see also Blum, *Love Canal Revisited*, 68, 74–75.
55. Like others who lived in Love Canal, Griffon Manor residents have held several reunions in recent years. See the Facebook post about one such recent event at https://www.facebook.com/events/450772188276078/.
56. Gibbs, *Love Canal*, 40.
57. Ibid., 2.
58. *NG*, August 5, 1978.
59. Ibid.
60. On the Wilcox visit, see *NG*, Aug. 5, 1978.
61. Lois Gibbs, *Love Canal*, 41–42; 66.
62. Wilcox quoted in *Buffalo Courier Express*, Aug. 6, 1978.
63. Thomas Casey, Acting Deputy Director of the FDAA, quoted in *Buffalo Courier Express*, Aug. 8, 1978.
64. LaFalce quoted in *NG*, Aug. 8, 1978.
65. On federal disaster relief and cultural notions of disaster, see the following important works: Theodore Steinberg, *Acts of God: The Unnatural History of Natural Disaster in America* (New York: Oxford University Press, 2000), and Kevin Rozario, *The Culture of Calamity: Disaster and the Making of Modern America* (Chicago: University of Chicago Press, 2007).
66. See Karen Tumulty, "Love Canal Reborn," *Los Angeles Times*, Aug. 14, 1990.
67. See "Brown Family Relocation Materials, 1978," and "Personal Papers, 1985–1992," in Ecumenical Task Force of the Niagara Frontier Records," Series II, "Pat Brown as Executive Director, 1978–1995," Box 9, Folder 10–11.

68. See Brown quoted in Newman, "From Love's Canal to Love Canal," in Cowie & Heathcott, *Beyond The Ruins: The Meanings of Deindustrialization* (Ithaca: Cornell University Press, 2003), 133–134. On Pat Brown more generally, see especially Patricia Donovan, "Collections Tell Love Canal Story," UB *Reporter*, June 22, 2000.

69. See Testimony of James Clark, Mar. 29, 1979, before the Senate Sub-Committee on Hazardous Waste, conveniently reprinted in the SUNY-Buffalo Love Canal Collections' online website: http://library.buffalo.edu/specialcollections/lovecanal/.

70. Gibbs, *Love Canal*, 42.

71. *NG*, August 5; *Buffalo Courier Express*, Aug. 6, 1978.

72. Ibid., 54.

73. Love Canal "Neighborhood Profile," in Emergency Needs Grant Application, 1980, Love Canal Area Revitalization Records, University Archives, SUNY–Buffalo, MS 74, Box 4, Folder 11, 19–25.

74. Shribman phone interview with the author, Sept. 8, 2005.

75. Gibbs, *Love Canal*, 68. For background, see especially Blum, *Love Canal Revisited*, especially Chapter 2, which focuses on women's struggles at Love Canal. On women and environmentalism more generally, see also Carolyn Merchant, *Earthcare: Women and the Environment* (New York: Routledge, 1996), especially Part Three. Among other works in the still-growing subfield, see also Mary Joy Breton, *Women Pioneers for the Environment* (Boston: Northeastern University Press, 1998). For global perspectives, see Maria Mies and Vandana Shiva, *Ecofeminism* (London: Zed Books, 1993).

76. Hillis, entry and draft of newspaper letter, June 30, 1979, in "Love's Canal Contamination: The Poisoning of an American Family."

77. Dudley Clendinen, "How Love Canal Mothers Became a Political Force," *N.Y. Times*, May 26, 1980.

78. Ibid.

79. "Family of 6 Happy to Be Out," *Buffalo Courier Express*, Aug. 9, 1978.

80. *NG*, Jan. 8, 1979.

81. *NG*, Aug. 8, 1978.

82. *Buffalo Courier Express*, Aug. 9, 1978.

83. Ibid.

84. Emphasis in original. See the Penny Ploughman Collection, ETF Records, SUNY–Buffalo, Love Canal Collections, MS65.D.17. Image of the sign is available at the Love Canal Collections website.

85. Photo by Robert F. Bukaty, in *Buffalo Courier Express*, Aug. 9, 1978.

86. An historic image taken by Penny Ploughman of the "Newco Chemical Waste Systems Water Treatment Facility" is available on the Love Canal Images website, SUNY–Buffalo, available online at http://digital.lib.buffalo.edu/items/show/16494.

87. *NG*, Aug. 7, 1978.

88. Michael Desmond, *Buffalo Courier Express*, Aug. 8, 1978.

89. Gibbs, *Love Canal, My Story*, 55–57.

90. Gibbs, *Love Canal, My Story*, 55–59.

91. Ibid. See the photograph taken by Penny Ploughman of "Emergency Evacuation Buses on 95th Street," at the Love Canal Images website, available online at: http://digital.lib.buffalo.edu/items/show/16488.

92. Levine donated her material to SUNY Buffalo and the Buffalo and Erie County Historical Society. On Levine's early conclusions about the disaster, see "The Love Canal: A Sociologist's Perspective," paper by Adeline Levine, March 1979, in Ecumenical Task Force of the Niagara Frontier Records, Box 38, Folder 6.

93. See "Interview forms for Adeline Levine's Love Canal research project, 1978–1979," in Adeline Levine Love Canal Research Materials (Part I), 1953–1981, University Archives, State University of New York at Buffalo, Box 1, Folder 34.

94 Adeline Levine, *Love Canal: Science, Politics, and People* (Lexington, Mass.: D.C. Heath & Co., 1982) 1–5. On Levine (1925–2015), see the obituary posted on the SUNY–Buffalo "News Center" website, available at: http://www.buffalo.edu/news/releases/2015/03/012.html.

95. Gibbs, *Love Canal*, 44–45.

Chapter 6

1. Luella Kenny, "Statement to the Annual Meeting of Occidental Petroleum Share Holders Corporate Responsibility Resolution," May 21, 1980, reprinted in Payne & Newman, eds., *Palgrave Environmental Reader*.

2. Eckardt C. Beck, "The Love Canal Tragedy," *EPA Journal*, January 1979, online at http://www2.epa.gov/aboutepa/love-canal-tragedy.

3. Michael H. Brown, "Love Canal and the Poisoning of America," *The Atlantic*, December 1979, 33–47.

4. *Buffalo Evening News*, Feb. 15, 1979.

5. Anne Hillis, journal entry, Fall 1979, in "Love Canal's Contamination: The Poisoning of an American Family," Box 38, Folder 9-38.10, Ecumenical Task Force of the Niagara Frontier Records, 1946–1995, University Archives, The State University of New York at Buffalo. [Hereinafter, ETF Records, SUNY–Buffalo.]

6. On the Vores and the Love Canal, see *NG*, Feb. 10, 1979.

7. Brown, "Love Canal and the Poisoning of America," 46–47.

8. See "Report of the Executive Director," "Progress Report of the Ecumenical Task Force of the Niagara Frontier" (Niagara Falls, 1980), 9. This report was the first of many issued by the group at Love Canal.

9. Testimony of Marie Pozniak before the Senate Subcommittee on Toxic Substances and Chemical Wastes, May 3, 1979, in Love Canal Collections, SUNY–Buffalo, online at: http://library.buffalo.edu/libraries/specialcollections/lovecanal/documents/pdfs/pozniak.pdf

10. See Gaylord Nelson, et al., *Beyond Earth Day: Fulfilling the Promise* (Madison: University of Wisconsin Press, 2002). See also Denis Hayes, quoted in the anthology *Earth Day: The Beginning* (New York: Bantam Books, 1970), iii.

11. Rachel Carson, *Silent Spring* (New York: Houghton Mifflin, 1962), 14. On Carson, see especially Linda J. Lear, *Rachel Carson: Witness For Nature* (New York: Henry Holt and Co., 1997).

12. Clifton Fadiman & Jean White, *Ecocide: And Thoughts Toward Survival* (New York: Interbook, Inc., 1971), 9.

13. See Charles O. Jones' review of *Ecocide*: "From Gold to Garbage: A Bibliographical Essay on Politics and the Environment," in *American Political Science Review*, Vol. 66, No. 2 (June 1972), 588–595.

14. Among the many works on second-wave environmentalism, see Philip Shabecoff, *A Fierce Green Fire: The American Environmental Movement* (New York: Hill and

Wang, 1993); Robert Gottlieb, *Forcing the Spring: The Transformation of the American Environmental Movement*, rev. ed. (Washington, D.C.: Island Press, 2005). See also Samuel P. Hays, *A History of Environmental Politics Since 1945* (Pittsburgh: University of Pittsburgh Press, 2000).

15. "Statement of the Hon. John J. LaFalce," May 19, 1979, in Hazardous and Toxic Waste Disposal Field Hearings, Joint Hearings Before the Subcommittees on Environmental Pollution and Resource Protection of the Committee on Environment and Public Works, U.S. Senate, 96th Congress, 1st Sess., May 19, 1979—Niagara Falls, N.Y., Vol. 2, 11.

16. Christopher J. Basso, *Environment, Inc.: From Grassroots to Beltway* (Lawrence: University Press of Kansas, 2005), 33–34.

17. See Gibbs' perspective in Newman, "From Love's Canal to Love Canal," in Cowie & Heathcott, eds., *Beyond the Ruins*, 128.

18. Gibbs, *Love Canal: My Story* (1982 edition), 138.

19. Gibbs in Hazardous and Toxic Waste Disposal Field Hearings, Vol. 2, 29–30.

20. See Walker's tale in *NG*, Aug. 9, 1978.

21. For a catalogue of Love Canal pictures, see SUNY–Buffalo's "Love Canal Images" link, at http://digital.lib.buffalo.edu/cdm/landingpage/collection/LIB-003.

22. "Deadly Drums," from AP Sunday Illustrations, Sunday, Jan. 27, 1985. Image by Mary Esch.

23. Gibbs to David Axelrod, May 24, 1979, in Lois Gibbs Papers, Tufts University, Special Collections.

24. Ibid.

25. Gibbs, *Love Canal*, 33.

26. Luella Kenny quoted in Ronnie Greene's story, "From Homemaker to Hellraiser in Love Canal," *Center for Public Integrity*, April 2013.

27. "Why Should I Listen to Lois Gibbs," in the Citizens' Clearinghouse for Hazardous Waste newsletter, *Everyone's Backyard*, Vol. 1, No. 1 (Fall, 1982), 1.

28. Gibbs, "Learning From Love Canal: A 20th Anniversary Retrospective," *Orion Afield*, Spring 1998, available online at http://arts.envirolink.org/arts_and_activism/LoisGibbs.html.

29. Dudley Clendinen, "A Boyhood Is Poisoned," *NYT*, June 19, 1980.

30. Anne Hillis, journal entry, Fall 1979. "Love Canal's Contamination," ETF Records, SUNY–Buffalo.

31. Ibid.

32. "LCHA Chronological Report," April 1978–January 1980, in Love Canal Collections, SUNY–Buffalo, available online at http://library.buffalo.edu/specialcollections/lovecanal/documents/pdfs/lcha_chron.pdf.

33. Ibid., June 26, 1979.

34. Stephen Lester quoted in "Happy Birthday, Love Canal," in *Chemical & Engineering News*, Vol. 86, No. 46 (Nov. 17, 2008), 46–53; available online at https://pubs.acs.org/cen/government/86/8646gov2.html.

35. LCHA Chronological Report, "Definitions," 3–4.

36. See Levine, *Love Canal, Science, Politics, and People*, 116–117, 121–122.

37. Gibbs, *Love Canal*, 66.

38. Gibbs, *Love Canal: My Story*, 113; see also Gibbs, "Housewife's Data," in "Voices From the Past," *American Journal of Public Health* (September 2011), Vol. 101, No. 9, 1556–1559, available online at: http://ajph.aphapublications.org/cgi/content/extract/101/9/1556.

39. See Adeline Levine, *Love Canal: Science, Politics, and People*, 88–99.

40. See "Lessons from Love Canal," a website produced by the Boston University School of Public Health, at http://www.bu.edu/lovecanal/main2.html. See also "Happy Birthday, Love Canal!" in *Chemical & Engineering News*, Vol. 86, No. 46 (Nov. 17, 2008), 46–53. While not every one of Paigen's claims had been verified, many were supported by subsequent studies. In the words of the reporter who interviewed state health officials about follow-up results, "[c]hildren born at Love Canal were twice as likely as other children in other parts of the county to be born with a birth defect, a statistically significant finding. Children conceived at Love Canal were more than twice as likely to be female compared with children conceived after the mother left the neighborhood." See http://pubs.acs .org/cen/government/86/8646gov2.html.

41. See, for example, "Technical Advisor Sub-Agreement," between the Committee for a Clean Environment (Hope, Maine) and Dr. Beverly Paigen, of Jackson Laboratories, in *Superfund Record of Decision, Union Chemical, Maine*, December 1990.

42. Allan Mazur, *A Hazardous Inquiry: The Rashomon Effect at Love Canal*, (Cambridge: Harvard University Press, 1998), 79–80.

43. Overview, "Love Canal Health Studies," at the National Academy of Engineering Online Ethics Center, especially the "Low Birth Weights Study" and the "Paigen Follow-Up Study," at http://www.onlineethics.org/cms/6541.aspx.

44. See "Happy Birthday, Love Canal," in *Chemical & Engineering News*, 46–53.

45. See Testimony of Anne Hillis and Jim Clark before the Joint Senate Subcommittee on Environmental Pollution and Hazardous Waste, Mar. 28–29, 1979, in Love Canal Collections, SUNY–Buffalo, available online at http://library.buffalo. edu/libraries/specialcollections/lovecanal/documents/pdfs/clark.pdf

46. Ibid.

47. Testimony of Grace M. McCoulf before the Senate Subcommittee on Toxic Substances and Chemical Wastes, Apr. 5, 1979, available online at: http:// library.buffalo.edu/libraries/specialcollections/lovecanal/documents/pdfs/ mccoulf.pdf

48. Testimony of Pozniak before the Senate Subcommittee on Hazardous Waste, May 3, 1979 . . .

49. See Culver's speech in "Hazardous and Toxic Waste Disposal: Joint Hearings. . . . Before the 96th Congress," 15, available online at http://archive .org/stream/hazardoustoxicwa01unit/hazardoustoxicwa01unit_djvu.txt.

50. Chafee quoted in Ibid., 1–3, 7–16.

51. See "Evacuation of Residents" section in "Love Canal: A Special Report to the Governor and Legislature, April 1981," available at https://www.health.ny.gov/ environmental/investigations/love_canal/lcreport.htm.

52. Gibbs, *Love Canal*, 93–95.

53. LCHA Chronological Report, Mar. 25, 1979, 14.

54. See Blum, "Parting the Waters," in Michael Egan & Jeff Crane eds., *Natural Protest: Essays on the History of American Environmentalism* (New York: Routledge, 2009), 266.

55. Margeen Hoffman quoted in *Buffalo Courier Express*, Sept. 12, 1979.

56. Ibid.

57. See "Progress Report of the Ecumenical Task Force," 1980, 1–10.

58. Joann Brietsman quoted in ibid., "Acknowledgements" page.

59. KJB, Genesis 26:1.

60. Paul L. Moore, "The Land is Cursed," in "Progress Report of the Ecumenical Task Force," 1980, iii.
61. The photograph by William D. Cecil, Jr., appears on the cover of the ETF's first "Progress Report": http://library.buffalo.edu/libraries/specialcollections/lovecanal/documents/pdfs/etf_progress1.pdf.
62. Ibid., ii.
63. See "Historical Note" in "The Finding Aid for the Ecumenical Task Force of the Niagara Frontier Records 1946–1995," See: http://purl.org/net/findingaids/view?docId=ead/archives/ubar_ms0065.xml.
64. See Moore, "The Land is Cursed," in "Progress Report of the Ecumenical Task Force," 1980, iii.
65. See the "Foreword" to the "Progress Report of the Ecumenical Task Force," 1980, i–ii.
66. See Moore, "The Land Is Cursed," in "Progress Report of the Ecumenical Task Force," 1980, ii–iii.
67. See Mazur's critique of Love Canal activism and reportage, A Hazardous Inquiry, Introduction.
68. Hoffman, "Report of the Executive Director," in Progress Report of the Ecumenical Task Force, 1980, 9.
69. Progress Report II of the Ecumenical Task Force…Aug. 1, 1980–Sept. 15, 1981 (Niagara Falls, 1981), 3 (emphasis in original).
70. Ibid., "Notes to Financial Statements," 74–79.
71. Gibbs, testimony presented to the House Subcommittee on Oversight and Investigations, Mar. 21, 1979, in Love Canal Collections, SUNY–Buffalo, available online at: http://library.buffalo.edu/libraries/specialcollections/lovecanal/documents/pdfs/gibbs.pdf; see also Gibbs, Love Canal, My Story, 3.
72. Grace M. McCoulf, testimony before Senate subcommittee on Toxic Substances and Chemical Wastes, Apr. 5, 1979, in Love Canal Collections, SUNY–Buffalo.
73. Jim Clark, Congressional Testimony, Mar. 28–29, 1979.
74. Hillis, NG, Feb. 23, 1979, reprinted in her unpublished memoir, "Love Canal's Contamination: The Poisoning of an American Family," ETF Records, Love Canal Collection, SUNY-Buffalo.
75. Progress Report of the Ecumenical Task Force, 1–9.
76. Ibid., 9.
77. See "Toxic Wastes and Race: A National Report on the Racial and Socio-Economic Characteristics of Communities with Hazardous Waste Sites," Commission for Racial Justice, United Church of Christ (New York, 1987), available online at http://d3n8a8pro7vhmx.cloudfront.net/unitedchurchofchrist/legacy_url/13567/toxwrace87.pdf?1418439935.
78. The classic study is Robert D. Bullard, Dumping in Dixie: Race, Class and Environmental Quality (Boulder, Colo.: Westview Press, 1990). For more recent assessments, see works by David Naguib Pellow, especially Resisting Global Toxics: Transnational Movements For Environmental Justice (Cambridge: MIT Press, 2007).
79. Gibbs, "Learning From Love Canal: A 20th Anniversary Retrospective," Orion Afield, Spring 1998, available online at http://arts.envirolink.org/arts_and_activism/LoisGibbs.html.
80. Lois Gibbs, Mar. 21, 1979, Testimony presented to the House Subcommittee on Oversight and Investigations, SUNY–Buffalo, available online at http://library.buffalo.edu/libraries/specialcollections/lovecanal/documents/pdfs/gibbs.pdf

81. Willard C. Richan, *Lobbying For Social Change* (Binghamton, N.Y.: Howarth Press, 1996), 257–258.

82. LCHA handbill, reprinted in Gibbs, *Love Canal, My Story*.

83. Nor could they sue the school board or the company. See *Buffalo Courier Express*, Aug. 6, 1978.

84. Eileen Matsulavage, "Love Canal Testimony," Apr. 5, 1979; Matsulavage to David Axelrod, Apr. 9, 1979, both available online at: http://library.buffalo.edu/libraries/specialcollections/lovecanal/documents/pdfs/matsulavage.pdf.

85. Loretta Gambino, congressional testimony Apr. 5, 1979, available online at: http://library.buffalo.edu/libraries/specialcollections/lovecanal/documents/pdfs/gambino.pdf.

86. Hillis, Congressional Testimony Mar. 28–29, 1979, in ibid.

87. Progress Report of the Ecumenical Task Force, 9.

88. Ibid., 7–8.

89. "Cathy Hinds...Battles Poison in Maine," oral history recollection with Mary Joy Breton, in *Women Pioneers for the Environment* (Boston: Northeastern University Press, 1998), 128.

90. Ibid.

Chapter 7

1. Edmund S. Muskie Archives, Bates College, Lewiston, Maine. Edmund S. Muskie Papers. Series V.A.11: U.S. Senate: Washington Office, 95th Congress (1977–1978). Edmund S. Muskie Collection. Series 23A. Sound Recordings: Cassette Tapes. Event No. 1,224. CBS interview, date unknown. Box 2166— Press Files. My thanks to Brian Powers for working on this material.

2. Edmund S. Muskie Collection. Library of Congress, Series 23A. Sound Recordings: Cassette Tapes. Event No. 1,224. CBS interview. Date unknown, circa 1978–1979.

3. Muskie eventually cited Hillis's testimony in a speech before the American Society of Civil Engineers in Boston, Apr. 2, 1979.

4. *NG*, Jan. 12, 1979.

5. *NG*, Aug. 10, 1978.

6. *Buffalo Evening News*, Aug. 8, 1978; *NG*, Aug. 10, 1978.

7. *Buffalo Courier Express*, Sept. 26, 1978.

8. Ibid.

9. "609...and Counting, Hazardous Wastes and the Public's Health in New York State" (Albany, 1980), 1–40.

10. LaFalce, May 18, 1979, in Hazardous Waste and Toxic Waste Disposal Joint Hearings Before the Subcommittees on Environmental Pollution and Resource Protection of the United States Congress, Vol. 2: Field Hearings, 2–7.

11. LaFalce, to Jimmy Carter, Nov. 9, 1979, in Box 1, Folder 39, Adeline Levine Love Canal Research Materials (Part 1), 1953–1981 (1978–1981 bulk), University Archives, The State University of New York at Buffalo.

12. LaFalce, May 18, 1979, in Hazardous Waste and Toxic Waste Disposal Joint Hearings Before the Subcommittees on Environmental Pollution and Resource Protection of the United States Congress, Vol. 2: Field Hearings, 2–7.

13. Ibid., 8–12.

14. LaFalce interview with the author, July 16, 2009.

15. LaFalce, May 18, 1979, in Hazardous Waste and Toxic Waste Disposal Joint Hearings Before the Subcommittees on Environmental Pollution and Resource Protection of the United States Congress, Vol. 2: Field Hearings, 2–7.

16. LaFalce interview with the author, July 16, 2009.

17. LaFalce, testimony, Mar. 28, 1979, Hazardous Waste and Toxic Waste Disposal Joint Hearings Before the Subcommittees on Environmental Pollution and Resource Protection of the United States Congress, Vol. 1, 188–192.

18. LaFalce, to Jimmy Carter, Nov. 9, 1979, in Box 1, Folder 39, Adeline Levine Love Canal Research Materials.

19. LaFalce interview with the author, July 16, 2009.

20. "Bury Now, Pay Later." See, for example, Desmond's *Buffalo Courier Express*, Sept. 22, 26 1978; see also report in the *Buffalo Courier Express*, Feb 9, 1979 on "The Today Show" follow up on Desmond's story.

21. *Buffalo Courier Express*, Sept. 26, 1978.

22. For a summary of the original "The Killing Ground" documentary and its follow-up, Richard F. Shepard, "The Killing Ground Is Updated," *NYT*, Aug. 21, 1980.

23. John Dowling Jr. in *The Bulletin of Atomic Scientists*, Vol. 36, No. 9 (November 1980).

24. See *NYT*, May 7, 1954.

25. *NYT*, Nov. 11, 1977.

26. Wyss, *Covering the Environment*, 7.

27. On Bethlehem Steel, see the EPA's report, "Air and Water Compliance Summary for the Iron and Steel Industry" (1977).

28. Shribman interview with the author, Sept. 5, 2005.

29. *Buffalo Evening News*, Aug. 8, 1978.

30. See Brown's "Cityscape" story, *NG*, July 30, 1978.

31. Brown, *NG*, Aug. 2, 1978.

32. "Nightline" transcript, May 21, 1981, Adeline Levine Love Canal Research Materials, Box 33, Folder 13.

33. See the following *NYT* stories by Brown: "New Jersey Cleans Up Its Pollution Act," Nov. 23, 1980; "Is Hemlock Being Slowly Poisoned?" July 15, 1979; "A Wasted National Resource," May 4, 1980.

34. See Brown, "Love Canal and the Poisoning of America," *Atlantic* (December 1979), 33–47. This essay also became the basis for Brown's book, *Laying Waste: The Poisoning of America by Toxic Chemicals* (New York: Washington Square Press, 1979, 1981).

35. Irene Kiefer, *Poisoned Land: The Problem of Hazardous Waste* (New York: Atheneum, 1981), 3–12.

36. David Morell & Christopher Margorian, *Siting Hazardous Waste Facilities: Local Opposition and the Myth of Pre-Emption* (Cambridge, Mass.: Ballinger Publishing Co., 1982), 1–8.

37. Paul A. Argenti & Janis Forman, "Should Business Schools Teach Aristotle?," *Strategy+Business*, (Third Quarter, July 1, 1998).

38. *Buffalo Courier Express*, Aug. 8, 1978.

39. Bruce Davis, quoted in ibid.

40. See Davis. quoted in Hazardous Waste and Toxic Waste Disposal Joint Hearings Before the Subcommittees on Environmental Pollution and Resource Protection of the United States Congress, Vol. 1, Davis, 248–59.

41. Jim Clark, attachment to Senate testimony, Mar. 28, 1979, in ibid., 22.

42. See Factline No. 3. The first Factline, "A Hard Look at the Love Canal," was dated April 1979. See also Adeline Levine, Love Canal Research Materials, Factline Newsletters 10–12, 1980, Box 1, Folder 33.

43. Factline 1, April 1979.

44. *Buffalo Evening News*, Aug. 6, 1978.

45. Donald L. Baeder to Financial Community Representatives, July 31, 1980, in New York City, in "The Other Side of Love Canal: Facts vs. Fallacies" (July 1980), 5. On RCRA and hazardous waste, see the EPA's website at: http://www .epa.gov/wastes/laws-regs/rcrahistory.htm.

46. "What Hooker Told Whom, When About Love Canal," *Wall Street Journal*, June 19, 1980. See also Factline No. 10, 1980, which reprinted *Wall Street Journal* editorials that supported Hooker's claim it had attempted to keep the Love Canal dump safe and secure before deeding it to Niagara Falls.

47. Donald L. Baeder, quoted in story on *L.A. Times-Wash. Post* News Service, reprinted in *Sarasota Herald Tribune*, Sept. 7, 1979.

48. Factline 3.

49. "A Message from the Industrial Chemicals Group, Executive Vice President Bruce Davis," submitted to Congress, Mar. 29, 1979, in Hazardous Waste and Toxic Waste Disposal Joint Hearings Before the Subcommittees on Environmental Pollution and Resource Protection of the United States Congress, Vol. 1, 239–241. See also Davis' Testimony to the Subcommittee, 249–259; and his written statement, 289–310.

50. Ibid.

51. Ibid.

52. On Hooker's ads, see, for instance, Gibbs' recollections in *Love Canal*, 98. See also the photographs in the Penelope D. Ploughman Love Canal Collection, University Archives, SUNY–Buffalo, available online at: http://digital.lib.buffalo .edu/collections/show/54.

53. Erin E. Robinson, 144–145, "Community Frame Analysis," *Sociological Spectrum* 22 (2) (April 2002): 139–169.

54. See *NG*, Feb. 1, 1979. For a summary of federal action, see also Ralph Blumenthal, "Residents Attack Accord on Hooker Corp. Cleanup," *NYT*, Feb. 6, 1981. Scorecard, the Pollution Information Site, Pollution Locator for Hyde Park, N.Y., HTTP:// scorecard.org/env-releases/land/site.tcl?epa_idNYD000831644#description

55. EPA Press Release, Dec. 20, 1979, at: http://www.epa.gov/history/topics/ Lovecanal/02.htm. See also "Love Canal: A Special Report to the Governor and Legislature: April 1981" (Albany, 1981), section entitled "Litigation," available online at: https://www.health.ny.gov/environmental/investigations/love_canal/ lcreport.htm

56. See *NYT*, Dec. 13, 1981. On Syosset, see the EPA Superfund site: http://cumulis .epa.gov/supercpad/cursites/csitinfo.cfm?id=0201187.

57. John M. Shauver, quoted in a national story picked up in *the Sarasota Herald Tribune*, Sept. 7, 1979.

58. Michigan Attorney General Frank J. Kelley, quoted in "The Other Side of Love Canal: Facts vs. Fallacies" (Los Angeles: Occidental Petroleum, 1980), 4; conveniently available online at the SUNY–Buffalo "Love Canal Collections" website: http://library.buffalo.edu/libraries/specialcollections/lovecanal/documents/ disaster_gif/records/prese1.html.

59. The Michigan settlement allowed Hooker/Occidental to take the high road and "forego possible legal defense," in Kelley's words. Ibid.

60. Bruce Davis, quoted in *Sarasota Herald Tribune*, Sept. 7, 1979.
61. See Harry S. Boyte, *The Backyard Revolution* (Philadelphia: Temple University Press, 1981), cover description.
62. Armand Hammer, quoted in "The Other Side of Love Canal: Facts vs. Fallacies" (July 1980), 4.
63. Ibid.
64. John W. Johnstone, interview with James Traynham, Chemical Heritage Foundation Oral History Transcript 0156, Feb. 11, 1997 (Enfield, Conn), 27. Johnstone was hired by Oldbury Electrochemical Company in Niagara Falls, which was purchased by Hooker.
65. Ibid., 10.
66. Ibid.
67. Ibid., 27.
68. Ibid.
69. Ibid., 17, 18, 27.
70. J. Roger Hirl, interview with James Traynham, Chemical Heritage Foundation Oral History Transcript 0177, Jan. 29, 1999, Dallas, Tex., 8–11.
71. Davis, Testimony, Mar. 29, 1979, in Hazardous Waste and Toxic Waste Disposal Joint Hearings Before the Subcommittees on Environmental Pollution and Resource Protection of the United States Congress, Vol. 1, 249–259; see also Davis' statement at 289–310.
72. Ibid., 249–259.
73. Ibid.
74. Davis, quoted in *Sarasota Herald Tribune*, Sept. 7, 1979.
75. Luella Kenny, interview with the author, Apr. 17, 2006.
76. Kai T. Erikson, review of *Laying Waste*, *NYT*, May 18, 1980.
77. Ibid.

Chapter 8

1. See "Love Canal" entry on EPA website, "Region 2, Superfund," available online at http://www.epa.gov/region2/superfund/npl/Lovecanal/.
2. Josh Barnabel, "Peaceful Vigil Resumed at Love Canal"; Robin Herman, "Accord Is Reached on Evacuation of Last 710 Love Canal Families"; Dudley Clendinen, "New Study Finds Residents Suffer Nerve Problems", all *NYT*, May 21, 1980.
3. Philip M. Boffey, "Study of Love Canal Finds No Direct Link to Genetic Diseases," *NYT*, May 18, 1983. See Michael Brown's comments on the study a decade later in "A Toxic Ghost Town," *The Atlantic* (July 1989), available online at: http://www.theatlantic.com/magazine/archive/1989/07/a-toxic-ghost-town/303360/.
4. See the United Press International story in the May 20, 1980, edition of the *Sarasota Herald-Tribune*; see the AP Story on May 20, 1980, in the *Lakeland Ledger* (Florida). On the situation leading to the incident, see also Ronnie Green, "From Homemaker to Hellraiser in Love Canal," *Center for Public Integrity* web article, May 19, 2014, available at: http://www.publicintegrity.org/2013/04/16/12465/homemaker-hell-raiser-love-canal.
5. *NYT*, May 21, 1980; John LaFalce, interview with the author, July 16, 2009.
6. *NYT*, May 20, 1980; see also *NYT*, May 23, 1980; *NG*, May 22, 1980.
7. *NYT*, May 22, 1980.
8. "Carter Signs Cleanup Bill on Upstate Toxic Wastes," *NYT*, Oct. 2, 1980.

9. Gibbs, *Love Canal*, 140.
10. *NYT*, May 22, 1980.
11. Irvin Molotsky, "U.S. Agrees to $7.5 Million for Love Canal Residents, Along With Loans," *NYT*, Aug. 23, 1980.
12. Gibbs, *Love Canal*, 136, 140, 162–164.
13. Ibid., 164.
14. *NYT*, Aug. 23, 1980.
15. *NYT*, Oct. 2, 1980.
16. On changes in the neighborhood, see New York Department of Health, "Love Canal: A Special Report to the Governor and the Legislature" (Albany, 1981).
17. "Notice to All Residents of Love Canal," handbill, November 1980, "Superfund" Folder, Center for Health, Environment and Justice Records, Tufts University. Hereinafter CHEJ Records. CHEJ superseded the Citizens' Clearinghouse for Hazardous Waste.
18. Rae Tyson, "A Year Later, Canal Homes Sit in Silence," *NG*, May 17, 1981.
19. Dorothy Little, quoted in ibid.
20. Rae Tyson (UPI), "[M]ost Love Canal residents have left homes," *Utica Daily Press*, May 18, 1981.
21. Gibbs, *Love Canal*, 172.
22. Shabecoff, "Waste Cleanup Bill Approved by House," *NYT*, Sept. 24, 1980.
23. Richard Lazarus, *The Making of Environmental Law* (Chicago: University of Chicago Press, 2004), Ch. 6, 99.
24. Ibid., 108–109.
25. John Johnstone interview, CHF.
26. Irving S. Shapiro, quoted in Philip Shabecoff, "DuPont Official Urges Compromise on Cleanup Fund," *NYT*, Nov. 20, 1980.
27. See Michael Brown's article in the *Niagara Gazette*, Jan. 18, 1979. For summaries of the proposed law, see: https://www.govtrack.us/congress/bills/96/hr1048; and https://www.govtrack.us/congress/bills/96/hr1049.
28. Moynihan, quoted in Hazardous and Toxic Waste Disposal, Joint Hearings Before the Committees on Environmental Pollution and Resource Protection of the United States Congress, Field Hearings, May 18, 1979, 1–2.
29. Ibid.
30. Ibid.
31. For good coverage of Superfund's evolving status in Congress, see *NYT*: Philip Shabecoff, "Waste Cleanup Bill Approved by House," Sept. 23, 1980; David E. Rosenbaum, "One Last Poll: Campaign Fog Obscures the Sharp Contrast on Most Issues," Nov. 2, 1980; Editorial, "Save the Superfund," Nov. 22, 1980.
32. See "Save the Superfund," *NYT*, Nov. 22, 1980.
33. Ibid.
34. "News From Congressman John J. LaFalce," Mar. 24, 1982, including copy of draft law, in "LaFalce" Folder, 1–2, CHEJ Records, Tufts.
35. Ibid.
36. "Landfill Use for Wastes is 'Last Resort,'" *Tonawanda News*, Mar. 22, 1982.
37. "Congressman John LaFalce's Update," August 1981, "LaFalce" Folder, 1–2, CHEJ Records, Tufts.
38. Ibid., 2.

39. LaFalce to Anne M. Gorsuch, EPA, Mar. 9, 1982, LaFalce folder, ibid. (emphasis added).
40. Jacob I. Bregman & Kenneth M. Mackenthun, *Environmental Regulations Handbook* (Boca Raton, Fla.: CRC Press, 1992), 22.
41. Lazarus, *The Making of Environmental Law*, Ch. 6.
42. On the aims of the Massachusetts law, see: http://turadata.turi.org/WhatIsTURA/OverviewOfTURA.html
43. Ibid.
44. See Eleanor Torcasio quote in Tyson, "[M]ost Love Canal residents have left homes," *Utica Daily Press*, May 18, 1981.
45. *NYT*, June 19, 1980;
46. The term was used in various places; see, for instance, *Social Policy*, a journal dedicated to grassroots causes, "Special Issue," Part II (Winter, 1990), 36.
47. See the "Baffled by the Terms" section in *Everyone's Backyard*, the newsletter published by the Citizen's Clearinghouse for Hazardous Wastes, Vol. 1, No. 1 (Fall, 1982), 7.
48. See the CCHW's outreach claims in *Social Policy*, 1990, 36.
49. "I Think There's a Dump in My Backyard—What Do I Do Next?" *Everyone's Backyard*, Vol. 1, No. 1 (Fall, 1982), 8.
50. See Teri Naugler of "Save Our Planet" to Stephen Lester and the CCHW, circa 1990 (New Mexico); Theresa Pisano to CCHW, Oct. 8, 1988 (New Jersey).
51. Pisano to CCHW, Oct. 8, 1988, New Jersey folder, Tufts.
52. *Social Policy*, 1990, 36–37.
53. Ibid.
54. Lynn Hill to CCHW, Dec. 9, 1987, "Kansas" Folder, CHEJ Records, Tufts University Library, Special Collections.
55. Gibbs to Lynn Hill, Dec. 29, 1987, in ibid.
56. "Leadership Handbook on Hazardous Waste," CCHW Publication (Arlington, Va., 1983), cover page, 1–10, 11–58.
57. Ibid., 2.
58. Gibbs, interview with the author, Feb. 5, 1999; see also Gibbs, *Love Canal*, 1–2.
59. Gibbs, *Love Canal*: 10.
60. See the *NYT*, "Movies" database: http://movies.nytimes.com/movie/29840/Lois-Gibbs-and-the-Love-Canal/overview.
61. See P. Michael Saint, Robert J. Flavell, & Patrick F. Fox, *NIMBY Wars: The Politics of Land Use* (Saint University Press, 2009), NIMBY image on the cover.
62. Kent Portney, quoted in William Glaberson, "Coping in the Age of Nimby," *NYT*, June 19, 1988.
63. Ibid.
64. See Cerrell Associates Inc., "Political Difficulties Facing Waste-to-Energy Conversion Plant Siting" (Los Angeles, 1984). On the Cerrell Associates report, which discussed ways to overcome activist resistance to hazardous waste incinerators, see also Kristin Demetrious, *Public Relations, Activism, and Social Change* (New York: Routledge, 2013), 63.
65. On the matter of community environmentalists and Green Knowledge, see especially Andrew Jamison, *The Making of Green Knowledge: Environmental Politics and Cultural Transformation* (New York: Cambridge University Press, 2001), 147–175.
66. See the EPA's web page on the "Emergency Planning and Community Right-to-Know Act (EPCRA)," which was part of the 1986 SARA process that established requirements for Federal, state and local governments, Indian Tribes, and industry

regarding emergency planning and "Community Right-to-Know" reporting on hazardous and toxic chemicals. The EPA site can be found at http://www.epa .gov/emergencies/content/lawsregs/epcraover.htm.

67. Diane Heminway, Assistant Director, CEC, presentation at the 20th Anniversary of Love Canal: Lessons Learned: Conference, SUNY–Buffalo, October 8–9, 1998. Spring, 2001, 8 Buff. Envt'l L.J. 271

68. *Social Policy*, 1990, 37.

69. "A Message from the Executive Director," Margeen Hoffman, ETF Annual Report 1985–1986, 8–9.

70. "Summary of Activities and Significant Accomplishments of the Ecumenical Task Force.... 1985–86 Fiscal Year," in ibid., 10–12.

71. "Activities of the ETF Resource Center," ibid., 14.

72. See, for example, Sam Howe Verhovek, "After 10 Years, the Trauma of Love Canal Continues," *NYT*, Aug. 5, 1988.

73. David Shribman, "Even after 10 Years, Victims of Love Canal Can't Quite Escape It," *Wall St. Journal*, Mar. 9, 1989. See the reprint in *Family Circle*, Aug 15, 1989.

Chapter 9

1. *Buffalo News*, Sept. 28, 1988; see also *Buffalo News*, Sept. 25, 1988.

2. *Christian Science Monitor*, Sept. 25, 1988.

3. *Buffalo News*, Sept. 28, 1988.

4. *NG*, Sept. 29, 1988.

5. *NG*, Sept. 30, 1988.

6. New York State Environmental Quality Review, Finding Statement for LCARA, Draft, 3, SUNY–Buffalo Love Canal Collection, Ms. 74, Box 1.

7. Dr. Lewis Thomas to Hugh Carey and Members of the New York State Legislature, October 8, 1980, in Report of the Governor's Panel to Review Scientific Studies and the Development of Public Policy on Problems Resulting From Hazardous Wastes.

8. *Environmental Monitoring at Love Canal*, 3 vols., (EPA, Office of Research and Development, Washington, D.C., May, 1980).

9. Ibid., Vol. 1, 8–9, 11.

10. Ibid. See Deegan's two articles in the American Chemical Society's *Environmental Science and Technology* magazine: "Looking Back at Love Canal," *Environmental Science Technology*, Vol. 21, No. 4, 328–331; "Looking Back at Love Canal: Results and Conclusions of EPA's Investigations," Environmental Science Technology, Vol. 21, No. 5, 421–426 (1987) [Hereinafter Deegan I and Deegan II, respectively]. Quote at Deegan II, 425.

11. Ben Deforest Story, AP, reprinted in the (Fredericksburg, Va.) *Free Lance-Star*, Feb. 26, 1983.

12. The AP story made waves papers far from Niagara Falls, such as the *Southeast Missourian*, Feb. 24, 1983.

13. Josh Barbanel, "At Love Canal, Some Hope to Start Over," *NYT*, May 17, 1982.

14. *Habitability of the Love Canal Area: An Analysis of the Technical Basis for the Decision on the Habitability of the Emergency Declaration Area*: A Technical Memorandum, Washington, D.C.: U.S. Congress, Office of Technology Assessment, OTA-TM-M-I3, (June 1983). NTIS order #PB84-114917, 3.

15. Ibid., 3.

16. Ibid.

17. Ibid.
18. On science's evolution from romantic moral endeavor to a way of knowledge making subject to social and political pressures, see Steven Shapin, *The Scientific Life* (Chicago: University of Chicago Press, 2010), especially Chapter 8; see also Allan M. Brandt, *The Cigarette Century* (New York: Basic Books, 2007) and Pamela E. Pennock, *Advertising Sin and Sickness* (DeKalb: Northern Illinois University Press, 2007).
19. Buchwald, "Dinner For Two," *The Lewiston Journal*, Feb. 26, 1983.
20. Philip Shabecoff, "Rita Lavelle Gets 6-Month Term and Is Fined $10,000 for Perjury," *NYT*, Jan. 10, 1984.
21. See Buchwald's syndicated column and the "Annie" cartoon together in the (Fredericksburg, Va.) *Free Lance-Star*, Feb. 26, 1983.
22. Lowell T. Harmison, Ph.D., "Toxic Substances and Health," *Public Health Reports*, Vol. 93, No. 1 (January–February 1978), 3–10, quote at 4–5.
23. *Buffalo News*, Apr. 21, 1990.
24. On Borner's organization, see the EHMI's website history at: http://www.ehmi.org/about/timeline.php.
25. See the "About" section of the EHMI's website at: http://www.ehmi.org/about/index.php.
26. *Whole Earth Catalogue*, Fall 1968 cover.
27. Its motto declared that average "people" and not just professionals must be involved in hazmat issues.
28. See the Asahi-America ad in *HazMat World* Magazine, Vol. 2, No. 9 (September 1989), On Asahi-America, see the company's innovative history online at: http://asahi-america.com/about-us/company-history.
29. *HazMat World* Magazine, ibid.
30. Ibid.
31. Don Haycock, quoted in article by John Leckie, "Growing & Cleaning Up," *Canadian Consulting Engineer*, Dec. 1, 2006.
32. Ibid.
33. "Love Canal Emergency Declaration Area: Proposed Habitability Criteria," report submitted by the U.S. Department of Health and Human Services, Public Health Service, the Centers for Disease Control, and the N.Y. State Department of Health, November 1985, 294.
34. Ibid., 298.
35. Ibid., Appendix, 39–40.
36. Ibid., Appendix, 39–40.
37. AP story reprinted in *Ocala Star Banner*, June 18, 1982.
38. TRC Habitability, Appendix, 39–40.
39. Ibid., Appendix 6, 332.
40. Ibid., Appendix 6, 18
41. EPA Love Canal Report, Region 2, Jan. 25, 2010, "Clean Up Process," 2, at http://www.epa.gov/region2/superfund/npl/0201290c.pdf.
42. Frank Rovers, Hazardous Waste and Toxic Waste Disposal Joint Hearings Before the Subcommittees on Environmental Pollution and Resource Protection of the United States Congress, Vol. 1, 276–280.
43. Ibid., 276.
44. Ibid., 282.
45. See, for instance, Devra Davis, *The Secret History of the War on Cancer* (New York: Basic Books, 2007). Dr. Davis also started the Environmental Health Trust in 2007.

46. U.S. Department of Health and Human Services, et al., "Love Canal Emergency Declaration Area: Proposed Habitability Criteria Report" (November 1985), 3. [Hereinafter Proposed Habitability Criteria Report.]

47. Devra Davis, whose work on environmental pollution soon set a standard of excellence in the field, served on the blue-ribbon committee. So too did Jan Stolwijk, a highly regarded professor of medicine at Yale. Other members included Warren Winkelstein, a medical doctor and professor of epidemiology at Berkeley; Dr. Martha R. Fowlkes and Dr. Patricia Y. Miller, professors who had already written on the Love Canal disaster from sociological and anthropological perspectives; and Michael Stoline, an expert on the statistical analysis of environmental regulation.

48. Proposed Habitability Criteria Report, 20–23.

49. See "Criteria for Residential Viability as Criteria for Residential Habitability in the Love Canal EDA," a report issue by Fowlkes and Miller, in ibid., Appendix 8.

50. See Appendix 7, "Choice of the Comparative Approach Methodology for Habitability Decision-Making," in ibid.,15. This subsection is entitled "The Recommended Approach."

51. Ibid., 2.

52. Ibid., 2–3.

53. Ibid., 3–4.

54. Ibid., 8.

55. EPA head William K. Reilly, quoted in Philip Shabecoff, "Government Says Abandoned Love Canal Homes Are Safe Now," *NYT*, May 15, 1990.

56. Axelrod, "Love Canal Emergency Declaration Area: Decision on Habitability," Sept. 27, 1988, Department of Health website, https://www.health.ny.gov/environmental/investigations/love_canal/lcdec88.pdf.

57. See Philip Shabecoff, "Government Says Abandoned Love Canal Homes Are Safe Now," *NYT*, May 15, 1990, and Eric Schmitt, "Axelrod Says 220 Love Canal Families Can Return," *NYT*, Sept. 28, 1988.

58. *Buffalo News,* Sept. 28, 1988; see also *Buffalo News*, Sept. 25, 1988.

59. "What is Risk? What is a Stressor?" and "What is Risk Assessment," on EPA's "Risk Assessment" link. See also Eric Schmitt, "Anger Lives in Canal's Uninhabitable Zone," NYT, Sept. 29, 1988.

60. EPA "Risk Assessment" link. See also *Buffalo News,* Sept. 25 and 28, 1988; and Eric Schmitt, "Anger Lives in Canal's Uninhabitable Zone," *NYT*, Sept. 29, 1988.

61. Gibbs, in Shabecoff, "Government Says Abandoned Love Canal Homes Are Safe Now."

62. Gibbs (paraphrased by Shabecoff), in ibid.

63. Jacqueline M. Warren, a lawyer for the Natural Resources Defense Council, in ibid.

64. http://epa.gov/riskassessment/basicinformation.htm#risk

65. Shabecoff, "Government Says Abandoned Love Canal Homes Are Safe Now," *NYT*, May 15, 1990.

66. William K. Reilly (quoting report of EPA panel of scientific experts) to Lois Gibbs, May 14, 1990, published as an EPA press release on May 15, 1990, available at the EPA website: http://www2.epa.gov/aboutepa/reilly-responds-lois-gibbs-love-canal-habitability-and-related-issues.

67. http://epa.gov/riskassessment/basicinformation.htm#risk.

68. "Dear Friends," Lois Gibbs' appeal circa Spring–Summer 1990, CCHW archives, "LCARA" folder.

69. Sam Howe Verhovek, "At Love Canal, Land Rush on a Burial Ground," *NYT*, July 26, 1990.
70. Andrew J. Hoffman, "An Uneasy Rebirth at Love Canal," *Environment*, Vol. 37, No. 2 (March 1995), 25.
71. LCARA's James E. Carr, quoted in Verhovek, "At Love Canal, Land Rush on a Burial Ground."
72. *NG*, Aug. 19, 1990.
73. *NG*, Aug. 27, 1990. Forest Glen, a resident-owned trailer park at the edge of Niagara Falls, was evacuated between 1990 and 1992 when the EPA purchased over 150 properties and began a cleanup that lasted roughly a decade. See the EPA's website: http://www.epa.gov/superfund/accomp/success/forest.htm.
74. See *NG*, Aug. 27, 1990. See also Associated Press, "Love Canal Video Criticized as Misleading," *NYT*, Sept. 16, 1990.
75. Verhovek, "Land Rush on a Burial Ground."
76. See Saratoga Associates, "Love Canal Area Master Plan," draft (October 1989.) Boxes 1-2, Love Canal Area Revitalization Agency Records, University Archives, State University of New York at Buffalo, MS 74.
77. Saratoga Associates, Love Canal Area Master Plan, final report (1990), 56, available as above. It is also available at the Buffalo and Erie County Public Library and the Niagara Falls Public Library.
78. Saratoga Associates, Love Canal Area Master Plan final report, 1.
79. Ibid., 13.
80. Saratoga Associates, Love Canal Area Master Plan final report, "Land Use Advisory Committee Deliberations," 14.
81. Ibid.
82. Verhovek, "Land Rush on a Burial Ground."
83. William Broderick, quoted in Amy Brooke Baker, "Love Canal—10 Years After: A Cleanup Still Waiting to Happen," *Christian Science Monitor*, Sept. 22, 1988.
84. *Buffalo News*, Apr. 17, 1990. On Gibbs' prize, see the official site: http://www.goldmanprize.org/1990/northamerica.
85. *Buffalo News*, Apr. 19, 1990; *NG*, Apr. 20, 1990.
86. *Metro Community News* (Niagara Falls), May 15, 1990.
87. Pat Brown, quoted in Baker, "A Cleanup Still Waiting to Happen."
88. Sam Howe Verhovek, "After 10 Years, the Trauma of Love Canal Continues," *NYT*, Aug. 5, 1988.

Epilogue

1. Jane M. Kenny, in "EPA Removes Love Canal From Superfund List" (Sept. 20, 2004), available online at http://www.epa.gov/superfund/accomp/news/lovecanal.htm.
2. An online image of a field trip to the monument with the SUNY–Geneseo History Club, featuring Love Canal activist Luella Lenny in 2005, can be viewed online at: http://www.geneseo.edu/history_club/year-review-2004-2008.
3. "EPA Removes Love Canal From Superfund List," online.
4. See "Superfund's 25th anniversary: capturing the past, charting the future," EPA online archives, http://archive.epa.gov/region9/annualreport/web/pdf/r9-annual-report-2006.pdf, at 17.
5. See the Center for Public Integrity story, Feb. 22, 2011, at http://www.publicintegrity.org/2011/02/22/2121/epa-superfund-cleanup-costs-outstrip-funding.

6. Editorial, "Delisting Love Canal," NYT, Mar. 22, 2004. http://www.nytimes.com/2004/03/22/opinion/delisting-love-canal.html

7. Kenny in the *Buffalo News*, Mar. 30, 2004. See also Kenny, quoted in Laura M. Simna, "Recent Information About Love Canal," Online Ethics Center for Science and Engineering, posted at http://www.onlineethics.org/Resources/Cases/lcanal/recent.aspx. See also http://www.geneseo.edu/history_club/year-review-2004-2008

8. ETF, "Earthcare: Lessons from Love Canal" (Niagara Falls, 1987), 9–12.

9. See Kenny, interview with the author, May 3, 2004.

10. Kenny and Gibbs, quoted in Laura M. Simna, "Recent Information About Love Canal," Online Ethics Center for Science and Engineering, posted at http://www.onlineethics.org/Resources/Cases/lcanal/recent.aspx.

11. Quimby, quoted in Associated Press, "First Superfund Site, Love Canal, Now Said to be Clean," *USA Today*, Mar. 18, 2004.

12. Gibbs, to reporter Aaron Besecker, in the *Buffalo News*, Oct. 22, 2013.

13. See anonymous EPA official's comments, quoted in Carolyn Thompson (Associated Press), "Lawsuits: Love Canal Still Oozes 35 Years Later," *USA Today*, Nov. 2, 2013.

14. Pierre Nora, "Between Memory and History: Les Lieux De Memoire," *Representations* 26 (Spring 1989), 7–24.

15. See Scott Sandage, "A Marble House Divided: The Lincoln Memorial, The Civil Rights Movement and the Politics of Memory, 1939–1963," reprinted in Charles M. Payne & Adam C. Green, *Time Longer than Rope* (New York: NYU Press, 2002), 492–535. On contested memory more generally, see Pierre Nora, ed., *Realms of Memory: Rethinking the French Past* (Vol. I: Conflicts and Divisions) (New York: Columbia University Press, 1996).

16. See "Friends: A Newsletter for the Friends of Tufts Libraries" (Winter, 2000), available online at http://www.library.tufts.edu/Friends/nl_winter2000.html.

17. See "Newsworthy" section of *Tuftonia* (Spring 2000).

18. See the "Abstract" section of the homepage of the Finding Aid for Ecumenical Task Force of the Niagara Frontier Records, SUNY-Buffalo archives, at http://libweb1.lib.buffalo.edu:8080/findingaids/view?docId=ead/archives/ubar_ms0065.xml.

19. See the event posted at https://www.youtube.com/watch?v=SfjoeWIRJ6s.

20. Glenn Springs Holdings report in Carolyn Thompson (Associated Press), "Lawsuits: Love Canal Still Oozes 35 Years Later" (emphasis added).

21. Marlene Kennedy, "Years Later, Love Canal Stew Bubbles Up" (Lockport, N.Y.) Courthouse News Service, Feb. 24, 2014.

22. Thompson (AP), "Lawsuits: Love Canal Still Oozes 35 Years Later."

23. *Buffalo News*, Oct. 22, 2013.

24. Nancy Nichols, *Lake Effect* (Washington, D.C.: Island Press, 2008).

25. Ibid., IX.

26. Ibid., 128; 135; 35; 47.

27. Kelly McMasters, *Welcome to Shirley* (New York: Public Affairs, 2008).

28. See Sandra Steingraber's reference to Lois Gibbs and Beverly Paigen in *Living Downstream: A Scientist's Personal Investigation of Cancer and the Environment*, (New York: Vintage Books, 1997), bibliography, 339–44; Illinois farmland quote at 5.

29. Lois Gibbs, *Love Canal and the Birth of the Environmental Health Movement* (Washington, D.C.: Island Press, 2011). Kindle edition, Introduction.

30. "Lois Gibbs Urges Strong Voice for Environmental Justice," University of Maryland School of Public Health homepage story, Apr. 18, 2014, at http://sph .umd.edu/news/lois-gibbs-urges-strong-voices-environmental-justice.

31. Ted Schettler et al., eds., *Generations at Risk: Reproductive Health and the Environment* (Cambridge: MIT Press, 1999), xvii, 282–283.

32. See Love Canal Medical Fund (LCMF) Inc., Annual Report for 1997, 1–5, available online at: http://www.lcmf.org/annual-reports.php (emphasis added).

33. Love Canal Medical Fund Bulletin - Health News and Benefits, Issue 9 (Summer 2001).

34. On Love Canal Health updates, see Love Canal Medical Fund Bulletin - Health News and Benefits, Issue 10 (Winter 2002); Issue 12 (Fall 2002); Issue 22 (Winter 2008).

35. Love Canal Medical Fund 1997 Annual Report, 1998 Annual Report, 4. LCMF Annual Reports are available on the Fund homepage: http://www.lcmf.org/annual-reports.php.

36. See Love Canal Medical Fund, Inc., Annual Report for 2010, 1–7, 1–4.

37. LCMF 1997 Annual Report, 4.

38. See the FAQ Section of the LCMF website at http://www.lcmf.org/frequently-asked-questions.php.

39. See Love Canal Follow-up Health Study, Prepared by the Division of Environmental Health Assessment, Center for Environmental Health, New York State Department of Health, for the U.S. Department of Health and Human Services Agency for Toxic Substances and Disease Registry (Albany, N.Y., October 2008), online at https://www.health.ny.gov/environmental/investigations/love_canal/docs/report_public_comment_final.pdf.

40. New York State Department of Health, "Love Canal Follow-up Health Study" (September 2002),online at: http://www.health.ny.gov/environmental/investigations/love_canal/902news.htm. For a stand-alone article on the results of the health study that discusses elevated cancers in certain categories, as well as some of the health study's inherent limitations, see also Lenore J. Gensburg, et al., "Cancer Incidence Among Former Love Canal Residents," *Environmental Health Perspectives*, Vol. 117, No. 8 (August 2009), available online at: http://ehp.niehs.nih.gov/0800153/.

41. The report's authors wrote that "such limitations as a relatively small and incomplete study cohort, imprecise exposure measurements, and the exclusion of cancers diagnosed before 1979" made the Love Canal health study's understanding of the link between toxic waste and "excess [public health] risks" somewhat "unclear." See "Conclusions" section of the 2009 stand-alone study, in ibid.

42. 1999 LCMF Annual Report, 5–8.

43. There were several court cases at Love Canal. In the major federal case, Judge John T. Curtin determined that Hooker was "negligent" on several fronts but not liable for $250 million in potential damages (which would have been paid to New York State); see "Ex-Owner of Toxic Site Wins Ruling on Damages," *NYT*, Mar 18, 1994. A second major case, in which New York sued to recover cleanup costs, resulted in a $98 million settlement; see Matthew L. Wald, "Out-of-Court Settlement Reached Over Love Canal," *NYT*, June 22, 1994. See also Michael Parrish, "Occidental Agrees to Pay $98 Million in Love Canal Case," *Los Angeles Times*, June 22, 1994, at: http://articles.latimes.com/1994-06-22/business/fi-7158_1_love-canal-site.

INDEX